# The United States, the Soviet Union and the Arab–Israeli conflict, 1948–67

Manchester University Press

# The United States, the Soviet Union and the Arab–Israeli conflict, 1948–67

Superpower rivalry

Joseph Heller

Manchester University Press

Copyright © Ben-Gurion Research Institute for the Study of Israel
and Zionism 2010

The right of Joseph Heller to be identified as the author of this work has
been asserted by him/her in accordance with the Copyright, Designs and
Patents Act 1988.

Published by Ben-Gurion Research Institute for the Study of Israel and
Zionism (Sede Boqer) 2010

First English-language edition published in 2016 by
Manchester University Press
Altrincham Street, Manchester M1 7JA
www.manchesteruniversitypress.co.uk

British Library Cataloguing-in-Publication Data
A catalogue record for this book is available from the British Library

Library of Congress Cataloging-in-Publication Data applied for

ISBN 978 1 5261 0382 6 hardback
ISBN 978 1 5261 2735 8 paperback

First published in hardback by Manchester University Press 2016
This edition first published 2019

The publisher has no responsibility for the persistence or accuracy of URLs
for any external or third-party internet websites referred to in this book,
and does not guarantee that any content on such websites is, or will remain,
accurate or appropriate.

Typeset by Out of House Publishing

# Contents

| | | |
|---|---|---|
| List of figures | | *page* vii |
| Acknowledgments | | ix |
| Abbreviations | | xi |
| | Introduction | 1 |
| 1 | The Soviet Union and Israel: from the Gromyko declaration to the death of Stalin (1947–53) | 6 |
| 2 | The United States and the Cold War: from Truman to Eisenhower (1948–53) | 19 |
| 3 | Israel and the Soviet Union prior to the Suez Crisis (1953–56) | 33 |
| 4 | Sharett versus Eisenhower and Dulles (1953–56) | 47 |
| 5 | Israel and the United States on the road to war (November 1955–November 1956) | 63 |
| 6 | The Eisenhower Doctrine and Israel (November 1956–January 1958) | 78 |
| 7 | Soviet–Israeli relations after the Suez War (1956–61) | 92 |
| 8 | How the Middle East crises affected US policy toward Israel (1958–60) | 106 |
| 9 | Kennedy, Israel and the Cold War before the Cuban Missile Crisis (1961–62) | 120 |
| 10 | Was Kennedy the 'father' of the US–Israeli alliance? (1962–63) | 135 |
| 11 | Khrushchev, Israel and Soviet Jewry (1961–64) | 154 |
| 12 | Was Johnson the 'father' of the US–Israeli alliance?: the Memorandum of Understanding (1964–65) | 168 |

| | | |
|---|---|---|
| 13 | Johnson, Israel and the Cold War: testing the Memorandum of Understanding (1965–67) | 185 |
| 14 | The Soviet Union, Israel and Soviet Jewry (1964–67) | 204 |
| 15 | The United States and the crisis of the Six Day War (May 14–June 5, 1967) | 220 |
| 16 | The Soviet Union and the Six Day War (May 14–June 5, 1967) | 241 |
| | Conclusions | 259 |
| Bibliography | | 269 |
| Index | | 282 |

# Figures

1 'Anyhow, thank you' by Kariel Gardosh (Dosh), October 1, 1962, from *So Sorry We Won!* (Tel Aviv, 1967), p. 148. Reproduced by kind permission of Michael Gardosh. *page* 134

2 'The Soviet government cancels the exchange of orchestras with Israel' by Yaakov Farkash (Ze'ev), September 26, 1966, from *Al Kol Panim* (Tel Aviv, 1975), p. 90. Reproduced by kind permission of Naomi Farkash Fink and Dorit Farkash Shuki. 218

3 'Moscow is ready to send its football team to Israel' by Yaakov Farkash (Ze'ev), September 27, 1966, from *Al Kol Panim* (Tel Aviv, 1975), p. 90. Reproduced by kind permission of Naomi Farkash Fink and Dorit Farkash Shuki. 219

4 'The chef's specialty' by Kariel Gardosh (Dosh), May 15, 1967, from *So Sorry We Won!* (Tel Aviv, 1967), p. 238. Reproduced by kind permission of Michael Gardosh. 239

5 'Did you say something?' by Kariel Gardosh (Dosh), May 25, 1967, from *So Sorry We Won!* (Tel Aviv, 1967), p. 247. Reproduced by kind permission of Michael Gardosh. 240

6 'The chicken refused to be sacrificed' by Yaakov Farkash (Ze'ev), October 13, 1967, from *Package Deal: 170 Political Cartoons by Ze'ev* (Tel Aviv, 1972), p. 12. Reproduced by kind permission of Naomi Farkash Fink and Dorit Farkash Shuki. 256

7 'No withdrawal without peace' by Yaakov Farkash (Ze'ev), October 17, 1967, from *Package Deal: 170 Political Cartoons by Ze'ev* (Tel Aviv, 1972), p. 11. Reproduced by kind permission of Naomi Farkash Fink and Dorit Farkash Shuki. 256

8 'Five points' by Yaakov Farkash (Ze'ev), October 20, 1967, from *Package Deal: 170 Political Cartoons by Ze'ev* (Tel

Aviv, 1972), p. 11. Reproduced by kind permission of Naomi
Farkash Fink and Dorit Farkash Shuki. 257

9 'The Israeli scorpion in the Sinai Desert', *Krokodil*, 18
(1967), p. 269. Reproduced by kind permission of 20 Century
Crocodile (20centurycrocodile.ru). 257

10 'We are determined', *Krokodil*, 18 (1967), p. 271.
Reproduced by kind permission of 20 Century Crocodile
(20centurycrocodile.ru). 258

# Acknowledgments

My thanks to Israeli diplomats Mordechai Gazit, Baruch Gilad, Yosef Govrin and Moshe Yegar, who participated in the events recounted here and whose generosity in sharing their knowledge and experience enabled me to absorb the zeitgeist in which they lived and operated. I am grateful to my colleagues at the Hebrew University International Relations Department, Uri Bialer and Amnon Sella, who graciously read a large part of the manuscript and whose comments greatly improved it. I also owe much to other colleagues – Zvi Ganin, Yehoshua Porath, Shimon Redlich, Eli Tsur and Norman Rose – who encouraged me during difficult times, and to the late Avraham Greenbaum and to Dan Charuv, who helped me with translations from Russian. Special thanks go to the staff of the Israel State Archive, in particular to its director, Yehoshua Freundlich, and his deputy Yemima Rosenthal. I also owe a debt of gratitude to the staff of the National Library of Israel and to the Hebrew University Library on Mount Scopus.

I could not have carried out my research without the dedicated assistance of many Americans, including the staffs of the National Archive at College Park, Maryland, the National Security Archive at George Washington University, especially William Burr, the John F. Kennedy Library in Boston, and the Lyndon B. Johnson Library in Texas. I owe no less gratitude to the British National Archives in Kew, London. I also wish to thank the Ben-Gurion Heritage Institute at Sede Boqer and the chairman of its editorial board, Tuvia Friling, and the editor Smadar Rotman, who initiated the book's original publication in Hebrew. Last but not least, my wife Shulamit for her constant encouragement and my sons Yair and Danny, and my daughter Dina who guided me through the mysteries of the computer. I am grateful to Haim Watzman for translating the book into English. I am particularly grateful to Elizabeth Yuval for editing and abridging the manuscript with efficiency and astuteness, producing an excellent and much shorter book. Special thanks are due to Tony Mason, senior editor at Manchester University Press, and to Alun Richards, editorial assistant, for their efficiency in editing the manuscript.

Joseph Heller, Jerusalem, October 2015

# Abbreviations

| | |
|---|---|
| AAPBRD | Akten zur Auswärtigen Politik der Bundesrepublik Deutschland |
| APC | armored personnel carrier |
| ARAMCO | Arabian-American Oil Company |
| BGA | Ben-Gurion Archives, Sede Boqer |
| BGD | Ben-Gurion's diary |
| CENTO | Central Treaty Organization |
| CWIHP | Cold War International History Project, at the Woodrow Wilson International Center for Scholars, Washington, DC |
| DEE | Department of Eastern Europe (Israel's Foreign Office) |
| DDF | Documents diplomatiques français |
| DFPI | Documents on Israeli Foreign Policy |
| DISR | Documents on Israeli–Soviet Relations, for which see Ro'i et al., 2000 |
| FRUS | Foreign Relations of the United States |
| IAEA | International Atomic Energy Agency |
| ICAB | Israeli Cabinet |
| ICFADC | Israeli Cabinet Foreign Affairs and Defense Committee |
| IDEEM | Israel Diplomatic Missions to Eastern Europe |
| IDF | Israel Defense Forces |
| IDM | Israel Diplomatic Missions |
| IFM | Israeli Foreign Ministry |
| IMM | Israeli Mission to Moscow |
| IMUN | Israeli Mission to the United Nations |
| IMW | Israeli Mission to Washington |
| ISA | Israel State Archives, Jerusalem |
| JCS | Joint Chiefs of Staff |
| JFKL | John F. Kennedy Library, Austin, Texas |
| KFADC | Knesset Foreign Affairs and Defense Committee |

| | |
|---|---|
| KR | Knesset Records |
| LAD | Latin American Department (Israel's Foreign Office) |
| LBJL | Lyndon Baines Johnson Library |
| LPA | Labour Party Archives (Beit Berl) |
| Mapam | United Labour [Marxist-Zionist] Party |
| MBR | British Commonwealth Department (Israel's Foreign Office) |
| MCC | Mapai Central Committee |
| MEC | Middle East Command |
| MED | Middle East Department (Israel's Foreign Office) |
| MFAC | Mapai Foreign Affairs Committee |
| MFASC | Mapai Foreign Affairs and Security Committee |
| MPC | Mapai Political Committee |
| NA | The National Archives, Kew, London |
| NARA | National Archives and Records Administration, College Park, Maryland |
| NPT | Non-Proliferation Treaty |
| NSC | National Security Council |
| NSF | National Security Files |
| PPS | Policy Planning Staff (US State Department) |
| SDMEC | Soviet Documents on the Middle East Conflict (1947–67) |
| UAR | United Arab Republic |
| UNEF | United Nations Emergency Force |
| USD | United States Department (Israel's Foreign Office) |
| WED | Western European Department (Israel's Foreign Office) |

# Introduction

Histories of the modern Middle East, and of the Arab–Israeli conflict in particular, generally focus on regional participants. Some work has been done about the relations between the region and the two superpowers (the United States and the Soviet Union), but little has put the Arab–Israeli conflict into the context of the Cold War. Both East and West sought influence and favor, juggling ideology and geopolitics. Between the end of World War II and the collapse of the Eastern bloc, the superpowers, fighting proxy wars in Korea and Vietnam and contending over Berlin and Cuba, calculated their national interests in the Middle East according to bilateral global factors. For Israel, those factors determined the nature of its relations with each of the superpowers.

David Ben-Gurion, Israel's first prime minister and defense minister, was not like many of his colleagues led astray by ideology or stereotypes. He understood that as a democracy Israel was a part of the West and that only the United States could provide Israel with the economic aid it needed to ingather Jewish exiles from all over the world. However, Ben-Gurion was faced with a paradox. Following the exodus of the Jews from the Arab-Muslim countries after the creation of the State of Israel, the Soviet Union's Jewish population was the largest reservoir of potential immigrants: the well-off Jews of the United States, he realized, would never move en masse to Israel. Thus, preserving correct relations with the Soviet Union and persuading it to allow its Jews to emigrate was critical for Israel and kept Ben-Gurion, at least initially, from explicitly aligning the country with the West.

That failed because the Soviet Union quickly concluded that its strategic interests lay with the Arab world. While Israel did have two political parties strongly identifying with the Soviet Union, the Soviets realized that the road to Soviet-style socialism in the Middle East would not be paved through Israel. The Arab world offered not only oil but strategic depth, and Soviet penetration of the Middle East began with the Czech–Egyptian arms agreement.

By all accounts, Israel's decision to join the Suez Campaign in 1956, either in collaboration with Britain and France or based on calculating national security interests, determined the country's short- and long-term strategies. The Sinai Campaign immediately worsened relations with the Kremlin and the Arab states, eventually leading to the Six Day War in 1967. Furthermore, cooperation with France contributed to Israel's deterrence when France helped set up Israel's nuclear reactor and provided a steady supply of aircraft and surface-to-surface missiles.

However, had Washington acceded to Israel's demands for security guarantees and heavy weapons, a mortal blow would have been dealt to the fundamental assumptions of US Cold War strategy. The United States would have lost its strategic interests in the Middle East, the oil, military bases and transportation routes, as well as the loyalty of the moderate Arab governments to the West, and the defection of the radical Arab states to the Soviets would have become a fait accompli. According to US policy at the time, giving Israel security guarantees (that is, an alliance) would have worsened the East–West conflict in the Middle East.

US administrations up to and including that of John F. Kennedy considered the Arab refugee problem the tinder most likely to set off a Middle East war, a volatile issue the Soviets could exploit. Throughout the period, the Washington mindset was global and regional issues were variables in the larger equations presented by the conflict with the Soviets. Israel could only try to influence the United States and other Western countries to pursue policies favorable to it, or at least keep harm to a minimum.

Israeli–Soviet relations cannot be fully explained without taking the Cold War into account and, given the lack of sources to explain decision-making in the Kremlin, nothing can be determined with the same certainty as in the relations between Israel and the United States. However, recently published Soviet diplomatic material offers a glimpse of the Soviet leadership's global and regional calculations. Like the United States, the Soviet Union took a regional approach and ignored Israel's vital interests.

The Kremlin may have been satisfied with making Israel a scapegoat, and Soviet support of the so-called 'progressive Arab states' held the promise of tipping the global balance of power in Moscow's favor. In all probability, the determined and unconditional Soviet support of the Arabs, and its contempt for Israel's capabilities, shaped the Kremlin's refusal to allow Soviet Jews to emigrate freely. While common wisdom is that the Kremlin kept its internal and external considerations completely separate, the members of the Central Committee and the Politburo who made the decisions about the Middle East were most likely anti-Semitic or influenced by anti-Semitism. However, we lack the tools to gauge this influence. The Kremlin may well have been satisfied to make Israel not only a scapegoat, but a victim of the Cold War.

I have not devoted Israel's domestic policy (*Innenpolitik*) the attention it deserves. For all intents and purposes, Mapai, Ben-Gurion's party, controlled foreign policy. Even when the leftist parties (Mapam and Ahdut HaAvodah) and those on the right (the General Zionists) participated in the government, their influence on foreign policy was negligible compared with Ben-Gurion and Moshe Sharett, and, afterward, Levi Eshkol, Golda Meir and Abba Eban. Both the United States and the Soviet Union understood the ideological and practical significance of Mapai's control. The United States viewed its rule as better than one led by the extreme right-wing Herut movement, which advocated a nationalist policy of economic and territorial expansion. The extreme left sought to establish closer ties with the Soviets, so that both left and right were liable to endanger US strategic interests. The Soviet Union was hostile to Mapai because of its pro-Western orientation, bourgeois character and opposition to Communist ideology.

The goal of this book is to examine decision-making processes in Israel, the United States, and, to the extent possible, in the Soviet Union during the first twenty years of the Cold War. Since the minutes of the Israeli cabinet meetings during these years are partly classified, important information on Israeli government decisions is lacking, particularly regarding the nuclear facility in Dimona. Nevertheless, there are a great many sources offering a reasonable picture of the decision-making process.

In effect, for better or for worse, Israel's fate was determined by the United States and the Soviet Union. France, Britain and West Germany also played roles in ensuring Israel's survival, albeit generally in coordination with, or at least with the knowledge of, Washington. The exception was France, which did not always notify the United States about its arms deals with Israel.

A word on methodology: I do not accept the view that Israel's history is a series of missed opportunities. That is merely hindsight and misses the spirit of the times (zeitgeist). I take a simple historical approach that does not preoccupy itself with theoretical assumptions and assumes rather that worldviews (weltanschauungen) guide and shape policy. A single pioneering study written by Uri Bialer tried to examine Israel's foreign policy within the methodological framework of the Cold War. The current study continues and updates Bialer's work.

Four more books deal with the Middle East in general, paying marginal attention to the impact of the Cold War on Israel. They are Yezid Sayegh and Avi Shlaim, eds., *The Cold War and the Middle East* (Oxford

1997); Michael B. Oren, *The Six Days of War and the Making of the Modern Middle East* (Oxford 2002); Yaacov Ro'i and Boris Morozov, eds., *The Soviet Union and the June 1967 Six Day War* (Stanford 2008); Wm. Roger Louis and Avi Shlaim, eds., *The 1967 War Arab-Israeli War: Origins and Consequences* (Oxford 2012). In addition, the abovementioned books focus mainly on the 1967 war itself and except for Oren, who begins as late as 1965, none of them uses the highly important material in the Israel State Archives (ISA).

During the Cold War, most of the countries of the world had to adjust themselves, one way or another, to its realpolitik and Israel was no exception. In large measure, its geopolitical position at a strategic crossroads in the very heart of the Arab world determined its fate. One basic assumption of this study is that Israel's proximity to the Middle East's large oil reserves, strategic transport routes, and the large military base in the area of the Suez Canal did not allow it the luxury of neutrality in the Cold War. Once the Czech–Egyptian arms agreement was concluded in 1955, the Cold War was a powerful regional presence.[1]

That raises the question of whether the Soviet threat was inherent or conditioned by Israeli behavior. The basic goal of the Soviet Union was to demolish the capitalist world and it made its own rules.[2] The United States had limited control over Israel, but it was completely different from the Soviet control of the Arabs. The Middle East was particularly important during the Cold War because of the strategic routes controlling access to it. Lacking a border with the Soviet Union, Israel did not play a direct or vital role in the West's strategy, but, because of its identification with the West, it could not avoid becoming a pawn in the East–West struggle.

Ideology was also a decisive factor in the Cold War. Beyond the ideological struggle, Israel exerted constant pressure on the Kremlin for Jewish immigration, something its rulers regarded as a direct threat. Thus, the Soviets regarded Israel as a double enemy, both Western and Zionist. Ultimately, the Soviet Union's efforts to gain a firm foothold in the Middle East, in particular in Syria and Egypt, led it to support its radical nationalist leaders. The Kremlin never adopted their program of seeking to destroy Israel, but it did not try to curb them. The United States found itself caught between its commitment to Israel and its strategic interests in the Arab world. While it was not dependent on

---

1 Arne Westad (2005) thinks that the Arab–Israeli wars had a special rationale stronger than that of the Cold War.
2 Heikal, 1978: 22–3.

Arab oil, its Western European allies were, and it feared that supporting Israel too strongly might directly cause economic chaos and enable the Soviet destabilization of Europe. Furthermore, the war in Vietnam limited US ability to firmly oppose Soviet encroachment in the Middle East. Ultimately, the Six Day War was a product not only of the Arab desire to wipe Israel off the map or of Israel's imperative to survive, but also of the complex global web of superpower conflict which led inexorably toward a Middle East war.

# 1

# The Soviet Union and Israel: from the Gromyko declaration to the death of Stalin (1947–53)

During World War II, the Yishuv leadership and the American Zionist leadership made a great effort to convince the Soviet Union to be more open to Zionism, regarding the effort as a long-term investment. The investment paid off when the Soviet ambassador to London announced in 1943 that his country would support Zionism.[1] Thereafter, the Soviet Union took an increasing interest in the region and, toward the end of the war, the Soviet foreign ministry recommended opening a consulate in Palestine. The Soviet Union had property valued at £1 million and there were 240 Soviet citizens and thousands of Jewish emigrants from the western Soviet Union there as well.[2]

However, Soviet Premier Joseph Stalin had not abandoned anti-Semitism. Asked by US President Franklin D. Roosevelt after the Yalta Conference whether he supported Zionism, Stalin responded that it was difficult to solve the Jewish problem because the Jews were 'middle-men, profiteers, and parasites.'[3] Immediately after the war, the Soviet Commission for the Preparation of Postwar Peace Treaties recommended transferring responsibility for Palestine from the British to the 'collective trusteeship' of the United States, the Soviet Union and Britain.[4] The first sign of the Cold War came when the Soviet envoy to Beirut opined that resolving the issue of Palestine was in the Soviets' interests because it was situated close to transportation routes that would become vital to the Soviet Union.[5]

Britain and the United States wanted to limit Soviet influence in the Middle East and refused to allow the Soviets to participate in the

1 DISR 1: 25–8, 68, 71.
2 DISR 1: 95.
3 Bohlen, 1973: 203.
4 DISR 1: 100–5.
5 DISR 1: 121–3.

Anglo-American Committee of Inquiry on Palestine and the Displaced Jews of Europe (1946). The Soviets argued that the Jewish question in Europe could not be solved by immigration to Palestine, but rather by uprooting fascism and establishing 'people's democracies' that would allow Jews to live 'normally.' They recommended a trusteeship for an independent, democratic Palestine.[6]

The Kremlin's anti-Zionist sentiments were reflected in *Novoye Vremya* (New Times), which claimed that Zionism served British imperialist interests and was supported by influential Americans.[7] A Soviet diplomat in Cairo argued that Ben-Gurion admired Hitler's methods of educating the youth, and that Sharett was no better.[8] The Soviets proposed that the British army withdraw from Palestine and that the Mandate be revoked.[9] The United States gave Britain a free hand, seeking for itself economic benefits and air routes, access to oil free of British influence, and a Zionist revival of the Peel partition plan of 1937.[10] According to the Soviets, oil and American Jewry determined US interests and President Harry S. Truman's support for Zionism was part of a plan to seize the Middle East and turn it into a US base. The UN, the Soviets maintained, should engineer a constitution that would grant equal rights to the entire population. Transferring the Palestine question to the UN would give the Soviet Union its first opportunity to influence Palestine's future.[11]

The Soviet foreign office warned that the conflict with the Americans was getting worse. The United States was meddling to gain control of oil fields, establish air routes, supply military raw materials to regional governments, send in advisors and grant loans.[12] The Kremlin interpreted Truman's October 4, 1946, statement of support for the partition of Palestine as an attempt to establish control over the region's oil. The route of a planned pipeline would pass through it and the United States would build refineries as well as air and naval bases. Palestine, with its exceptional economic and strategic importance, would serve as a US bridgehead in the Eastern Mediterranean. The Soviets, the foreign ministry said, should support the demand that Palestine become an independent democratic state.

6  DISR 1: 126–9 (May 15, 1946).
7  K. Seriojin, 'Problems of the Arab East,' *Novoye Vremya* (1946): 15.
8  DISR 1: 33–53.
9  DISR 1: 144–6.
10 DISR 1: 161–3, 166–8.
11 DISR 1: 169–72.
12 DISR 1: 173.

On May 14, 1947, to counteract the potential Western position in the Middle East, Andrei Gromyko, the Soviet Union's representative to the UN, made a speech before the General Assembly stating that, while a binational state was the ideal, under the current circumstances the USSR would support partition. He spoke of the British failure in Palestine and said that he identified with the 'exceptional sorrow and suffering' of the Jewish people during World War II. He ended by saying he empathized with Europe's displaced Jews who wanted a state of their own. He balanced the Jewish and Arab demands, maintaining that the legitimate interests of both sides required a binational state that could guarantee their interests. However, if relations between the two peoples deteriorated, such a state might not succeed and thus it was necessary to consider the alternative: a partition of the land into two independent countries.[13]

It is not clear why Gromyko abandoned the Soviet opposition to Jewish immigration, or why he specified partition as a second choice even before the United Nations Special Committee on Palestine (UNSCOP) had supported it. It may have been an attempt to enlist the sympathy of America's Jews.[14] When they met, Ben-Gurion tried unsuccessfully to persuade Gromyko to renounce his support for a binational state and to sanction the Jewish Agency's construction of settlements and economic projects throughout Palestine. Gromyko rejected the request on the grounds that it would not receive the necessary two-thirds majority.[15]

After UNSCOP issued its report, the Soviets supported partition as better reflecting their position.[16] Gromyko was instructed to consult with the Jews on all major issues, Jerusalem in particular, a policy formulated by Stalin himself. A special Security Council commission would determine the borders between the two states and governing councils would be chosen in consultation with the democratic parties in both states. Democratic constitutions would be formulated and an armed police force would prevent border incidents. The UN commission would oversee political and military issues.[17] The Kremlin's decision to support partition was at odds with the recommendations of Soviet diplomats in the Arab world. The Soviet envoy to Iraq argued that, for the Arabs, the Zionists were enemies and more dangerous than the British and that a

13  United Nations, 1947: 128–32.
14  DISR 1: 232–4.
15  Ben-Gurion, 1993: 121–2.
16  DISR 1: 226–7.
17  DISR 1: 235–6.

Jewish state in the very heart of the Arab world would jeopardize the dream of Arab unity.

Soviet support for Zionism reached its zenith on November 26, 1947, with Gromyko's pro-partition speech. Partition, he declared, served the legitimate interests of the Jewish people and their desire for a homeland. He also hoped that the Arabs would turn their eyes toward Moscow for help in their 'just struggle.'[18] When the Americans did an about-face and began to advocate a trusteeship rather than partition, the Soviets feared Western aggression, suspecting the Americans of wanting to turn the region into a new Cold War battleground.[19] The Kremlin, motivated by a desire to obtain a tactical advantage, recognized Israel *de jure* just three days after it had declared its independence. The Kremlin also recommended to Yugoslavia and Czechoslovakia that they help Israel acquire artillery and aircraft, since the Arabs were receiving materiel from the British.[20]

Israeli diplomats told the Soviets that while Israel realized aligning itself with the Eastern bloc could help its desire for Jewish immigration and Communist aid, it had to maintain its friendship with the United States; the Soviets did not seem opposed. The Soviets would never accept exclusion from the Middle East because it bordered on the Soviet sphere of influence and was rich in oil, and, in an emergency, the local Communists might turn from being a marginal factor to becoming a major influence.[21] Thus, as long as Israel fought the British-supported Arabs it could be assured of Soviet support, but it still required huge resources from the West.[22]

The Soviet position toward Israel was clearly that a Jewish problem existed only in states not progressing toward socialism, and therefore Jews could only emigrate to Israel from such states. Furthermore, emigration would not solve the Jewish problem because Israel was a small country and had the capacity to absorb only a limited number of immigrants.[23] Israel's representatives in Moscow reported that the Soviet foreign ministry had adopted a dangerous position on Jewish emigration, arguing that Jews should fight for socialism wherever they lived rather than congregate in a Jewish state. On September 21, 1948, the argument was given a Jewish imprimatur by Ilya Ehrenburg, who at Stalin's behest

18 Dagan, 1970.
19 DISR 1: 270.
20 DISR 1: 291.
21 DFPI 1: 155–6.
22 DFPI 1: 512–14.
23 Namir, 1971: 52–6.

wrote in *Pravda* that the theory that all Jews were connected by secret ties was a lie, and that there was no such thing as the 'Jewish nation.'

In effect, Moscow linked Israel's relations with the Soviet Union to Soviet Jewry's sympathy toward Israel. The chairman of the Kremlin's Council of Religions and Sects had closely watched the 'huge demonstration' of tens of thousands of Jews around Moscow's central synagogue on the High Holy Days, and ordered the chief rabbi to keep his connections with the Israeli legation to a minimum. Indeed, Golda Myerson (who changed her name to Meir in 1956), the first Israeli envoy, was the main attraction for the Jewish demonstrators. For Stalin, the demonstration was proof that Soviet Jews in fact supported the United States in the Cold War.[24]

Israel officially appealed to the Soviet Union for military aid, even though it had little expectation of receiving it. Israel's military attaché in Moscow asked for help in training and for weapons captured from the Germans, and was turned down. At the same time, Israel's foreign minister told the government that the Soviet Union resolutely supported Israel and did not demand that Israel identify with the Eastern bloc in the Cold War.[25] Israel tried to explain to the Soviet foreign ministry that the Israel Defense Forces (IDF) needed sophisticated weapons for defense, and was told that the world would turn against the Soviet Union if it were discovered supplying arms to Israel in violation of the UN resolution.[26]

It was Ehrenburg who personally warned Israel's representatives of the essential difficulty in the relations between the two countries. Since there was no Jewish problem in the Soviet Union, Israel had to stop luring Soviet Jews to Israel. Soviet Jews, he claimed, were absolutely loyal to the motherland. Furthermore, Israel could not avoid identifying with the United States in the Cold War. Ehrenburg warned that Soviet Jews would fight against Israel in a third world war. Mordechai Namir, Golda Meir's successor, had every reason to believe that Ehrenburg was speaking for the Kremlin itself.[27]

It was inevitable that relations would deteriorate. When Ben-Gurion did not include Mapam, the left-wing party, in the governing coalition, the Soviet Union classified Israel as bourgeois, nationalistic and leaning toward the West.[28] The first crisis was over the issue of immigration.

24 Service, 2004: 568.
25 DFPI 2: 29–30.
26 Namir, 1971: 74–6.
27 Namir, 1971: 88–91.
28 DFPI 2: 414–16, 421.

The Soviets charged that the Israeli legation was encouraging Soviet citizens to renounce their citizenship; the legation denied the charge.[29] The Soviets refused to accept the Israeli explanation that immigration was vital for a 'progressive fortification' against the Arab world.[30] According to Namir, Israel's pressure for immigration left the Kremlin with three options: (1) transferal of all Soviet Jews to Birobidzhan to create a new Soviet-Jewish nation; (2) complete assimilation; and (3) officially sanctioned emigration to Israel. If the danger of a third world war disappeared or became less urgent, the Kremlin might attempt to implement all three options at once simply to rid itself of the irksome issue.[31] To guarantee some chance for immigration, Israel ostensibly committed itself to tactical neutrality ('non-identification') in its foreign policy, promising that no foreign bases would be established in the Negev once it had been liberated.

However, from the start neutrality was at odds with the goal of Jewish immigration, which was the very life-blood of Zionism.[32] Despite the difficulties, Israel decided it would be best to send an envoy to Moscow to balance Anglo-American pressure about borders, refugees and Jerusalem. For the Soviets, the Palestine question was just one facet of the general deepening crisis. The Soviet Union insisted that only they supported the aspirations of both Jews and Palestinian Arabs for freedom, as well as the return of the refugees to the independent Arab state that the UN was obligated to establish.[33] The Soviet approach was to cool relations and instruct its envoy to Israel to track US and British activities in the region.[34] Soviet Jews who wished to move to Israel were required to give up their Soviet citizenship, and each case would be considered by the Supreme Soviet. The Soviet Union rejected Israel's request for financial credits and also rejected assurances that the IDF was not commanded by the Pentagon.[35]

The Soviet regime's campaign against 'cosmopolitan' Jewish scientists and writers appalled the Israelis and it was suggested that a campaign be launched to leak information about the persecution of the Soviet Jews.[36] Regarding immigration, it was suggested the Soviets be told they

29 DISR 1: 436–8.
30 DFPI 2: 424–5, 522.
31 DFPI 2: 455–6.
32 KR 1: 764 (June 20, 1949).
33 DISR 2: 521–8.
34 DISR 2: 535–8.
35 DFPI 4: 524–5.
36 DISR 2: 551.

were missing an opportunity to affect the future of Israel, and that they could wield influence by providing the IDF with equipment and training, and by expanding trade, cultural, and scientific relations.[37] As far as the Kremlin was concerned, Ben-Gurion was the ringleader of anti-Soviet propaganda and Israel's 'reactionary' press was spreading rumors, claiming there was no difference between the Soviet regime and fascism.[38] Yet, despite deteriorating relations, the USSR continued to support the UN partition plan, which included the establishment of Jewish and Arab states and the internationalization of Jerusalem.[39]

While Israel viewed immigration as the central Israeli–Soviet issue, for the Kremlin the main issue was Israel's identification and solidarity with the West. The Soviet government was angry with Israel for not officially supporting the Soviet proposals for arms reductions and a nuclear weapons ban, and for not yet according diplomatic recognition to the People's Republic of China. Furthermore, the Soviet authorities claimed, Israel's economic policy had failed, chauvinism was on the rise and the Arab population was oppressed. Israel's 'reactionary' policies were moving it toward an alliance with the United States and the issue of the Soviet Jews was leading to an 'unavoidable clash' between the two countries.[40] Assurances that Israel would not become a US vassal state went unheeded.[41] In 1949, the Soviets reversed their position and advocated the partition of Jerusalem,[42] and, on the eve of the Korean War, the Kremlin designated Israel as a hostile state identifying entirely with the West.[43]

The Korean War brought a sharp decline in Israeli–Soviet relations. The Israeli government voted in favor of the Security Council decision to send military forces to fight North Korea, in practice abandoning its Cold War tactic of non-alignment.[44] Ben-Gurion shrugged off the condemnations of the Israeli left. Israel, he maintained, could not be 'indifferent and neutral' to world events, and its conscience was not for sale, neither to the Americans nor the Russians.[45]

37 DFPI 4: 566–7.
38 DISR 2: 562–70.
39 DFPI 4: 686, 712–13.
40 DISR 2: 601–14.
41 DISR 2: 615–19.
42 DISR 2: 635.
43 DISR 2: 635.
44 ICAB, July 2, 1950, ISA.
45 KR 7: 2058–60, 2082–3.

However, the escalation in Korea did not end the era of non-alignment. Israel rebuffed the US request to send the IDF to participate in the war and offered medical assistance instead. Ben-Gurion did not shrink from an internal debate. 'The Western countries,' he said, 'need to know that we are a serious nation.' Israel vainly tried to persuade the Soviets that it was in their own interest to allow the Jews to emigrate, arguing that the Anglo-American alliance threatened to turn the Middle East into a launchpad for a war against the Soviets.[46]

In February 1951, General Brian Robertson, the commander-in-chief of the British army in the Middle East, came to Israel to request that it play an important role in regional defense. Ben-Gurion was willing, on condition that peace treaties be signed with the Arab states and that nothing be done to prejudice immigration from the Soviet bloc.[47] The Soviet mission reported to the Kremlin that Israel's growing dependence on the United States was leading to a loss of Israeli sovereignty. Mass immigration was strengthening the reactionary forces and making Israel into one of the strongest states in the region.[48] The Soviets regarded Ben-Gurion's US visit in 1951 as another stage in Israeli enslavement to imperialist interests. Israel's request for $150 million, if granted, would lead it to make further concessions to the West. *Pravda* claimed that the two countries had signed political treaties during the visit, completing Israel's transformation into an American possession.[49] The mutual trade and shipping agreement, they claimed, was the first stage toward a defense treaty.[50]

Yet the Israeli foreign ministry still remained optimistic about relations with the Soviets. The Kremlin had not abandoned its anti-Arab ideological stance, being of the opinion that time was working in Communism's favor, but that the time had not yet come for a social revolution in the Arab world because the Arab proletarians and *fellahin* (peasant farmers) were still weak. Islam, according to the Soviets, was keeping its adherents from adopting a secular ideology like Communism.[51] Israel believed the Soviet Union would settle for obstructing the Western effort to establish a military presence in the area, threatening the Arabs that they would share Korea's fate if they permitted the West to turn them into strategic targets, and targeting Iranian and Iraqi oil. Israel assumed that the Soviet

46 Levavi to IFM, February 13, 1951, ISA 2410/10.
47 DISR 2: 689–90.
48 DISR 2: 693–4.
49 DISR 2: 702.
50 DISR 2: 715–17.
51 Soviet Policy in the Middle East, June 20, 1951, ISA 2507/1.

Union would not start a regional war unless it had decided on a world war. Oil was the main issue, even though the Soviet Union did not itself need Middle Eastern oil.[52]

Ben-Gurion had a low opinion of Soviet nuclear power and was opposed to foreign bases in Israel, but if the Soviets turned into aggressors he would reconsider.[53] He did not believe Stalin when he said he would not attack the United States. Ben-Gurion's strategy was clear: Israel could shore up its military and economic power only with Western help, but the Soviet Union was a great power and home to two million Jews.[54] Israel's tactic of non-alignment prevented the government from reading the writing on the wall, and the Soviet abstention in September 1951 regarding the Egyptian blockade of Israeli shipping through the Suez Canal was not viewed as a bad omen.[55] However, the official US invitation to the region's countries to join the Middle East Command (MEC) heralded conflict. In November 1951, the Kremlin sent Israel a communiqué in which it argued that the purpose of the Western proposal was to bring Israel into NATO military missions against the Soviet bloc. If Israel joined, it would gravely damage relations between the two countries, as well as regional peace and security.[56]

Israel defended its position, claiming it had not received an official invitation to join the MEC. It would not consent to aggression against the Soviet Union and there were no foreign bases on its territories. The ingathering of the exiled Jewish people was the country's raison d'être, a goal consistent with Soviet policy, which was based on the equality of nations and the right to self-determination. The Soviet foreign ministry, however, charged that Israel published anti-Soviet material,[57] and the Kremlin considered Israel as having identified with the United States, saying it did not believe Israel's reservations about the MEC. Rather, said the Soviets, Israel did not want to join because of its conflict with the Arabs and its desire for immigration from the Soviet Union.[58] Israel mistakenly believed that regional security and immigration were bilateral issues that could be isolated from the Cold War. The Soviets argued that there were no candidates for immigration: Jews occupied senior positions in the Soviet regime and Birobidzhan had a Jewish majority. The

52  Soviet Policy in the Middle East, June 20, 1951, ISA 2507/1.
53  DISR 2: 735–7.
54  KFADC, November 20, 1951, ISA.
55  DFPI 6: 593–4.
56  DFPI 6: 821–2.
57  DISR 2: 758–9.
58  DFPI 6: 808–19.

Israeli government was leading the country into political subjugation to the United States, having received $100 million from the United States for an anti-Soviet vote.[59]

It was no longer possible to halt the deterioration of Soviet–Israeli relations, as illustrated in November 1952 by the arrest and trial of a group of Jewish Communist leaders in Czechoslovakia. Their trials in Prague were accompanied by a wave of Soviet anti-Zionist and anti-Semitic propaganda,[60] and strengthened Ben-Gurion's conviction that Israel had to oppose the Soviet Union. He was certain that the West would win a world war, but Israel could be defeated. 'It would be enough to destroy Tel Aviv and its surroundings, and we would be done for,' he said. He raised the plight of the Soviet Jews and their aspiration to emigrate to Israel,[61] but if the Kremlin permitted its Jews to leave, it would be tantamount to acknowledging the failure of the Soviet system.[62] The Soviets began to adjust their Middle East policy according not to Arab power but to Western strategy.

The Prague trials sent Soviet–Israeli relations hurtling into an abyss.[63] Israel's envoy to Prague was designated persona non grata and expelled. He said the situation there was 'without precedent' in the history of anti-Semitism, with the exception of Tsarist Russia and Nazi Germany.[64] According to the prosecutor, the Americans had promised Ben-Gurion they would support the establishment of the Jewish state if Israel agreed to organize groups for subversion and espionage in the Soviet bloc.[65] The downturn in the Soviet approach to Israel began when at the seventh session of the General Assembly in December 1952, the Soviet Union voted against direct negotiations between Israel and the Arab states.[66] It quickly became clear that the Kremlin had coordinated with Prague. The Israeli envoy explained to the Czechoslovakian government that the reparations agreement with West Germany was not an anti-Soviet plot and that Israel had also demanded reparations from East Germany, but his explanations were rejected.[67]

---

59  DISR 2: 765.
60  DFPI 6: 873–5.
61  ICAB, October 28, 1951, ISA.
62  DFPI 7: 65.
63  DFPI 7: 581–2.
64  DFPI 7: 654–5.
65  DFPI 7: 659–60.
66  DFPI 7: 678, 718, 721; Eban, 1977: 169.
67  ICAB, December 3, 1952, ISA.

The Israeli government was horrified by the Prague trials but remained silent, fearing a reaction would further complicate the plight of the Jews of the Eastern bloc.[68] Ben-Gurion sharply censured the Israeli extreme left, which continued to support Stalin unreservedly and frightened the public by claiming Israel was a US satellite.[69] The dynamics of the increasingly better relations with Moscow were reversed. In January 1953, some of the Soviet Union's most important physicians, most of them Jews, were charged with attempting to poison the Soviet political and military leadership and the Soviet people were called on to be vigilant regarding the 'fifth column.'[70]

Within the Israeli foreign ministry a debate raged between those who cautioned against involvement in the Cold War and their opponents. It was suggested that the Doctors' Plot was anti-Zionist but not anti-Israeli,[71] perhaps the result of a power struggle in the upper echelons of the Soviet leadership where some of the contenders sought to show that they could rule with an iron fist. The argument was academic because *Novoye Vremya* accused Israeli public figures of being US State Department stooges and helping defeat Soviet peace proposals at the UN.[72]

Israel decided not to be more anti-Soviet or to openly join the West in the Cold War, even though the Doctors' Plot looked like preparation for war.[73] The Kremlin was told that the atmosphere in Israel was 'hysterical' and there were reports of an anti-Soviet campaign being waged to increase fundraising for Israel in the United States. The insistence on Jewish immigration was demagoguery and meant to strengthen Israel's demand for US aid, distract public opinion from economic woes, and reinforce national sentiments in preparation for a political offensive.[74]

The Doctors' Plot set Israel and the Soviet Union on the road to inevitable collision, which occurred in February 1953 when a bomb went off in the courtyard of the Soviet legation in Israel. The Soviet envoy, Pavel

---

68 ICAB, November 23, 1952, ISA.
69 MCC, November 23, 1952, LPA.
70 DFPI 8: 20.
71 On Stalin's orders, the security ministry accused (in January 1953) a group of mostly Jewish physicians for plotting to kill army, party, and government officials, and tortured them into confession. Only after Stalin's death did the Kremlin's new leadership admit to provocation.
72 Eliashiv to FO, January 21, 1953, ISA 6/2325; Brent and Naumov, 2003.
73 DFPI 8: 98–9; FRUS, 1952–1954, viii: 1073–75.
74 DISR 2: 868–9.

Yershov, claimed the bombing was the result of the Israeli government's official anti-Soviet campaign and recommended severing diplomatic relations. He rejected Israel's apology as hypocritical, given its record of 'incitement' against the Soviet Union,[75] and diplomatic ties were in fact severed. Israel claimed that the Kremlin had been responsible for poor bilateral relations since 1949 because the Soviet regime denied the Soviet Jews' connection to Israel and had no respect for Israeli democracy.[76] The Soviets, Israel told both the United States and the UN, were suffering from two of Hitler's ailments: insecurity and paranoia.[77] In the case of a world war, Ben-Gurion said, there were two possibilities: Israel would be conquered either by the United States or by the Soviet Union. A US occupation would be temporary and would not ban immigration, but a Soviet occupation would lead to the imposition of a totalitarian regime and the prohibition of Zionism.

However, Israel was not yet aware of the extent of Stalin's hatred for Soviet Jews. In a secret meeting of the Communist Party Presidium, he had defined Jews as those of Jewish national identity who believed that the United States had saved the Jewish people, and called them 'American spies.' The Jews would destroy the Soviet Union and it would never again be able to rise.[78] Thus Stalin's death in March 1953 presaged the end of an era of steadily deteriorating Israeli–Soviet relations. Israel did not abandon the immigration issue, infuriating the Kremlin, even after the Soviets had labeled Israel as completely aligned with the West.[79] From a historical perspective, Israel was naive to believe it could separate the question of the immigration of Eastern bloc Jews from that of Israel's joining a regional defense organization. It can be argued that, even without the issue of immigration, the Kremlin would not have regarded Israel as a friendly country. In effect, Israel's unavoidable economic and military dependence on the West placed it squarely in the bloc hostile to the Soviet Union.

Stalin's death and the beginnings of détente that followed it worked in Israel's favor. Diplomatic relations were resumed, but quickly ran aground again. As Israel oriented itself ever more completely with the West and gradually abandoned any pretense of neutrality, it increasingly endangered its relations with the Soviet Union. The Eisenhower

---

75 DISR 2: 874–5, 879–90.
76 DISR 2: 139.
77 Summary, Session of IMUN, February 12, 1953, ISA 2/2507.
78 Van Ree, 2008: 206–7.
79 Ro'i, 2003: 21–36.

administration's distance from Israel did not encourage the Kremlin to moderate its attitude toward Israel. The Arab world gradually rose in the Soviet list of priorities, a situation overlooked by Israel because it was eager to get closer to the American hand feeding it. It did not take into account the damage that would cause to Soviet Jews and their ability to immigrate to Israel.

# 2

# The United States and the Cold War: from Truman to Eisenhower (1948–53)

As early as 1947, the US State Department was worried by Soviet penetration of the Middle East, even before any decision had been made about the issue of Palestine – although the lack of a decision would only hasten Soviet expansionism.[1] The State Department believed that partition would undermine international stability, and claimed the Arabs were emotional and liable to view the United States as their principal enemy. Soviet anti-Semitism reinforced opposition in principle to the establishment of a Jewish state.[2] The CIA and the Pentagon were concerned that the United States and the Soviet Union might have to send military forces into Palestine following the British evacuation, gravely endangering regional security.[3]

There was other opposition to partition. The State Department felt that Palestine had great strategic importance, with US oil concessions, air bases in Saudi Arabia and trade with the Arab world at risk if the Soviets gained a foothold. Without the Middle East's 800,000 barrels a day to Western Europe, the Marshall Plan to rebuild postwar Europe's economies would be endangered. If the Soviet army participated in implementing the partition plan, its presence might turn the Middle East into a Cold War arena. Thus the State Department sought an alternative to partition, along the lines of an international trusteeship or federal state.[4] The Zionists responded that US–Soviet relations had never been perfect.[5] US forces outnumbered Soviet forces and there was no real danger of Soviet penetration. Canceling contracts with American oil

---

1 FRUS, 1947, V: 1004–5.
2 FRUS, 1947, V: 1122, 1153, 1155, 1176–7.
3 FRUS, 1947, V: 1236.
4 FRUS, 1948, V (2): 546–54, Memorandum by George F. Kennan, Director of the Policy Planning Staff, to Secretary of State Marshall, January 19, 1948; cf. Costigliola, 2014: 210–11 (Gaddis, 2011: 296); FRUS, 1948, V (2): 622, 666–75.
5 Yogev, 1980: 221–2.

companies would be suicidal for the Arab countries, which could not sell their oil to the Soviet Union because its currency was worthless. There was no basis for the American fear that a Jewish state would turn into a Soviet puppet.[6]

The US Department of Defense opposed Zionism as being contrary to US strategic interests, but the White House counsel, Clark Clifford, argued that a Jewish state in Palestine would strengthen the American position. The test of the UN resolution would be its implementation. The UN was supposed to decide how the partition resolution would be carried out, but in light of the hostilities in Palestine that had been put on hold. At the time, Washington was focused on the Berlin crisis and worried the Soviets would take military action. The National Security Council (NSC) considered the Middle East the most vulnerable region after Europe,[7] and warned that an Arab invasion of Palestine was liable to spark an all-out war, giving the Soviet Union an opportunity to send in forces.[8] Truman met with his advisors on May 12, 1948, and decided, against Secretary of State George Marshall's advice, to recognize Israel before the Soviet Union did,[9] taking into consideration strategic imperatives, economic interests, and ideological preferences.[10]

The NSC was warned there were risks involved in defending a Jewish state. Support for partition would risk vital US interests, threaten to dissolve Western unity toward the Soviet Union and destroy the UN.[11] The State Department opposed granting Israel *de jure* recognition, fearing it planned to conquer Amman and that Communists would take over the country.[12] Withholding recognition also gave it leverage over the new country's government, and Israel's request for a loan was postponed.[13] The State Department opposed lifting the embargo on arms to Israel. It feared Israel would topple Arab regimes and that the resulting chaos would invite Communism into the region, ultimately harming it and ending the rehabilitation of Europe.[14] The CIA warned that the Soviet Union would obstruct any Jewish–Arab compromise.[15] The State

6  Yogev, 1980: 276–7.
7  FRUS, 1948, V: 560–5; Ganin, 1979: 185–7; M. Cohen, 1982: 345–66.
8  FRUS, 1948, V: 882–6.
9  Yogev, 1980: 775–6; Clifford, 1991: 21.
10 Cumings, 1995: 54–5.
11 FRUS, 1948, V (2): 1021–30, 1047–9.
12 DFPI 1: 94–5.
13 DFPI 1: 54–5, 114, 141, 1261–2.
14 FRUS, 1948, V (2): 1217–18.
15 FRUS, 1948, V (2): 1240–8.

Department was influenced by the British, who argued that the Kremlin had a real interest in the Middle East. The situation in Palestine was as dire as that in Berlin, where the United States and Britain had to prevent the Soviets from acquiring an important strategic asset.[16]

In the absence of great power intervention, Israel was free to expand its borders beyond those laid out by the UN resolution.[17] Furthermore, Ben-Gurion rejected the implied US threat of sanctions if the Arab refugees were not allowed to return.[18] It was clear to Israel that the United States wanted a calm Middle East so that it could concentrate on the crisis in Germany.[19] Up to that point, Truman's support for Israel had been merely verbal; the implementing of decisions lay with the State Department. *De jure* recognition of Israel was regarded as a test case, because of the danger that it would enrage and ignite the Muslim world.[20] The US administration's dilemma worsened following Israel's conquest of the northern Negev in October. The Pentagon argued that US obligations were already too numerous, especially when the Cold War in Europe was liable to turn into a global conflict.[21] In the end, however, Truman prevailed over State Department opposition. The test was the IDF's penetration of the Sinai Peninsula at the end of December 1948. The administration threatened to reconsider Israel's application to the UN and to reevaluate US relations with Israel if the IDF did not withdraw.

The US ambassador to Moscow warned Washington that the Kremlin's attitude toward Israel was worsening, and that marked the turning point in US–Israeli relations. With the objective of weakening Israel, the Soviet leadership had demanded its boundaries be limited to those laid out by the UN partition plan; it also intended to halt Czechoslovakian military aid.[22] In light of the threat, the US administration began to listen to Israel's basic requests and to oppose the British demand for sanctions. The real strategic need was not to restrict Israel's borders, but to encourage it to join the West.[23] For the first time, there was talk of Israel's geopolitical importance. The land routes from Turkey to Suez passed

---

16  FRUS, 1948, V (2): 1272–3, 1291–2.
17  FRUS, 1948, V (2): 1328–9.
18  FRUS, 1948, V (2): 1334, 1336–9.
19  DFPI 1: 541–9, 553–7.
20  FRUS, 1948, V (2): 1366–8, 1391, 1408–9.
21  FRUS, 1948, I (2): 656–62.
22  FRUS, 1949, VI: 656–8.
23  FRUS, 1949, VI: 658–61.

through it and its port in Haifa, and its airports could block Soviet transports from oil fields. Cooperation with Israel could greatly benefit the West if there were a conflict with the Soviets,[24] and, for the United States, Israel was best as an ally or even a friendly neutral state. Israeli leaders had secretly declared that their sympathies lay with the West, but apparent neutrality was essential because they needed Soviet support in the UN and Jewish immigrants from the Soviet Union.[25]

However, the State Department threatened that if Israel did not consent to the principles of the UN's decision of December 11, 1948, which called for withdrawal and the return of the Arab refugees, the United States would have to revise its position.[26] Ben-Gurion replied that Israel could be destroyed, but it did not intend to commit suicide. The State Department believed that Israel wanted guarantees against Arab aggression, but not if they were liable to be seen by the Soviet Union as being anti-Soviet.[27] It was clear to the Israeli leadership that its Soviet card against the United States was weak. The West would establish a regional defense organization, and in a bipolar world Israel had limited maneuverability. It would not be able to remain neutral because capital for immigrant absorption could only be raised in the West.[28] Abba Eban, Israel's envoy to the UN, warned that the choice was between the return of 100–200 thousand Arab refugees and an open clash with the United States, and that, when international tensions relaxed, Washington would turn its attention to the Middle East.[29] The best tactic was to bargain with non-alignment: 'We should claim that our status is undecided internally,' Ben-Gurion argued, 'and that they must pursue a cautious policy so as not to push us into the arms of the East.'[30]

Israel's primary objection to adopting an overtly Western orientation was that it would endanger immigration from the Soviet bloc, but Israel was, in fact, an anti-Communist democracy. Its best option was tactical non-alignment, although that did not keep it from supporting NATO and the rehabilitation of Western Europe. If another war broke out, Israel felt it could not remain neutral, and anti-Communist sentiments

24  FRUS, 1949, VI: 1009–12.
25  FRUS, 1949, I: 342.
26  FRUS, 1949, I: 1072–4.
27  McGhee, 1983: 36.
28  DFPI 4: 96–8.
29  ICAB, June 28, 1949, ISA.
30  DFPI 4: 225.

were deeply rooted.³¹ Maintaining its neutrality reflected Israel's desire to receive US aid, keep Soviet support and expedite immigration from the Soviet Union. If peace were not achieved between Israel and the Arab states, Israel would pay a heavy economic and psychological price, and would have to be on constant military alert. An unstable Middle East would put US national interests at risk. It was vital for Israel to reach a compromise with the Arabs so they could work together against possible Soviet aggression.

Ben-Gurion admitted that economic sanctions would be enough to bring Israel to its knees.³² There was no doubt that orienting to the West was a strategic imperative, and the United States proposed that Israel, given its serious economic plight, forsake neutrality. Aid could only come from the United States, because the Soviet Union was committed to 'Russifying' its Jews. Better, then, that Israel join the West openly and benefit from its economic prosperity.³³ There was a danger that the Israeli government would be deluded into thinking that Israeli interests were identical to those of the United States and there were calls for caution, stressing that the State Department felt Israel was an impediment to regional stability and peace and suspected of being uncooperative in the fight against Communism. Its policy toward mass immigration was a threat to its own economy and Israel could not survive even two weeks without financial aid. The $100 million granted to Israel by the Export–Import Bank of the United States was an anomaly, given lest Israel threaten to request arms from the Kremlin if the United States refused.³⁴

It was generally agreed in Washington that no Middle Eastern country could withstand a massive Soviet invasion. Some coordination with Britain and France would be needed, including a joint declaration against regional aggression directed against the Soviets.³⁵ Thus the oil-rich Middle East was taken into account in the formation of US strategy for the Cold War, which called for the tripling of the US defense budget, signed by Truman after the outbreak of the Korean War.³⁶ Despite Truman's directive to supply Israel with defensive arms, the operative decision remained the domain of the Pentagon and the State Department, both of which regarded Israel as aggressive and more powerful than the

31 DFPI 4: 471.
32 FRUS, 1949, VI: 718–19.
33 DFPI 4: 731.
34 Keren to USD, March 28, 1950, Top Secret, ISA 2479/8.
35 FRUS, 1950, V: 135–8.
36 FRUS, 1950, I: 249.

Arab countries.³⁷ The most that the West would do to prevent a regional war was issue the Tripartite Declaration (by the United States, France and Britain) to allay suspicions and tensions. The Arabs were apprehensive about Jewish immigration and territorial annexation, while Israel feared a second round of war. The Declaration endorsed the status quo and tried to convince the local countries that their true security problem was a corollary of the Soviet threat to the West.³⁸ The Declaration was also intended to prevent Israel from turning to the Soviet bloc.³⁹ Israel cited its need for Soviet support in the UN. The Arabs would not alter their positions on the questions of refugees, borders, or peace, even if Israel openly announced a pro-Western orientation.⁴⁰

The Israeli ambassador to Washington viewed the Tripartite Declaration as an extremely important accomplishment. It received a guarantee for its borders, an acknowledgment that it was seeking peace, and a promise of defensive arms.⁴¹ Ben-Gurion was pessimistic, fearing that, '[The agreement] might serve some [of the powers] in the Cold War, and [Israel] should not get involved.'⁴² The Israeli cabinet's position, however, was that everyone knew where Israel stood ideologically.⁴³ The Korean War turned Israel sharply toward the West. Ben-Gurion defended the military action, but said that the Soviets, who were boycotting the UN because China's permanent seat on the Security Council had gone to Chiang Kai-shek's regime in Formosa, should be induced to return to the Security Council.⁴⁴ The immediate benefit was that for the first time the United States promised arms to Israel.⁴⁵ The foreign ministry warned that if Soviet aggression in Korea were not stopped it would spread to Indochina, Iran, Yugoslavia, Berlin, and West Germany.⁴⁶

Israel's dependence on the United States was unprecedented. More than 40 percent of its imports were American and funds for development programs, debt payment, arms acquisition, immigrant absorption, and preparations for emergencies were obtainable only in the United States. In addition, Israel could not hope to receive reparations from Germany without US involvement and Israel did indeed get special treatment,

37  DFPI 5: 315–17.
38  FRUS, 1950, V: 138–41.
39  FRUS, 1950, V: 163–6.
40  DFPI 5: 328–9.
41  DFPI 5: 346.
42  KFADC, May 30, 1950, ISA.
43  ICAB, May 31, 1950, ISA.
44  ICAB, July 2, 1950, ISA.
45  DFPI 5: 421–2.
46  Rafael to IFM, July 6, 1950, ISA 2405/1.

receiving $100 million. However, Washington was concerned about how the Arabs would react. US officials were also wary about how the Israeli parties on the left, Mapam and Maki (the Israeli Communist Party), would act in the event of a Soviet attack.[47]

For Israel, the Korean War was a window of opportunity. By siding with the United States, Israel's population could be increased by two million in the space of three years, non-alignment could end, and an army of a quarter of a million soldiers could be equipped with US arms to repel 'Russian aggression.' It was a crossroads in history. The United States was certain that Israel would fight a Soviet invasion with the same degree of anxiety it had had when fighting the Arabs, and believed that Israel was pro-Western because it would not bite the hand that fed it.[48] However, the State Department opposed supplying arms to Israel, arguing that the enlargement of the Israeli population and strengthening of the IDF ran counter to US plans and obligations.[49] General Omar Bradley, Chairman of the Joint Chiefs of Staff (JSC), and Air-Marshal Arthur Tedder, chief of the Royal Air Force in Britain, agreed that the IDF was already the most effective army south of Turkey.[50] While President Truman sympathized with Israel, it was the State Department, headed by Secretary of State Dean Acheson, that had to carry out the policy and its compliance was not a foregone conclusion.[51]

Ben-Gurion said that North Korea's aggression should be viewed in the same light as Arab aggression against Israel in 1948, but because of the dangers it faced only a symbolic Israeli contingent of 150 volunteers should be sent to the UN force in Korea.[52] Other cabinet members argued that only a medical team should be sent, arguably allowing Israel to retain its non-aligned position. Escalation in Korea made Israel more valuable to the West despite its fundamental weakness.[53] As far as the State Department was concerned, Israel had come over to the West. Although an estimated 18 percent of Israel's population was pro-Soviet, the government was in control, not the pro-Soviet faction. However, the IDF alone could not hold back a Soviet invasion, it could only serve as an auxiliary force along with Jordan's Arab Legion and the reconstituted

47 USD, Israel–US Relations, July [1950], 2463/2, ISA.
48 FRUS, 1950, V: 960–2.
49 FRUS, 1950, V: 965.
50 FRUS, 1950, V: 189.
51 M. Comay, Report on Conversation with A. Feinberg, July 26, 1950, ISA 2460/9.
52 ICAB, August 3, 1950, FRUS, 1950, V: 966.
53 FRUS, 1950, V: 193–6.

Egyptian army. The United States could expect support from regional countries only if the West staged a successful counteroffensive during a war.[54]

China's entry into the Korean War in November 1950 increased the risk of escalation. Israel, with its army of 200,000 men, could help defend the Middle East against a Communist invasion and had to persuade the Truman administration that it was a strategic asset. Despite the arguments, Israel's requests for 150,000 rifles and machine guns, and for funds to improve the ports of Haifa and Eilat, were rejected.[55] The severity of the Arab–Israeli conflict made Washington reject the proposal that Israel serve as an emergency stockpile. In principle, Israel had to solve its food and oil problems by making concessions on territorial and refugee issues, regarded as the way to end the Arab boycott.[56] The NSC agreed that technical and financial assistance to Israel was in US interest[57] and the administration knew Israel had no bargaining strengths, only weaknesses. Internal problems made the adoption of a pro-Western orientation difficult, its stability was threatened by the lack of peace and it was almost complete dependent on foreign aid. Furthermore, its plans for mass immigration weakened it and exacerbated Arab fears. However, the State Department adhered to its goals, seeking to prevent a war between Israel and the Arab states and to reach a general settlement before the Soviet Union initiated a major war.[58] The State Department did regard Israel as an important factor, although in a major war Israel could be cut off from its sources of supply in the West.[59] Israel, the State Department maintained, should be seen as a fait accompli and be included in the aid being provided to the region. The goal was to ensure stability to reinforce the defense of Greece, Turkey, and Iran.[60]

Israel's dependence on the United States was obvious in the UN vote on a US resolution to condemn Communist China, when Israel voted with the West.[61] Nevertheless, Ben-Gurion and Foreign Minister Moshe Sharett demanded that no public identification with the United States be made, although Israel had no other option. The Swiss model of neutrality

54  FRUS, 1950, V: 221–30.
55  DFPI 5: 718–29.
56  DFPI 5: 723.
57  FRUS, 1950, I: 446.
58  FRUS, 1950, V: 271–8; Louis, 1984: 604–31, 757–90.
59  FRUS, 1950, V: 17–21, 561–2.
60  FRUS, 1950, V: 21–7.
61  ICAB, February 1, 1951, ISA.

was misleading, because the Swiss were willing to fight to maintain their neutrality.[62] Israel, however, still did not fulfill the State Department's expectations of a compromise with the Arabs, reinstating the flow of Iraqi oil and benefiting from passage through the Suez Canal to save its economy. The State Department warned that the United States ought not to be 'unduly committed' to Israel economically, militarily, or politically.[63] The idea of a 'Middle East Command' was abandoned in the face of escalation in the Far East. The Middle East was important because of its oil and as a gateway to Africa, but there were no forces available to defend it.[64] Israel was told that even if it stood in a void it would not receive another penny.[65]

The State Department feared that the $1.5 billion Israel had requested for absorbing half a million Jews over a period of three years would rouse the fury of the Arabs, who had not yet decided whether to side with the East or the West.[66] Giving Israel preferential treatment would deal a mortal blow to US standing in the Muslim world, and the State Department maintained that had to be prevented,[67] but escalation on the Syrian border was a new threat to the stability of relations. US public opinion viewed Israel's bombing of al-Hammah in April 1951 in retaliation for the Syrian killing of seven Israeli policemen as disproportionate. US support for a UN resolution condemning Israel was unavoidable,[68] as the influence of the Jewish lobby was limited. The Truman administration was preoccupied with saving Korea, Iran, and Western Europe. If Iran and the Arab states were to fall into Soviet hands, Israel was warned, it would find itself in an untenable situation.[69] Ben-Gurion exploited an unofficial visit to the United States in May 1951 to belittle the Arabs' military ability to cope with the threat to world peace.[70] The State Department, determined to counter the image that the United States was an Israeli pawn, equivocated and would not endorse Israel's request for raw materials.[71]

---

62 ICAB, February 8, 1951, ISA.
63 FRUS, 1951, V: 570–6.
64 FRUS, 1951, V: 27–42, 44–7; M. Cohen, 1997: 250–2.
65 DFPI 6: 102–4.
66 FRUS, 1951, V: 599–600.
67 FRUS, 1951, V: 608–10.
68 DFPI 6: 258–9.
69 DFPI 6: 213–14, 256.
70 FRUS, 1951, V: 667–70.
71 ICAB, June 13, 1951, ISA.

Ben-Gurion's position was that the West should base its regional defense on Turkey and Israel.[72] He maintained that the Cold War prevented the United States from fully understanding the serious nature of the Arab–Israeli conflict, and revolutionary leaders with only weak connections to the West were liable to rise among the Arabs.[73] In addition, Israel's concerns about a third world war had reached apocalyptic proportions. He feared that if Israel joined the MEC it would give the Soviets an excuse to halt immigration from Eastern Europe.[74] However, it was no use, Israel's unilateral dependence on the United States was again painfully evident when it submitted a request for a grant of $126 million.[75] Israel had received more financial grants than any other country, $50 per capita, in comparison with ten cents per capita for Britain and five cents for France.[76] However, Ben-Gurion was not mollified: 'I am apprehensive about what will happen to our grandchildren and their great grandchildren … around us is an [Arab] nation 60 million strong, that will soon be 100 million, it is a single bloc and they will destroy us.'[77]

Israel was aware of the paradoxical nature of its situation. If the United States concluded that Israel was apathetic about the MEC and not concerned about a Soviet invasion, it would withhold aid and thus lead to Israel's destruction,[78] yet Israel's value to the administration was constantly rising. A US intelligence evaluation supported covert cooperation with Israel, but also stressed that Israel was exploiting Western fear of the Soviets to improve its military position.[79] Israel's standing in Washington improved in April 24, 1952, when the NSC (129/1) reformulated US strategy in the Middle East[80] to prevent Soviet aggression and defend Western interests in the regional resources. Israel's strategic value was recognized, thanks to its geographic location, military bases, roads, railways, airways, and refineries. However, a revision of its immigration policy was necessary to reduce internal stress and lessen pressure for territorial expansion.[81]

72  DFPI 6: 708–11.
73  ICAB, October 17, 1951, ISA.
74  DFPI 6: 775–8, 808–19.
75  FRUS, 1951, V: 971–2.
76  KFADC, January 3, 1952, ISA.
77  ICAB, September 12, 1951.
78  MPC, January 3, 1952, LPA.
79  National Intelligence Estimate, March 7, 1952, FRUS, 1952–1954, IX: 195–9.
80  'United States Objectives and Policies with Respect to the Arab States and Israel,' FRUS, 1952–1954, IX: 222–6.
81  FRUS, 1952–1954, IX: 222, note 1.

The United States felt that the British and Turkish armies, along with the Arab Legion or the IDF, were not capable of defending the region. It was therefore imperative to improve the IDF's effectiveness and to strengthen the Egyptian army so that it could defend the Suez Canal.[82] The United States responded positively to most of Israel's emergency financial requests, regarding them as contributions to political stability in the region.[83] The Israeli embassy in Washington had a positive opinion of the American attitude toward Israel, and Israel's military attaché in Washington said that it was necessary to reinforce Israel's Western orientation in light of the world's division into ideological, economic and societal blocs. Israel received better treatment in Washington than did any other country, the embassy maintained. An escalation of tensions in the Middle East could be expected once West Germany was brought into the European Defence Community. Close cooperation with the West was thus essential, and the only obstacle was Israel's responsibility for Soviet Jewry.[84]

US policy toward Israel was reversed with the appointment of Henry Byroade as Assistant Secretary of State for the Middle East, South Asia and Africa in the spring of 1952. His tour of the region convinced him that the Arabs genuinely feared Israel because of its desire to expand and what he called its 'arrogance' (he said Israel's attitude was, 'If a single Jew is killed, we will kill sixteen Arabs'). Byroade told Eban that the Arabs complained that the United States was rescuing Israel from its economic woes, while at the same time refusing to implement the 'moral aspect' of the Arab refugee question and demanding West Germany pay reparations to help absorb Jewish refugees into Israel. The proper concern of the United States was regional security, given the weakened positions of Britain and France.[85] Byroade was particularly apprehensive about Israel's reprisal operations and the way, he claimed, that Israel's youth were being educated to 'hate the Arabs.' In a hot war, such a small country, with only 200,000 armed men, would not be of much use. On the other hand, in the Cold War it gave the Soviet Union an opportunity to maneuver between the Arab states.[86] The Pentagon also argued that, despite the great importance of the Middle East, priorities should not be revised. Korea, Indochina and NATO came first. The US strategy

82 FRUS, 1952–1954, IX: 232–4.
83 DFPI 7: 199–201, 219–20.
84 FRUS, 1952–1954, IX: 251–4.
85 FRUS, 1952–1954, IX: 942–4.
86 DFPI 7: 331.

of defending the area, from Turkey to Iran, required the full cooperation of the Arabs.[87] The critical step was taken in June 1952, when the Middle East Defense Organization (MEDO) was established to replace the MEC, and Israel was not asked to join. Despite Israel's valuable contribution to the MEC, the United States felt its participation would have a negative impact on cooperation with the Arabs.[88]

At the beginning of the Cold War, the Middle East was a second-tier US priority, along with Southeast Asia and North Africa; the first tier was Western Europe, West Germany, and Japan. The third tier was to weaken the Soviet Union and to cause internal change.[89] Byroade went directly to Truman with his unpleasant findings from the Arab countries. They were not particularly afraid of Communism, he said. Truman responded that agriculture had to be developed in Iraq, Egypt, and northern Syria (where the Palestinian refugees could be settled). Truman, as the end of his presidency approached, vowed that Egypt would under no circumstances receive military aid without showing willingness to reach peace.[90] Given that the Arab states were explicitly neutral, a small country like Israel was a strategic, if marginal, player.

Israel had, in fact, given up its neutrality the minute it submitted its requests for economic and military aid.[91] Its request for preference in receiving military aid was turned down. Israel was of equal weight with any one of the Arab states, Byroade said, but not with all of them together. He first proposed that Israel agree to unfreeze the bank accounts of Arab refugees and follow with consent to repatriate between 50,000 and 60,000 of them. The refugees, he argued, would strengthen its economy. Israel argued that if it took in any more than the 170,000 Arabs it already had, they would turn into a fifth column.[92] Of limited consolation to Israel was the JCS evaluation that in 1955 the West would have an attack force of eighteen divisions and 620 aircraft deployed in the Middle East, among them two divisions and eighty aircraft from Israel (Iraq would have two divisions). Britain and Turkey were supposed to bear the major burden, without a US contribution.[93] Characteristically, the US ambassador to Lebanon recommended to the State Department

---

87 FRUS, 1952–1954, IX: 237–47.
88 DFPI 7: 251–4.
89 FRUS, 1952–1954, II: 62–3.
90 DFPI 7: 734, note 2.
91 'Israel and Middle East Defense,' in L. Kohn, Political Planning Council, November 4, 1952, ISA 41/7.
92 FRUS, 1952–1954, IX: 1065–9.
93 FRUS, 1952–1954, IX: 1082–3.

that it disregard both Zionist and Arab extremist pressures. If the United States did not act objectively the region would be engulfed by chaos. It was entirely possible that even the Soviet anti-Semitic attitude would strengthen the Kremlin's standing among the Arabs.[94]

Truman's final days in office were marked by Israel's desperate attempt to persuade the administration not to supply weapons to Egypt without conditioning them on peace with Israel. Israel could not remain silent when the balance of power was being upset.[95] The US assessment was that the Middle East was an internationally weak spot like Western Europe and the Far East and that therefore aid to the Arabs should not be conditioned on peace with Israel. Of the two dangers threatening Israel, the Arabs and the Soviets, in the US assessment the second one was greater.[96] The joint intelligence evaluation prepared by the administration warned of an ongoing deterioration in the region that played into Soviet hands. The refugee problem, it said, was the greatest obstacle to stability, and the Arabs feared Israeli expansionism because of its demographic growth and its shortage of economic resources, water in particular.[97]

A reassessment of the Truman era does not support the myth of unreserved US backing for Israel. On the contrary, the Truman administration based its policies almost entirely on the danger of a projected Soviet takeover of the region. Truman himself was sympathetic to Israel in principle, but did not control the implementation of policy orchestrated by Secretary of State Dean Acheson. The expectation of an approaching third world war influenced geopolitical and economic thinking far more than emotional and electoral factors. Arab animosity became a permanent influence on US policy, with the result being that Israel was low priority. While the accepted rules of the patron–client relationship had not yet been fixed, Israel did not dictate US positions in any way and critical economic support was given to Israel because of its contribution to regional stability.[98] In anticipation of a new administration, the State Department prepared the ground for policy changes detrimental to Israel, giving attention to Arab expectations for a change in their status.[99] It was in these doubtful circumstances that Israel entered the Eisenhower–Dulles era.

94  FRUS, 1952–1954, IX: 1082–3.
95  FRUS, 1952–1954, IX: 1086–7.
96  S. Bendor, Report on Conversation with F. Russell, Adviser to the American Embassy in Tel Aviv, January 7, 1953 12/2445a, ISA.
97  National Intelligence Estimate, January 15, 1953, FRUS, 1952–1954, IX: 334–43.
98  MPC, August 24, 1952, LPA.
99  FRUS, 1952–1954, III: 67–9.

The historiographical consensus so far has been that Truman was pro-Zionist only out of internal political considerations, namely, as a result of the Jewish lobby. However, this version of events is true only until 1948. After that his involvement gradually diminished and the State Department and the Pentagon made Middle East policy.[100] The recognition of Israel was not a decisive factor and Truman does not deserve to be blamed for the emergence of the Arab–Israeli conflict.[101] Stalin, who did not offer unambiguous military and political support for the establishment of Israel, was more responsible for exacerbating the conflict than Truman.

The position of the State Department, the Pentagon, and the Mutual Security Agency (which oversaw military, economic, and technical aid to US allies) on the eve of Dwight Eisenhower's entry into the White House stressed the Soviet threat, especially to Iran, but also the Arab states' hatred of Israel. Alongside the new administration's recommendation that the American presence in the region be augmented, it had to demonstrate openly and clearly that Israel would not be given preferential treatment over the Arab states.[102]

---

100 Offner, 2002: 274–306; Gaddis, 1997: 156.
101 Kuniholm, 1989: 317–28.
102 FRUS, 1952–1954, IX: 220.

# 3

# Israel and the Soviet Union prior to the Suez Crisis (1953–56)

At the time of Stalin's death, Israel and the Soviet Union were poles apart. For Ben-Gurion, Jewish immigration from the Soviet Union and orientation toward the West were conditions for Israel's survival, while for Stalin's heirs it was ideologically imperative to deny the existence of a Jewish issue in the Soviet Union and to demand Israel's neutrality.[1] In April 1953, the Soviet government publicly acknowledged that the Doctors' Plot had been a fabrication, but for Israel the basic facts remained unchanged. The Soviets were not interested in regional accommodation, the official condemnation of Zionism voiced at the Prague purge trials had never been altered, and Soviet Jews were still forbidden to emigrate to Israel.[2] The Soviet attitude toward Israel was part of its strategy of breaking Western containment. The tactics they employed included conducting an anti-NATO propaganda campaign and working to perpetuate the Arab–Israeli conflict.[3] When a bomb went off at the Soviet embassy in Ramat Gan in 1953, the Kremlin severed diplomatic relations, which would be renewed only if Israel did not join military alliances or sign anti-USSR treaties.[4] Israel said it had not signed any military agreements and had no intention of doing so. It wanted bilateral relations renewed and did not want to become embroiled in the Cold War.[5]

Nevertheless, it was generally accepted that no matter what Israel did, it would be virtually impossible for it to maintain amicable relations with the Soviet Union. Nothing could make the Kremlin amenable to Israel or induce the Soviets to let the Jews emigrate.[6] Furthermore, attempts to

1 DFPI 8: 258–60.
2 DFPI 8: 268, 270, 315–16, 335–8.
3 Summary, Session of IMUN, April 21, 1953, ISA 2511/9.
4 DISR 2: 897–901. FRUS, 1952–1954, vii: 1140–3.
5 DFPI 8: 443–4.
6 DISR 2: 912–15.

revive the issues of immigration and to preserve Soviet Jewish national culture failed, as did the attempt to obtain Soviet support in the UN for Israeli sovereignty in the demilitarized zone along the Syrian border. Large-scale immigration was rejected and the Kremlin demanded that Israel reach an agreement with the Arabs without third-party mediation.[7]

On January 24, 1954, the Soviets cast their first veto against Israel at the UN Security Council over the issue of Israel's water diversion project in the demilitarized zone on the Syrian border. The Soviet Union was realigning its Middle East policy in favor of the Arabs, forcing the United States to compete with it for the friendship of the Arab world.[8] The veto meant that the growing Arab–Israeli conflict was being brought into the Cold War arena. At first, Israel did not realize the importance of the veto, mistakenly believing that the reestablishment of relations with the Soviet Union was a victory for the policy of Western orientation. The Soviets tried to minimize the significance of the veto and claimed that direct negotiations were needed to resolve the Arab–Israeli conflict.[9]

According to British assessment, Israel had no choice but to belong to the Western camp, because it would be destroyed if the Soviet Union won a third world war, and thus sought defense arrangements with the West. If a war broke out, the Soviet Union might force Israel to disavow its commitments to the West by threatening Nazi-type reprisals against Soviet Jews. The Soviets could not, however, compel Israel to act against the United States because Israel was economically dependent on it.[10] However, if Israel participated in a war against the Soviet Union, the Soviets might well deport its Jews, and local pogroms were also likely.[11] Only after a second Soviet veto on March 29, regarding free navigation in the Suez Canal and the Gulf of Aqaba, did Israel understand the Kremlin had decided to take a harder line.[12]

Another blow fell in July 1954 when Britain and Egypt signed an agreement ending British military presence in Suez. Israel was stunned.[13] The Soviet Union could now establish a huge bridgehead throughout the Mediterranean and the West, not wanting to be held responsible

---

7 DISR 2: 940–1.
8 DFPI 9: 44–6.
9 Y. L. Gideon, Conversation with G. Zeitsev (Head, Middle Eastern Department, Soviet Ministry for Foreign Affairs) to DEE, January 21, 1954, ISA 3492/17II.
10 A. Moore to A. Eden, February 23, 1954, Classified, NA, FO371/111124/R1223.
11 Sir W. Hayter to R. Allen, March 10, 1954, Confidential, NA, FO371/1111064/VR10338/1.
12 Sharett, 1978, 2: 421.
13 Louis, 1989: 43–71.

for the outbreak of a third world war, would hesitate to intervene. The agreement, Israel argued, should include a provision regarding an attack against any state in the Middle East, without mentioning Israel explicitly, and Israel should also be provided with defensive weapons.[14]

Two factors were behind the deterioration of Israel's relations with the Soviet Union: the issue of Soviet Jewry and the Kremlin's turn toward the Arabs. Nahum Goldmann, president of the World Zionist Congress, was asked to speak to Vyacheslav Molotov, Soviet Minister for Foreign Affairs, about immigration.[15] Molotov evaded the question and the Israeli envoy in Moscow suggested that the Kremlin readopt a neutral position toward the Arab–Israeli conflict.[16] Israel had no way of maneuvering the Soviets against the United States because it did not have the option of buying arms from the Soviet Union. However, there was support for expanding trade with the Soviet Union, including oil, which might herald better diplomatic relations and might also strengthen the connection with Soviet Jewry. Even though Soviet Jewish immigration was imperative, Israel, faced with a categorical Soviet refusal, ceased to press for mass immigration and made do with family reunification in keeping with the Soviets' new, more liberal, domestic policies.[17] The Kremlin's attitude toward Israel was also influenced by Israel's position on Western defense plans. Small countries, the Soviets insisted, should turn down US offers of military aid and demand that the superpowers cease manufacturing nuclear weapons, like India, which advocated non-alignment.[18]

Diplomatic relations between Israel and the Soviet Union were reestablished in July 1953, but Israel refused to commit to not entering into a military alliance against the Soviet Union; the Soviets accepted the Israeli position.[19] Ben-Gurion believed that the Kremlin might not want war, but it would continue to seek world domination. The Soviets would attack when they grew stronger, but that might not be for another twenty years, while the Arabs could wait a century to attack.[20]

The Israeli ambassador to Moscow reported that the Kremlin's greatest fear was West Germany's rearmament, prompting the Soviet leadership

14 Eytan to Sharett, August 2, 1954, ISA 2403/16.
15 See Chapter 4.
16 DFPI 9: 525, 642–3, 696–7.
17 DFPI 9: 917–19.
18 E. Sasson to Director WED, October 8, 1954, 2421/21, ISA.
19 S. Lebovitz to A. Aroch, May 22, 1955, ISA 2511/9.
20 BGD, May 12, 155, BGA.

to sign a peace treaty with Austria.[21] In dealing with the Soviet leadership Israel stressed that its agreements with the United States were the result of its isolation and should not interfere with its relations with the Soviet Union.[22] However, every attempt to approach the Soviet Union based on the quid pro quo of Israeli opposition to the rearming of West Germany in exchange for Jewish immigration was rejected.[23] In reality, Nikita Khrushchev, effectively the new ruler in the Kremlin, was hardly seeking a deal with Israel. *Izvestia* published an article entitled 'Attempts to Drag Israel into a Military Bloc.' It asked whether Israel's pursuit of a military alliance with the West was consistent with the commitments it had made when it reestablished diplomatic relations with the Soviet Union, and accused Israel of 'fraud' and 'breach of trust.'[24] The article received considerable attention in Israel. Israel accused the Soviet Union of using its veto at the UN Security Council to encourage the Arabs to attack Israel. Why was Israel under the threat of an attack, its leaders asked, if the Soviet Union supported world peace?[25]

Given the prevailing tension, Israel realized it was pointless to raise the question of immigration.[26] Molotov warned that in any 'commitment' between Israel and the United States, the latter would have the last word. The Soviet Union did not fear an Israeli attack per se, but it would regard Western bases on Israeli territory as it viewed the bases in Turkey.[27] Israel defended its pursuit of a defense pact with the United States on the grounds that it was not an anti-Soviet move, but rather that the regional balance of power had been upset. However, the Soviet ambassador said that allowing Jewish emigration from the Soviet Union depended on Israel.[28] Signing a defense pact with the United States meant that Israel could be used as a base for an aerial attack on the Soviet Union. Moshe Sharett replied, 'If the United States were to invade Israel and bomb Odessa from there, it would almost certainly be able to do so,' whether or not it had signed a pact with Israel.[29] The Soviets stated also that Israel's pursuit of a military alliance with the West justified the dismantling of Jewish cultural institutions in the Soviet Union,

21 Avidar to DEE, May 18, 1955, ISA 2507/1.
22 Yachil to Avidar, 'Ambassadors' Convention,' Classified, May 24, 1955, ISA, 12/450.
23 DFPI 9: 917–19.
24 Sharett, 1978, 4: 1049.
25 DEE to IMM, June 13, 1955, ISA 2326/3.
26 Sharett to Avigur, June 26, 1955, ISA 2397/18.
27 DEE to IMM, June 28, 1955, ISA 2326/3.
28 Sharett, 'Conversation with Abramov,' July 14, 1955, SDMEC 1: 299–303.
29 Sharett to Shek, May 3, 1956, ISA 2410/20.

which under the influence of American Zionists could serve as 'instilling anti-Soviet ideas.'[30]

Israel felt it unlikely that a new world order would be established following the Geneva Summit on nuclear disarmament held in July 1955. East–West relations were heading for coexistence while leaving the Jewish problem unsolved. Israel needed broad coverage in the Western press, because the Kremlin was highly sensitive to criticism for human rights violations. Israel was prepared to abandon a defense pact with the United States, the chances for which were bleak in any case, in exchange for Jewish immigration from the Soviet Union.[31] However, it was already too late, Khrushchev had closed a deal with Egyptian President Gamal Abdel Nasser.

A clear sign of the worsening relations was the expulsion of members of Israel's embassy staff connected with an Israeli agency called Nativ, which worked secretly to encourage the immigration of the Soviet Jews. According to the Soviets, they were spies and were in contact with 'criminals.'[32] Israel decided to make Jewish immigration from the Soviet Union and Eastern Europe an international issue but without referring to the Soviet Union as a totalitarian state, which would have made Israel look like an enemy.[33] Israel's representatives throughout the world were told to exploit every opportunity to raise the problem of Eastern European Jewry.[34] However, as part of the Kremlin's tactics to ease tensions, the Soviets ridiculed the Arab threats to drive the Jews into the sea, saying that eventually one Arab country would make peace with Israel and, after it, Lebanon.[35]

Israel learned that the Soviet ambassador to Cairo had proposed the construction of Soviet military industries and steel factories in Egypt and to supply all the arms Egypt wanted as a way of thanking Egypt for not joining a Western defense alliance. Egypt notified the United States, fishing for a counteroffer from Washington, but the United States would not commit to supplying arms immediately.[36] Nasser told the Soviets he

30 Argaman (Bucharest) to DEE, August 5, 1955, 'Conversation with F. Didushkin,' 2410/21/6.
31 Sharett, 1978, 4: 1121–3.
32 Avidar to Sharett, August 18, 1955, Personal, ISA 2326/4.
33 'Summary of Consultation Concerning Aliyah from the USSR,' August 21, 1955, Top Secret, ISA 2397/8.
34 Harman to Heads of IDM, September 5, 1955, ISA 2496/18.
35 Razin to Sharett, September 7, 1955, in Dinur to Sharett, September 20, 1955, ISA 2390/20.
36 DEE to IMM, August 28, 1955, ISA, 2326/3; Sharett, 1978, 4: 1148.

needed arms to keep Israel from defeating his army, and that an Israeli victory would allow Western agents to incite the Egyptian people against him and replace him with a pro-Western regime.[37]

The Egyptian arms deal with Czechoslovakia did not look dangerous, since the United States alone determined Israel's fate. Israel called the deal a game that Egypt was playing with the two superpowers.[38] The Soviet denial of the significance of the deal was ideological. The Soviet Union, the Soviets argued, had always operated according to Lenin's precept of supporting all anti-colonialist countries, such as Egypt. It had no intention of harming Israel,[39] the arms deal was nothing more than a commercial transaction.[40] Israel protested that the Kremlin should pay attention to the saber rattling of the Arab leaders and the Soviets replied that, while they opposed an arms race, every country needed a minimum supply of defensive arms. On September 12, 1955, the Czech–Egyptian arms deal was signed in Prague[41] and made public by Nasser two weeks later.[42] Israel protested that Egypt was a strongly hostile country,[43] and that it had no choice but to renew its efforts to achieve a defense pact with the United States.[44] Israel claimed that the deal was 'a very serious shift.' It was 'the first real response' to the region's integration into the Western defense system and to Israel's status as a US ally, and ended an era in Israeli–Soviet relations.[45]

Prime Minister Sharett acknowledged in his diary his failure as the country's leader. There was no hope of receiving either arms or security guarantees from the United States and the only option was a preemptive war, which he opposed in principle: 'What is our vision of living in this land – perpetual war and living by the sword?'

The foreign ministry mistakenly thought that Israel's attempts to achieve a defense pact with the United States had not affected Soviet

37 'Memorandum of Conversation between Solod and Nasser,' September 15, 1955, Top Secret, CWIHP.
38 Sharett in KFADC, September 6, 1955, ISA.
39 Margalit (Bucharest), Conversation with Kokarko, September 11, 1955, ISA 2507/9.
40 'An Intelligence Brief Submitted by Hassan Tuhami, Head of the Intelligence Branch at the President's Office, to Gamal Abd al-Nasser,' June 15, 1955, CWIHP.
41 SDMEC 1: 328–34.
42 Bar-On, 1994: 1–2.
43 USD to IMW, Sharett-Klimov, Soviet Chargé, Meeting, September 29, 1955, ISA 2775/10.
44 Levavi to Eytan, September 30, 1955, ISA 2403/16.
45 Gefen, October 11, 155, Special Survey, 250, ISA 2492/17.

policy in the Middle East. Sharett accused the Soviets of having begun a war of annihilation against Israel and was able to obtain a broad consensus in the government and the Knesset on a pro-US policy.

It was now clear to Israel that the only place in the world where East and West had agreed to cooperate was Austria, and that the Soviet Union had been blocking a solution to the Arab–Israeli conflict since December 1952.[46] It also became clear how isolated Israel was. One exception was France, which promised an immediate supply of arms, but Israel was hugely disappointed by Secretary of State John Foster Dulles, who turned down Israel's request for a defense pact and armaments.[47] Israel warned of a war that would suck in the entire world, while the Soviet Union argued that Israel was strong and Egypt was weak. Israel supported the West, it was pointed out, but the West was not rushing to help it.[48]

The Soviet Union had realized the traditional Russian goal of penetrating the Middle East, which had been blocked by the West after World War II, and its goal was to pressure Israel to abandon its Western orientation.[49] Israel viewed the Czech–Egyptian arms deal as an offensive against the West as well as a blow to Zionism and Israel. According to Israeli assessment, Soviet regional policy was a facet of its global policy and its aim was to exploit the spirit of the Geneva Summit to weaken the West. The Kremlin, Israel predicted, would support Arab demands for the 1947 partition boundaries as a basis for a solution to the refugee problem. It was argued that the government had not understood the Kremlin's intentions.[50] Nothing would persuade the Soviets that Israel could sign a security pact with the West without offering military bases, and Sharett's talks in Geneva only strengthened the Soviets' conviction that Israel was a Western puppet.[51]

The Czech–Egyptian arms deal shook the leadership and the Israeli government finally realized the extent of the disaster. Minister of Labor Golda Meir accused the Soviet Union of planning to annihilate Israel.[52] Ben-Gurion acknowledged that the situation was 'extremely grave.' The Soviet Union had a strategic interest in the Middle East: forty million

---

46 Eban to Sharett, October 18, 1955, ISA 2505/23.
47 Sharett, 1978, 5: 1249–54.
48 Sharett, 1978, 5: 1272–5.
49 Argaman on a November 7 party at the Soviet embassy, November 10, 1955, ISA 24933/1.
50 Avidar to Eytan, November 17, 1955, ISA 2505/23.
51 Aivdar to Eytan, December 2, 1955, ISA 2410/18.
52 Yachil to Meroz, November 28, 1955, ISA 2496/18.

Arabs and their oil fields were more important than a million and a half Jews on a small patch of land.⁵³

Only at the beginning of December did it become apparent that the arms deal had altered the balance of power. The Egyptians would receive 200 MiGs, dozens of bombers, 150 heavy tanks and an unknown number of torpedoes and submarines. Israel had yet to receive Mystère jets from France and had nothing to counter the thirty-two Centurion tanks Egypt already had. Furthermore, Israel's very existence irritated the Kremlin and was a thorn in its domestic policy because it was an obstacle to the assimilation of Soviet Jews. Ben-Gurion opposed a preemptive attack against Egypt, predicting that Britain would intervene against Israel, but that the Soviet Union would stay out as it had done in Korea. If Israel attacked it would not be able to receive arms from anywhere, its economic strength would be exhausted, and a second round of war would lead to a third.⁵⁴ The deal was assessed in the context of the Cold War. Israel could prepare for the worst in three ways: exclusive dependence on the United States, reconciliation with the Kremlin via neutrality, or by attempting to walk a tightrope, alternating back and forth between both positions. Ben-Gurion feared that the Soviet Union would send 200 'volunteer' pilots from Romania or Czechoslovakia to assist Nasser in a war against Israel.⁵⁵

Israeli–Soviet relations were beyond repair. On December 29, 1955, Khrushchev gave a speech at a meeting of the Presidium of the Supreme Soviet in which he condemned an Israeli reprisal operation which had left fifty-four Syrian and six Israeli soldiers dead. Israel, he claimed, was supported by imperialist countries seeking to take over the region's natural resources.⁵⁶ Ben-Gurion understood the great danger of the Soviet Union, whose *Great Soviet Encyclopedia* officially libeled both the Jewish people and the Bible. It was not at all clear that Khrushchev wanted peace. Angry and on the verge of despair, Ben-Gurion claimed that the speech had made very real threats and that the Soviets were sending strategic weapons to Israel's enemies.⁵⁷ Israel's plight forced it into closer relations with West Germany. The talk of playing off East

---

53 KFADC, November 30, 1955, ISA.
54 Ben-Gurion in ICAB, December 4, 1955, ISA.
55 ICAB, February 25, 1955, ISA.
56 A. Chelouche (Moscow) to DEE, December 30, 1955, ISA 2327/1.
57 Ben-Gurion in ICAB, January 1, 1956, ISA.

against West was groundless, despite Ben-Gurion's posturing in secret cabinet sessions, in which he raged against the Kremlin.[58]

When the Knesset voted against a no-confidence motion submitted by the Israeli Communist Party, the Kremlin took it as proof of Israel's desire for a military alliance with the United States. Israel replied that it had not granted bases to other countries. Molotov answered that 'official circles' in Israel were taking an extreme anti-Soviet position and that the importance of the Czech–Egyptian arms deal had been overrated. It was inconceivable that the Soviet Union would not help countries that had liberated themselves from the yoke of colonialism and were still fighting for independence. Israel responded that its policy reflected only its own vital interests.[59] Israel understood that alone it could not overcome the dangers of world Communism. Lenin and Stalin had opposed Zionism and the Jewish people's right to exist. Israel's fate was of no concern to the Communist world, it cared only whether Soviet penetration of the Middle East strengthened or weakened the United States.[60] Israel needed allies at any price and, while there was a huge difference between West and East, it hardly made a difference to a country that had been set adrift by both.[61]

Israel's room for tactical maneuvering against the Soviet Union grew narrower. Khrushchev's claim that his policy was not anti-Israel and that relations depended on Israel's behavior had become a dangerous game of words.[62] According to Ben-Gurion, the Soviet Union had been hostile to Zionism since Lenin's death. Khrushchev's historic speech of February 25, 1956, at the Twentieth Congress of the Soviet Communist Party, in which he condemned Stalin's crimes without condemning Communism, did not fool him. Furthermore, Israel would be finished if all the Arab states went Communist, and if the Soviets sent a million Jews to Birobidzhan it would also be tantamount to destroying Israel.[63] The Kremlin warned Israel that chasing alliances with the West would be catastrophic, and claimed that the Arabs should be given more support in the UN and their demands for the return and compensation of Palestinian refugees be backed.[64]

Israel made a final tactical effort. The best guarantee against the outbreak of war in the region would be to supply Israel with a hundred

---

58 Ben-Gurion in ICAB, January 8, 1956, ISA.
59 DFPI 11: 106–10; Sharett in KFADC, February 7, 1956, ISA.
60 Sharett, 1978, 5: 1349.
61 Eshel to Kadar, March 5, 1956, ISA 2507/4.
62 Chelouche IMM to DEE, March 5, 1956, ISA 2326/7.
63 ICAB, March 4, 1956, ISA.
64 DEE Director to Sharett, 'Conversation with Uri Ra'anan', *Ha'aretz* Political Correspondent, March 21, 1956, ISA 2507/4.

jet planes and anti-tank weapons. The Soviets were not impressed. The Arab countries, it claimed, were weak and the disadvantaged parties in the conflict, and Israel was strong.[65] Despite Soviet denials, Ben-Gurion reported to the cabinet that he personally had seen photographs of Ilyushin IL-28 bombers in Alexandria.[66]

In April 17, 1956, the Soviet foreign ministry announced publicly that it was concerned about the worsening situation in the Middle East, India and Afghanistan. To the dejected Sharett, who had retained the foreign minister's portfolio in Ben-Gurion's new government, it sounded as though the Soviet position had taken a turn for the better. There was no mention of the UN partition boundaries of 1947 or of the return of the refugees. However, it soon transpired that the Soviets' announcement disregarded the violation of the balance of power in the Middle East, stressed the principle of neutrality and, generally speaking, supported the Arabs.[67] The Soviets, responding to a request for clarifications, said that Israel's refusal to understand the Soviet declaration would have grave consequences.[68] Israel, said the Soviets, was aggressive and had appropriated 6,000 square kilometers of territory that, according to the UN resolution, did not belong to it.[69] Khrushchev also claimed that external forces were encouraging Israel to go to war.[70]

Shocked by the Czech–Egyptian arms deal, the Israeli government put a moratorium on its program to revive Jewish national life in the Soviet Union, lest continuing it would embroil Israel in the Cold War. At the same time, Sharett cautioned that if the Jews around the world remained indifferent it would be doomed to failure. Everything had to be done to create the impression of a 'spontaneous awakening in the Jewish world.'[71] The Kremlin had forced Israel to face reality, warning that it could not compete with Arab power. Israel concluded that only a Western threat of military intervention that ignored a Soviet veto at the UN Security Council could provide Israel with a deterrent to Soviet support for possible Arab aggression.[72] In fact, interviewed by the Egyptian

65 DFPI 11: 298–300.
66 Avidar to DEE, April 10, 1956, ISA, 449/9.
67 Sharett, 1978, 5: 1394.
68 DFPI 11: 374–9.
69 [No author], Report of Meeting between M. Argov and B. Razin with the Soviet Ambassador, April 24, 1956, ISA 2410/20.
70 Discussions with Mr. Bulganin and Mr. Khrushchev at No. 10 Downing Street, April 20, 1956, Secret, NA, PREM 11/1463.
71 DFPI 11: 400–5.
72 Katz (Budapest) to Eytan, June 25, 1956, Top Secret, ISA 2507/4.

daily *Al-Ahram*, Khrushchev called Nasser a 'great hero,' and said that time was on the side of the Arabs, who had to remain patient and preserve the peace. A war between Israel and the Arabs, he said, would mean a third world war.[73]

The Kremlin stressed the ideological aspect of Soviet foreign policy. Communism, it reiterated, was based on an eternally true scientific theory, which was why it supported free shipping in the Formosa Straits but not in the Suez Canal. Nasser was a leader of national liberation, whereas Chiang Kai-shek was the opposite.[74] The Kremlin moved the Cold War to the center of its relations with Israel, making it impossible for the Soviets to be persuaded to support a four-power agreement on the Arab–Israeli balance of power.

In an attempt to save the situation, Israel conveyed to the Kremlin its regret that the new Soviet foreign minister had not visited Israel and that it was still expecting a visit from Deputy Prime Minister Anastas Mikoyan. The Soviet declaration of April 17, 1956, could still serve as a window for cooperation, as for several months Israel had not done anything about a defense pact with the United States.[75] However, all was for naught. After Nasser nationalized the Suez Canal in July 1956 (a surprise to the Soviets),[76] *Izvestia* wrote that, with Western assistance, ruling circles in Israel had considerably increased their military activity.[77]

Ben-Gurion answered that neutrality was an entirely fraudulent Soviet slogan, since Czechoslovakia and Poland were not required to be neutral, but Israel was. How could Israel be neutral toward the United States when American Jews aided Israel and Soviet Jews were not permitted to?[78] Golda Meir, the newly appointed foreign minister, was not impressed by the announcement that the Supreme Soviet had decided on general disarmament and said that Israel would purchase the weapons it needed for survival.[79] She said she knew Muslim pilots from the Soviet Union would volunteer during a war, as they had done in Korea.[80] Ben-Gurion's greatest fear was of a coalition of Nehru, Tito, Khrushchev, Eden, and perhaps the United States, which would pressure Israel to return to the 1947 partition borders, thus denying it the Western Galilee

---

73 [No author], Khrushchev interview with *Al-Ahram*, July 1, 1956, ISA 2505/24.
74 Chelouche to DEE, 'Conversation with Solod', July 4, 1956, ISA 2505/24.
75 DEE to IMM, July 10, 1956, ISA 2507/4.
76 Rucker, 2001: 67; Kyle, 2003: *passim*; Lucas, 1996: *passim*.
77 IMM to DEE, July 29, 1956, ISA 2326/7.
78 KFADC, August 7, 1956, ISA.
79 KFADC, July 23, 1956, ISA.
80 KFADC, September 11, 1956, ISA.

and much of the Negev. The Cold War threatened the Jewish people in both the Eastern and Western blocs. Israel's only loyal allies were the American Jews, a determining factor in US–Israeli relations. Israel was not demanding new territories, but rather new Jews.[81]

The Soviet Union increased its attacks on Israel, claiming it had received large amounts of heavy arms in preparation for an operation against Egypt. A thousand Israeli officers, it charged, were training in NATO countries.[82] The IDF had in fact doubled its armored force and strengthened its air force, but Egypt still had naval and aerial superiority. Israel had no bombers, while Egypt had sixty Ilyushins. The Mystère was superior to the MiG, but Egypt enjoyed numerical superiority. Israel had no heavy tanks. The breakthrough came in June 1956 when France secretly promised Israel the arms it needed, especially aircraft.[83] The Soviet deputy foreign minister complained that Israeli pressure on Egypt originated in the West. Gromyko reported to the Central Committee that Israel was preparing for war and recommended a warning be issued.[84] It was also argued that Arab actions were 'retaliation for retaliation,' and it was difficult to establish what came first.[85]

However, the government did not despair, sensing that the tensions were the result of a consistent and calculated Soviet line. The response was to implement a policy that would burden the Kremlin. The Soviet Union was searching for allies in anti-US non-Communist countries, in church circles and among progressive intellectuals, all places where Israel had friends.[86] The Soviet Union, it was felt, would not risk a war at the expense of economic development. It did not want a war, it wanted tension which served its interests.[87]

The decisive moment came on October 24, 1956, when Israel secretly signed the Sèvres agreements with Britain and France regarding a military action against the Arabs.[88] On October 28, the Israeli cabinet decided to go to war. The goals were to destroy the Gaza Strip bases of the *fedayun*, the Arab irregulars who were infiltrating Israel and attacking civilians and property, and to capture military outposts in Sinai and Tiran Island in the northern Red Sea Straits of Tiran, which controlled access to Eilat.

81  ICAB, August 5, 1956, ISA.
82  IMM to DEE, September 22, 1956, 2503/14.
83  Bar-On, 1994: 169–71, 197–8.
84  DFPI 11: 721–3.
85  DFPI 11: 745–8.
86  Eshel to Meir, October 21, 1956, ISA 2507/4.
87  ICAB, October 21, 1956, ISA.
88  Bar-On, 1994: *passim*.

Ben-Gurion told the government he could not promise that the Soviet Union and the United States would not demand that Israel withdraw.[89]

By disregarding the two superpowers, the three parties in the war ensured its failure. On November 5, Khrushchev sent threatening warning letters to Britain, France and Israel. For Israel, such an ultimatum was unprecedented. Soviet Premier Nikolai Bulganin (although Khrushchev was the decision-maker) accused Israel of playing criminally and irresponsibly with the fate of the world and its own people, and sowing such animosity for Israel as to question the very existence of Israel as a country.[90] In response Ben-Gurion stated that the Soviet Union ignored the fact that the Israeli operation was a requirement of self-defense.[91] The territories conquered were a bargaining chip for direct peace talks with Egypt.[92] However, the chip was not worth much. West Germany warned Israel that if the Soviet Union attacked, the United States would probably not come to its aid. France also feared the results of an Israeli refusal to withdraw. Ben-Gurion thought the Soviets were bluffing. For the moment, he ignored the opposition of the superpowers and allowed himself to be swept up in the euphoria of victory.[93]

The Israeli assessment was that the Soviet Union had been badly hurt by the deterioration of its position in the Middle East, but that it might increase arms shipments and send 'volunteers' to Syria. The Soviets' intention was to prove to the world and to the Soviet satellites that the Hungarian crisis had not damaged its political or military power.[94] Israeli leaders were pleased that diplomatic relations had not been severed and hoped the Kremlin might recognize Israel's regional importance. However, a Soviet display of animosity was liable to worsen the situation for Soviet Jewry and end the tiny immigration from the Eastern bloc.[95] Despite the Israeli military victory, the government feared a strong Soviet response. It had no doubts about the Kremlin's goals, two of which were Israeli withdrawal to the 1947 partition borders and the creation of a common Egyptian–Jordanian border. Ben-Gurion feared that the Soviets were likely to bomb Israel as they had done to Hungary.

89 Ben-Gurion, 1972: 527–8.
90 KR 21: 259.
91 KR 21: 259 (November 14, 1956).
92 ICAB, November 3, 1956, ISA.
93 ICAB, November 8, 1956, ISA.
94 In October 1956, Hungarian nationalists had rebelled against the pro-Soviet regime in Budapest. After the Hungarian government announced its intention to withdraw from the Warsaw Pact, the Soviet army crushed the revolt.
95 DEE to IDM, November 7, 1956, ISA 2507/4.

He dreamed of new borders in place of the armistice lines, but the Soviet intention to send an international force did not fool him into thinking that Israel could drag out its presence in Sinai indefinitely.[96]

Israeli–Soviet relations deteriorated after the Suez War. Had France not come to the rescue, Israel's fate would have been bitter. Today it is known that the Soviet threat was a bluff, as the Soviets themselves admitted.[97] Ben-Gurion's confidence that getting rid of Nasser would solve the conflict with Egypt overcame his concerns about Soviet intervention. The United States had not promised to back Israel, but France's promise of planes was enough for Ben-Gurion. He realized that he was taking a calculated risk, but if France and Britain could, so could Israel.

---

96 Ben-Gurion in ICAB, (108), November 8, 1956, ISA; KFADC, November 9, 1956, ISA.
97 Vassiliev, 1993: 40–1.

# 4

# Sharett versus Eisenhower and Dulles (1953–56)

Before the Eisenhower administration consolidated its Middle East policy, it was suggested by the US Ambassador to Israel that the State Department take note of the blows Israel had received. There had been the Prague trials, the Arab boycott and the jets Britain had given to the Arabs.[1] Enhanced US support could prevent Israel's economic collapse, but at the price of Arab enmity, which would be harmful to US interests.[2] The US embassy in Amman said peace negotiations would only be possible if Israel made concessions. It would have to internationalize Jerusalem, recognize the Arab refugees' right of return, make reparations and adjust borders to permit villagers to return to their lands, otherwise the spread of Communism would be encouraged.[3]

The new Secretary of State, John Foster Dulles, blamed Israel for the border incidents and jeopardizing regional stability. Syria, he said, was prepared to accept 80,000 refugees and Egypt appeared ready to enter into peace negotiations.[4] Arab ambassadors warned that US support for Israel would facilitate the Soviet penetration of the Middle East. The State Department promised them the Kremlin would never agree to mass Soviet Jewish emigration.[5] Nevertheless, Ben-Gurion proposed that the new administration enter into emergency negotiations with Israel. Israel could train 250,000 men and serve as a center for Western forces.[6] While American Jews had not voted en masse for Eisenhower, it did not mean the administration should court the Arabs.[7] Israel had two assets: the

---

1 FRUS, 1952–1954, IX: 1002–3.
2 FRUS, 1952–1954, IX: 1107–9.
3 FRUS, 1952–1954, IX: 1118–20, 1130–1.
4 FRUS, 1952–1954, IX: 1128–9, 1131–3.
5 FRUS, 1952–1954, IX: 1136–8.
6 FRUS, 1952–1954, IX: 1140–2.
7 DFPI 8: 189–209.

IDF and American Jewry. Ben-Gurion said that, if Eisenhower sought reelection, American Jewish attitudes would be a factor at the polls.[8]

Despite its marginality to US global strategy, the new administration regarded Israeli stability as an asset and granted short-term loans.[9] Israel assumed its relations with the United States were governed by its strength, American public opinion and a common democratic culture, making Israel a good ally for defending the Middle East.[10] However, the administration determined that Israel had to be prepared to adjust its borders and take back a small number of refugees. Sharett rejected the proposals,[11] although he acknowledged the administration's anxiety for the fate of the region, which was wide open to Soviet penetration.[12]

The US envoy to Israel warned of renewed hostilities and claimed Israel was economically weak; the world powers were unfavorably disposed to it and it was suffering from siege trauma.[13] The State Department agreed, having long since concluded that, while Israel was not a viable state, its financial collapse might lead to regional instability. The United States did not, however, give Israel a no-strings-attached grant. For the administration, the conflict precluded Israeli membership of the MEC, but the situation would be reconsidered in light of developments. The administration suggested solving the refugee problem by resettling displaced Arabs in other Arab countries, but Israel would have to pay reparations and repatriate 100,000 of them.

Israel, with only 1.4 million inhabitants, was not considered able to play a role in regional defense,[14] although the State Department did call Israel a vigorous, progressive state. The United States felt that in return for economic support all it had received was Zionist pressure, and said the relations between the two countries were lopsided. The Eisenhower administration rejected the Arab demand to compel Israel to return to the 1947 borders, but it did not accept Israel's demand for recognition of the 1949 armistice lines as its permanent boundaries.[15]

Dulles visited the Middle East with Harold Stassen, director of the Mutual Security Agency (MSA). Middle Eastern oil was a US national

8  DFPI 8: 259–61.
9  FRUS, 1952–1954, IX: 1156–7.
10 DFPI 8: 271–7.
11 FRUS, 1952–1954, IX: 1164–70.
12 DFPI 8: 282–5.
13 FRUS, 1952–1954, IX: 1185.
14 FRUS, 1952–1954, IX: 1188–99.
15 FRUS, 1952–1954, IX: 1215–18.

interest and there would be serious consequences if it fell into Soviet hands.[16] In Cairo, Dulles explained to Nasser that Eisenhower feared the Communist threat. The Communists controlled a third of the world and were expanding into Indochina. He said the new administration was seeking a balance in the conflict with Israel and, if Egypt wished, the United States would build up its army. The administration wanted to support nations that had liberated themselves from colonialism and the military base at Suez was important for deterring the Soviets, who had their eyes on the Persian Gulf.[17]

When Dulles arrived in Israel, Sharett told him the true danger to Israel was the Soviet threat.[18] Ben-Gurion reminded him that, except for Turkey, Israel was the only country in the region prepared and able to fight as part of the free world. He said the US role in the Middle East should be to compete with the Soviet Union, otherwise it would become a second Korea. Dulles said that the United States was prepared to test the Kremlin's good faith regarding détente, but that Communist aggression in the Far East and Germany made the international situation dangerous. Without the Arabs' good will, he said, the United States could not usefully defend the Middle East. Eisenhower supported Israel because it represented a great achievement, but he also had to persuade the Arabs of US interest. Dulles added that the success of Eisenhower's policy in the Middle East depended on the support of American Jews, otherwise the President would abandon responsibility for the region.[19]

Jordan promised Dulles the Arabs would maintain their hostility to Communism, but insisted that peace with Israel had to be based on the UN partition resolution of 1947.[20] Dulles replied that the UN resolutions could not be implemented at that time[21] and told Syria that the United States opposed Israel's expansion beyond the 1949 borders, but would not support the reimposition of the 1947 lines.[22] The United States, he reassured his Arab hosts, would not support massive Jewish immigration to Israel and would not permit undue Jewish influence on its policies.[23]

16 FRUS, 1952–1954, IX: 376–7.
17 FRUS, 1952–1954, IX: 8–18, 19–28.
18 DFPI 8: 370–2.
19 DFPI 8: 376–87, 388–90.
20 FRUS, 1952–1954, IX: 46–8.
21 FRUS, 1952–1954, IX: 48–50.
22 FRUS, 1952–1954, IX: 56–64.
23 FRUS, 1952–1954, IX: 64–71, 76–8.

Dulles also met with Colonel William Eddy, consultant for the Tapline and ARAMCO oil companies, who advised him that the United States had lost its bargaining power and that the Arabs considered using oil to leverage their demands. He said that Israel would invade neighboring Arab capitals and the United States would have to send its army in. Dulles rejected the view as extreme. He said it would be better to give the Arabs more aid, preserve the balance of power and condition aid to Israel on its renouncing territorial expansion.[24] Only in Iraq did Dulles find an Arab partner against Soviet aggression, but Arab confidence in the West was questionable because of its position in the Arab–Israeli conflict.[25] Turkey was the only country that expressed approval of Israel and had reservations about the Arabs.[26] Meeting with Dulles and the Egyptian ambassador, Eisenhower said the Jewish lobby would not influence him and that unity in the face of the Soviet threat was the most important issue.[27] Dulles reported to the NSC that Egypt would not play a key role in defending the region. The problem was that the Arabs ignored the gravity of the Soviet threat. The new focus of the MEC should be the 'Northern Tier' – Pakistan, Turkey, Iran, Syria, and perhaps Iraq – and economic development in Iraq and Syria would make it possible to resettle the Palestinian refugees there.[28]

As soon as the Eisenhower administration was sworn in, Israel realized it had lost its influence in the White House[29] and that the State Department would now determine policy.[30] The President told Abba Hillel Silver, an important Jewish lobbyist, that there was no way Israel would be given preference over the Arabs. Israel's plans to absorb another two million Jewish refugees would destroy all hope for its economic stability and the Arabs would be the victims.[31] Israel, he said, could participate in the MEC only when the regional conflict had been resolved. US support was conditioned on peace, border disputes should be resolved through Israeli concessions and no mass immigration would be allowed.[32] Given the diplomatic stalemate, it was proposed that the refugees be settled

24 FRUS, 1952–1954, IX: 81–4.
25 FRUS, 1952–1954, IX: 90–4.
26 FRUS, 1952–1954, IX: 148–54.
27 FRUS, 1952–1954, IX: 381.
28 FRUS, 1952–1954, IX: 378–9.
29 DFPI 8: 84.
30 DFPI 8: 507.
31 FRUS, 1952–1954, IX: 394–8.
32 FRUS, 1952–1954, IX: 399, 406.

along the Jordan–Syria border, and the area could be made productive with an irrigation project. The Israeli claim that the return of 100,000 *fellahin* to Israel would threaten its security was rejected.[33] The administration argued that peace in the region was years away but that hostilities would not resume as long as a balance of power existed. Since its founding, Israel had received more than $1 billion in foreign aid, of which $800 million had come from the United States.[34] The US dilemma was the West's conflicting interests: it needed the MEC to strengthen the Arab world against the Soviet threat, but it also needed to bolster Israel against an Arab attack.[35]

Globally, the State Department was concerned about the vacuum on the Communist world's southern perimeter between Turkey and India, a territory whose military weakness was an open invitation to Soviet expansion. Israel's claim, that a properly armed Jewish state could serve as a bulwark against Communist penetration of the region, looked preposterous to the Americans. However, Israel should not worry, the State Department maintained, the United States had not given it $300 million so that it could be cast into the sea. US military aid and the promotion of Israeli security would ensure that the Soviets did not bomb it.[36]

US–Israeli relations were, as always, subject to the dynamics of the US–Soviet conflict. The world reacted with shock and anger when Israeli soldiers killed Arab civilians in a reprisal in the West Bank village of Qibya in October 14, 1953, but ignored the Arab terrorist attacks that had led to it. Israel's reputation was at stake and a project to divert the Jordan River was postponed lest it result in the loss of the US grant.[37] Ben-Gurion defended the West Bank operation[38] and the United States responded by suspending its annual aid to Israel, claiming it was destabilizing the region.[39] In March 1954, when Arab terrorists attacked a bus and killed eleven Israelis, given the predictable Soviet response, Israel debated whether even to lodge a complaint with the UN Security Council.[40]

Dulles was concerned Israel had decided that, with the Soviets backing the Arabs, a peace that came only after another war would be better

---

33 FRUS, 1952–1954, IX: 1269–75.
34 National Intelligence Estimate, in FRUS, 1952–1954, IX: 1280–1.
35 FRUS, 1952–1954, IX: 1290.
36 FRUS, 1952–1954, IX: 1294–8.
37 ICAB, October 18, 1953, ISA.
38 ICAB, October 19, 1953, ISA.
39 FRUS, 1952–1954, IX: 1384–7, 1406–9.
40 Eban–Wainhouse Conversation, March 31, 1954, ISA 2480/2.

than a shaky armistice.[41] But it was Byroade who publicly called on the Israelis to integrate into the Middle East instead of serving as a headquarters for religious groups. Moreover, it 'should drop the attitude of a conqueror and the conviction that force is the only policy that your neighbors will understand,'[42] later denying it was a racist remark. The US consul in Jerusalem warned the State Department that Soviet entry into the region was extremely dangerous for Israel, which could be defeated by the surrounding forty million Arabs. The country's arrogance, he said, and its refusal to recognize the practical implications of its actions were liable to bring about its annihilation: 'It may be asked if qualities which led to Maccabeeian and Bar Kochba ... still exist in the Jews today.'[43] Even though US policymakers depicted Israel as the most dangerous country in the region,[44] anything was preferable to an all-out war like Korea and Indochina. Economic aid amounting to $200 per capita (as opposed to $1 per capita for the Arab states), they felt, afforded Israel substantial security.[45]

Sharett was disappointed and in despair. The United States could blockade and starve Israel,[46] it did not need a treaty with Israel; Israel had no friends and no one would save it, he lamented.[47] The president of the American Jewish Committee complained to the State Department that a recent arms shipment to Iraq endangered Israel,[48] and the State Department replied that the arms were meant to enable Iraq to resist Communism, warning the Jewish lobby that anti-Semitism would increase if a war broke out in the Middle East.[49] Dulles told Israel not to think the administration would abandon its 'historical friendship' with the Jewish state.[50] Although preoccupied with the fate of Indochina after the French defeat in Dien Bien Phu, Dulles promised he would not neglect the Middle East.[51]

The principal concern of the annual meeting of the heads of US diplomatic missions in the Middle East was that the Soviets might exploit the

41 FRUS, 1952–1954, IX: 1513–14.
42 Byroade, 1954, 1–14.
43 FRUS, 1952–1954, IX: 1518–20.
44 FRUS, 1952–1954, IX: 1528–9.
45 FRUS, 1952–1954, IX: 1538.
46 Sharett in KFADC, April 19, 1954, ISA.
47 Session in Sharett's house, with Shiloah, April 19, 1954, Top Secret, ISA 5934/3.
48 FRUS, 1952–1954, IX: 1555–6.
49 Isaiah L. K[enen], 'Meeting with Henry A. Byroade and the American Zionist Committee for Public Affairs,' April 30, 1954, ISA 2480/3.
50 Myerson in ICAB, May 2, 1954, ISA.
51 FRUS, 1952–1954, IX: 1557–61.

Arab–Israeli conflict to their own ends.[52] Israel had the best army in the region with the exception of Turkey, the envoys said, and giving it arms would keep the Arabs from participating in the MEC.[53] While the meeting recommended that Israel be given a solemn guarantee against aggression,[54] Israel worried that an Arab attack could take place while the West was preoccupied with the threat of global war. Guarantees would be of value only if they included a commitment for an immediate US response to Arab aggression.[55] The meeting claimed that the real danger lay with a 'foolish Israeli move.'[56]

The chief of army intelligence, General Arthur G. Trudeau, joined Israel's opponents in the administration, claiming it was uncertain which bloc Israel would ultimately support. At most, if the Soviets broke through the northern defense line, the IDF could defend the Suez Canal.[57] However, congressmen who visited Israel doubted whether Israel would stand by the West, since it had not sent soldiers to Korea, it had opposed the regional defense plans and it had close ties with 2.5 million Jews in Eastern Europe.[58] To allay Israel's concerns it was pointed out that the United States had sent a military delegation to Iran when it had been on the verge of a Communist insurrection, implying that Israel, too, should accept such a delegation.[59] Byroade warned IDF Chief of Staff Moshe Dayan that the Communist threat was growing while Israel was undermining regional defense by considering another attack like the one in the West Bank. Dayan protested that the United States was weakening Israel, which expected to face an Arab attack within five to ten years. In its defense, Byroade said, it was determined to prevent Israel's destruction, even if it required sending in the army.[60]

On July 22, 1954, Dulles told an NSC meeting that the United States could not commit to sending military forces into the Middle East in cases of Arab aggression because that required UN sanction and congressional approval. President Eisenhower maintained that none of the parties should be told precisely what the administration would do in such an eventuality. The majority in Congress believed that aggressive

52 FRUS, 1952–1954, IX: 1561–4.
53 FRUS, 1952–1954, IX: 506–10.
54 W. Eytan, 'Note of Conversation with the American Chargé d'Affaires, F. Russell, June 17, 1954,' ISA 2455/1.
55 L. Kohn, Memorandum, June 18, 1954, ISA 2415/1.
56 FRUS, 1952–1954, IX: 1572.
57 DFPI 9: 323–4.
58 W. Eytan, 'Note of a Conversation with F. Russell, May 24, 1954,' ISA 2415/1.
59 'Lavon's Conversation with Mr. Russell, July 7, 1954,' ISA 357/44.
60 FRUS, 1952–1954, IX: 1588–90.

action had to be taken to restrain Israel, which was perceived as the most dangerous and provocative state in the region. Most members of Congress supported the administration's efforts to be fair and objective, claiming that despite the cuts in economic aid, Israel was better off than it had been in the past. Vice-President Richard Nixon commented that the Republicans did not need the Jewish vote. In any case, he said, Eisenhower would receive the support of what he called 'moderate and wise Jews.'[61]

The next day, NSC staff drafted a secret memorandum entitled 'United States Objectives and Policies with Respect to the Near East' (NSC 5428), which claimed the balance of power was in Israel's favor, but that Israel had to be given appropriate guarantees. The role of the United States was to deter the Israelis and Arabs from acts of aggression. If Israel attacked the Arabs and the West failed to stop Israel, the Soviet Union would gain control of the region. Israel and its US supporters had to be persuaded not to abuse Israel's military power, to abandon plans for mass immigration from the Soviet Union and to cease seeking regional hegemony.[62]

The State Department feared that US–Israeli relations would deteriorate if Israel continued sabotaging US policy in the Middle East.[63] Sharett called the charges of Israeli aggression insulting[64] and the product of State Department animosity toward Israel.[65] The Anglo-Egyptian treaty created a new balance of power, he said, and the Sinai Peninsula was no longer a buffer zone. If the United States did not restore the balance, Israel would become a 'nervous embattled camp obsessed with military preparedness.' Dulles reassured him that the United States would not tolerate injury to Israel, although it needed congressional sanction for military intervention.[66]

Eban proposed that the status quo in the Arab–Israeli conflict be preserved to maintain US cooperation, on the grounds that the world was facing a very swift advance of Communist power. Israel was cautiously optimistic, thanks to the protest lodged by 150 members of Congress against

---

61 Memorandum, Subject: Discussion at the 207th Meeting of the National Security Council, Thursday, July 22, 1954, Eisenhower Library, Ann Whitman File, 1953–61, NSC series, Box 5.
62 FRUS, 1952–1954, IX: 525–36.
63 FRUS, 1952–1954, IX: 1592–3.
64 FRUS, 1952–1954, IX: 1596.
65 Sharett to Isser Harel, May 1954, ISA 7226/3.
66 FRUS, 1952–1954, IX: 1600–2.

the arming of Iraq. Israel's strength in Congress had enabled it to receive $350 million over the previous three years, giving it military superiority. The United States did not press Israel on vital issues and economic aid continued, and good Israeli public relations could be very helpful in improving US–Israeli relations.[67] Sharett explained that Israel might act out of desperation to frustrate US plans for a Middle East defense pact against the Soviet Union. Israel did not, he said, want to create the impression of a head-on collision with the United States,[68] which was why it did not have diplomatic relations with Communist China.[69] He categorically opposed any thought of a preemptive war to take control of the West Bank, which had occasionally been considered.[70] He also had little difficulty overcoming the left-wing parties' proposal to break free of the United States and reject a proposed grant of $40–$50 million, which he called an 'act of suicide.' Given the difficulty of its economic position, Israel had to avoid a break from the United States and exploit its fear of Communism.[71]

The main opposition to a defense treaty with Israel came from the US chargé d'affaires in Israel, Francis Russell, who warned that Israel's well-known 'dynamics' prevented it from acting moderately. A defense treaty would establish a 'special relationship' that the United States did not want. It could make the United States a 'semi-combatant,' and cause problems regarding its obligations to countries in the region.[72]

With the Eisenhower administration's opposition to a defense treaty with Israel and the fear of a war between Israel and its neighbors, the State Department drafted a plan called Project Alpha, intended as part of a treaty between the West and the countries of the Middle East. Inauspicious for Israel, its goal was not peace but a formal settlement of the Arab–Israeli conflict within two years in a way not detrimental to the US Northern Tier alliance. A balanced US policy had to reject Israel's pretensions as the defender of Western civilization in the Middle East and the center of the Jewish world, although Israel would be promised US approval for the use of force if necessary,[73] and receive economic aid as a reward for its cooperation with the West.[74]

---

67 Eban in KFADC, August 17, 1954, ISA.
68 Sharett, 'Assessment of our Relations with the US and Suggestions for Action', August 18, 1954, ISA 2414/28.
69 Sharett to Kadar, August 10, 1954, ISA 2414/3.
70 Shek to Eytan, August 19, 1954, ISA 2488/6.
71 ICFPSC, August 25, 1954, ISA.
72 FRUS, 1952–1954, IX: 1627–9.
73 FRUS, 1952–1954, IX: 1695–7.
74 FRUS, 1955–1957, XIV: 9–14.

Project Alpha's terms were not good for Israel. It would have to agree to border adjustments in Jordan's and Syria's favor and give up two triangular patches of territory north of Eilat to create a corridor between Jordan and Egypt. It would also have to take back 50,000–75,000 refugees and give them financial compensation, or allow double the number to return if the Gaza Strip were handed over to Israel (the others would be settled in the Jordan Valley and Sinai Peninsula, while the refugees in Syria and Lebanon would be integrated into the local populations). Haifa would serve as a free port for Jordan and security guarantees would be given to Israel and the Arabs. In exchange, Israel would enjoy free passage through the Suez Canal and the Arab boycott would end. The core of Project Alpha was that Egypt would be the West's major Middle Eastern ally. Dulles hoped to enlist the American Jewish leadership to tell Israel that, if it did not cooperate, Jewish aid to Israel would stop, as they would not throw away their money on a risky enterprise.[75]

The operation in Gaza on February 28, 1955, in which thirty-eight Egyptian and eight Israeli soldiers were killed, caused a crisis in US–Israeli relations, and Nasser used it as an excuse to close a deal with the Soviet bloc. Ben-Gurion argued that because of Cold War considerations the State Department would court Nasser in any case and supply him with arms. The operation had undermined Dulles's trust of Israel and his efforts to strengthen the region in the face of the Communist threat. The United States and Britain wrongly assumed Nasser's objections to Project Alpha could be overcome through military and economic aid to Egypt.[76] The British ambassador to Israel stopped defending Israel after the Gaza operation and slandered the country by saying it was mentally ill and suffering from a variety of complexes, the product of 2,500 years of Jewish history. If the issues were not treated, he said, Israel was liable to become suicidal.[77] According to Dulles, Israel was lucky that Nasser had done his best to sabotage Project Alpha by demanding that he be given the entire Negev south of Beersheba.[78]

Sharett argued that Ben-Gurion was too reliant on Israeli military power and disdainful of other factors.[79] Ben-Gurion he said had yet to

75 Sharett, 1978, 3: 691; Shamir, 1989.
76 FRUS, 1955–1957, XIV: 98–107.
77 Jack Nicholls to Shuckburgh, March 8, 1955, Secret, NA, FO371/7715/VR1051/86; Shuckburgh to Nichols, March 25, 1955, Secret, NA, FO371/7715/VR1051/86; Ovendale, 1996: 118–19.
78 FRUS, 1955–1957, XIV: 151–5, 159–60, 296–7.
79 ICAB, April 24, 1955, ISA.

see a defense treaty ratified by the Senate. Eisenhower, he said, was leery of such an agreement, fearing a world war starting in the Middle East. While France did indeed help Israel, it was weak, and West Germany was not yet a world power, so Israel could depend only on itself.[80] Sharett told Dulles categorically that Israel could not defend itself against Soviet aggression if a security treaty were to demand concessions on the issues of refugees and borders.[81] However, Sharett and his advisors did not fear imminent Soviet aggression and he believed that reprisal operations against Palestinian guerrilla attacks would undermine his efforts to achieve the long-sought defense pact with the United States.[82]

According to Abba Eban, Eisenhower had solved crises in Iran, Suez, Trieste and Austria, granted sovereignty to West Germany and said nuclear power should be available to other countries for peaceful purposes. His policy toward Israel and the Middle East was a product of the Cold War, Eban claimed. He argued that $260 million in aid to Israel over four years showed the US administration sought to strengthen Israel. Both the Western and Soviet blocs opposed the use of force and considered borders inviolable. Borders had to be respected, otherwise 'the world would stand on the edge of annihilation.'[83] Ben-Gurion believed American superiority and nuclear technology deterred the Kremlin and that there would be peace with no surprises for five to ten years.[84] Sharett had to accept that he could no longer steer Israeli policy in what he thought was the correct direction. He stopped pressing for a defense pact with the United States, believing that this would enable him to persuade the Soviets to permit its Jews to emigrate to Israel.[85] In effect, however, Israel had no room to maneuver, because the Kremlin had decided against Israel and its arms deal with Egypt was underway. Israel's future looked gloomy, and then Nasser set off a bombshell by telling Byroade he had decided to accept the Soviets' proposal to supply military equipment.[86]

On the eve of the Czech–Egyptian arms deal, US intelligence reported that only Turkey and possibly Israel were capable of defending themselves against a Soviet attack.[87] Yet, despite Israel's stability and

---

80 ICAB, April 28, 1955, ISA (Ben-Gurion).
81 FRUS, 1955–1957, XIV: 170–4.
82 Sharett, 1978, 4: 1018, 1022–5.
83 ICAB, May 29, 1955, ISA.
84 Ben-Gurion, 1954, 5: 176–8.
85 Sharett, 1978, 4: 1121–3, 1059–60.
86 FRUS, 1955–1957, XIV: 237–40, 270–3, 327–8, 497–8.
87 FRUS, 1955–1957, XII: 77–97.

opposition to Communism, the US Joint Chiefs of Staff continued to oppose a defense pact with Israel.[88] In a war, they felt, the Soviet Union would target Egypt and Kuwait to destroy its Western bases, cut off the flow of oil and seize the Bosporus.[89] The administration learned that the Kremlin had promised Egypt 100 MiG combat planes and 200 tanks.[90] Dulles argued that by upsetting the balance of arms the Soviet Union could force the United States to support Israel in a much more aggressive way.[91] Nevertheless, on 26 August he announced a new Middle East policy centering on Project Alpha.[92] Sharett was 'shaken and frightened' by Dulles's announcement. He warned the United States against acting hastily and causing irreparable damage.[93]

Not wanting to seem to be appeasing, Dulles warned Molotov that the arms deal could cause an Arab–Israeli war and that, in such an eventuality, the United States would not stand aside. British Foreign Secretary Harold Macmillan also warned Molotov of severe consequences for the region.[94] Yet Dulles continued to oppose supplying Israel with either arms or a defense pact on the grounds that it would set off an arms race. He proposed instead that the Czechoslovakian arms deal be used to pressure Israel to give up a larger chunk of the Negev.[95] He told Eban that the deal's implications were among the most serious since Hitler's defeat and were part of the global confrontation with Communism. The regional balance would be upset within twelve to fifteen months, Dulles admitted, but arms to Israel would not prevent the deal and a defense pact with Israel would have a negative impact on the Arab world.[96]

Sharett waited until Nasser officially announced the arms deal before blaming the United States.[97] While the Israeli Cabinet was stunned, Sharett hoped it would now be possible to obtain US arms, believing, naively, that within twenty-four hours Washington would impose its will on Egypt, force it to cancel the deal and forego Soviet aid for the Aswan

88 FRUS, 1955–1957, XII: 98–101, 103–6, 136.
89 FRUS, 1955–1957, XIX: 136–42.
90 FRUS, 1955–1957, XIV: 355–8; for a detailed list of Czech arms supplied to Egypt: 'Ministry of Foreign Trade to Major L. David', 22 July, 1955, CWHIP.
91 FRUS, 1955–1957, XIV: 368–9 Willie Morris to Rose, August 23, 1955, Top Secret, NA, FO/371/115874/VR1076/194/G.
92 FRUS, 1955–1957, XIV: 366–7.
93 Sharett, 1978, 4: 1147.
94 FRUS, 1955–1957, XIV: 483.
95 Catterall, 2003: 517–19.
96 FRUS, 1955–1957, XIV: 540–1; Sharett, 1978, 5: 1180.
97 USD to IMW, September 28, 1955, ISA 2430/19.

Dam.[98] The NSC deliberated the Czech–Egyptian arms deal on October 6, 1955. The CIA's position was that the deal advanced Soviet interests and that Israel would demand arms and guarantees. Dulles argued that if a war broke out the United States would have to intervene.[99] However, he was anxious to prevent escalation at any price. Fearing a strong Soviet reaction, he turned down Iran's request for military and economic aid. Saudi Arabia was liable, he feared, to follow Egypt into the Soviets' lap. His inclination was to think the Czech–Egyptian arms deal would not be repeated and that Nasser would prefer accommodation to war.[100] British Prime Minister Anthony Eden opined that the Kremlin had to be warned that it was risking a global conflagration by aggravating tensions between Israel and Egypt.[101]

Sharett suggested four options to the Americans. The first was to compel the Soviets to cancel the deal. The second was for Israel to launch a preemptive strike, although it would not solve all of Israel's problems. The third was for the United States to supply Israel with arms in quantities equal to those received by Egypt. The fourth was a US–Israeli defense treaty. All were rejected,[102] because the US administration was not prepared to risk an altercation with the Soviet Union[103] and Dulles refused to bring the Cold War into the Middle East. He found himself in a quandary of huge risks and options: one, to enter into negotiations with the Kremlin about establishing spheres of influence; two, to view the Czechoslovak arms sale as the end of the Geneva spirit and to prepare for war; three, to compel Israel to take in a large number of refugees and cede a large part of the Negev; four, to ruin the Egyptian economy; and, five, to reinforce the Northern Tier economically and militarily.[104]

A US intelligence estimate found that the danger of a preemptive Israeli strike had grown. The arms deal would block an Arab–Israeli accommodation, prevent the establishment of a regional defense organization and give Egypt military superiority. Israel was also capable of conquering the Jordan-ruled West Bank and the parts of Egypt, Syria and Lebanon lying close to its borders.[105] The administration recommended that Israel be deterred from launching a preemptive strike by threatening to halt aid.

98  ICAB, October 3, 1955, ISA.
99  FRUS, 1955–1957, XIV: 553–7.
100 FRUS, 1955–1957, XIV: 558–62.
101 Middle East Supply of Arms, October 4, 1955, C.M.34 (55)8, NA, CAB128/29.
102 FRUS, 1955–1957, XIV: 590–1; Sharett, 1978, 4: 1209–10, 1214, 1226.
103 ICAB, October 16, 1955, ISA.
104 FRUS, 1955–1957, XII: 172–3.
105 Intelligence Estimate in FRUS, 1955–1957, XIV: 577–86.

An NSC memorandum stated that it would be simple to impose sea and air embargoes on Israel, but that it would alienate Israel and American Jewry, require the diversion of forces from other arenas and risk a Soviet reaction. The NSC recommended economic sanctions and an embargo, and, if that did not work, subject to congressional approval, military force could be used against Israel.[106]

At an NSC meeting on October 20, 1955, Dulles argued that the United States and the Arabs were partners in repelling Communism, noting the close economic ties between the United States and the Arab countries. Israel, he claimed, was the only country separating the United States from the Arabs. He was convinced that Israel would launch a preemptive strike if it did not receive arms and/or a defense pact. The Eisenhower administration's lack of popularity in the American Jewish community, he said, would not induce it to enter into an arms race with the Soviets because tiny Israel was in any case unable to absorb as many arms as the Arabs. The CIA's position was that the arms deal was liable to cause the free world devastating damage in the Near East.[107] Dulles thought it unlikely that the Senate would ratify a defense pact with Israel, but there was no way of knowing what might happen in an election year. He felt he could not recommend a pact to the Senate without a border agreement between Israel and the Arabs.

The NSC accepted Dulles's position that Israel should not be supplied with arms or money to buy arms, and that Israeli aggression would trigger economic sanctions.[108] Dulles said he and Macmillan had agreed that Israel should be pressured to accept Project Alpha, including giving up Eilat. He argued that the Israelis believed, like Formosa and South Korea, that their only hope lay in a global war, because they could not defeat the Arabs alone.[109]

Dulles badgered Sharett, telling him a comprehensive settlement would require concessions and a defense pact was not practical. He added that the Arab–Israeli problem would be decided in accordance with US national interests, not internal political considerations. Israel, he said, could not save itself with a preemptive attack. Sharett, whose only consolation was a commitment from France to supply aircraft and artillery,[110]

106 FRUS, 1955–1957, XIV: 592–603.
107 FRUS, 1955–1957, XIV: 617–32.
108 FRUS, 1955–1957, XIV: 617–30.
109 FRUS, 1955–1957, XIV: 650–5; Catterall, 2003: 495–6.
110 Sharett, 1978, 5: 1249–50, 1254–5.

replied that, in desperation, Israel would fight.[111] According to the NSC assessment, war would soon break out between Israel and the Arab countries, and the final decision was that troops would not be sent and the aggressor would be hit only with economic sanctions.[112] Meeting in Geneva, Dulles warned Molotov of the dangers of war. Molotov replied that the arms deal was small, commercial and defensive. Israel was the country threatening a preemptive war, he said, not Egypt.[113] Dulles answered that Arab declarations about destroying Israel were the product of Soviet arms deals.[114]

Sharett pressured Dulles, saying it was better that the United States join the Baghdad Pact and grant Israel a defense agreement. (However, the Baghdad Pact was planned to defend the Northern Tier against Soviet invasion, not Israel. It was signed on February 24, 1955, between Turkey and Iraq, later to be joined by Britain and Iran. The United States preferred to remain behind the scenes. The Pact was opposed by the radical Arab states, chiefly Egypt.) Dulles replied that the Czech–Egyptian deal threatened not only Israel, but the entire free world.[115] Sharett had little bargaining power. While the Americans claimed the Soviets could be negotiated with only from a position of strength, it was preaching the opposite to Israel. In the end, Dulles promised that if it turned out that Nasser was lost to the West, a defense pact might be possible. However, Dulles was more concerned about the fate of Iran and Iraq in the Cold War than about what would happen to Israel.[116] The US position was that Communism was Islam's 'mortal enemy' and that no Arab government would cooperate with it.[117]

The only bright spot for Israel was France, with which it had signed an arms agreement in November 1955. However, France was also concerned about the growing gulf between Israel and the Arabs.[118] Dulles wrote to Eisenhower that Molotov had been entirely non-committal.[119] In a conversation with Spain's dictator, Francisco Franco, Dulles argued that a new front opened by the Soviet Union in the Middle East would be a threat to the West's oil supply, the mainstay of the entire Western

111 Eban to IFM, October 26, 1955, ISA 12403/9.
112 FRUS, 1955–1957, XIV: 661–8.
113 FRUS, 1955–1957, XIV: 680–3.
114 FRUS, 1955–1957, XIV: 685, 689.
115 FRUS, 1955–1957, XIV: 683–4.
116 'Records of meeting between Mr. Macmillan and Mr. Dulles at Geneva', November 9, 1955, NA, FO800/680.
117 FRUS, 1955–1957, XIV: 692–3.
118 Tsur, 1968: 216–18.
119 FRUS, 1955–1957, XIV: 650.

European economy. It would also be a direct threat to North Africa and in fact to the entire African continent. In any case, although 'explosive,' the situation did not call for an anti-Arab policy.[120]

Sharett's failures as prime minister were not the result of a lack of leadership, but rather of Israel's objectively dangerous situation within the East–West conflict. The main goal of the United States and Britain was to save the Middle East from Communist penetration, and the Arab–Israeli conflict was the major obstacle.[121] The British ambassador to Moscow warned that both Israel and the Arabs would lose their racial and national character if Communism were imposed on them.[122] Ben-Gurion's new government did not see any alternative: it was time to defeat Nasser. The government did not take into account the negative consequences for Israel's relations with the Soviet Union, but, as far as Israel was concerned, after the Czech–Egyptian arms deal there was no hope for good relations with the Soviets in any case.

---

120 FRUS, 1955–1957, XXVII: 548.
121 Shuckburg, 'Notes on the Arab–Israel Dispute, Annex: The Elements of a Settlement, December 21, 1954,' NA, FO371/111095.
122 Sir William Hayter, 'Notes on Arab-Israel Dispute (Version December 13, 1954),' NA, FO371/411095.

# 5

# Israel and the United States on the road to war (November 1955–November 1956)

Contradicting the government's official guarantee of neutrality,[1] Ben-Gurion's new government wanted a defense pact with the United States.[2] Israel requested US weapons and planes even though it had already signed an arms deal with France.[3] While US participation in the Baghdad Pact increased the value of the pact, it would also involve the United States in local disputes, escalate the arms race and push the Arab countries toward greater dependence on the Soviet bloc. Israel had no choice but to press the United States more urgently. US intelligence actually predicted a scenario more like the Six Day War than the Suez Crisis. Israel would hold onto its acquisitions to bargain for a peace agreement, while the West would not persist with economic sanctions. An Israeli victory would cause turmoil in the Arab countries, create opportunities for the Soviets and act as an incentive for the Arabs to prepare for a new round of even fiercer fighting.[4]

Dulles navigated US policy in the Middle East through the shoals of the Cold War. He strove for a modus vivendi with the Soviet Union, emphasizing that the United States was doing nothing more than setting up a defense system. In a secret memorandum to Macmillan, he said the United States should only join the Baghdad Pact and offer Israel guarantees if the ties between Egypt and the Soviet Union grew stronger. If Israel wanted to survive, it would have to compromise between the 1947 and the 1949 borders, and should not be given arms to balance those acquired by the Arabs. On the other hand, to induce Nasser to break with the Soviets, Egypt should be offered economic benefits and weapons. Nasser should also be encouraged to accept the Johnston Plan for

---

1 KR 29: 229 (November 3, 1955).
2 Levey, 1997: 23; generally, cf. Alteras, 1993; Ben-Zvi, 1993; Hahn, 2004.
3 ICAB, November 6, 1955, ISA.
4 National Intelligence Estimate, November 8, 1955, in FRUS, 1955–1957, XIV: 131–6.

the division of water resources between Israel and its neighbors, as well as the proposal to resolve the Arab refugee problem by settling them in Arab countries.⁵

The State Department assumed Nasser would not attack. Israel's increasing use of its military power, Dulles argued, provided fodder for those in the United States who regarded Israel as a questionable ally and liable to involve the Americans in a world war. A reprisal on the Egyptian border on November 2, 1955, showed Israel's disinclination to resolve conflicts peacefully. After six months of deliberations, the US administration reaffirmed its policy of trying to limit Soviet influence on Nasser. Soviet penetration of the region urgently required a resolution of the Arab–Israeli conflict. In the meantime, Israel would have to rely on the Tripartite Declaration and on the US promise not to abandon it.⁶

On November 5, Eden gave a speech at London's Guildhall advocating territorial compromise and causing great consternation in Israel. At a secret meeting, he warned the Israeli ambassador his country was being strangled, not only because of Soviet arms in the Middle East but also because of the increasing wealth of the Arabs, and it was imperative that Israel make concessions. Ben-Gurion praised Eisenhower's declaration that the United States and Western countries would supply arms to Israel for self-defense, and condemned Eden's speech.⁷ Dulles was intransigent, saying that Israel needed shock treatment on the territorial issue.

Behind the scenes was the Anglo-American consensus that the Soviets were losing control over its satellites. Its resistance to elections in both parts of divided Germany showed that the Kremlin had abandoned the spirit of Geneva. Because of the threat to the oil fields in Baku, Dulles feared the Soviets would react negatively if Iran joined the Baghdad Pact. He ignored the intelligence assessment that the Egyptian receipt of Soviet arms would upset the balance of power and believed that Nasser would play the two superpowers off against each other.⁸ Project Alpha, aimed at protecting the region and the free world, remained the Anglo-American miracle cure. Sharett rejected it out of hand because it would mean Israel's relinquishing its claim on Eilat and parts of the Negev.⁹ At

---

5 FRUS, 1955–1957, XIV: 728–32.
6 Raphael to Eytan, November 11, 1955, Immediate, ISA 330/14.
7 Eisenhower's declaration, however, also included support for Dulles's speech (August 27, 1955): 'Statement by the President on the Hostilities between Egypt and Israel in Violation of the General Armistice Agreement, November 9, 1955,' in Public Papers of the Presidents of the United States, 234.
8 FRUS, 1955–1957, XIV: 720–3, 733 note 4, 750–2.
9 FRUS, 1955–1957, XIV: 793–6.

an NSC meeting in November 1955, Dulles acknowledged that, unlike Britain, the United States could not ignore Israel's existence. The Arab–Israeli conflict was no graver than other difficulties that the United States had overcome, he said, but might entail the loss of oil, which would be a disaster.[10]

Israel found itself with no leverage and nothing to do except wait for Nasser's final break with the West. The issue of Soviet Jewry could not be raised if Soviet military aid to Egypt was at the center of the inter-bloc conflict.[11] Ben-Gurion felt that, given the pressing need to correct the balance of power, a defense pact was becoming irrelevant. The coming year was a US election year and a Democrat president would be no different from a Republican, but public opinion would play an important role and act in Israel's favor. He hoped to obtain arms from France, and concluded there was no cause for despair.[12] He misunderstood Eisenhower's speech, thinking the administration had abandoned Project Alpha,[13] one reason he continued to oppose a preemptive war. Egypt would receive Soviet MiGs and British Centurion tanks, and, if Israel were seen as the aggressor, it would not be able to obtain weapons. Another reason was that a war was liable to destroy a large portion of the country. 'Our economic strength will be exhausted,' Ben-Gurion said. 'They will do a second round, and a third, and then we will be lost.'[14] However, by the end of December he was convinced, despite Sharett's objections, that war was unavoidable.[15]

The reprisal against Syria on December 11, which left six Israeli soldiers and fifty-four Syrians dead, took Sharett by surprise.[16] The result, he thought, would be a preemptive war, in which case the British might shell Haifa from Cyprus and the conflict with the Arabs would not be resolved. A war initiated by Israel would antagonize global public opinion and lead to sanctions and internal devastation.[17] The US administration's predictable reaction to the reprisal was to suspend the supply of arms.[18] Ben-Gurion remained firm in his position that it had been justified and necessary. If the administration used it not to send Israel arms,

10  FRUS, 1955–1957, XII: 200–3.
11  Harman to IDM, 'Jews in the Soviet Union,' November 23, 1955, ISA 382/10.
12  KFADC, November 11, 1955, ISA.
13  Shiloah to Sharett and Eban, December 1, 1955, ISA 2403/9.
14  ICAB, (133) December 4, 1955, December 11, 1955, ISA 2403/9.
15  MPC, December 27–8, 1955, LPA.
16  Sharett, 1978, 5: 1307.
17  MPC, December 27–8, 1955, LPA.
18  Bendor, 'Conversation with F. Russell, Paris, December 17, 1955,' ISA 188/1.

he was certain, it would only be an excuse for something it had already decided on. In early 1956, Ben-Gurion supported a preemptive strike to break the blockade of Eilat. Sharett was opposed, fearing the reaction of Washington and the UN if Israel took the initiative,[19] and was certain a preemptive war would lead to 'Third Temple destruction.' Ben-Gurion may have believed that only a preemptive strike wiping out Egyptian arms could prevent such a catastrophe.[20]

The gap between the United States and Israel was unbridgeable. Dulles lacked confidence in Israel, although he had not opposed France's supplying it with twelve Mystère fighter planes. The decision was the prerogative of the NATO supreme commander, and Dulles saw it as preserving the balance of forces.[21] Macmillan and Dulles thought that the situation in the Middle East was much like that of Czechoslovakia in 1948 before it fell to the Communists, but both were more concerned about possible Soviet expansion in the Persian Gulf and Kuwait.[22] Eisenhower sent Robert B. Anderson, former Secretary of the Navy and Deputy Secretary of Defense, to the Middle East to promote a settlement. Dulles did not dare undermine the Egyptian cotton sector or revoke aid for the construction of the Aswan Dam, which he could have done to pressure Nasser. Britain and France were also unwilling to pay the price of supporting Israel against the Arabs. Anderson was supposed to prevent a situation in which the Soviet Union supplied arms to Egypt and the United States supplied Israel with arms and money.[23] US interests required that any discussion about Israel be conducted in the context of the Cold War. The United States would not accept a situation in which aiding Israel threatened the Baghdad Pact, a top priority for both the United States and Britain.[24]

Ben-Gurion tried to convince Anderson that Israel's qualitative advantages were more important than the Arabs' quantitative advantages, and would ensure an Israeli victory; relinquishing territory would be suicidal. Nasser was a Soviet pawn, and Soviet arms, which would be unlimited, would enable Nasser to destroy Israel in revenge for the defeat of 1948. His bombers were ten minutes away, Ben-Gurion said. Israel would not agree to be the sacrificed so that the West could make treaties with the

19 ICAB, January 8, 1956, ISA.
20 Sharett, 1978, 5: 1334.
21 FRUS, 1955–1957, XIV: 890–2.
22 'Record of Conversation in Paris, Middle East General, 15.12.1955,' Top Secret, NA, FO/800/678.
23 FRUS, 1955–1957, XV: 20–3.
24 FRUS, 1955–1957, XII: 216–28.

Arabs.[25] Dulles rejected Israel's urgent request for arms, but reassured Ben-Gurion they would be available if Nasser did indeed have bellicose intentions.[26] He also rejected Israel's request to maintain military superiority, on the grounds it would drive the Arabs into the Soviet embrace all the more quickly.[27] The administration viewed the Czech–Egyptian arms deal as a product of the Cold War rather than as directly targeting Israel.[28]

Dulles stopped appeasing Nasser upon learning he had lied when he privately affirmed that a settlement with Israel was possible. Presenting the new Egyptian constitution, Nasser said that its objective was for Arab unity and the restoration of Palestine.[29] Nevertheless, the US administration categorized both Israel and Egypt as potential aggressors. Blockading both Israel and Egypt was possible, but in response the Soviets might deploy their fleet to break the embargo.[30] In Formosa it had been clear who the enemy was; the Middle East was murkier territory. However, after the arms deal with Czechoslovakia, Egypt was clearly the greater potential aggressor.[31] Dulles committed himself to 'the preservation of Israel in all its essentials,'[32] but without arming it. The United States did not want to leave Israel weak, but neither did it want to endanger the region. Eban told Dulles that the balance of power had been altered and to preserve it Israel needed forty-eight F-86 fighter planes. Dulles believed Israel had no future as an embattled state without accommodating its neighbors and was endangering itself for short-term gain. He promised Ben-Gurion steps would be taken to strengthen Israel, but warned against political pressures that would yield the opposite results.[33] Byroade warned Dulles that supplying arms to Israel would nullify US progress in Egypt and increase Soviet involvement. He recommended the President explain US interests to the public in a way that would destroy Zionism as a political force, weakening the American Zionist lobby.[34] Israel did not understand how precarious

25 FRUS, 1955–1957, XIV: 63–6.
26 FRUS, 1955–1957, XIV: 74–7, 84.
27 FRUS, 1955–1957, XIV: 91–3.
28 'Eden talks, Washington (January 30,–February 1, 1956), General Estimate of Soviet Objectives and Policies with Particular Reference to Colonial and Under-Developed Areas,' January 25, 1956, Secret, NARA, Lot 62 D 18 CF 648.
29 FRUS, 1955–1957, XV: 243–4.
30 FRUS, 1955–1957, XV: 110–12.
31 FRUS, 1955–1957, XV: 160–1.
32 DFPI 11: 138–9.
33 FRUS, 1955–1957, XV: 163–6.
34 FRUS, 1955–1957, XV: 208–12.

its position was within the US administration. Ben-Gurion still believed the United States could be persuaded to supply Israel with the arms it needed to achieve parity with the Arabs.[35]

Dulles told the Senate Foreign Relations Committee that the UN and the Tripartite Declaration could provide Israel with more protection than could mere arms. Edward Lawson, the US ambassador, was convinced territorial concessions would destroy Israel. He agreed with Ben-Gurion that, with a quarter of the quantity of Nasser's planes, Israel could provide itself with a minimum of security.[36] Eban noted the discrepancy between Dulles's promise in Geneva and his statements before the Senate committee, enraging Dulles, who attacked Israel for conducting 'political warfare' against the administration. Israel, he said, had no consideration for NATO's need to preserve the supply of Middle Eastern oil. Dulles did not want to transform the Middle East into another Cold War front. Nasser was warned, to no avail, that under no circumstances would the United States cut funding intended to defend Israel from the Soviets.[37] Nasser replied that he refused to meet an Israeli or American Jewish representative to discuss a settlement, claiming he might be assassinated like King Abdullah of Jordan, and persisted in demanding the entire Negev.[38]

Eisenhower learned that Soviet arms were again en route to Egypt. He said that, if the arms supply continued, the United States would give Israel defensive weapons. Feeling abandoned by both the UN and the United States, Sharett publicly attacked Dulles, saying the War of Independence had proved the few could withstand the many.[39] Frustration had led the entire Israeli political spectrum to advocate asking the Soviet Union for arms, Sharett claimed. However, Ben-Gurion did not believe he would receive arms from a country that denied the very existence of the Jewish people.[40] Ben-Gurion did not want a war, but the situation worsened. He believed in a victory because, according to the annual enlistment data in Egypt, 60 percent of the draft candidates were disqualified on medical grounds and 90 percent were illiterate. If the United States did not prevent a war, it would bear the moral responsibility for the consequences. His policy was approved in a Knesset vote of confidence.[41]

35 FRUS, 1955–1957, XV: 255–7.
36 FRUS, 1955–1957, XV: 269–72.
37 FRUS, 1955–1957, XII: 277–8, 299.
38 FRUS, 1955–1957, XII: 249.
39 FRUS, 1955–1957, XII: 307–8.
40 ICAB (310), March 4, 1956.
41 KFADC, March 6, 1956, ISA; KR 20 (1), March 6, 1956: 1308.

Eisenhower became convinced that Nasser would not compromise with Israel and that Soviet arms had emboldened the Arabs.[42] Ben-Gurion was encouraged by Egypt's unwillingness to compromise, and Israel did not need parity in arms with Egypt in order to defeat it. If Egypt had 200 MiGs, Israel could make do with between seventy-five and a hundred planes, he said. The administration promised to reexamine the arms supply issue in a more positive light.[43] Eisenhower understood that Israel wanted US arms, even though European arms were available, because it needed a reliable ally. However, he acknowledged that he had no plan to resolve the conflict.[44]

From Israel's perspective, the Egyptian rejection of the US overture reinforced the moral obligation of the United States to supply Israel with arms and funds. Israel warned that if it had not received a positive US answer by the end of March, it would go it alone, devoting all its resources to defense. The US State Department, however, was more concerned about the future of Libya and Saudi Arabia than that of Israel,[45] and, while the United States dithered, France resolved to send twenty-four Mystère IV planes to Israel without Washington's knowledge.[46] Britain was more aware of Israel's strategic weakness and of the existential dangers it faced,[47] but did not yet regard Israel as an ally on the same plane that France did, whose prime minister, Guy Mollet, compared Nasser to Hitler on the eve of World War II. The United States was leading to the destruction of the free world, he claimed, and he was determined to restore the balance of power by providing Israel with arms.[48]

In March, the State Department asked the Pentagon what kinds of arms requested by Israel could be granted without harming US interests.[49] Dulles did not want to give Nasser preferential treatment, but he rejected what he called Israeli anti-Arab antagonism. The US loan would be granted only if the project to divert the Jordan River ceased, and the F-86 planes were to be supplied if and when the United States lost its

---

42 FRUS, 1955–1957, XV: 326–7.
43 FRUS, 1955–1957, XV: 333–6.
44 FRUS, 1955–1957, XV: 342–3, 348–51.
45 FRUS, 1955–1957, XV: 367–71; on Nasser's threats to topple the Arab monarchies, see FRUS, 1955–1957, XV: 364–5.
46 ICAB, March 18, 1956, March 25, 1956, ISA.
47 Sir John Nicholls to Selwyn Lloyd, 'Survey of Israel's Armed Strength and Military Thinking,' March 10, 1956, Secret, NA, PREM11/1462.
48 [Mollet and Eden], 'Records of a Meeting, March 11, 1956', Secret, Guard, NA, FO800/734.
49 FRUS, 1955–1957, XV: 403–4.

influence in the Arab world.[50] The US administration forbade supplying Israel and its neighbors with heavy weapons on the grounds that a war would only benefit the Soviets.[51] Dulles was prepared to give Israel only anti-submarine weapons and mines, warning that the administration would not consent to political attacks from Israel.[52]

US policy was slowly changing in Israel's favor. The Eisenhower administration decided that Canada and Britain would supply Israel with planes, rather than the United States, so as not to accelerate Soviet penetration of the region as the direct US provision of arms was likely to.[53] Blocking the Suez Canal was a nightmare. Every day 1.2 million barrels of oil passed through the canal in tankers and 900,000 in pipelines to the Mediterranean ports. Dulles finally accepted Israel's assessment that Nasser was heading toward war, but his basic approach had not changed, namely that Israel could not serve Western interests unless it was part of a regional defense pact. If it were, the United States could easily identify the aggressor in any conflict, but the US need for Arab oil prevented it from entering into such an agreement. Saying that the United States was committed to Israel's existence lacked strategic force, since he was not authorized to deploy forces without congressional approval. Aggression could only be defined according to international law, and US support for an Israeli military action that was not a response to an overt attack was liable to topple world order.[54]

Defining Nasser as a potential aggressor prompted the United States to establish emergency arms stockpiles in Cyprus, including between twenty-four and forty-eight F-86 planes, which could be transferred to Israel in a crisis.[55] The US concept of the future of the Cold War in the Middle East was that both the regional and international situations were liable to deteriorate.[56] Dulles was pleased that Israel had received Mystère planes and promised that he would speak with Canada about supplying F-86 planes. The country's security would improve if the Arabs realized that the free world would defend it. At a NATO meeting in Paris on May 6, 1956, Dulles showed greater understanding than in the past about the deterioration of Israel's security, and promised a reevaluation. Planes, he

50 FRUS, 1955–1957, XV: 405–8, 410–16.
51 FRUS, 1955–1957, XV: 419–21.
52 FRUS, 1955–1957, XV: 427–9.
53 FRUS, 1955–1957, XV: 430–45, 453–4.
54 FRUS, 1955–1957, XV: 504–5.
55 FRUS, 1955–1957, XV: 532–7; cf. 575–7, 628–32, 637–8.
56 FRUS, 1955–1957, XV: 589.

said, were a psychological issue. In the end, Ben-Gurion had to content himself with receiving US money to buy planes from France.[57] Israel now requested US helicopters, cargo planes, half-tracks and increased financial support. Above all, it needed at least seventy-two planes to counter the threat of Egypt's 250 military aircraft.[58] Dulles refused, insisting that what remained of Western influence in the Arab world had to be preserved, although without deserting Israel. Dulles maneuvered fruitlessly between the Arabs and Israel. On June 28, he told the NSC he was concerned the Arabs were using oil as leverage, which was why absolute support of Israel had to be avoided. He proposed building large tankers that could circumnavigate Africa, obviating the need to ship oil through the Suez Canal, an idea rejected as impractical.[59] Israel directly benefited from the worsening US–Egyptian relations. Dulles promised Eban he would support Israel in a time of crisis, told him about the 'stockpile' of weapons in Cyprus and promised that the United States would train Israeli pilots, even if there were a delay in Canada's delivery of the F-86 planes.[60]

Two weeks before the Suez Canal was nationalized, Dulles agreed to supply Israel with defensive weapons, including light planes, heavy machine guns, half-tracks and helicopters. Israel would not receive transport planes, which were considered offensive weapons. Dulles had accepted Israel's assessment of a dramatic increase in Soviet influence and the Egyptian threat to the independent Arab countries.[61] The US State Department's Policy Planning Staff (PPS) upgraded Israel to being the United States' number two priority in the Middle East, second only to the preservation of its oil interests. Aggression against Israel would, the PPS maintained, be an intolerable affront to the United States. If an attempt were made to destroy Israel, the Americans would have to fight by its side. The United States should, however, condition economic assistance to Israel on the cessation of provocative acts.[62] US disappointment with Nasser created a window of opportunity for Israel. There were a number of encouraging signs, including a possible ongoing stable loan on terms that would not have to be renegotiated annually.[63] However,

57 FRUS, 1955–1957, XV: 618.
58 FRUS, 1955–1957, XV: 692–4, 698–701.
59 FRUS, 1955–1957, XV: 308–9, 754–6.
60 FRUS, 1955–1957, XV: 723–4.
61 FRUS, 1955–1957, XV: 786–9, 818–19, 858–9.
62 S/P [J. G. Mathews], 'US Policy in the Middle East,' July 18, 1956, Top Secret, NARA, RG 59, NEA, Lot 59 D 518 Box 37.
63 DFPI 11: 575–6.

Israel reacted angrily to being preached at about ending its reprisals, especially when the preaching was accompanied by a threat to stop the supply of arms.[64]

On July 26, 1956, Nasser nationalized the Suez Canal, the point of no return for Britain, France and Israel. While the United States reneged on its promise to supply planes via Canada or France, the State Department still felt an aggressive stance was called for, but not one involving military intervention.[65] Eisenhower wanted to threaten the use of force against Egypt if it interfered with the operation of the canal, but Dulles opposed.[66] Israel assumed Nasser had nationalized the canal with Soviet knowledge, and that the United States would do no more than mediate between Israel and Egypt. Foreign Minister Golda Meir thus recommended non-action, assuming the West would boycott Egyptian cotton.[67] The United States had still not declared that the Cold War had reached the Middle East. Israel could serve as a Western stronghold, Eban said.[68]

Ben-Gurion assumed Washington was competing with the Soviet Union to save Nasser, that the United States had no policy, that Britain would not fight and that France would not act alone. The Arabs, he warned were liable to destroy Israel with war and organized terrorism. In the event of war, he planned to occupy part of the West Bank, not wanting to bring too many Arabs under Israeli rule. He dreamed of establishing connections with the Christians in Lebanon and with the emerging countries in Asia and Africa. He had no illusions about the limited influence of American Jewry in an administration hostile to Israel. Dulles, he said, was behaving despicably on the question of arms and the administration was a disaster for world peace, because it was nurturing 'a snake named Nasser.' In the next war, Beersheba would be destroyed and so would a third or a half of Tel Aviv.[69]

Israel suggested to Dulles that the United States construct atomic power plants to be less dependent on Arab oil. Oil from pro-American Saudi Arabia and the Persian Gulf protectorates could be transported on supertankers capable of circumventing the Cape of Good Hope without passing through the Suez Canal. Israel also proposed the construction of a canal from Eilat to the Mediterranean and an oil pipeline passing through Israel, and suggested the West establish military bases in Israel if

64  ICAB, July 22, 1956, ISA.
65  FRUS, 1955–1957, XVI: 24–5.
66  FRUS, 1955–1957, XVI: 26–7, 38–9.
67  ICAB, July 29, 1956, ISA.
68  FRUS, 1955–1957, XVI: 136–8.
69  ICAB, August 5, 1956, ISA.

the peace process failed. Dulles rejected everything.[70] By now, Israel had given up on both blocs. Neither side would do anything for Israel, Meir said, although the United States was still providing Israel with money.[71] Despite his reservations about war, Dulles was intent on preserving the balance of power in the Middle East, but without giving Israel the military advantage that might tempt it to attack Egypt. If the British and French occupied the Canal and parts of Egypt, he maintained, the Middle East and most of Africa would become enemies of the West and the Soviet Union would reap the benefits.[72] A US intelligence estimate backed the State Department, predicting that Britain and France would soon seize key positions in Egypt, and that Soviet-encouraged Egyptian acts of sabotage could be expected. Israel would not act because France and Britain would do all the work. Even if the United States did not participate in the Anglo-French attack, the Third World would accuse it of being in secret collusion with Britain and France, resulting in new opportunities for the Soviet bloc.[73]

Ben-Gurion was skeptical. Nasser would not tolerate an insult to his prestige and it would be impossible to open the Suez Canal by force. However, Egypt could be defeated if Soviet and Czechoslovak pilots could be prevented from participating in the battles.[74] Despite Dulles's equivocation, Ben-Gurion acknowledged that relations with the United States were 'the cornerstone of our entire foreign policy.'[75] Despite an Israeli reprisal in the West Bank (in Hussan) in response to the murder of four Israelis, Dulles did not renege on the promise of F-86 combat aircraft via Canada.[76] Israel's bargaining position was still weak and it remained concerned about its economic dependence on the United States and its Jewry, the danger of a US embargo and the Soviet threat.[77] According to Meir, the US administration could not be trusted because, while Dulles had been disabused about Nasser, he was not prepared to go beyond exerting economic pressure to destabilize the Egyptian regime.[78] Ben-Gurion conditioned Israeli participation in an anti-Egyptian operation on British consent and US knowledge.[79]

70 FRUS, 1955–1957, XVI: 178–81.
71 ICAB, 12 August 1956, ISA.
72 FRUS, 1955–1957, XVI: 334–7, 403–4, 435–8.
73 FRUS, 1955–1957, XVI: 382–91.
74 FRUS, 1955–1957, XVI: 400–3.
75 Ben-Gurion to Eban, [no date], ISA 7224/11.
76 FRUS, 1955–1957, XVI: 608–10.
77 Bar-On, 1994: 234–9, 204–10.
78 KFADC, October 9, 1956, ISA.
79 DFPI 11: 734.

It was questionable whether the royal regime in Jordan world survive Nasser's subversion, as was whether Israel could tolerate an Iraqi army in Jordan. The United States viewed Iraq's prime minister, Nuri Said, as a stabilizing factor and supported the entrance of his army into Jordan to save King Hussein. Israel was opposed, fearing that such a move would preface Jordanian–Iraqi unification, and agreed only to the temporary presence of a small force.[80] The State Department was worried Israel would cross the Jordan River and Egypt would react by moving toward an alliance with the Soviet Union. Israel's failed attack on the West Bank city of Qalqiliya on October 10, 1956 (eighteen Israeli soldiers dead), made Eisenhower suspect Ben-Gurion wanted to destroy Jordan. If Israel initiated an unjustified war, the Soviets would send significant assistance to Israel's enemies. It would be shameful, the State Department maintained, for the United States to make decisions out of keeping with its national interest.[81] The end result would be the Sovietization of the entire region. In the long run, Israeli aggression would bring catastrophe.[82] However, to maintain the status quo, Washington suspended support for Project Alpha. The administration objected to Israel's reprisals, which it feared could deteriorate into a general conflagration. It preferred an Iraqi to an Egyptian presence in Jordan, preventing Israel from claiming *casus belli*. Despite the reprisals, the United States had not reneged on the advances promised for weapons purchases or the delivery of helicopters. In the end, the US policy of preventing Soviet expansion in Asia and Africa, and Nasser's aggression, provided Israel with what it had wanted from Washington, namely a restoration of the balance of power and economic reinforcement.[83]

On October 24, 1956, the die was cast and Britain, France and Israel secretly met in Sèvres, France, and agreed to cooperate in a military action against Egypt. US intelligence did not doubt that Israel would occupy the West Bank, penetrate Syria as far as Damascus, penetrate Egypt to the Suez Canal, and end the Egyptian blockade of the Gulf of Aqaba. The war against Egypt would be successful, it estimated, as long as the Soviet Union was busy in Eastern Europe.[84] Dulles told Eisenhower that, if Israel had not withdrawn funds from New York banks, it meant that it was not headed for war.[85] On the morning of October 28, the eve

80 ICAB, October 7, 1956, ISA.
81 FRUS, 1955–1957, XVI: 722–4.
82 FRUS, 1955–1957, XVI: 724–33.
83 KFADC, October 22, 1956, ISA.
84 FRUS, 1955–1957, XVI: 798–9.
85 FRUS, 1955–1957, XVI: 810–11.

of the war, Ben-Gurion warned of Soviet intervention on the one hand and US intervention, intended to force Israel to withdraw, on the other. The occupation of Gaza might be embarrassing. 'If I believed in miracles, I would pray for the sea to swallow it,' he declared.[86] In an emergency meeting on October 29, Dulles noted that France had exceeded the agreed amount of Mystère planes supplied to Israel. Eisenhower mentioned the United States' Tripartite Declaration to assist any victim of aggression and asked if a blockade of Israel would be effective. Dulles's main concern was that the United States would be dragged into another war. The problem was not Suez, but rather France's questionable future in Algeria, and Britain's influence in the Persian Gulf and Iraq.[87]

The United States moved quickly to punish Israel. Two days after the military operation began, all monetary assistance was stopped, goods and money could not be sent to Israel and its military personnel could not be trained.[88] Dulles admitted a serious political and intelligence error. He assumed that the next step would be an Israeli strike against Jordan. Britain and France had deceived him, he felt. Annoyed, he suggested imposing moderate sanctions on Israel. He suggested suspending military and economic aid, but not freezing assets. If the United States did not demonstrate leadership, the emerging countries in Asia and Africa would go over to the Soviet Union. It would be tragic if, instead of opposing Soviet colonialism in Eastern Europe, the United States supported Anglo-French colonialism in the Middle East. Eisenhower supported Dulles completely. If the UN declared Israel an aggressor, aid from the International Cooperation Administration (ICA) would be suspended and sanctions against Israel tightened.[89]

There was also a genuine fear that the Middle East would turn into a new Cold War front, and that the Cold War would develop into a real war. Dulles was wary of Soviet infiltration and the possibility that the war would spread to the Persian Gulf and North Africa, and suggested only a suspension of the supply of war materiel and economic aid, but not the imposition of sanctions.[90] Eisenhower emphasized that it was vital to deny the Soviets global leadership at any price. The United States was the last hope for genuine political and economic unity in the Muslim world, he said.[91] Dulles did not convey to Israel the decision to suspend

86 Ben-Gurion, 1972: 526–7.
87 FRUS, 1955–1957, XVI: 851–5.
88 FRUS, 1955–1957, XVI: 890–1.
89 FRUS, 1955–1957, XVI: 902–16.
90 FRUS, 1955–1957, XVI: 918–19.
91 FRUS, 1955–1957, XVI: 924–5.

aid. Eban, unaware, was elated. The fall of Nasser was a historical crossroads. The spread of Communism had been halted. The United States, Eban told Dulles, should exploit the opportunity for peace. Dulles was not impressed. The invasion was a serious blow to the UN and to the cause of peace. Would Pakistan now be permitted to attack India? If every country were to resort to force, the result would be anarchy.[92]

Ben-Gurion realized Eisenhower was motivated by a fear that every additional day of war provided opportunities for the Soviets. The Kremlin was encouraging coups in Syria and Jordan and might cut off relations with Israel and expel it from the UN.[93] British intelligence warned that, while the Soviet leadership did not want war, a world war could nevertheless result from a chain of circumstances and miscalculations. The Soviet air force would not be capable of attacking the United States for the next few years, but the United States was capable of dealing the Soviet Union a fatal blow. The Kremlin would therefore act carefully.[94]

Israel disregarded US considerations. Ben-Gurion maintained that Israel should hold on to the Straits of Tiran, propose an international regime in the Sinai and avoid provoking the Soviet Union by publicly displaying captured Soviet weapons.[95] While he enjoyed the euphoria following the victory and his government enjoyed unprecedented support, he warned the public not to be deluded regarding future dangers.[96] On November 5, the Soviets suggested that the United States join an immediate military action in the Middle East to stop the fighting. Eisenhower did not respond even when the Soviet foreign minister said the Soviet Union did not intend to use force against Britain and France, but rather to have the superpowers impose a ceasefire.[97]

Concerned about Soviet military involvement in Egypt, Eisenhower suggested warning the Soviets against sending 'volunteers' to Egypt and asking the Arabs if they wanted the Soviets to treat the Middle East the way they were treating Hungary.[98] The United States also needed to reassure France, which interpreted the Soviet suggestion as a desire to settle the conflict in the entire region by means of force.[99] Eisenhower said he

92 FRUS, 1955–1957, XVI: 925–7.
93 FRUS, 1955–1957, XVI: 968–72.
94 Joint Intelligence Committee, Soviet Designs in the Middle East, November 11, 1956, Top Secret, Guard, J.I.C.(56)117 (Final), NA, CAB 158/26.
95 ICAB, November 3, 1956, ISA.
96 ICAB, November 7, 1956, ISA; KR 21: 197–215 (November 7, 1956).
97 FRUS, 1955–1957, XVI: 984–6, 989–94.
98 Referring to the Soviet army's crushing of the Hungarian revolt in October 1956. FRUS, 1955–1957, XVI: 1001–2.
99 FRUS, 1955–1957, XVI: 1003–7, 1023–5.

did not wish to threaten Israel, but that he would embargo the transfer of funds if it did not withdraw. Dulles demanded categorically that Ben-Gurion announce his agreement to withdraw from Sinai forthwith. If he did so, the friendly relations between the two countries would not be damaged.[100] Dulles's deputy, Herbert Hoover Jr., warned that the Soviets were exploiting the situation. Israel might be expelled from the UN and subjected to heavy sanctions.[101]

Dulles, more of a pragmatist than a crusader, was adamant about containing the boundaries of the Cold War. He did not exploit the Hungarian crisis because it was taking place in the Soviet sphere of influence. His refusal to cut off Nasser grew out of his conviction that he was neutral, but not a Communist. Although what Dulles called Israel's 'collusion' with Britain and France had been carried out behind America's back, the Israeli leadership felt that it had no choice. Ben-Gurion had no doubt that the Sinai War was justified and that its results were absolutely positive for Israel's future security.[102]

---

100 FRUS, 1955–1957, XVI: 1049–53, 1061–4.
101 FRUS, 1955–1957, XVI: 1065–7.
102 Shlaim, 2000: 169–78; Brands, 1989: 305–7; Immerman, 1990: 280; Karabell, 1999: 111–12.

# 6

# The Eisenhower Doctrine and Israel (November 1956–January 1958)

The Sinai Campaign could have meant turning acquired territory into diplomatic victory. Eban suggested Israel announce that it had no territorial ambitions and, in exchange for withdrawal, ask Eisenhower to get the Soviets to remove their aircraft from Syria.[1] Ben-Gurion, however, believed there was no cause for alarm. CIA Director Allen Dulles told the NSC that with Soviet aid Nasser had regained his standing as Egyptian leader. The situation in Syria needed to be monitored and Soviet and Chinese volunteers might still arrive in the Middle East. He did not think the Kremlin would initiate a world war, but acknowledged that events might have a domino effect. He was more concerned with Soviet threats against Iran and Iraq than against Israel.[2]

Eisenhower thought Soviet repression in Hungary had given him bargaining power in the Middle East. The United States could offer Egypt arms on condition it did not accept Soviet weapons. Israel should also be given arms and the $75 million loan it had requested.[3] Israel demanded that its withdrawal from the Sinai Peninsula be accompanied by free passage for its vessels through the Suez Canal and security guarantees, demands rejected on the grounds of 'endangering world peace.'[4] Eban feared the Soviets would replay the invasion of Hungary in the Middle East, but the real question was what the United States would do.[5]

Ben-Gurion wanted a new order that would guarantee Israel's future. He wanted the demilitarization of the Sinai Peninsula, internationalization of the Suez Canal, direct negotiations between Israel and its neighbors, Israeli control of the Gaza Strip and the Straits of Tiran, and keeping the Soviets out of the region. However, he received a letter from

1 DFPI 12: 94–5.
2 FRUS, 1955–1957, XVI: 1070–6.
3 FRUS, 1955–1957, XVI: 1088–9.
4 FRUS, 1955–1957, XVI: 1090–1.
5 'Eban's Survey to the Embassy Staff, November 9, 1956,' ISA 5936/8.

Eisenhower warning Israel that if it did not withdraw from the Sinai Peninsula it could expect UN condemnation, which would damage US–Israeli cooperation.[6]

Secretary of State Dulles believed the Suez Campaign had weakened the Baghdad Pact and would increase Soviet involvement in the Middle East,[7] but that in the long run the United States could not compete with the Soviet Union for the allegiance of the Arabs.[8] The Eisenhower administration was more concerned with preserving the balance between pro-Western Arab states and the region's radical regimes. The status of the Middle East was upgraded, having become the most strategic region in the world because of Western Europe's dependence on its oil.[9] However, the administration claimed Israel and Egypt had been equally responsible for the conflict[10] and continued to regard Israel as an obstacle to regional stability.

However, Israel believed Nasser had been weakened by the campaign, which had revealed the extent of Soviet penetration of Egypt.[11] According to a US Special National Intelligence Estimate, the region had been turned into a major trouble spot. The Soviet Union would use the outcome of the campaign against NATO and would support Nasser to deflect world attention from events in the Soviet satellites, particularly Hungary. Syria had been given tanks, APCs (armored personnel carriers) and aircraft. Israel regarded Syria as Soviet-supported and capable of taking hostage the oil pipelines running through its territory. According to the Special Estimate, the Soviet Union would not carry out its threats against the West if it meant risking the outbreak of a third world war.[12] Eisenhower was advised to issue a warning to the Kremlin and to send troops to the Middle East if the Soviets sent their army into Syria or technicians to Egypt, since Congress could grant the President special powers.[13] At the same time, the administration resolved not to suspend aid to Israel officially, but rather to slow it down.[14]

Ben-Gurion knew US support was vital, and ordered Dayan to withdraw IDF forces to a point 30 miles distant from the Suez Canal as

6 Meroz, 'Conversation with Bergus, November 15, 1956,' ISA 7226/5a.
7 FRUS, 1955–1957, XII: 330–7.
8 FRUS, 1955–1957, XVI: 1158–62.
9 FRUS, 1955–1957, XII: 340–2.
10 FRUS, 1955–1957, XII: 344–52.
11 ICAB, November 25, 1956, December 2, 1956, ISA.
12 'Special National Intelligence Estimate, November 29, 1956,' in FRUS, 1955–1957, XII: 355–60.
13 FRUS, 1955–1957, XVI: 1219–29.
14 FRUS, 1955–1957, XVI: 1236–8.

a goodwill gesture. He was also concerned about the Egyptian–Soviet rumor that Israel was concentrating forces on the Syrian border, fearing Khrushchev would use it as an excuse to use Soviet missiles and planes deployed in Syria to destroy Israel. By this time, he was convinced that there would be no return to the status quo ante. The minimum, he said, was maintaining an Israeli presence at Sharm el-Sheikh. However, he realized the United States would not end its efforts to restrict Soviet rule throughout the world just because Israel wanted to annex territories.[15]

The State Department felt the Soviet threat was so severe that a new treaty organization was needed to replace the Baghdad Pact, making Israel's position in Washington more precarious. Israel, according to the State Department, had no choice but to abandon its reprisals because, if it refused, economic sanctions would be imposed.[16] Knowledge of the State Department's decision, which made no mention of Israel's demands, would have shocked the Israeli government. There was no intention of including Israel in the new alliance, although it would require some sort of US guarantee for Israel. The State Department claimed that Israel should put its trust in the UN Secretary General, while Israel demanded that Nasser be removed.[17]

The United States opposed the use of force to resolve international disputes. The US sanction of Israel's attack on Egypt might be seen as a precedent and other countries might be tempted to seize territory by force. Dulles felt political and economic pressures would be enough to influence Nasser. He now admitted that underestimating the Soviet–Egyptian arms deal had been a mistake, but maintained that the Sinai Campaign had only worsened the situation. It would be difficult for the United States to grant guarantees to Israel because it lacked stable borders, he said. The administration was concerned Israel would seize the opportunity created by increasing Soviet hostility to pressure the United States for security guarantees.[18]

A group of senators, headed by Jacob Javits, tried unsuccessfully to pressure Dulles into giving Israel security guarantees without an Israeli withdrawal from Sinai.[19] Ben-Gurion, believing reports in the largely pro-Israel American press, thought that there had been an important change in US policy and that Israel need not hurry to withdraw its forces.

15 ICAB, December 23, 1956, ISA.
16 FRUS, 1955–1957, XVI: 383–7.
17 Meroz (Washington) to USD, Conversation with J. M. Ludlow, December 7, 1956, Top Secret, ISA 3088/4.
18 FRUS, 1955–1957, XII: 407.
19 A. Yaffe, USD, to IMW, Visit of Senator-Elect Javits, November 30, 1956, ISA 406/24.

In the end he was a realist and planned, if grudgingly, to withdraw in stages to El-Arish, but no further, until Israeli ships could freely pass through the Suez Canal.[20]

Meir told Dulles that Israel did not want to annex Sharm el-Sheikh or the Gaza Strip. An end to the blockade of the Straits of Tiran and Israeli administration of the Gaza Strip until a permanent solution could be found, she believed, would suffice. Dulles warned that, if Israel attacked, it would remain surrounded by hostile forces no military force could defend it from. The Sinai invasion had set back the assurance of Israel's future by a generation, he said. Meir told him Israel wanted close relations with the United States, but Dulles claimed that Israel's reprisals made correct relations with the Arabs impossible. Dulles said that he recognized the Gulf of Aqaba as international shipping waters, but would make no commitment regarding the Gaza Strip. She should rest assured, however, of US friendship and sympathy for Israel.[21]

Lawson, the US ambassador, asked Ben-Gurion what the 'end of Israel' would be. Ben-Gurion said he was optimistic. The United States had fought for its independence for thirteen years, he said, and twenty years then passed before it doubled its population. However, he was pessimistic about the Arabs. Their education was based on the Muslim concept of *Dar al-Islam* and *Dar al-Harb*, the lands already ruled by Islam and the rest of the world, which was slated for conquest. He said the United States alone would decide whether the Arabs would succeed in destroying Israel, adding that for 2,000 years the Jews had been hated but had survived.[22]

Ben-Gurion knew that the United States would not promise Israel it would open the Gulf of Aqaba if Egypt blocked free navigation, and that Israel had no hope of keeping Sinai.[23] He was prepared to take an economic blow if Israel did not withdraw and called for an emergency plan that would lower living standards and redouble the campaign to raise money from Jews overseas. However, Levy Eshkol, minister of finance, asked if Israelis would be willing to live like the Arab *fellahin* if the sanctions included restrictions on oil and if Israel had no money. Mordechai Namir, then minister of labor, claimed that a nation with 30,000–60,000 hungry people could not survive.[24] Ben-Gurion lowered his expectations. American Jewry was leaderless and a lower standard of living would

---

20 ICAB, December 9, 1956, December 13, 1956, ISA.
21 FRUS, 1955–1957, XVI: 1341–3.
22 ICAB, December 31, 1956, ISA.
23 MPC, January 10, 1957, LPA.
24 KFADC, January 8, 1957, ISA.

threaten Israeli public fortitude. Although the opposition vigorously opposed the withdrawal from the Sinai Peninsula, it was obvious Israel would not be able to withstand US sanctions and the vote passed in the Knesset.[25]

The US administration realized that Dulles's programmatic speech from August 26 was not sufficient to defend US interests in the Middle East. Eisenhower issued a call for US military and economic cooperation with interested Middle Eastern states. The UN helped defend small countries, he said, but not in the face of Soviet aspirations. On January 5, 1957, Eisenhower asked Congress to authorize aid to prevent aggression by any Communist country, known as the 'Eisenhower Doctrine.'[26] The need to decide was fast approaching. On February 2, 1957, the UN General Assembly called for a total Israeli withdrawal from the Sinai Peninsula and Eisenhower warned Ben-Gurion that refusing to withdraw would damage US–Israeli relations. It was clear that the United States was prepared to impose sanctions,[27] but as long as the UN had not yet decided on them Ben-Gurion could play the role of the determined national leader. His first priority was planning for another round of war. The United States refused to free up $50 million in aid, which from his point of view was a sanction.[28] Israel could not, he realized, withstand the withholding of basic raw materials. France had recently supplied gasoline, despite the fuel shortage in Europe, sufficient for a fortnight. Ben-Gurion worried that withdrawal under threat of sanction would set a precedent to force Israel to withdraw to the 1947 partition borders. He gradually lost confidence in Israel's ability to hold on to Gaza, but insisted on Israeli control of the Straits of Tiran.[29]

Dulles was inclined to impose sanctions on Israel unless it withdrew. As far as he was concerned, Israel was more belligerent than the Arabs (in every Israeli reprisal, more Arabs had been killed).[30] Yet, at the same time, he claimed he was not threatening sanctions and that the United States and Israel had to work together, following the highest moral standards.[31] He thought for a while that it would be almost impossible for the United States to implement any policy regarding Israel without the consent of

25 KR 21: January 15, 1957: 749–52.
26 FRUS, 1955–1957, XII: 437–9.
27 FRUS, 1955–1957, XVII: 82–3.
28 ICAB, February 6, 1957, ISA.
29 KFADC, February 8, 1957, ISA.
30 FRUS, 1955–1957, XVII: 109–12, 121–2.
31 FRUS, 1955–1957, XVII: 125–31.

American Jewry.³² The pro-Israel lobby recruited Lyndon Johnson, the Senate majority leader, who criticized the UN and said that he had not seen any proposal to impose economic sanctions on the Soviet Union, which was also occupying another country's territory.³³ Dulles warned that, if Israel did not withdraw from the Sinai Peninsula, he would raise the issue of sanctions at the UN. Israeli opposition to withdrawal gradually diminished. Ben-Gurion was finally persuaded that the United States was committed to keeping ships in the Gulf of Aqaba and that there was a chance that oil tankers could reach Eilat and an international oil pipeline could be built from Eilat to Haifa. However, he had little hope that deploying the United Nations Emergency Force (UNEF) in the Sinai Peninsula would effectively prevent Egyptian aggression.

The Israeli cabinet, taking into consideration the threat of sanctions and the fear of war, voted in favor of the US proposal on condition that certain revisions were made. Ben-Gurion's resolve stiffened again, declaring he chose sanctions, although there was a two-thirds majority in the UN in favor, even with a US abstention. However, in the end realism conquered national honor. 'I think that if there were a war between us and America, America would win,' Ben-Gurion said.

The CIA did not think Canada, West Germany or France would participate in sanctions against Israel, but the economic damage would still be severe. Israel's imports far exceeded its exports, and US funding was critical to the Israeli economy ($45 million in governmental aid and $150 million in private funding; Israeli imports amounted to $357 million, covered by $103 million Israeli exports and $40 million in German compensation).

There could be little doubt that economic sanctions would compel Israel to fold within three months to a year.³⁴ In the meantime, it became obvious that Israel's conviction that Congress was on its side was a chimera. Dulles kept threatening, and if Israel did not withdraw, he said, the Arab guerrilla campaign would expand and the world order would collapse, and the Arabs would turn to the Soviet Union. The Israeli attack on Egypt was like the Communist attack on Korea, he claimed. Eisenhower declared that no one wanted to impose sanctions on Israel when other countries were also to blame for the situation.³⁵ Eventually, however, Israel was forced to give in.³⁶

32  FRUS, 1955–1957, XVII: 136–7.
33  FRUS, 1955–1957, XVII: 139–44.
34  FRUS, 1955–1957, XVII: 210.
35  FRUS, 1955–1957, XVII: 214–24.
36  DFPI 12: 602–3.

Ben-Gurion pretended he had not surrendered and called for the demilitarization of Sinai and an Israeli civilian administration in the Gaza Strip. The final decision was made on February 21, with Ben-Gurion fearing Eisenhower would incite American Jewry against Israel. He acknowledged that the debate was over, the fight was lost and Israel had 'lost America.' The United States recognized the Straits of Tiran as an international waterway, but there was no guarantee that Israeli ships would be protected. The United States assumed only moral responsibility and each country would have to defend its own ships. The Israeli cabinet was persuaded that UNEF's presence in Sharm el-Sheikh was necessary until peace was assured. It might be necessary to go to war again in five years if Israel were attacked, Ben-Gurion said.[37] Dulles argued that the United States would not support a guarantee in the Gulf of Aqaba unless Israel agreed to return the Gaza Strip to Egyptian control. The legal counsel of the State Department argued that the law of innocent passage (through the Straits of Tiran) did not apply to countries at war, but that Israel did have the right to defend itself pursuant to Article 51 of the UN Charter,[38] according to which: 'Nothing ... shall impair the inherent right of individual or collective self-defense if an armed attack occurs against a member of the United Nations.' Ultimately, the US administration's major concern was the fate of Western Europe, not Israel.

Eventually, Ben-Gurion agreed to a French proposal to internationalize the Gaza Strip, tying Nasser's hands. Israel would be entirely isolated unless it agreed to US terms, he maintained, predicting terrorist attacks Israel would not be able to overcome.[39] Dulles, determined to prevent further Soviet penetration of the Middle East, was eager to turn over a new leaf with the Arab states. He told them that Israel would withdraw unconditionally, that the United States had no secret agreement with Israel, and that he hoped they would not again blockade Israel at the Straits of Tiran.[40]

Dulles told Eban that the United States had recognized the Gulf of Aqaba as an international waterway and that Egyptian rule of the Gaza Strip was over. The Arabs had expected Israel would refuse to withdraw, that its friendship with the United States would weaken and that it would be destroyed. Ben-Gurion, however, had no illusions and knew it was a gamble. Israel would have to trust the IDF's strength if attempts

---

37 ICAB, (360) (359) February 25–26, 1957, ISA.
38 FRUS, 1955–1957, XVII: 291–5.
39 ICAB, February 27, 1957, ISA.
40 FRUS, 1955–1957, XVII: 332–6.

were made to curtail its rights, and Western support was not legally guaranteed. He reminded the cabinet of the gamble taken on the eve of independence to declare the state and how practical considerations had won. However, he admitted failure. Holding Sharm el-Sheikh would not ensure free navigation and Israel would have to fight after the Egyptian army returned. War was not a solution because, no matter how many times Israel beat Egypt, it would still be there. If Egypt beat Israel, that would be the end. The government voted to withdraw,[41] and Foreign Minister Meir admitted that the Soviet threat to bomb Israel was the main reason for withdrawal.[42]

IDF Chief of Staff Moshe Dayan met with General E. L. M. Burns, the UN Chief of Staff of the Truce Supervision Organization, to arrange a staged withdrawal. Ben-Gurion admitted there was no certainty that the United States would actively support free navigation. Eisenhower's commitment, he said, was quite general and promised nothing in regard to the Gaza Strip.[43] Dayan feared that Egyptian forces would return to Gaza and that Israel's economy and immigration from the Soviet Union would be adversely affected.[44] Meir warned that the United States would not implement the Eisenhower Doctrine unless Israel retreated from Sinai. She blamed UN Secretary General Dag Hammarskjöld for not helping Israel obtain a better deal in Sinai and Gaza, and acknowledged Eisenhower's fear of a world war.[45]

Ben-Gurion informed Eisenhower that Nasser was generating tension in the Gaza Strip and that Arab terrorists were again operating, overseen by the Egyptians. Radio Cairo had announced Egypt would not allow Israeli ships to pass through the Straits of Tiran. Ben-Gurion warned it would be necessary to use force. Dulles was defensive, claiming Israel should rely on the UN. Meir warned him that Soviet technicians and pilots were being sent to the Middle East. She told the cabinet that Israel's expectations of the United States were too high. The United States acted to promote its own interests, in this case the prevention of the Sovietization of the Arab countries. If Dulles did something really despicable against Israel, all that had to be done, she said, was to assemble 20,000 Jews in Madison Square Garden to shout 'gewalt! [help!]'[46]

---

41 ICAB, March 1, 1957, ISA.
42 ICAB, March 24, 1957, ISA; MFAC, March 24, 1957, LPA.
43 ICAB, March 3, 1957, ISA.
44 MPC, March 3, 1957, LPA.
45 MPC, March 13, 1957, LPA.
46 ICAB, March 24, 1957, ISA.

Unknown to the Israeli government, Eisenhower and Macmillan had met in Bermuda to discuss world affairs and the Middle East; they devised what they called a 'long-haul piecemeal settlement' for the Arab–Israeli conflict. After the failure of Project Alpha, the United States told Britain that the American public would not support economic pressure on Israel for concessions. However, it was possible to cooperate with the Arab states against the Soviet threat.[47]

The State Department understood Israel could not publicly identify with the United States regarding the danger of Communism. It understood Israel's concern about Jewish immigration from the Soviet Union and its fear of the reactions of the Asian and African countries with which it had established commercial and military relations. However, the United States would intervene only if the Soviets sent 'volunteers' to the Middle East.[48] Israel understood that the Eisenhower Doctrine's goal was to win over the Arabs and that it might worsen Israel's situation, yet Israel could not manage without the promised US aid. Israel's leaders were unhappy but realized the new doctrine was the least of all possible evils.[49]

Meeting Eisenhower's special envoy, James P. Richards, Ben-Gurion asked how the Eisenhower Doctrine would defend Israel. He feared that with Soviet support the Arabs could destroy the country before outside help arrived. Meir said Israel was doomed to live or die with the free world and could not harass Communism. If the United States declared that Syria and Egypt were controlled by Communism, Israel could stop worrying, she opined, because the United States would defend it against Communism, if not against the Arabs. Ben-Gurion requested an explicit commitment for rapid assistance if Syria attacked with planes manned by Soviet pilots, saying Communism could not be cited in an official Israeli announcement of support for the Eisenhower Doctrine because of Israel's left-wing parties.[50] Ben-Gurion believed that the United States would defend Israel, but he and Meir were concerned that American Jewry would be confused if Israel did not acknowledge US aid. He asserted that the two countries were committed to cooperation.

47 Bermuda Conference, March 1957, 'Middle East Prospect of Palestine Settlement, Secret Joint Paper,' Minutes of Second Plenary Meeting, March 21, 1957, Top Secret, NA, FO 371/123114/VR107222G.
48 Gazit to Navon, '*Ha'aretz* Political Correspondent Uri Ra'anan, Conversation with Lawson, May 7, 1957,' ISA 7226/6a.
49 ICAB, April 28, 1957, ISA.
50 FRUS, 1955–1957, XVII: 454–7, 529–30, 597–601.

Ben-Gurion wanted the United States to promise Israel it would provide military assistance in case of attack. The United States had taken note of Israel's announcement that it supported US goals in the Middle East – namely, the Eisenhower Doctrine – but Ben-Gurion feared that the Doctrine would not prevent Syria from turning into a 'popular democracy' like Hungary. He argued that a separate Israeli announcement without mentioning the Eisenhower Doctrine would be equivalent to omitting Hamlet from Shakespeare's plays. It would deter both the Arabs and the Soviets. While both the United States and Soviet Union officially opposed war, the Kremlin might support an Arab attack. In any case, such an announcement would not carry the weight of a mutual defense pact. Had Dulles stated his readiness for such a pact, the Israeli government would have signed it regardless of the political fallout, meaning the resignation of Mapam left-wing ministers. Even the State Department, which viewed Israel as a nuisance, did not want to see it destroyed, Ben-Gurion maintained. Based on its declaration of support for the Doctrine, Israel could request armaments for free or cheaply.

In the final analysis, Ben-Gurion viewed the Eisenhower Doctrine as a moral commitment. What was really needed, he believed, was a plan for the coming decade that would include a million immigrants, nuclear power, completion of the national water carrier and aid from the United States and the European Economic Community for the establishment of large economic enterprises.[51] In addition, Israel had to cultivate unofficial allies, such as West Germany and France, to bolster its standing in its dealing with the United States.[52]

The State Department's realpolitik approach rejected Israel's request for emergency aid because the Arabs would regard it as Israel's being rewarded. However, Israel's preoccupation was with Jewish immigration, not Arab refugees. Eshkol ridiculed Dulles's fear that immigrants from Poland and Hungary were Communists, saying they had had enough of Communism.[53] To Dulles's credit, as far as Israel was concerned, he rejected the Arab position on the refugees question.[54] The NSC no longer regarded Israel as a militaristic state[55] and, to Eban, Dulles stressed the mutual understanding and confidence that the United States and Israel shared. Dulles hoped the Soviets would refrain from provocations that could lead to US military involvement. There was, he said, too much

51  ICAB, June 16, 1957, ISA.
52  Shaltiel, 1996: 405.
53  ICAB, July 7, 1957, ISA.
54  FRUS, 1955–1957, XII: 559–63.
55  FRUS, 1955–1957, XVII: 694–5.

evil loose in the Middle East, and problems had to be dealt with on a crisis-to-crisis basis until fundamental Soviet thinking on the region had changed.[56] The United States still refused to sell Israel heavy weapons, despite the Soviet threat from Syria and the presence of Soviet submarines in the Mediterranean.[57]

Ben-Gurion noted Soviet press reports that Eilat had been handed over to the United States as a military base, and that France and Israel were planning to attack Syria. Israel saw as especially menacing a statement made by the Soviet ambassador to the effect that Israel had still not been bombed from the air. Ben-Gurion waited in vain for the United States to take a bold stance against the Soviet threat.[58] Dulles carefully avoided calling Syria a Soviet-ruled country, but the British Foreign Secretary was extremely concerned about what appeared to be the Sovietization of Syria.[59] According to a British military intelligence assessment, a nuclear war between East and West could break out in the Middle East.[60]

The United States would never agree to Israel's requests as long as no Arab country had a Communist regime, and would not supply Israel with warplanes despite the large number of aircraft that Syria had received from the Soviet Union.[61] As a rule, the State Department was more attentive to Arab than Israeli envoys.[62] Dulles was serious about blocking a Communist takeover of Syria, but he did not think Israel would be threatened by a Communist Syria, especially given that the CIA had concluded that Syria was not a Soviet puppet.[63] The prospect of war with a Soviet-backed Syria was a source of endless anxiety for Israel's leaders. Ben-Gurion accused Eisenhower of bringing a holocaust on the world because of laziness and fear of the Soviet Union, comparing the President and Dulles with the capitulation of Neville Chamberlain and Edouard Daladier in Munich. He warned that a single bullet could kill King Hussein and bring a pro-Soviet regime into Jordan. Then Iraq could fall and perhaps even Saudi Arabia. Israel thus had to act with

---

56 FRUS, 1955–1957, XVII: 706.
57 ICAB, August 18, 1957, ISA.
58 FRUS, 1955–1957, XIII: 648–50.
59 'Conversation between the Secretary of State and Israel Ambassador, September 11, 1957,' Secret, NA, FO 371/128107/VR1052/23.
60 Arab-Israeli Dispute (6), September 20, 1957, J.I.C. (57) 62, NA, CAB158/29.
61 ICAB, September 1, 1957, ISA.
62 FRUS, 1955–1957, XVII: 713–21.
63 FRUS, 1955–1957, XIII: 500–2, 680.

maximum caution. Meir went so far as to call Israel's northern frontier the 'Israeli–Soviet border.'[64]

US intelligence was more concerned about the possibility of pro-Soviet regimes in Lebanon, Jordan and Iraq than the Syrian threat against Israel. It wanted 'quiescence,' but was not at all sure it could get it. Dulles believed that the United States was facing the gravest danger since the Korean War and that the Soviet regime's objective was to divert public attention from internal problems. He argued that Khrushchev was dangerous, crude and impulsive, resembled Hitler more than any other Soviet leader and was no less erratic. It was clear to Eisenhower and Dulles that the Arabs sought jihad against Israel, and Dulles feared that the Soviet success in Syria would go to Khrushchev's head.[65]

Israel demanded clarifications. The United States, Dulles said, had no illusions that, globally speaking, the regional situation was very serious, and he acknowledged that Israel's neighbors were liable to turn into Communist client states. However, he was prepared to promise no more than intelligence cooperation on the Jordanian question in the event of Soviet aggression. Israel believed, perhaps too strongly, that if it were attacked the United States would not stand on the sidelines.[66] Israel tried to obtain a firm commitment from Dulles for protection against a Soviet attack. The crisis in the Middle East, Israel maintained, was not the result of the Arab–Israeli conflict, but rather a function of US–Soviet relations. Israel asked that the United States not initiate any plan regarding the refugee problem, so as not to distract the Arab states from the Communist threat. Dulles made do with warning Egypt of the danger of the Hungarian-style enslavement of Egypt by the Soviet Union.[67]

Meir explained to Christian Herter, Dulles's deputy, that what Israel needed were bomber planes and aircraft that could counterbalance the MiG-19s, but was told that Israel should appeal to France. The State Department was still concerned about Israel's plans for immigration, which frightened the Arabs. Meir claimed that she wanted to know if there would be an end to Soviet extortion.[68] According to a US National Intelligence Estimate, any attempt to intervene in Syria would lead to war. Israel's strength, according to the estimate, depended on strong

---

64 ICAB, September 1, 8, 1957, ISA (Ben-Gurion); MFASC, August 30, 1957, LPA (Meir).
65 FRUS, 1955–1957, XIII: 685–9, 698–9.
66 ICAB, September 15, 1957, ISA.
67 FRUS, 1955–1957, XVII: 743, 747–9, 752–5.
68 FRUS, 1955–1957, XVII: 760–2.

deterrence, and within a year it would be able to defend itself and strike Egypt and Syria, although it would be vulnerable to surprise aerial attacks. Israel's fear of Arab military superiority, achieved through Soviet aid, could lead it to make a preemptive strike. The development of water resources on its northern border and hatred from extremist Arab states also increased the risk of war. The Soviets would take a bellicose position, but would not knowingly risk a third world war.[69] Dulles believed that the lack of a solution to the Palestine problem enabled the Soviets to benefit from regional instability.[70] The US administration understood Israel's position better as Dulles's attitude toward Nasser became more negative. He felt that Nasser, with his attempts to incite the two superpowers against each other, was leading Egypt into a trap and toward catastrophe, and had not learned that any country that cooperated with the Soviets would regret it.[71] Soviet propaganda was increasingly anti-Israel, Dulles acknowledged, but the Soviet Union would not deliberately provoke an Arab attack on Israel. The United States would have to live with the Arab–Israeli conflict for a long time, Dulles thought, and had little room to maneuver, and in case of aggression might eventually have to resort to military intervention. There was no practical way, he maintained, of achieving a modus vivendi with the Soviet Union, which was threatening its neighbors.[72]

Ben-Gurion believed the American people were decent and that they did not want to see Israel destroyed. However, he feared that the Soviets could demolish Israel in a few hours and destroy twenty American cities in just half an hour.[73] The Israeli government feared the Soviet Union had concluded that an attack on Israel would not demand a serious American response or cause a world war.[74] Israel realized that, had the United States allowed it to purchase US arms, the Eisenhower Doctrine would have collapsed, explaining Israel's eagerness to obtain weapons secretly from any available source. Behind Israel's desperate search for new sources of arms was Ben-Gurion's fear that Egypt would compel the UN force to evacuate Sharm el-Sheikh. Israel, he felt, could be destroyed quite rapidly, and US intervention would be of no value.[75]

69 National Intelligence Estimate, October 8, 1957, in FRUS, 1955–1957, XII: 594–611.
70 FRUS, 1955–1957, XVII: 767–70 (October 21, 1957), 774–5.
71 FRUS, 1955–1957, XVII: 776–7.
72 FRUS, 1955–1957, XII: 619–36.
73 ICAB, December 1, 1957, ISA.
74 [No author,] November 11, 1957, Top Secret, ISA 3105/13.
75 ICAB, December 24, 1957, ISA.

Israel was disappointed by Dulles's insistence that it was the totality of US policy that provided Israel with real defense. Dulles disagreed that strengthening the Israeli army could provide it with sure defenses, stating that Israel's lack of recognized borders prevented the United States from providing it with defense guarantees.[76] Israel's attempts to establish ties with NATO were fruitless and its application for a loan from the Export–Import Bank of the United States was suspended pending its consent to restrict immigration and allow Arab refugees to return.[77] The State Department accepted the stalemate, but the Pentagon maintained that the situation in the Middle East was a threat to free world security, and the Soviet Union had to be prevented from exploiting regional instability.

The Eisenhower Doctrine improved Israel's standing in the US administration solely because of the danger of a Soviet takeover of Syria, Lebanon and Jordan. The State Department had given up on Nasser, but not on pro-Western countries like Iraq and Saudi Arabia. Israel's greatest disappointment was that the administration still refused to supply it with heavy weapons. The Eisenhower Doctrine was intended to block the Soviet Union by strengthening relations between the United States and moderate Arab regimes. As long as Israel could obtain the weapons it needed from Europe, mainly France,[78] and as long as US financial and economic aid continued flowing, Israel's existence could be guaranteed without its becoming a burden – or an asset – to the United States. The only way for Israel to ensure its survival and to prevent Soviet penetration of the region was to depend on the West (especially on the United States), to seek guarantees and to strengthen its defensive capabilities by integrating into the defense of the free world.[79] Ever present were the dubious arrangements left behind by Dulles regarding freedom of navigation in the Gulf of Aqaba and the problematic mandate of the UN forces in Sinai and the Gaza Strip. Thus Israel had to strengthen its military power to be able to deter its enemies and prevent them from launching a war. At the same time, it was paying a heavy price for the preference Dulles gave to the Cold War in Europe and the Far East over the Arab–Israeli conflict.

---

76 FRUS, 1955–1957, XVII: 779–85, 792–3, 828–30.
77 FRUS, 1955–1957, XVII: 841–6.
78 Tsur to MPC, to Shiloah, 'Israeli–French Relations,' November 17, 1957, ISA 3120/23II.
79 M. S. Komay to G. Avner (London), Personal and Secret, November 8, 1957, ISA 3085/12.

# 7

# Soviet–Israeli relations after the Suez War (1956–61)

After the Suez War, Ben-Gurion, fearing Soviet 'volunteers' would participate in hostilities against Israel, tried to persuade the West that the Soviet Union was committed to Arab radicalism. The Israeli left warned against doing anything that would be tantamount to declaring war against the Soviet Union; rather, it was proposed, Israel should concentrate on defending itself.[1] Bulganin (that is, Khrushchev) sent a second threatening letter to Ben-Gurion calling Israel a 'tool of foreign forces seeking to restore a colonial regime.' The Israeli embassy in Moscow believed that the Soviet Union would not use force against Israel, but that it would work to prevent the Arab states from reconciling with the West.[2] Khrushchev ridiculed Israel and praised Nasser. An article headlined 'The Way to Suicide: Where is the Reckless Policy of the Ruling Circles in Israel Leading?' appeared in *Izvestia*, claiming that Israel was seeking lebensraum just as Hitler had, and that its leaders were war criminals.[3] The Soviet position had hardened because Israel had allegedly caused damage to its strategic assets in the Middle East. Israel regarded the article as a declaration of war,[4] and told the US ambassador that Khrushchev stated that the Soviet Union did not need to send forces against Israel because it could be destroyed with missiles alone. It warned that the danger of a Soviet miscalculation had grown, adding that Bulganin was bluffing but to a certain degree the Kremlin was genuinely dangerous, and that Israel needed a US guarantee that would deter the Soviet Union. While Soviet Jews supported Israel, they were increasingly fearful of state persecution.[5]

1 ICAB, November 10, 15, 18, 25, 1956, ISA; Govrin, 1998: *passim*.
2 Bulganin to Ben-Gurion in Ben-Gurion, 1997: 251, 253–4; IMM to DEE, November 19, 1956, ISA 48/3.
3 IMM to IFM, November 29, 1956, ISA 2236/7.
4 DEE to IFM, December 7, 1956, ISA 330/14.
5 Avidar to DEE Director, December 2, 1956, Secret, ISA 3115/8.

Ben-Gurion attacked Communist ideology, saying it was hypocritical and deceitful, even if it was backed by hundreds of armored divisions. He said that Israel should not give up hope for Soviet Jewish immigration when the current regime in Moscow was replaced.[6] Israel hoped the flow of immigrants from Hungary and Poland would not be ended, despite the *Stürmer*-like anti-Jewish incitement in the Soviet press.[7] The Kremlin announced that, despite the huge anger against Israel, it would not send 'volunteers' to Egypt, confirmation that it had in fact intended to send them. Ben-Gurion hoped Soviet animosity would be channeled into the Soviet Union's problems in Hungary, and its fear of rebellions in other satellite states, making it possible for Soviet Jews to emigrate to Israel.[8] He also hoped Soviet policy toward Israel would improve when it realized that its Arab policy had been a failure.[9]

The Soviet foreign minister, Dmitry Shepilov, called on February 11, 1957, for excluding the Middle East from the East–West conflict, saying the region should focus only on economic development. Ben-Gurion, however, feared the Soviet Union still intended to destroy Israel.[10] After learning the Kremlin had discussed permitting the revival of Jewish culture in the Soviet Union, he instructed Israel's envoys in the free world to make the Eastern bloc's Jews a priority. The Kremlin had decided that Jewish prayer books could be printed, Jewish folk songs could be performed and the number of exit permits to Israel would be increased. It had recently permitted Chechens to return to their native land from internal exile, and Bulgaria, Yugoslavia and Poland allowed Jews to emigrate, proving that emigration did not harm Communist regimes or economies or contradict Communist principles.[11] However, the Soviet threat remained constant. Dayan maintained that Israel was stronger than all the Arab armies put together, but could be defeated if the Arabs were armed with atomic weapons, if Israel suffered economic collapse (especially because of an oil shortage), or if 'volunteer' Soviet pilots were sent to the Middle East, and if the Arabs staged a surprise attack like Rommel's offensive in Tobruk (1941).[12]

---

6  Ben-Gurion, Histadrut Council, December 5, 1956, Protocol, 15–16.
7  *Der Stürmer* was an anti-Semitic weekly tabloid published in Nazi Germany. ICAB, December 9, 1956, December 13, 1956, ISA.
8  KFADC, December 11, 1956, ISA.
9  Avni to Tsur, Meeting with the Adviser to the Russian Ambassador, December 28, 1956, January 6, 1957, 1957, ISA 3115/8.
10  DFPI 12: 537–8.
11  Eytan to IDM, February 26, 1957, ISA 335/14.
12  KFADC, February 26, 1957, ISA.

Ben-Gurion acknowledged Israel had withdrawn from the Sinai Peninsula because the Soviets had threatened to attack and because it had no option but to bow to US wishes.[13] He accepted the Western premise that the Soviet Union did not want an all-out war, and Khrushchev advocated negotiations because he knew the West had hydrogen bombs.[14] The US ambassador to Moscow did not believe the Soviets would have a change of heart and were, he said, prepared to deal Israel a heavy blow. If the United States rejected the Soviet disarmament offer, more Soviet arms would be sent to Egypt and Syria. Clearly, he said, Khrushchev was not only anti-Israeli, but also anti-Semitic.[15]

All signs indicated the Kremlin was taking a tough line. The Soviet press called the Israeli government a clique and took anti-Israeli propaganda to unprecedented levels. It claimed that the funds collected in the United States were used to arm the IDF and were financing 'imperialism.'[16] The Israeli embassy in Moscow appraised the Soviet Union had become so deeply involved in the Middle East that it could not back out without losing face.[17] Little wonder the Soviets accused France and Israel of plotting to attack Syria. Ben-Gurion remarked that, while such charges appeared almost daily in the Soviet press, it was worrying because Soviet military instructors had arrived in Syria, and, despite his concern for the Soviet Union's Jews, the decisive factor would be whether the United States would provide immediate assistance if the Communists attacked.[18]

The Cold War made mending Soviet–Israeli fences impossible. Israel accused the Soviet Union of threatening it and calling it a US base, even though the US fleet was anchored in Beirut. The Soviets claimed their attitude was a function of Israel's relations with the United States. The world, the Soviets cautioned, was on the brink of a third world war, waiting only for the West to arm West Germany. Israel noted that it had no interest in what it called 'graveyard socialism,' the kind of Soviet socialism that would take an enormous toll of life.[19] Ben-Gurion told the government that the Kremlin would be wary of an Israel it considered

13  ICAB, February 26, 1957, ISA 359, 360.
14  ICAB, February 27, 1957, ISA 359, 360.
15  Argaman (Washington) to USD, March 15, 1957, ISA 3088/5b.
16  Eshel, DEE to IMM, April 24, 1957, ISA 2327/1.
17  Chelouche to Avidar, 'Our Policy Regarding the Soviet Union,' April 30, 1957, ISA 3115/8.
18  ICAB, May 7, 12, 1957, ISA.
19  Y. Ariel (Brussels), 'Conversation with the Soviet Ambassador Avilov', May 10, 1957, ISA 3115/8.

backed by the United States. Some leftist government ministers countered that the Soviets would see it as a matter of competition between military alliances and it would thus escalate the Cold War.[20]

*Pravda* claimed that Israel had capitulated to the United States and that the Eisenhower Doctrine was linked to a US desire to deploy atomic weapons in the Middle East for a war against the Soviet Union.[21] However, a record of a stormy Politburo meeting showed that Israel was a secondary factor in the US–Soviet conflict. Molotov said that, according to Lenin's principles, a joint US–Soviet force should be sent to the Middle East to oppose Britain and France. Mikoyan, defending his superior, said Khrushchev had shown the United States that the Soviets had teeth, had helped bring the Suez War to an end, and had proved that the Soviet Union was capable of fighting on two fronts simultaneously, that is, in Hungary and in the Middle East.[22] Khrushchev called Molotov a dogmatist divorced from reality and accused him of pushing Turkey and Iran into the arms of the West. Molotov, he said, should not teach him about Leninist foreign policy. The warnings he issued to the West proved he knew how to exploit the contradictions in the imperialist camp. The steps taken by the Soviets during the Triple Aggression against Egypt, he said, had prevented a new world war, the Soviet Union had retained the initiative, and the Kremlin's peace-seeking policy had put the West on the defensive.[23]

Israel was caught between the fear of more Soviet weapons on its borders and the hope that the Israeli victory in Sinai would jumpstart a national awakening of the Jews of the Soviet Union. If the Soviets could be persuaded to open their gates, half a million Jews would emigrate to Israel immediately and another million would follow. However, the Soviets were arming the Syrians with $140 million worth of weapons and Ben-Gurion acknowledged that the danger of the Soviet Union destroying Israel kept him awake at night.[24] The Israeli cabinet's fundamental assumption was that, given Israel's poor relations with the Soviet Union, there was nothing to lose by allying with the United States and that Israel should prepare a counteroffensive for Western public opinion

20 ICAB, May 20, 26, 1957, ISA.
21 IMM to DEE, March 24, 1957, ISA 4330/8.
22 'Minutes of a Meeting of the CPSU CC [Communist Party of the Soviet Union Central Committee] Plenum on the State of Soviet Foreign Policy,' June 24, 1957, CWIHP.
23 Transcript of a CSPU CC Plenum, June 28, 1957, CWIHP.
24 ICAB, July 7, 1957, August 18, 25, 1957, ISA.

to increase its nuisance value.²⁵ The possibility of a Soviet-triggered Syrian attack increased after the cabinet voted to continue draining the Hula swamp and diverting the Jordan River. Khrushchev may have denounced Stalin,²⁶ but he was capable of behaving just like him. Israel would continue its development project because the danger of the 'volunteers' the Soviets would send was indirect and only the United States could prevent it.²⁷

Khrushchev called Soviet Jews 'aliens,' unlike the other nationalities in the Soviet Union,²⁸ and claimed that the cause of the 'Jewish problem' was the dispersal of Jews throughout the state. It was not his fault, he claimed, that the Birobidzhan initiative had failed. As far as he was concerned, he said, the Jews could build synagogues, community organizations and theaters, and produce literature with their own money. If they had not done so thus far, it was because they did not want a cultural life of their own.²⁹ Gromyko was no less disappointing to Israel. When Meir asked for a promise that Syria would not attack, he said he could not speak for Syria. She called the conversation 'difficult and terrible ... sitting before us was a man who without the slightest hesitation could destroy us himself or look on complacently as others destroyed us.'³⁰

Ben-Gurion hardened his anti-Soviet line after the successful Sputnik launch on October 4, 1957. Until then he had been convinced that the Soviet Union did not want war, but the launch made him less certain. He took Sputnik as a sign the Soviets had weapons capable of destroying the United States, without whose help Israel would be unable to defend itself.³¹ The Kremlin redoubled its offensive and Gromyko, now the new Soviet foreign minister, warned the UN General Assembly that, if Israel attacked Syria, its very existence would be at risk.³² The missile base built in Egypt by the Soviets and the possibility that they would build another in Syria heightened Ben-Gurion's fears. He then learned that the Kremlin planned to provoke Israel and bomb Haifa and Tel Aviv. However, he felt Khrushchev could not be certain the United States would not fight for Israel and feared an attack on Israel would also mean

25 [No author,] 'How to Bring About a Softening of the Soviet Attitude to Israel,' August 1, 1957, ISA 3115/8.
26 See Chapter 3.
27 ICAB, September 1, 15, 1957, ISA.
28 B. Eliav to G. Avner (London), June 14, 1967, ISA 335/14.
29 M. Rivlin to DEE, September 5, 1957, Top Secret, ISA 382/10.
30 Gromyko–Meir Conversation, October 1, 1957, ISA 330/14.
31 ICAB, October 13, 1957, ISA.
32 Levavi to Eytan, October 23, 1957, ISA 3115/8.

war with the Americans. He was anti-Semitic, but he did not want to conquer Israel and would not risk a world war just to attack it. What Israel needed was a Western deterrent against the Soviet threat.[33] Ben-Gurion's fears reached new heights. The Soviet Union had twice threatened to destroy Israel, but had made no threats against NATO, thus Israel was isolated. He worried endlessly about the possibility that Tel Aviv might be bombed. However, he pointed out that Khrushchev would not be master of the Soviet Union forever. Soviet officials told Israeli diplomats that the conflict between the two Cold War blocs lay at the root of the problem in the Middle East. The United States had constructed a belt of bases around the Soviet Union, which the Soviets had to break through. While it was true that the Soviet Union was seeking to strengthen Egypt by supplying it with arms, the Kremlin had forbidden the weapons to be used against Israel.[34]

On December 10, 1957, and January 19, 1958, Israel and the Soviet Union exchanged communiqués about the nuclear threat and reinforcing peace. The optimists in the Israeli cabinet who advocated neutrality and the left-wing ministers who had still had hopes for the Soviet Union were at a disadvantage in debating the pessimists. Even if the two superpowers decided that Israel remain neutral, how would that help if Syria and Egypt wanted to destroy it?[35] The Soviets made it clear that relations could not be improved. Vladimir Semyonov, the Soviet deputy foreign minister, claimed that Israel was a tool of colonialism and had joined the forces that were doomed. Furthermore, in 1948, the Soviet Union had not known what kind of country Israel would become, and, had it known, Israel would not have received Soviet support. For Meir, that ended any hope of progress with the Soviets. Worse, Israel still had no concrete guarantees from the West.[36] Despite the cabinet's negativity, Ben-Gurion demanded that Israel maintain correct relations with the Soviets. However, the Soviets had to be told that Israel was entitled to accept assistance from any country willing to help it, 'just as [the Soviet Union] had the right to accept help from Hitler.' He also warned against being misled by Soviet sloganeering about nuclear disarmament.[37] The question was not whether relations could be improved, but whether the

33 KFADC, December 11, 1957, ISA.
34 Col. A. Yariv, 'Conversation with Commander Galinsky from the Soviet Navy', December 12, 1957, ISA 3115/8.
35 ICAB, December 15, 1957, ISA.
36 DFPI 13: 615, 617.
37 ICAB, January 26, 1958, ISA.

Soviet Union still accepted the principle of Israel's independence and territorial integrity.[38]

Ben-Gurion said that Israel could hardly tell the United States not to supply missiles to Turkey, as the Soviets demanded, as that would make Israel look like a Soviet pawn. On the other hand, Israel should not make itself appear anti-Soviet, which, with three million Jews in the Soviet Union, would be contrary to Israeli interests. He feared the worst, that the Soviets might give Egypt an atomic bomb. Israel was developing peaceful atomic power, he said, which would give it an answer to Arab oil.[39]

On February 1, 1958, a surprised Israel learned that Egypt and Syria were uniting to form the United Arab Republic (UAR). Israel claimed the Soviet Union had to have known about it beforehand and might take control of it. Thus, in any future war, Israel would face both the Arabs and the Soviets.[40] Khrushchev did in fact regard the establishment of the UAR as a victory for Communism.[41] Ben-Gurion expected that historical dialectic would bring about a change in the Soviet Union and asked his ministers not to accuse the Soviet Union of anti-Semitism, lest it worsen relations. The establishment of the Soviet-favored UAR showed that the situation was getting worse.[42] The Israeli foreign ministry did not believe Arab hostility could be brought to an end, maintaining that fundamentally the Arabs wanted to destroy Israel. Even if the Arab leftists were to emerge victorious, the policies of the Arab countries toward Israel would not change.[43] The Soviet–Arab alliance would not dissolve as long as the Soviet Union had not lost in the international arena. Thus a summit meeting would be of no avail because neither of the superpowers would make concessions on fundamental issues such as military alliances and bases.[44] The Soviet Union's declaration that it accepted the status quo was no more than a ruse, since its official position was that it recognized only the UN partition borders of 1947. Israel was completely marginalized when East and West were vying for influence in the Arab states, thus it would be foolish to expect a Soviet guarantee of the 1949 borders or Soviet adherence to the Tripartite Declaration.[45]

\* \* \*

38  Eban to Shiloah, February 3, 1958, ISA 3088/II6.
39  ICAB, February 2, 1958, ISA.
40  Podeh, 1999: 25–48.
41  Zivkov's Report at the CC [Central Committee] B[ulgarian] Plenary Session on the Middle East Crisis, February 10, 1958, CWIHP.
42  ICAB, February 16, 1958, ISA.
43  Shimoni to Harel, March 4, 1958, Personal, ISA 3105/13I.
44  Levavi to Harel, March 11, 1958, ISA 3105/13II.
45  Avidar to Shiloah, March 24, 1958, Secret, ISA 208/11.

On April 4, 1958, Khrushchev wrote to Ben-Gurion asking him to support a moratorium on nuclear testing, the same request sent to the leaders of other countries and not indicating a change in policy. Ben-Gurion reminded the Soviet ambassador that Nasser had received a nuclear reactor from the Soviet Union and called the letter a fraud. The Soviets, he said, believed the West was doomed and did not value coexistence. As far back as the nineteenth century, Russia had believed the West was corrupt and that Russia's mission was to save the world. Once a dream, it was now a religion. Time was on their side, why start a war when the United States was strong? The United States had to display its determination to fight Communism for the long haul, Ben-Gurion said. Other countries would lose their faith in the West if it did not.[46]

Interviewed by *Le Figaro* on April 9, Khrushchev again blamed the Jews for the failure of the Birobidzhan initiative. They had, he claimed, been unable to organize to live together. He would not deviate from the Soviet theory of nationalities and pointed out that his grandson was half-Jewish, and claimed that half of the members of the Central Committee were married to Jewish women. Furthermore, he said, his best friend was a Jewish engineer, the classic claim of every anti-Semite.[47]

Israel feared that the two blocs would reach an accommodation at its expense. The West did not understand the Soviet talk of coexistence, which really meant subversion. The Soviets wanted the United States to withdraw its missiles unilaterally from Turkey, they wanted the dissolution of the Baghdad Pact and the end of what they called 'economic imperialism,' namely the oil concessions Western countries had received from the Arabs. The Soviets had no intention of observing a moratorium in East–West tensions, as proved by their conduct in Korea, Indochina and Berlin.[48]

Nasser's visit to Moscow in 1958 (April 29–May 14) showed the extent of Soviet involvement in the Middle East. A joint communiqué was issued, stating that the Arab refugee problem was a threat to peace and regional security, and that the refugees had legal rights to Palestine. Israel assumed that the Soviets would increase their pressure in favor of the refugees, which could encourage Nasser to take hasty and aggressive steps.[49] The Kremlin reassured Israel that it had given Nasser no

---

46 Ben-Gurion to ICAB, April 20, 1958; 'Interview, May 16, 1958, with the Prime Minister of Israel, Mr. David Ben-Gurion, and 31 Members of the National War College,' Washington, D.C., ISA 7226/6a.
47 ICAB, April 27, 1958, ISA.
48 Levavi to the Inner Circle of IFM, April 18, 1958, ISA 4316/17.
49 DFPI 13: 631.

promises regarding the 1947 borders, as Egyptian propaganda claimed, because the Soviet Union did not want war.[50]

Ben-Gurion proposed that the two countries improve their relations. He asked the Soviets for arms and called for an Israeli–Egyptian peace agreement. The proposal was rejected because, the Soviets said, Israel was negotiating the purchase of submarines from West Germany and airplanes from France.[51] Robert Oppenheimer, 'father' of the American atomic bomb, advised Ben-Gurion to construct an atomic power plant. If the West developed a weapon to blow up a Soviet atom bomb in flight, it would deter war, he said. His advice caused Ben-Gurion great concern.[52] Israel realized that the Soviet Union's principal grievance remained Israel's Western orientation, not its pressure regarding Soviet Jews.[53] The only solution was a clear Western declaration that it would defend those countries that did not surrender to Nasser and the Soviets.[54] The Soviet attitude toward Israel was a combination of Cold War imperatives, the nature of the Soviet regime and the Jews' status within it. The Soviet Union would not attack Israel to destroy it because its opposition to Israel was tactical, not fundamental.[55] Soviet manipulation included, as usual, charges that the IDF was concentrating forces in Israel's north. Meir told Ben-Gurion to issue a public denial and in vain invited the Soviet ambassador to tour the north to see with his own eyes that Israel had not called up reserves.

Israel became more pessimistic about the chance for improved relations with the Soviet Union, although it was argued by Aryeh Harel, the left-oriented ambassador to Moscow, that relations could be improved if an Arab working class were to emerge in the Middle East.[56] The Middle East was evidently important to the Soviet Union, obvious from the huge amounts of money it was pouring into the UAR. Discrimination against the Jews was producing a Zionist revival and the only solution for both the Soviet government and its Jews was Jewish emigration to Israel. The Kremlin would not deport half a million Jews to Birobidzhan and would not intervene during hostilities against Israel because it feared a global war.[57] It was also argued that the Soviet Union was weighing

50  DFPI 13: 632–3.
51  DFPI 13: 635–6.
52  ICAB, June 1, 1958, ISA.
53  DFPI, 13: 66–7, 95–6, 636–8.
54  DFPI, 13: 682–3.
55  KFADC, November 5, 1958, ISA.
56  Harel to Shimoni and Peled, April 16, 1959, ISA 3115/18.
57  ICAB, November 23, 1958, December 28, 1958, ISA.

the advantages and disavantages of its relationship with Israel, and was therefore open to compromise.

Ben-Gurion sought to establish diplomatic relations with West Germany. To opponents he said that West Germany did not need to be rehabilitated by Israel. It was already a member of NATO and East Germany was a member of the Warsaw Pact and had not paid reparations to the Jewish people as West Germany had. He said that Khrushchev was 'head over heels in love with East Germany,' so it would be naive to assert that Jewish immigration from the Soviet Union would be affected by Israel's sale of arms to West Germany.[58] The Soviet Union and its satellites launched an extensive anti-Israel campaign, attacking it for signing an arms deal with Hitler's successors. West German reparations payments, said the Red Army newspaper, were intended to procure arms for Israeli militarists, who were imperialist agents in the Middle East.[59]

Ben-Gurion termed Soviet policy, which sought to buy the friendship of seventy million Arabs, 'Machiavellian.' The Kremlin, he said, intended to make Israel repugnant to the Soviet Jews by calling Israel an inferno. If Israel wanted to enjoy free navigation in the Red Sea and Suez Canal, claimed the Kremlin, it had to resolve the Arab refugee and border issues.[60] Moreover, while the Soviet Union's stated position might have been the possible reinstatement of cultural and commercial ties, its actions contradicted its declarations.[61] According to IDF intelligence, the Soviet Union had thus far supplied the UAR with $400 million worth of weapons and Iraq with $140 million. Since Eastern bloc prices were lower than the rest of the world market's, it meant more than at first glance, including heavy and medium tanks, bombers, submarines, destroyers, MiG-17s and cannons.[62]

The Khrushchev–Eisenhower summit of September 1959 caused concern in Israel. Meir feared Khrushchev would make a deal with the United States over Israel's head in disregard of its vital security interests and of the right of Soviet Jews to emigrate. In fact, Eisenhower did bring up the subject of Soviet Jewry, but to no avail. Khrushchev claimed that the Jews in his country had the same status as all other citizens.[63]

58 DFPI, 13: 644–6.
59 *Krasnaya Zvezda*, July 5, 1959.
60 ICAB, June 7, 1959, ISA.
61 DFPI 13: 647–9, 650–2.
62 Col. Haim Herzog to G. Meir, 'Soviet Military Assistance to the Arab States,' August 15, 1959, ISA 3115/19.
63 DFPI 13: 660–5.

Disappointed by the summit meeting, Israel advocated a doctrine of coexistence to reduce Nasser's power to extort, and to strengthen Israel and perhaps improve the lot of the Soviet Jews. It was proposed that Israel recognize Communist China as a way of improving relations with the Soviets, but the cabinet rejected the idea.[64]

A Jewish woman was burned to death in an arson attack on a synagogue in Malakhovka, 30 km from Moscow, in October 1959, a sign that the plight of the Jews in the Soviet Union was getting worse. Initially, the Soviet authorities denied that the attack had taken place, but eventually had to put the alleged murderers on trial. A proposition was made, and rejected, that Malakhovka be made a symbol of Soviet Jewry's struggle for its rights, but without getting dragged into the Cold War.[65]

There were three theories in Israel about Soviet Jewry. The first was that the Soviet Union wanted a sympathetic West and was thus sensitive to Western pressures, and feared that a marginal issue such as Soviet Jewry could sabotage the spirit of détente. The second was that public pressure would force Khrushchev to permit Jewish emigration as part of détente. The third was that Khrushchev had to be cautious because détente could weaken his position in the Soviet Union.[66] Israel's position was that the Kremlin's official campaign of anti-Semitism and anti-Israel incitement was a reaction to Israel's support of France in Algeria. The conclusion was that Soviet policy toward its Jews and Israel was determined by the Arab factor, but was also a product of deep-rooted anti-Zionism. The Soviet Union waffled between four options: total assimilation of the Jews, concentrating them in Birobidzhan, cultural autonomy and, some in Israel worried, mass annihilation.

Eban told the Knesset's Foreign Affairs and Defense Committee that relations with the Soviet Union were in a very bad situation and that international détente had not had a positive influence on Soviet–Israeli relations.[67] Nasser had received $487 million from the Soviet bloc and $175 million from the West. Nevertheless, Ben-Gurion believed that Israel could find non-Arab Middle Eastern allies in countries such as Iran and Turkey. Although the Arabs did not in fact constitute a majority in the Middle East, Israel could lose its qualitative advantages in three to five years. Egypt was about to receive Ilyushin bombers at a time when Israel did not have even one, and would receive MiG-19s in 1962.

64 Peled to Meir, August 19, 1959, ISA 3105/13II.
65 Harel to G. Meir, October 26, 1959, ISA 4316/9.
66 Harman to B. Eliav, November 10, 1959, ISA 4309/10.
67 KFADC, January 12, 1960, ISA.

The UAR could then block the shipping lanes to Eilat, capture Sharm el-Sheikh and the Red Sea islands of Tiran and Sanafir, and obstruct Israel's water project on the Upper Jordan River.[68] Israel remained anxious. The Russian people would not, Ben-Gurion prophesied, tolerate the Communist regime for long, and it would end within twenty years. Israel needed, within the space of two years, to build a deterrent force.[69]

Israel's leaders distrusted the Soviet claim that it was sending the Arabs the message that Israel was a fait accompli they had to take into account and that they should stop talking about destroying it because the Soviets would not permit it. Israel, therefore, rejected the Soviet demand for cooperation, especially regarding West Germany, which was a true friend to Israel. Ben-Gurion met with Konrad Adenauer, postwar chancellor of West Germany, in New York in March 1960, angering the Kremlin even more.[70] The clearer it became to Israel that the Soviet position in the Arab–Israeli conflict would not change, the more urgent the question of Soviet Jewry became. Ben-Gurion did not believe that a US–Soviet accommodation was in the offing, because Khrushchev rejected coexistence. He told Adenauer that when Khrushchev said 'peaceful coexistence,' he meant a variation of 'what's mine is mine and what's yours is mine.'

On August 9, 1960, the newspaper *Kommunist* in Buynaksk, Dagestan, published an article headlined 'Even Without God the Road is Open.' It accused Jews of being religiously obligated to drink Muslim blood. It was a notorious display of anti-Semitism and Israel was stunned. Could something like that happen forty-three years after the October Revolution? The Jews of Dagestan sent a protest to Anastas Mikoyan, Soviet deputy prime minister, and to Mikhail Suslov, the Communist Party's chief ideologue. Ben-Gurion was not in the least surprised and praised the Dagestan Jews for their courage.[71] Nevertheless, the decisive factor was that Israel was a de facto ally of the West. Had Israel conducted an independent foreign policy, the Soviet Union would not have cared if Israel's regime was extreme rightist and capitalist.[72] The Israeli foreign ministry concluded that Soviet support for the Arabs, as on the

---

68 ICAB, January 17, 1960, February 7, 1960, ISA.
69 ICAB, January 31, 1960, ISA.
70 ICAB, June 18, 1961; DFPI, 14: 337–42; Tsur to Peled, February 5, 1960, Secret, ISA 3332/1.
71 Harel to T. Kollek, October 28, 1960, Top Secret, ISA 6382/2c.
72 Y. Herzog (Otawa) to DEE Director, 'Conversation with the Soviet Ambassador,' July 31, 1960, ISA 3332/1.

refugee question, was increasing the risk of war in the Middle East, despite the Soviet Union's policy of détente.[73]

Ben-Gurion feared that Israel would be defeated if attacked by the Soviet Union. The Soviets were spreading disinformation, such as that Israel was planning to attack Egypt because of the latter's surprising deployment of forces in the Sinai Peninsula.[74] Ben-Gurion told the French president, Charles de Gaulle, that the United States did not understand the true nature of Soviet Communism, according to which the ends justified all the means, including deception, intrigue, violence, subversion and war.[75] The Soviets complained that, in addition to Israel's complete identification with the West and the growing importance of the issue of Soviet Jewry, Israel was developing advanced nuclear technology with the objective of producing nuclear weapons, which could cause severe tension beyond the Middle East. The superpowers, they said, could do a great deal to deter new countries from joining the nuclear club.[76]

Khrushchev told various Soviet forums (on January 6, 1961) that socialism was defeating capitalism and that the Third World would join the Communist camp. The growing rift with Communist China was also evident when Khrushchev condemned Chairman Mao as a hard-liner willing to risk a nuclear war. Support for the 'sacred' struggle for decolonization and independence offered Communism a shorter road to the defeat of imperialism, he maintained. A nuclear war was unthinkable, but wars of national liberation such as those in Algeria and Vietnam were inevitable and worthy of Soviet support. Khrushchev distinguished between a worldwide nuclear war, local wars and wars of national liberation. The Soviet Union, he said, should help colonized peoples throw off the yoke of imperialism, and could legitimately do so while advocating coexistence.[77]

Khrushchev referred to Israel only indirectly, but the implication was obvious. It was no coincidence that newly elected President John F. Kennedy ordered his staff to read the speeches in full.[78] During Kennedy's term, Khrushchev would spark international crises in Germany and Cuba. Unsurprisingly, the United States was now affording Israel stronger backing in its conflicts with the Arabs and the Soviet Union.

73  Raphael to Y. Herzog, August 8, 1960, ISA 3332/1.
74  KFADC, February 26, 1960, March 23, 1960, ISA.
75  Shaltiel, 1996: 432–4.
76  SDMEC 2: 358–9 (Menshikov–Robert Kennedy meeting, January 11, 1961).
77  Rubinstein, 2008, 88–91; Zubok and Pleshakov, 1996: 208; Fursenko and Naftali, 2006: 73.
78  Hilsman, 1967: 414.

Paradoxically, Israel's international and regional status was improving, ignored by Khrushchev because of his overwhelming confidence that the Soviet Union could bury the West. Israel could now only hope that it would not have to pay too heavy a price for increased US support and for growing Soviet enmity.

# 8

# How the Middle East crises affected US policy toward Israel (1958–60)

The secret US Near East policy proposed by the National Security Council on January 15, 1958, was disappointing as far as Israel was concerned (NSC5801/1).[1] It contained a section calling for limiting immigration, which had serious implications for Israel and had not appeared in the previous version (NSC5482, July 23, 1954). It also stated that regional public opinion opposed the establishment of a mutual regional defense organization aimed against the Soviet Union. Secretary of Defense Neil McElroy warned the NSC that a third world war could be triggered in the Middle East and it was urgent for the United States to find a solution for the Arab–Israeli conflict. Dulles blamed Israel for keeping the problem from being resolved. He said proof of the power of so-called 'international Jewry' was that the Soviet Union, which hinted it would help the Arabs dismember Israel, had never offered more than hints.[2] The situation was precarious, he warned, but not hopeless.

United States Information Agency director George Allen said the problem of immigration to Israel was more important than the issue of the Arab refugees and suggested that only Jews undergoing religious persecution be allowed to immigrate, claiming that Soviet Jews were not more persecuted than the Christians. Dulles agreed that the loan from the Export–Import Bank should be conditioned on a new immigration policy, but doubted that would be possible in an election year. Atomic Energy Commission chairman Admiral Lewis Strauss said that if the United States sought to limit immigration to Israel it would lose the support of both the Zionists and the entire philanthropic community.[3] The new policy was based on the assumption that the Soviet Union had formed de facto alliances with Egypt and Syria, and that hostilities

---

1 'Long-Range Policy toward the Near East,' January 15, 1958, in FRUS, 1958–1960, XII: 4–5.
2 FRUS, 1958–1960, XII: 8.
3 FRUS, 1958–1960, XII: 6–14.

against Israel would be resumed. If the Soviets continued supplying the Arabs with arms, Western aid to them would be restricted.

Dulles continued to lead the State Department. He had always advocated border adjustments requiring Israel to cede territory it had acquired in the 1948 war and considered the return of some Arab refugees to Israel as feasible. Israel and its neighbors would share the waters of the Jordan River, in return for which the Arab boycott against Israel would be eased and freedom of navigation in the Gulf of Aqaba guaranteed. However, now Israel would be required to limit immigration, a UN force would be deployed and Israel would be given only the minimum arms necessary for self-defense. If war broke out, the United States would act through the UN and impose a commercial embargo, prevent transfers of funds, weapons and manpower, and impose sanctions on the aggressor. Israel's existence within its current borders was recognized, conditional on Israel's acceding to a new regional system and a reduction in economic aid.[4]

Barely issued, the policy was overtaken by events. In February 1958, Egypt and Syria united to form the UAR. The United States did not recognize it and established the short-lived Iraq–Jordan Arab Federation two weeks later to counter it.[5] Israel's nightmare was a union of Egypt, Syria and Jordan, a single coordinated enemy flanking it on three sides. Had that happened, Israel would have had to demand additional guarantees from the UN.[6] Israel asked the United States to make it clear to the UAR that Israel's integrity and security were vital to US interests and that any violation would trigger US intervention. Israel wanted a plan for US aid if it were attacked by Arab states under Soviet direction, which was likely to happen now that the Soviets were constructing submarine bases at Latakya and Alexandria and supplying the Arabs with modern arms. Israel's efforts to join NATO had failed, but according to the Eisenhower–Macmillan Declaration of Common Purpose (October 25), aid was to be provided to free countries that were not officially Western allies.[7] The Soviets were intransigent and in any case Dulles had no faith in the Kremlin and was of the opinion that any Soviet–US compromise in the Middle East would have to come at Israel's expense.[8] Israel could do nothing about the West's courting of Nasser as long as there had been no major shift in the Cold War parameters.[9]

4 FRUS, 1958–1960, XII: 18–32.
5 DFPI 13: 327–8.
6 DFPI 13: 328–30.
7 DFPI 13: 676–7; Macmillan, 1971: 756–9.
8 Meroz to USD, March 31, 1958, ISA 3088II/6.
9 A. Levavi, 'Western Appeasement of Nasser,' June 13, 1958, ISA 3144/40.

Israel feared the merger of Egypt and Syria. Ben-Gurion took some consolation in the fact that the union was artificial, but he also took into account the possibility of a war in two years' time. Adenauer was the only person Ben-Gurion trusted who understood the situation.[10]

However, the United States was concerned about how the UAR would influence the moderate Arab regimes and thus agreed to the Saudi Arabian demand to remove Israeli frigates from the Gulf of Aqaba.[11] The outbreak of a crisis in Lebanon, where Nasser threatened to topple that country's pro-Western government, changed the status quo.[12] Israel warned that the same thing could happen in Jordan. Dulles was convinced that Nasser was intervening in Lebanese internal affairs to realize, with Soviet assistance, his pan-Arab dream. Eban warned that if the Lebanese regime collapsed, all the countries whose security had been guaranteed by the United States would doubt that they would, if challenged, stand behind the Eisenhower Doctrine. The United States would be weakened globally unless it intervened.

A US National Intelligence Estimate stated that, given the volatile situation in the region, a preemptive Israeli attack against Egypt was likely. In addition, the Soviet response to US intervention in Lebanon should be restricted to aggressive diplomacy. However, if the United States violated the territorial integrity of the UAR, the Soviets would respond with expanded military aid and 'volunteers,' and the risk of a direct Soviet–US confrontation, even if not an all-out war, would increase.[13] William M. Rountree, Assistant Secretary of State for Near Eastern and South Asian Affairs, opposed Israel's request for support according to the Eisenhower Doctrine on the grounds that, if granted arms, it could use them against moderate Arab regimes. Israel could, however, replace old weapons with new ones if it kept quiet.[14]

Given the danger to the Jordanian regime, Israel was forced to allow British aircraft to use its airspace to reach Jordan. Ben-Gurion agreed because Jordan's independence was in Israel's interest, but feared a Soviet reprisal. However, if Jordan became part of Nasser's empire, Israel would be virtually surrounded. Nasser had flown to Moscow and was probably plotting with Khrushchev to establish Communist regimes in Iraq and Jordan, he said. Both had already received Soviet and Western weapons

10 ICAB, July 20, 1958, ISA.
11 DFPI 13: 338–41.
12 Gendzier, 1997, claimed there was no Soviet threat: 295–337; Karabell, 1999: 136–72; Little, 1996: 17–47.
13 National Intelligence Estimate, June 5, 1958, in FRUS, 1958–1960, XII: 61–3.
14 FRUS, 1958–1960, XIII: 54–6, 357–8.

respectively, yet Israel remained without even a promise of arms.[15] The Arabs needed two years to prepare for war, which Israel would win thanks to the quality of its manpower and combat methods. According to Ben-Gurion, the IDF's most pressing problem was arms. Israel, he said, should concentrate on purchasing arms from Western Europe, with US consent.[16]

Ben-Gurion knew that the United States was a key factor in enabling Israel to offset Arab power and was angry with Eisenhower for doing nothing to stop Nasser from gaining control of the oil in the Arab states and Iran. Nasser's intentions were clear from his book, *The Philosophy of the Revolution*, as had Hitler's been in *Mein Kampf*. On the other hand, he was encouraged by US intervention in Lebanon (7,000 US Marines sent to Lebanon to protect Western interests) and hoped US aid would be forthcoming.[17] Israel, however, had its own considerations and had initially opposed the transport of British forces to Jordan through Israeli airspace.[18]

According to another US Special National Intelligence Estimate, Nasser might request emergency arms from the Kremlin and 'volunteers.' It also predicted that, if Hussein fell, Israel would occupy the West Bank or attack Nasser if the West also took action against him. The Soviet Union would not take any steps that might cause an all-out war and would do nothing more than hold military maneuvers along its borders with Turkey and Iran.[19] It was clear to Israel that, once Western intervention ended, the trend toward Arab unification would leave Israel surrounded by stronger enemies. Therefore, it demanded that the United States warn the Soviet Union against any infringement of Israel's independence. Eban asked Dulles how the United States and Israel could have such good mutual understanding of the regional dangers yet debate over a few dozen half-tracks and rifles. Dulles told him Israel should take heart from the US intervention in Lebanon, since, if it were in the same kind of trouble as Lebanon, the United States would respond.[20] King Hussein of Jordan was worried that the coup in Iraq might encourage a coup in his own country, especially given Nasser's efforts to subvert his regime. Dulles was worried that an Arab–Israeli war would break out if Hussein's regime fell and that the Soviet Union would become involved

15 DFPI 13: 6–7, 11–12, 366–7.
16 ICAB, July 20, 1958, ISA.
17 KFADC, July 16, 1959, ISA.
18 FRUS, 1958–1960, XII: 81–7.
19 Special National Intelligence Estimate, in FRUS, 1958–1960, XII: 87–93.
20 FRUS, 1958–1960, XIII: 67–73.

and expand the war. Heavy pressure would then be brought to bear on the United States to support Israel.[21]

Israel sought to use the British request to use Israeli airspace as a bargaining chip. If the West wanted Israeli airspace, Israel wanted guarantees for its territorial integrity. Furthermore, Eban told Dulles, the West was making demands on Israel as though the United States and Israel had a formal alliance, with Israel risking the dangers of being a US ally but without the benefits. Eisenhower and Dulles would say only that the United States had an interest in Israel's integrity and independence.[22] According to Dulles, US and British intervention in Lebanon and Jordan had panicked the Kremlin. The Soviets had to realize that their joint policy with Egypt could cause a world war. Dulles assumed the United States was militarily superior to the Soviet Union. Nasser, he said, would not allow the Arab refugees to settle anywhere permanently because they were important to his propaganda.[23]

Israel was fifth on the NSC Planning Committee's list of US priorities in the Middle East, after halting Soviet penetration, the oil supply to Western Europe, the construction of strategic bases, and transit privileges for American commercial and military needs. A solution to the Arab–Israeli conflict could only be achieved by permanent borders for Israel with guarantees provided by the UN or the great powers, and resettlement of the refugees elsewhere while allowing a certain number to return to their former homes in Israel and compensating the rest.[24]

The population in the West Bank was rebelling against the Hussein regime and, faced with the danger of its collapse, Israel proposed the establishment of an autonomous entity there. Ben-Gurion was not enthusiastic about invading, partly because he assumed the United States and the Soviet Union would force a withdrawal, but, more importantly, he did not want to add a million Arabs to Israel's population. Meir also warned that annexing the West Bank would prove to be both evil and bitter for Israel. In 1958, the United States again turned down Israel's demand for a defense pact, despite the claim that the US moral obligation to Israel had grown stronger.[25] At the same time, Ben-Gurion demanded that Britain immediately halt its overflights into Jordan because of Soviet

21 FRUS, 1958–1960, XI: 377.
22 DFPI 13: 49–52, 63–5.
23 FRUS, 1958–1960, XIII: 114–35.
24 FRUS, 1958–1960, XII: 145–52 (August 19, 1958).
25 DFPI 13: 67–8.

threats. Israel, he said, stood entirely alone and the Soviet Union could destroy it in minutes.[26]

Dulles asked Eban to what extent Israel was prepared to call the Soviet Union's bluff. Eban said that Israel had no US guarantees and affirmed that the Soviet Union could destroy it. Dulles was intransigent, and said that a treaty would require the approval of Congress. However, if the Soviet Union attacked Israel, the United States would certainly fight the aggressor. The Soviet Union's goal was to destroy US manufacturing power by denying it Middle Eastern oil. If that happened, everything, including Israel, would fall into Soviet hands, as Czechoslovakia had done in 1938. Ben-Gurion knew Israel was not free to choose between the two rival superpowers and could not even opt for neutrality, but would never surrender.[27] On the other hand, Israel could not achieve political goals solely by wielding military strength, and the country had no future without the support of American Jews. Only with US assistance could Israel absorb immigrants and establish settlements, and American Jewry was dependent on the US administration. There was nothing in writing, and Dulles had limited himself to oral assurances that the United States would aid Israel if it were attacked, a promise he could break at any time.[28]

Secretary of State John Foster Dulles also argued that the wave of Arab nationalism could not be stopped, and that the only solution was to pile sandbags to defend Lebanon, Israel and the Persian Gulf oilfields. The President, he said, still believed that, if not for Israel, the United States could conduct a sustainable policy in the region, insisting it could preserve its standing in the Middle East even if its position were not popular. His brother, CIA Director Allen Dulles, said the Arab world was in the throes of the same bloody processes that France had endured in the French Revolution.[29] Ben-Gurion told Eisenhower he believed in the United States' sincerity regarding its interest in Israel, but again pointed out that it had never guaranteed Israel's integrity or warned the Soviet Union and Nasser, as it had when the Soviet Union threatened Turkey.[30]

Fear of Soviet expansion in the Middle East improved Israel's standing in the Eisenhower administration, but the US promise to preserve Israel's independence was one thing, and the United States fighting for Israel was another. Eisenhower argued that the Arabs needed a larger

26 DFPI 13: 69–70.
27 DFPI 13: 79–82, 85–7; cf. FRUS, 1958–1960, XIII: 82–3.
28 ICAB, August 10, 1958, ISA.
29 FRUS, 1958–1960, XIII: 365.
30 FRUS, 1958–1960, XIII: 83–7.

military force than they currently had to be able to endanger Israel. Previously, the administration's concern had been Israeli aggression toward the Arabs, now the situation was reversed. The NSC concluded that the danger to Israel's security did not equal a Soviet takeover of the Middle East and with the need to preserve US and European access to the region's oil fields, despite the United States' displeasure, the door had to be left open for Nasser.[31] The US strategic shift was minimal. The State Department instructed that arms could be sent to Israel, but it did not want the United States to be Israel's major supplier, preferring it to be Britain and France. Nevertheless, it acknowledged that the regional situation had changed fundamentally. Israel was given credit for allowing the British to use its airspace, but the United States provided Israel with only 100 recoilless guns.[32] Ben-Gurion was dissatisfied. The United States was being evasive and he still had not received an explicit guarantee of Israel's territorial integrity.[33] Eventually, the US administration decided to supply Israel with half-tracks, anti-aircraft guns, helicopters and machine guns. Britain would supply Centurion tanks, while France and Italy would send surplus American Patton tanks.[34]

Resolution of the Arab–Israeli conflict was postponed until the two sides could find common ground. The chiefs of staff, wary of any new military obligations, advised the NSC that political action be taken to establish new borders for Israel and to resettle Arab refugees, with a large number allowed to return to their former homes. Dulles demanded that the United States seek a window of opportunity for a new initiative to resolve the conflict (which he likened to Kashmir), because a solution could not be imposed. He raised the issue of sanctions against Israel, should it be designated the aggressor in a war, and restrictions on immigration.[35] Israel had no knowledge of what was happening in Washington, but was pleased to see an improvement in British attitudes after the fall of the Iraqi monarchy and in view of the threat to the monarchy in Jordan. Moreover, the British regarded Israel's military power as an asset to the West.[36]

31 FRUS, 1958–1960, XII: 157–8.
32 DFPI 13: 373–4.
33 DFPI 13: 371.
34 DFPI 13: 374–83.
35 US Policy in the Near East (NSC 5820/1): FRUS, 1958–1960, XII: 162–6; cf. 175–86, 187–99.
36 Roger Stevens to Viscount Hood, November 7, 1958, Top Secret, NA, FO 371/134298/10710/10.

Eban, always an optimist, thought the West, specifically Britain and France, was turning toward Israel and saw relations with the United States improving. The United States, he said, was allowing Israel to purchase arms and exhibiting goodwill in economic negotiations. However, he noted, the improvement was almost entirely due to the administration's anti-Nasser position and its desire to preserve the status quo in Europe as well as in the Middle East. He argued the Americans would consider an attack on Israel as Communist aggression and defend it in accordance with the Eisenhower Doctrine.[37]

US policy fluctuated between assuming the United States would have been able to maintain control of the Middle East if Israel did not exist and assuming the Arabs were unstable and could not be trusted, but Israel could and should receive support. Israel had achieved some of its objectives, among them the promise of free navigation, increased economic aid and the receipt of oral security guarantees. In East–West negotiations, the Soviet starting point might be the 1947 partition borders, while the United States might propose a compromise. Dulles favored the border status quo because the dismantling of US bases in the Middle East would be detrimental to US strategy. Dulles regarded himself as divinely charged to prevent a Communist takeover of the Christian world and Eisenhower had total confidence in him.[38] Dulles's attitude toward Israel was a function of the dynamics of the Arab–Israeli conflict and its relationship to the Cold War. Growing tension between Israel and Syria in early December 1958 tested the Israeli policy of deterrence and Ben-Gurion believed the tension could lead to war. In such an event, US military might was an effective deterrent to war. In addition, he fully understood the theory of Military Assured Destruction (MAD), which held that US and Soviet nuclear capabilities would ensure stable peace.[39]

Dulles had become more aware of Israel's problems. Israel, he said, should benefit from US assistance like any other victim of aggression. Increased immigration from Eastern Europe was stoking Arab fears that Israel would annex further territories, although he received assurances that Israel would establish settlements only within its current borders.[40] For Israel, the US declarations of willingness to come to Israel's aid had always been vague, because the United States regarded an Arab attack on Israel as less serious than general Communist aggression. Israel redoubled its efforts to obtain arms by enlisting American public opinion, claiming

37 ICAB, November 2, 1958, ISA; KFADC, November 5, 1958; DFPI 13: 392–4.
38 KFADC, December 23, 1958, ISA (Yaacov Herzog).
39 KFADC, December 16, 1958, ISA; DFPI, 13: 399–403.
40 DFPI 13: 390–2.

that, by holding Nasser and Communism at bay in the Middle East, it was an asset to the free world.[41] Even though he understood the gravity of Israel's situation, Dulles refused to make a strategic move in Israel's favor because he would not sever ties with Nasser or intervene in Iraq.[42]

After the second Berlin crisis,[43] and following the coup in Iraq, Ben-Gurion made another bid to join NATO. Joint planning between Israel and NATO was an urgent Western interest, he said,[44] and he discounted NATO's concern that cooperation with Israel would harm Western interests in the Middle East and push the Arabs into the Soviet camp.[45] Given the rapid obsolescence of Israel's arsenal, he wanted to preserve a balance of power. Ben-Gurion was plagued by the fact that, with Soviet assistance, the Arabs could destroy Israel, and the knowledge gave him no rest.[46] The US State Department feared a Soviet takeover of the Middle East would disrupt the supply of oil to Western Europe and put an end to NATO.[47]

Israel worried about US acknowledgment of their common interests, but there was agreement about the dangers presented by the Cold War and the problems growing out of the regional conflict, such as Soviet arms shipments to Iraq. President Eisenhower admitted to Eban that he had no common ground with Khrushchev, beyond the fact that a war would be horrible. The President was disappointed by the Arabs' lack of interest in economic progress and because their extreme nationalist feelings were stronger than their economic logic.[48]

The US administration gradually learned to live with increased immigration to Israel from Eastern Europe and was not overly concerned about Arab protests. However, Rountree tried to stop the fundraising of the American Jewish organizations, which he thought made it seem that the United States supported Israel over the Arabs. He called for giving more attention to the Arab world on the grounds that Iraq was liable to join the Communist bloc. Furthermore, it could harm relations with Nasser,

---

41 DFPI 13: 397–8.
42 DFPI 13: 404–7, 414–15.
43 In 1958, Khrushchev announced a six-month time limit to negotiate a permanent solution to the German question in order to get recognition for two German states. If the West declined, he warned, a separate agreement would be signed only with East Germany. The West rejected the Soviet threat.
44 DFPI 13: 684–9.
45 Levant Department, 'Israel and NATO', May 6, 1959, Confidential, NA, FO 371/142317/VR1076/1.
46 ICAB, June 28, 1959, ISA.
47 FRUS, 1958–1960, XII: 210–12.
48 DFPI 13: 421–3 (May 16, 1959).

who seemed to have been persuaded of the dangers of Communism.[49] However, Eban opined that, 'since the Sinai war American support for Israel [was] "an essential asset," and not any more support because of "conscience," "beneficence," or "pity."' And the Americans accepted Israel's claim that Nasser was the warmonger of the Middle East and the American public viewed Israel as a partner and a friend. The conflict with the Arabs was a microcosm of East–West relations, defined by Eban as maximum hostility without war.[50]

Interestingly, the instructions given to the new US ambassador to Israel, Ogden Reid, show that there was indeed cause in the United States to be worried about the two countries' common interests. Israel indeed held 'a very special place' in US foreign policy, but it also needed to conduct 'very close attention' to the Arab world. Reid was told to be careful not to take any position identifying the United States with Israel's problems or interests.[51]

However, the US administration decided to improve relations with Nasser, who was prepared, so it claimed, to give precedence to economic development. It was agreed within the administration that, if Nasser acted independently of the Soviet Union, it would be a mistake to push him into Soviet arms.[52] Israel's greatest hope was that the upcoming Eisenhower–Khrushchev summit would not force a solution on the Middle East, which had to be removed from the Cold War arena without harming US interests in Turkey and Iran.[53] However, a US State Department assessment suggested that Khrushchev's support of détente might be a ploy to give the Soviets more opportunities to penetrate underdeveloped areas.[54] In practice, Dulles's policy had failed. Meeting with Rashid Karami, the Lebanese prime minister, Eisenhower said that Israel was a fait accompli and Karami ridiculed the idea.[55]

The real test was the issue of arms, even though economic aid alone would have been sufficient to define the relations as patron–client had Israel not been under siege. There was a growing gap in the balance of power because, since the 1956 war, the UAR had received arms worth $500 million (including 250 MiG-17 planes, 50 Ilyushin bombers and 600 tanks), while Israel had no official allies or a defense treaty. At the

---

49 FRUS, 1958–1960, XIII: 182–4.
50 KFADC, July 7, 1959, ISA.
51 FRUS, 1958–1960, XIII: 182.
52 FRUS, 1958–1960, XII: 12, 218–19.
53 Avner to IFM larger team, August 18, 1959, ISA 3105/13II.
54 FRUS, 1958–1960, XI: 490–1.
55 FRUS, 1958–1960, XI: 642.

same time, the US administration had accepted Arab claims of neutrality, despite their increasingly close relations with the Soviet Union.[56] Israel was dependent on arms from Europe and was asking for financial aid to buy them, and also wanted full official US protection in the face of growing Soviet involvement in the region.[57]

Israel expected far too much from the American Jewish lobby. The lobbyists were wary of opposing the Eisenhower administration's policy toward Israel. When the President of the Major Jewish organization Philip Klutznik contacted the US State Department, they were told everything was fine. Israel had received an average of $50 million a year since its founding and the request for aid for the national water carrier was being considered favorably. In the UN, the United States had supported the opening of the Suez Canal to Israel. There was no reason for pessimism on the refugee question; Israel's security needs were well known. The State Department also believed that Nasser was prepared to normalize relations with the West and reduce regional tensions.[58]

The refusal by the United States to be Israel's main arms supplier was a clear statement that the US administration did not want to grant Israel full client status, like Greece, Turkey and Iran. While the promise to defend it as part of the Eisenhower Doctrine was kept with economic aid, frozen East–West relations made it impossible for Israel to achieve more. Eban was satisfied with the status quo, since Israel had free navigation in the Gulf of Aqaba, the United States had opposed forcing Israel to make territorial concessions and Israel had received US economic aid. Israel opposed the Western desire for relations with Israel to be dependent on its relations with the Arab world, he said, and, while the situation was worrisome, there was no reason to despair.[59]

Israel felt that the Soviet arms and military advisors being sent to the UAR made it imperative to purchase heavy arms from the United States and Europe. Strengthening Israel's deterrent capabilities was vital, more important than seeking a formal relationship with the United States. In February 1960, Israel gave the United States a shopping list for fighter-bombers, heavy tanks, armored cars, cannons, air-to-air missiles, surface-to-air missiles, submarines and electronic equipment. Following Israel's claim that the UAR was engaging in a military build-up, the State

---

56 KFADC, December 29, 1959, ISA.
57 DFPI 13: 431–2.
58 FRUS, 1958–1960, XIII: 244–6; G. L. Jones to the Secretary, 'Call by Delegation of American Jewish Leaders,' December 7, at 2.30 p.m., NARA, NEA/NE79 D 215.
59 KFADC, January 12, 1960, ISA.

Department recommended to the Pentagon that the request be considered seriously. It also recommended that the purchases be funded covertly by the Development Loan Fund (DLF),[60] stressing that the Arabs' military advantage was entirely the result of Soviet intervention.[61]

The hope for better treatment from the United States did not mean a reversal of US policy. Israel's survival was an inseparable part of US policy, even if the US administration's continued refusal to make a public statement was a cause for concern. The administration still viewed Israel's requests as a function of its relations with the Arab world and its position in the Cold War.[62] The seriousness of Egypt's threat was demonstrated when its army secretly penetrated the Sinai Peninsula in February 1960, prompting Israel to call up reserves. Ben-Gurion said Nasser might start a war by denying Israeli ships entry to the Gulf of Aqaba, by seeking to divert the Jordan headwaters or by launching a preemptive strike against Israel.[63]

Ben-Gurion visited Washington in March 1960 and, prior to his arrival, the US administration sought to reassure Israel by reaffirming the Eisenhower Doctrine. The Soviet Union was certainly aware of the US commitment to assist Israel against what it saw as Communist aggression, but the administration remained apathetic regarding the issue of Soviet Jewry. Eisenhower acknowledged Israel's concern over the situation of Soviet Jews, but apparently accepted Khrushchev's assurances that there was no anti-Jewish discrimination in the Soviet Union and that in any case it was an internal matter.[64] Ben-Gurion expressed pessimism about Communism and the Soviet Union. The Communists, he told Eisenhower, believed that they would win in the end and coexistence was a sop they threw to the West while they were willing to make temporary compromises to help their satellites. He requested Eisenhower ask Khrushchev for a joint statement guaranteeing the independence and territorial integrity of all Middle Eastern countries. The Jews, he said, had struggled to survive for 4,000 years and the State of Israel was their last stand. The State Department did not attach much importance to the visit and was happy that Israel had agreed to keep it low key.

60 The DLF was established in 1957 in order to facilitate investments in developing countries as part of a revision of the Mutual Security Act, as an instrument to fight Communism.
61 DFPI 14: 195–204.
62 DFPI 14: 205–9 (Memorandum by G. Avner, March 3, 1960).
63 KFADC February 23, 1960, February 26, 1960, ISA.
64 'Prime Minister Ben-Gurion's Visit', Washington, March 9–12, 1960, Position Paper, Soviet Near East and Jewish Policies (to be Raised Only at Israel's Initiative), March 4, 1960, Secret, NARA, Lot 62 D 435, BG Visit, Box 3.

Ben-Gurion acknowledged failure. Eisenhower had again said that the United States did not want to be Israel's primary arms supplier, citing the usual excuses. Under Secretary of State Douglas Dillon tried to persuade Ben-Gurion to gradually repatriate Arab refugees. Ben-Gurion answered that, given Arab hostility, allowing the refugees to return to Israel would be tantamount to poisoning the Jewish state. Furthermore, he said, Israel was anticipating the immigration of two million Jews, half of them from the Soviet Union. However, the visit was not a total loss. The US administration believed that Israel needed help for aerial defense and was willing to provide surface-to-air missiles and early-warning systems,[65] Israel would receive Mirage combat aircraft from France and the United States would assist Israel in the event of Arab aggression.[66]

However, Washington delayed Israel's missile request on the grounds that NATO needed to deploy Hawks first. To reinforce Israel's claim that it needed them immediately, Meir provided the United States with new information about Soviet penetration of the Middle East. The United States argued that the Arabs could purchase surface-to-surface missiles to intercept the Hawks. The United States did not want to give Israel the missiles because, if showcase missiles were deployed in Israel, the UAR would ask the Kremlin for a similar system. According to George Lewis Jones, Assistant Secretary of State for the Near East, Israel had a magnificent air force that gave it a clear advantage and its friends would come to its aid in the event of a surprise attack. De Gaulle had promised to do so and the United States would deploy the Sixth Fleet. Nasser knew that, emphasized Lewis Jones.[67]

Israel's status had been upgraded from a non-confidential to a confidential country, but to get Hawk missiles it needed to be a secret country. The missiles were supplied only to NATO countries, with the exceptions of Greece and Turkey. Giving Israel the missiles would be seen as US acceptance of responsibility for its security at the expense of its relations with the Arab world, and so Ben-Gurion was informed the United States would not supply the missiles to prevent restarting the arms race. In addition, it might encourage her to behave aggressively in connection with the diversion of the Jordan River. Ben-Gurion told the US ambassador that Israel needed Hawks because Israel's cities could be destroyed by Egyptian bombers in a surprise attack. He also said that Nasser could attack the Straits of Tiran and demand the evacuation of the UN force in Sharm el-Sheikh. The UN and the United States might not arrive in time,

65 FRUS, 1958–1960, XIII: 280–300.
66 Peres in KFADC, March 15, 1960, ISA.
67 FRUS, 1958–1960, XIII: 344–9.

or be foiled by a Soviet veto, and in the meantime most of Israel would go up in smoke.[68]

Arab rhetoric had grown more strident. Despite the dangers Israel faced, its main problem was its standing in Washington in the context of the Middle East. The NSC shunted Israel to the sidelines on the grounds that Arab Nationalism, not Communism, was the prevailing regional ideology (NSC/6011, July 19, 1960). The greatest danger to the West's long-range interests was that many of the goals of Arab Nationalism were compatible with the goals of the Soviet Union.[69]

Eisenhower was surprisingly weak in his dealings with Nasser. He claimed to respect the UAR's neutral status and said that he had no objection to its purchasing Soviet weapons. He also did not mention the position of the US State Department, which was that most of Arab refugees would not return to Israel. Instead, he asked Nasser how many refugees should return and Nasser said 'all of them.' Eisenhower asked if he did not think it was a lot of Arabs for such a small country and Nasser answered that Ben-Gurion planned to bring 'three million' Jews from the Soviet Union and had declared he would not let a single refugee return.[70] Eisenhower said that, while Israel constituted a problem, it did exist. Nasser answered that to accept Israel as a fact would be to permit a thief to keep what he has stolen. Eisenhower did not take advantage of the opportunity to contradict him, only suggesting that he secretly send the US government a proposal for resolving the refugee problem, when he had one.[71]

By the end of the Eisenhower era, Israel had the status of a US economic and financial client. It had failed to obtain Hawk anti-aircraft missiles, but the US administration had recognized in principle that it needed them. From a historical point of view, Israel was in a much better position at the end of Eisenhower's presidency than it had been at the beginning. That was not the result of anything Israel itself had done, but rather a function of the East–West conflict. Even the détente following the Cuban Missile Crisis did not improve relations with the Kremlin. However, by that time Israel was contracting a nuclear reactor in Dimona in the Negev with French assistance, which reinforced its deterrent position and gave it leverage.

---

68 FRUS, 1958–1960, XIII: 350–3; DFPI 14: 275.
69 FRUS, 1958–1960, XII: 262–73.
70 It was unclear how many Jews lived in the Soviet Union. Estimates varied between two and three million.
71 FRUS, 1958–1960, XIII: 600–6.

# 9

# Kennedy, Israel and the Cold War before the Cuban Missile Crisis (1961–62)

When John F. Kennedy entered the White House, Israel's nuclear reactor in Dimona was the subject of considerable discussion in Washington and Dean Rusk, new Secretary of State, told the State Department and US intelligence to monitor it.[1] France told the United States that it had pressed Israel into accepting the International Atomic Energy Agency's (IAEA) standard of guarantees, which allowed the operation of nuclear reactors for civilian purposes. The outgoing US ambassador, Ogden Reid, said that an Israeli reactor would have no effect on the regional balance of power. The new US administration understood Israel's sensitivity regarding Egypt's military build-up, making it a good time for Israel to ask the United States for Hawk missiles, and for Israelis to be trained in the United States in their operation, in exchange for which Israel would not use the reactor to develop a nuclear bomb. There were more important issues at hand than nuclear reactors, Israel told the Americans, such as Communist penetration of Africa and US aid to the UAR.[2]

The United States was dubious about Israel's claim that Nasser was preparing a surprise attack on Israel, because it was generally accepted that Egypt would not be victorious and he could not risk losing a war to Israel. Furthermore, Nasser had not even challenged the presence of the UN force in the Sinai Peninsula. The balance of power had to be preserved, but Israel might be exaggerating Egypt's military build-up.[3] The new administration did not consider Nasser a new Hitler and the Arabs would not ignore his removal from the scene, and would be angry with Israel. The administration opposed signing a bilateral defense treaty with Israel and guaranteeing its territorial integrity. Such initiatives were opposed not only by the Soviet Union, but also by the United States' European allies. The Arabs would interpret an Israeli–US treaty and a

1 FRUS, 1961–1963, XVII: 9–10.
2 FRUS, 1961–1963, XVII: 26–31.
3 Harman to Bendor, March 23, 1961, Secret, ISA 19/3294.

pro-Israeli declaration as a US shift away from neutrality in the Arab–Israeli conflict. The new administration believed that an East–West arms race would be initiated if the United States served as an arsenal for Israel. However, the Americans would continue to supply surplus defense equipment and Israeli officers could continue to train in the United States.

The Jewish lobby failed to convince the US administration that Israel was anxious about Nasser. American Jewish leaders were told that Israel could take care of itself and that there was no proof the balance of power had tilted against Israel, which led the Jewish leaders to realize they had no real influence in Washington. In addition, Abba Eban, now minister of education and culture, warned the Israeli cabinet against illusions that Kennedy's election meant the Cold War had ended. Ben-Gurion feared the defense budget for the coming three to four years would be inadequate. In three years, he believed, the Arabs would be able to destroy Israel in a Pearl Harbor-like attack.[4] The government of Israel fluctuated between pessimism and optimism. The United States was focusing on the Cold War at Israel's expense, Ben-Gurion said, and Nasser was working for Khrushchev. However, the US administration claimed it was committed to Israel's survival and to increasing its strength. Meir was unreservedly pessimistic, claiming that the Americans honored the Arabs publicly and disparaged them in private, while they disparaged Israel publicly and honored it in private. The United States suffered, she added, from *Grüss mich nicht unter den Linden* (Don't greet me Unter den Linden) syndrome.[5]

The first positive signs came from Deputy Assistant Secretary of Defense William P. Bundy, who said he understood Israel's vulnerability to a surprise aerial attack and supported the request for Hawk missiles. In addition, he pointed out, Israel wanted to buy the missiles, not receive them as a gift, and said they were defensive, not offensive, weapons.[6] Kennedy, however, wanted new and different US–Arab relations and to keep the pro-Western regimes in the region out of the clutches of Nasser and Khrushchev. He wrote to Nasser in May 1961, referring to recent international crises, but without mentioning his blatant military intervention in Congo, the criticism of the Bay of Pigs invasion in the Egyptian press, and promising him economic aid and a solution to the Palestinian refugee problem.[7] The State Department believed Nasser was anti-Communist and that the Soviets needed him more than he needed them. It assumed Nasser had become more moderate and should be

---

4 ICAB, March 23, 1961, ISA.
5 IFM, Third Session, May 4, 1961, ISA 4328/7.
6 Little, 1988; 1993: *passim*.
7 FRUS, 1961–1963, XVII: 110–13.

invited to visit Washington. Kennedy was advised by Myer Feldman, Deputy Special Counsel to the President, that the United States should not guarantee Israel's defense or sell it Hawk missiles or aircraft. In addition, the refugee problem had to be solved and the United States should also warn Israel not to invade the West Bank.[8]

Ben-Gurion met Kennedy in New York on May 30, 1961. Kennedy told him he opposed Israel's entry into the nuclear club, lest Egypt seek to follow. He asked if Israel would allow international supervision of the Dimona reactor, to which Ben-Gurion said no, as that would entail Arab, Soviet or Indian oversight, although Israel would agree to Norwegian inspectors. He told Kennedy that Nasser intended to destroy Israel and that Israel had to have sufficient force to deter him. Kennedy said that selling Israel missiles would lead to an immediate regional escalation, but that the United States did not want Israel to be defenseless and, if its request for Hawk missiles were approved, it would no longer be in danger of defeat.

Ben-Gurion suggested that Kennedy and Khrushchev use the upcoming Vienna Summit meeting to issue a declaration supporting the territorial integrity of all Middle Eastern states. Kennedy said he doubted whether such a declaration would be of much use. Nasser would oppose it because he did not view Israel's current borders as final, and Nasser's opposition would make support from Khrushchev unlikely. Ben-Gurion played his last card, saying that if Nasser defeated Israel in a war he would destroy it. While Kennedy understood Israel's particular difficulties, it was more important for him to improve relations with Nasser because Nasser could create more trouble for the United States. The United States sent Egypt wheat and flour, hoping to weaken its ties to the Soviet Union.[9]

The Middle East was not on the agenda at the Vienna Summit and the situation stagnated. In a US intelligence assessment, Nasser would avoid total dependence on either East or West, but his fear and loathing of Israel would grow because of Israel's nuclear potential and its efforts to divert the Jordan River.[10] It was proposed to demand that Nasser trade economic aid for a less antagonistic policy toward Israel.[11] US policy did not satisfy Ben-Gurion. Nasser had said that, when the Arab refugees returned, there would be three religions in Israel and that the country

8 FRUS, 1961–1963, XVII: 129–32.
9 FRUS, 1961–1963, XVII: 142–5; Meeting of President Kennedy and Prime Minister Ben-Gurion, Waldorf Astoria Hotel, Suite 28A – 4.45–6.16 p.m., May 30, 1961, ISA 4361/8; FRUS, 1961–1963, XVII: 142–5.
10 National Intelligence Estimate, June 27, 1961, in FRUS, 1961–1962, XVII: 164–6.
11 FRUS, 1961–1963, XVII: 173; Bass, 2003: 87.

would be replaced by a state of all its citizens, which Ben-Gurion saw as tantamount to Islamic rule. He was determined to conclude an arms deal with West Germany so that the IDF would be well-enough equipped to prevent an Egyptian repetition of the Holocaust. He knew there was no chance of receiving a four-power guarantee that would include the Soviets and maintained it was up to the United States to neutralize the Soviet Union's influence in the Middle East.[12]

The chiefs of staff in the Kennedy administration felt that strategic Israeli nuclear capability would make regional and global tensions more acute, although Israel, fearing the strong response of the superpowers, would probably not use nuclear weapons. It would, however, use its nuclear potential as a psychological weapon against the Arabs. The United States would not punish Israel if it achieved nuclear capability but wanted to persuade Israel that it was contrary to its interests.[13] Kennedy was told that Israel had 'fantastic' planning and intellectual advantage and that Nasser did not really intend to destroy it. Israel protested that the Arabs hated Israel blindly and pathologically.[14] Israel was worried about the future of US–Israeli relations,[15] the danger of deeper Soviet penetration into the Arab world was increasing and Israel claimed the Kennedy administration had written off Israel's existence. According to an Israeli diplomat in Washington, the US State Department thought that the United States would learn of a plan to attack if Nasser had one. He had no Soviet support for military action and without Arab unity he could not undertake effective military action. The State Department maintained Nasser had other priorities, including the development of Egypt, his personal standing in the non-aligned world and pan-Arab unity.[16] However, the State Department's optimism did not keep Israel from doing its utmost to preserve the balance of power. Since the United States could not stop the arms race without reneging on its obligations to Turkey and Iran, Israel, its leaders said, deserved military aid.[17]

New Assistant Secretary of State for the Near East William Phillips Talbot argued that, despite being roundly hated by the Arabs, Israel

12 'Ben-Gurion Conversation with Adlai Stevenson,' June, 1, 1961, ISA 4316/8.
13 'A Strategic Analysis of the Impact of the Acquisition by Israel of a Nuclear Capability,' in FRUS, 1961–1962, XVII: 216–21.
14 Gazit to Meir, 'Conversation with Meyer,' August 10, 1961, Secret, ISA 2146/1.
15 'Conference of Heads of Israeli Legations in Western Europe', Zurich, August 28–30, 1961, ISA 3420/17.
16 Gazit to Harman, September 27, 1961, ISA 3026/3.
17 Harman to Avner, September 6, 1961, ISA 3300/3.

enjoyed military and civilian superiority. The UAR fell apart on September 28, 1961, Lebanon and Jordan did not want to fight Israel and the Syrian government was having difficulty controlling its army. Egypt could not face Israel on the battlefield alone and the Arabs knew the West would intervene if they attacked Israel en masse. While they did in fact want to destroy Israel, there was no sign they were trying to do so. According to Talbot, no Arab leader would risk defeat and Egypt desperately needed Western economic aid and would not stage a major attack unless provoked by Israel. However, Israel might be tempted to stage a surprise attack and, if the Arabs felt threatened by nuclear weapons and ballistic missiles, they might attack out of desperation, making it imperative to oversee Israel's atomic energy program.[18]

The Kennedy administration wanted rapprochement with Egypt (which officially continued to call itself the UAR even after Syria seceded). The Special Advisor to the President, Chester Bowles, was sent to persuade Nasser of the advantages of democracy and of the need for a moratorium on the Arab refugee problem. During Bowles' visit to Egypt in February 1962, Nasser seemed to be interested in improving relations and was termed a pragmatist who would exploit the Soviet Union but prevent Communist penetration. Egypt's rulers feared Israeli superiority and knew Israel enjoyed US support. It was made clear to Nasser that the United States could repel any Soviet attack and cause inestimable damage to the Soviet Union. Nasser promised Egypt would not attack first, but said the United States had to prevent a minority (by which he meant American Jews) from dictating policy. Although intelligence on Soviet intentions in the Middle East was vital for US decision-making, US intelligence did not have advance notice of the 1962 Soviet decision to send missiles originally intended for Egypt to Cuba.[19] No wonder an academic such as Henry Kissinger was pessimistic about Israel's survival, though he believed that nuclear weapons, once achieved, would change the situation in Israel's favor.[20]

The US administration believed solving the refugee problem was the key to the entire conflict and Kennedy's special envoy Joseph Johnson proposed offering the Arab refugees a choice between return and compensation. Meir claimed the result would be an Israel overwhelmed by returning refugees. Johnson, she said, disregarded the Arab boycott, the flow of Soviet arms to the Arabs and declarations that Israel would be driven into the sea. When the Arabs were openly preaching

---

18  FRUS, 1961–1962, XVII: 342–4.
19  Fursenko and Naftali, 2006: 170.
20  Argov, 'Conversation with Dr. Henry Kissinger,' March 8, 1962, Secret, ISA 3026/4.

the destruction of Israel, she said, the refugee problem could not be discussed.[21] The Americans preferred an indirect, gradual approach to the refugee issue, but the Cold War was an obstacle and determined the entire American outlook on the Middle East. Meir argued that with US aid Israel could achieve a modus vivendi with Egypt. Israel's standing in the Kennedy administration, she claimed, was miserable,[22] and the Jewish lobby needed to exert its influence on Kennedy before midterm elections in November.[23] Israel could accept US economic aid to Syria and Egypt if the United States gave more tangible reassurance of its commitment to Israel's territorial integrity. The best way would be for Kennedy to send Ben-Gurion a secret communiqué saying that the United States recognized the necessity to reinforce Israel's security and would take all necessary steps to foil an Arab attack. In such a case, Israel would not need to pursue an activist policy.[24]

Ben-Gurion was concerned that the Arabs would eventually close the qualitative gap. Furthermore, Nasser claimed that there would be no repeat of Israel's 1948 victory. Israel's only permanently loyal ally was the Jewish people of the Diaspora. France, currently Israel's most reliable ally, could change and Israel had to fortify its relations with West Germany.[25] Escalation could be caused by a variety of issues, from free navigation in the Gulf of Aqaba to the Jordan water diversion project to Nasser's rising star in an Arab world thirsty for revenge. A nuclear reactor was being built with Soviet assistance in Egypt and another was being planned, Egypt would be able to manufacture nuclear weapons in seven to eight years and German engineers were helping it build long-range missiles that would be operational within five years. The Arabs were paying for Soviet weapons, but at 40 percent of the world market price. Egypt had 250 combat planes and jet bombers, Syria had 78, Israel had 102. Israel's standing army totaled 43,000 troops, in contrast with 135,000 for Egypt and 65,000 for Syria. In a few years, Israel might buckle under the economic pressure of maintaining its air force and chances for peace were nil.[26]

---

21 KFADC, April 30, 1962, ISA.
22 KFADC, April 3, 1962, ISA; Ben-Gurion pointed out to de Gaulle rapprochement with West Germany as a model for Israel to be copied by Israel: ICAB, January 13, 1963, ISA.
23 'Consultations in Golda Meir's House with Ambassadors Harman and Comay,' May 4–5, 1962, ISA 4316/8.
24 FRUS, 1961–1963, XVII: 647–9.
25 KFADC, February 20, 1962, ISA.
26 KFADC, February 20, 1962, ISA.

Ben-Gurion knew Iraq and Egypt were too cautious to be drawn into a war because of incidents between Israel and Syria, but nevertheless a war could break out at any time. Eban thought Syria was not deterred by Israel, but Dayan, now Minister for Agriculure, said that, if the Syrians understood their provocations had a serious outcome, they would stop.[27] While Ben-Gurion was certain Israel could defeat Egypt and Syria, he knew Israel was weak economically and did not have many friends in the international arena. A peace policy, he said, had to begin with the two superpowers, not Israel, which had to defend its sovereignty. If necessary, he said, he would go to war for freedom of navigation at Sharm el-Sheikh and would have no compunction about destroying enemy aircraft or bombing Damascus.[28]

Visiting Washington in May 1962, Shimon Peres, Deputy Defense Minister and Ben-Gurion's right-hand man, requested a reevaluation of Israel's request for Hawk surface-to-air missiles. Nasser would certainly attack when he achieved military superiority, he said, and US aid to Nasser allowed him to devote himself to acquiring Soviet weapons. Peres was promised Israel's air defense would be reconsidered. Additionally, China might enter the region, and the Algerian struggle for independence could enhance Arab unity.[29] Asked by Walt W. Rostow, Chairman of the Policy Planning Council of State, if he really doubted the United States would intervene if Israel were attacked, he said he did, because there were no high-level military contacts. He warned the Pentagon senior clerks Rosewell Gilpatrick and Paul Nitze that Nasser was planning an attack for 1963 or 1964, and that Israel needed Hawk missiles immediately as well as a defense pact.[30] He added that if the United States could not guarantee Israel's borders or link it to NATO, it should at least supply Israeli with heavy weapons. Peres was told that the United States knew Israel lacked all-weather combat planes and had a genuine need for Hawks. In addition, US officials acknowledged that Egyptian technicians were being trained in the Soviet Union to operate SA-2 missiles.[31]

The US State Department deliberately cast Nasser as a moderate. Its experts claimed he had promised not to support Fidel Castro in Cuba and was improving his relations with Europe, and hoped increased US

27 ICAB, March 20, 1962, ISA.
28 ICAB, April 1, 1962, ISA.
29 FRUS, 1961–1963, XVII: 676–7.
30 Harman to Levavi, May 23, 1962, ISA 7226/6/1.
31 FRUS, 1961–1963, XVII: 671–4, 683; Peres to Ben-Gurion, Meir and Prihar, May 25, 1962, ISA 7226/6a.

aid would make him less dependent on the Soviets. US expectations of Nasser soared, but Israel rejected the American assumption that Nasser would ever truly be neutral in the East–West conflict.[32] New information supplied by Israel about the Egyptian military build-up made the State Department have a change of heart and, realizing Israel could be attacked from the air once Egypt received long-range bombers, it promised to reexamine the situation.[33] It was also proposed by Robert W. Komer, an NSC senior staff member in charge of the Middle East, that the United States strengthen Israel with a security guarantee and perhaps Hawk missiles and support for its Jordan River project, which would signal to the Arabs that the rapprochement with Nasser did not mean sacrificing Israel's security.[34]

A limited security arrangement was drafted by Talbot and his deputy, Robert Strong, including the possible provision of Hawks and stronger friendship with Israel plus financial support. Israel was to receive an unwritten promise of a pact in return for which it would be more restrained. The United States would supply Israel with weapons, but not have close military relations to avoid Arab animosity. Israel would not be given the status of an ally because that would destroy the United States' neutral position and push the Arabs toward a similar relationship with the Soviet Union. Israel and its supporters, the State Department claimed, needed to understand that good US–Arab relations were in Israel's interest, and such relations would be jeopardized if there were a special US–Israeli relationship. Furthermore, Israel's chief of staff, Zvi Tzur, had said that Israel had nothing to fear from the Arabs until 1966, certainly up to 1970, and, that being the case, there was no need to supply Hawk missiles. According to State Department thinking, Israel would be better off waiting until the Soviets deployed surface-to-air missiles in Egypt.

To soften the blow, the State Department recommended the Sixth Fleet visit Haifa and suggested a more liberal approach to Israeli arms purchases as well as help with its financial burdens. In addition, Nasser should be asked to freeze his own military build-up. Having been refused both a defense guarantee and Hawks, the Israeli leadership was unhappy, but considered the other promises a great diplomatic achievement which could be used for leverage in other vital issues.[35] Kennedy sent Ben-Gurion demands and promises. He wanted quiet on Israel's

32  ICAB, May 6, 1962, ISA (G. Meir).
33  FRUS, 1961–1963, XVII: 684–5.
34  FRUS, 1961–1963, XVII: 692.
35  FRUS, 1961–1963, XVII: 710–18; Raphael to Meir, Draft Letter-Cable from Harman, June 7, 1962, Top Secret, June 10, 1962, ISA 4312/5.

borders and cooperation with the UN, and obligated himself to Israel's territorial integrity and to advancing its economy.[36] Ben-Gurion, however, warned Kennedy that Israel was threatened with annihilation, as happened in the Holocaust, and had to have deterrence to prevent war.[37]

The State Department was still of the opinion that the most worrying issue in the Middle East was that of the Arab refugees. Since the Soviet Union supported the Arab solution, the State Department felt that the United States should not grant Israel a security guarantee. If it did, Israel might provoke the Arabs and the United States would be compelled to come to Israel's aid.[38] The State Department warned that a military alliance with Israel would destroy the current delicate balance in the Middle East, and Hawks should not be supplied to Israel unless the Soviets supplied similar missiles to Egypt.[39] However, in mid-July 1962, the Pentagon became convinced that Israel was in fact vulnerable to an Egyptian attack using Soviet bombers and that it required Hawk missiles for its defense.[40]

Kennedy had to make a decision. Talbot and Strong recommended he condition a security guarantee on slowing the arms race and on Israel's abandoning its demand for direct negotiations with the Arabs. However, if it became clear, within two months, that there was no way to limit the supply of Soviet missiles to Egypt, the United States should offer Israel Hawk missiles.[41] However, it was essential to promise Nasser that the United States was only declaring *in principle* that Israel should get Hawks. Israel's security was touted as a central principle of US policy, but the missiles would not be supplied until 1967. Ben-Gurion explicitly stated to Myer Feldman, Kennedy's special envoy, that any discussion of allowing refugees to return was delusional as long as Nasser, Iraq's Kassem and King Hussein of Jordan continued to proclaim their intention to destroy Israel, and Arab hate propaganda was so strong it was obvious there was no chance of resolving the issue. Kennedy should begin negotiations, not with Nasser but with Khrushchev. If the Soviet Union agreed to Arab–Israeli coexistence, Nasser would have to end his state of hostility. The only possible solution was a US–Soviet arrangement, but it was a distant possibility. Israel wanted not only the Soviet Union's two million Jews, it wanted the Jews of Morocco and Argentina as well. None of the millions of refugees created by World War II in Europe had

36  FRUS, 1961–1963, XVII: 734–6.
37  FRUS, 1961–1963, XVII: 751–4 (June 24, 1962).
38  FRUS, 1961–1963, XVII: 762–76.
39  FRUS, 1961–1963, XVIII: 2–7.
40  FRUS, 1961–1963, XVIII: 8–9.
41  'United States Policy Towards Israel,' in FRUS, 1962–1963, XVIII: 27–32, 33–8.

returned to their former places of residence, Ben-Gurion said.[42] The State Department categorically rejected any official US intervention on behalf of Soviet Jewry, maintaining that the Communist regime persecuted all religions equally and was not specifically anti-Semitic.[43]

Nasser clung doggedly to the position that a final solution for the refugee problem would be possible only if a majority were allowed to return to their former homes. He said that would mean that the Jewish state would become binational within seventy years.[44] However, he was told by the United States that, given the new missiles he had received from the Soviet Union and the lack of an arms control agreement, the United States would have no choice but to sell Israel Hawk missiles.[45] The State Department notified Israel that its intransigence regarding the refugees would force the administration to withdraw the preferential treatment it had given to the Hawk training program and delay delivery of the missiles. The United States would, the State Department said, take a firmer position on other issues as well. There would now be greater difficulties regarding the Jordan water diversion project, the demands for the creation of a Palestinian entity and a guerrilla war, Algerian style, against Israel.[46] The US administration would supply Hawk missiles to Israel, but they would be linked to resolving the issue of the Arab refugees, especially the return of 10,000–20,000.[47]

The Americans were increasingly concerned about Soviet involvement in the Middle East. Secretary of State Dean Rusk noted that Soviet policy in the region had cost the United States $470 million since 1947.[48] The NSC warned that overt capitulation to Israel would provoke a catastrophic Arab reaction and that Israel had to be compelled to cooperate, not just with regard to the refugees but also on the issues of the diversion of the Jordan River and border adjustments. The United States had to demonstrate that it would not be frightened into giving in to Israeli dictates.[49] The State Department believed that the Arabs had become rational and would eventually accept Israel's existence, yet Israel was

---

42 FRUS, 1961–1963, XVIII: 64–9, 73–4; 'Minutes of Meeting at the Prime Minister's Home in Tel-Aviv on 19th August 1962,' at 4 p.m., Strictly Confidential, ISA 4312/6.
43 FRUS, 1961–1963, V: 456–8.
44 FRUS, 1961–1963, XVIII: 76 (August 24, 1962).
45 FRUS, 1961–1963, XVIII: 71, 94–5; ICAB, August 26, 1962, ISA.
46 FRUS, 1961–1963, XVIII: 112–16.
47 'Note of a Meeting Held at the Ministry of Defense,' August 20, 1962, Secret, NA, FO 371/164348.
48 FRUS, 1961–1963, XVIII: 131–6.
49 FRUS, 1961–1963, XVIII: 143–4, 152–4.

not willing to compromise, even though by agreeing to sell it Hawks the United States had shown it was committed to Israel's defense.[50]

The US administration finally gave up trying to impose conditions on Israel, convinced by the increasing Soviet involvement in Egypt.[51] In addition, the war in Yemen had opened a new Cold War front and Nasser was fighting Britain in Aden.[52] Nevertheless, the United States still regarded the resolution of the refugee issue as the most important contribution to regional peace and stability. The administration did understand, however, that the creation of a large Arab minority in Israel would be detrimental to it.[53] Israel felt the public announcement of the sale of Hawk missiles on September 26, 1962, was linked to the United States' upcoming midterm elections, but the Israeli leadership understood the President would not have approved the sale without the consent of the State Department, the Pentagon and the NSC.[54]

However, as far as the State Department was concerned, selling Israel the Hawks was a one-time affair. The United States could not become Israel's principal supplier of arms, which would be an enormous blow psychologically as well as strategically. The United States had to be careful not to push Israel into a preemptive war.[55] There was no need to apologize to the Arabs for supplying Israel with Hawks as the United States was adamant about maintaining an evenhanded policy in the Middle East. The Soviet Union had made the sale necessary by supplying defensive weapons to the moderate Arab states Jordan and Saudi Arabia.[56] The Israeli government was satisfied with the Hawks, but the United States was not meeting all of its demands, despite the favorable change in the balance of power and the successful work of the American Jewish lobby. Eban viewed it as US recognition of Israel's vital interests. The most important thing, he said, was that the United States was committed to preserving the balance of power, even if it warned Israel against a preemptive strike. However, his claim that the United States could negotiate a Middle East settlement with the Soviets was an exaggeration.[57]

50 FRUS, 1961–1963, XVIII: 145–9, 156–7.
51 FRUS, 1961–1963, XVIII: 158–9; Ben-Zvi, 2002: *passim*.
52 FRUS, 1961–1963, XVIII: 162–70.
53 'Harman-Talbot Conversation Regarding Refugee Affairs,' October 22, 1962, Secret, ISA 4312/2.
54 Gazit to Yachil, Director General IFM, October 2, 1962, 'The Missiles,' Secret and Personal, ISA 4312/7.
55 Gazit to Yachil, October 3, 1962, 'Missiles – Future Weapon for Israel According to the State Department,' Top Secret, ISA 4312/7.
56 RWK [Komer] to Carl [Kaysen], September 27, 1962, JFKL, NSF, Komer, Box 428.
57 KFADC, October 2, 1962, ISA.

The end of October 1962 was critical for the Cold War. The Soviet deployment of missiles in Cuba brought the United States and the Soviet Union to the brink of a nuclear war, and the ensuing crisis affected the Middle East as well. Kennedy made a speech with serious implications for Israel. 'We no longer live in a world,' he said, 'where only the actual firing of weapons represents a sufficient challenge to a nation's security to constitute maximum peril.' In other words, the United States would respond to the change in the status quo caused by the Soviet Union's deploying of strategic nuclear weapons in the Western Hemisphere. Kennedy and Secretary of State Dean Rusk stated categorically that aggressive behavior not met by resistance could lead to a world war. In the same speech, Kennedy (22 October) said that '[a]ny hostile move anywhere in the world against the safety and freedom of peoples to whom we are committed ... will be met by whatever action is needed.' The Cuban Missile Crisis required every UN member to take a position in the Cold War, and non-alignment was not an option. It was not just 'seventy miles from our shore,' it was a struggle with the Soviet Union's use of Cuba as a missile base against the nations of the Western Hemisphere. In addition, it also raised the possibility of a worse conflict with the non-aligned states, which in practice supported the Soviet Union, making Cuba a test case of the conflict between East and West.[58]

The Joseph Johnson Plan committed the United States only to having 10 percent of the refugees return to Israel, while 90 percent would be resettled elsewhere. The United States also promised that Article 11 of UN General Assembly Resolution 194 (11) regarding the return of the Arab refugees would be buried. However, the United States did not control Nasser and could not promise he would not attack.[59] The Egyptian foreign minister gave a speech at the General Assembly in which he said that no individual refugee should be allowed to express his desire to choose the best option for him, not even in private.[60] Furthermore, in a conversation with a group of American senators, Nasser declared that the only solution for the refugee problem was the repatriation of all refugees. Israel's fate, he said, would be like that of the Crusader kingdom.[61] To

---

58 Harman to Arad, 'U.S. Policy and its Implications,' October 23, 1962, ISA 4312/2; Fursenko and Naftali, 1997: 216–56; Dallek, 2003: 535–74.
59 Harman to Meir, 'The Conversations with the US on Refugee Matters,' October 23, 1962, ISA 4312/2.
60 Harman, 'Conversation with Talbot, Notes,' November 2, 1962, ISA 4312/2.
61 John Badeau to Department of State, 'Memorandum of Conversation with Gamal Abdel Nasser, President of the UAR,' November 15, 1962, Secret, JFKL, NSF Countries, Box 168A.

Ben-Gurion and most of the Israeli population, it was obvious that the refugee issue was merely a function of the Arabs' desire to destroy Israel.

Meir noted that in Egypt, like in Cuba, there were Ilyushin bombers. There was a difference, Rusk replied, in that Cuba probably had nuclear bombs. In principle, she said, there was no basis for discussion as long as Nasser was preparing for war. She warned that Israel would discuss the refugee issue only within the framework of peace negotiations. His intervention in Yemen shows that he was not interested in a solution to the problem. The State Department feared that if the United States gave in to Israel, Israel would be uncooperative and intransigent in other matters.[62] The refugee issue, Komer argued, was a problem the two involved sides could not resolve on their own. Both faced a conflict which, in the absence of external intervention, could lead to war. Israel's tough policy led to border incidents that fanned the flames of Arab hatred. Within a decade, Nasser and others might obtain sufficient arms to risk a war. The threat of US intervention could serve as a deterrent, but the cost would be high and the United States was liable to find itself having to supply more than Hawks. The current administration had given Israel more than any of its predecessors, and without asking for anything in return, and Israel had prevailed on all major issues. A window of opportunity had opened allowing the United States to confront Nasser at a time when US prestige was at its height. The question of the Dimona reactor, which had been pushed to the sidelines, loomed large again. The United States accepted Israel's claim, verified by two visiting scientists, that it was building a reactor solely for peaceful purposes. That, Israel said, was what the United States should tell Nasser.[63]

The Cuban Missile Crisis did not lead to a fundamental shift in the US administration's attitude toward Israel. A Jewish state in the midst of an Arab region was considered unnatural and a main source of trouble in the Middle East. A newly resigned anonymous State Department source said that US policy was being swayed by the anti-Semitism of his former colleagues and by the huge influence wielded by the oil companies. Kennedy himself was the person who made the decisions about international issues, especially regarding Israel, but it would be a mistake to assume that the State Department could not maneuver.[64] The United States was still pressing for a solution to the refugee problem, but had agreed to shift the balance of power in Israel's favor. There was nothing Israel could do but hope that the Americans would sense Nasser's

---

62 Meir–Rusk Conversation, November 21, 1962, Top Secret, ISA 4312/3.
63 FRUS, 1961–1963, XVIII: 168–96, 211–18.
64 Raphael to Meir, November 8, 1962, ISA 3377/5II.

growing extremism, illustrated by his intervention in Yemen. The United States was faced with a dilemma regarding Nasser, given that the Soviets had rejected a Middle Eastern détente and were demanding East–West supervision of the supply of weapons to the Middle East. Yet the Soviets demanded the inclusion of US allies Turkey and Iran, which would show that the Arabs, not Israel, were at a disadvantage.[65]

Israeli Deputy Chief of Staff Yitzhak Rabin said that even if a limited war broke out between the two blocs, or a world war, the Soviet Union would have a clear advantage in the Middle East. It would be able to use air and sea bases in Egypt and Syria it had helped plan and build. The problem was that the West refused to believe that Egypt had become, in Cold War terms, a Soviet satellite. Had the West accepted Israel's view, it would have meant accepting the Middle East as a full-fledged Cold War arena, which would require a full-scale revision of Western strategy, he said.[66] Ben-Gurion had not abandoned his confidence in de Gaulle. The French ambassador to Israel had promised that France's new ties with the Arabs would have no effect on Israeli–French relations. Furthermore, Ben-Gurion was certain that, if Nasser attacked Israel, neither the United States nor the Soviet Union would aid Egypt. He acknowledged, however, that the danger presented by Nasser was growing.[67] Despite lukewarm support from Washington, Ben-Gurion feared that the Soviets, having backed down in the Cuban Missile Crisis, would pressure the West in Berlin. He was encouraged, however, by the Egyptian army's failures in Yemen.[68] Meir, seeking not to annoy the Kremlin, was more cautious, speaking in the Knesset, and carefully did not side with either Khrushchev or Kennedy in the Cuban Missile Crisis.[69]

Even though Israel had decided not to resume reprisal operations, the cabinet authorized Ben-Gurion to respond immediately to Syrian attacks on Israeli settlements on the eastern shore of the Sea of Galilee.[70] He took comfort only in the fact that Nasser had declared that the war to liberate the Arab states from their rulers took precedence over war with Israel, so the Jordan River diversion project could be completed by the summer of 1964. Ben-Gurion knew it was a casus belli for the Arabs, but he was fairly certain Kennedy would not let war break

---

65 Harman to Arad, December 3, 1962, ISA 3378/14.
66 Deputy Chief of Staff's Bureau to Bendor, 'Lecture by Y. Rabin,' November 17, 1961, ISA 3319/34.
67 ICAB, October 28, 1962, ISA.
68 ICAB, November 11, 1962, ISA.
69 KR 35: 93 (November 12, 1962).
70 ICAB, December 9, 1962, ISA.

out because of it, saying that if he could restrain Khrushchev, he could restrain Syria.⁷¹

After the Cuban Missile Crisis, Israel perceived Kennedy as the man who had saved the world from destruction. Eban quoted National Security Advisor McGeorge Bundy, who said making the Soviets back down was like forcing Hitler to withdraw from the Rhineland (1936). Eban argued that the Middle East was now of secondary importance, after the Caribbean, Berlin and the Congo. However, he said, the United States still believed Nasser was more interested in economic and social progress in Egypt than aggression, and that a solution for the refugee problem would bring peace closer. Israel said the opposite was true, that a peace agreement would bring a solution of the refugee issue closer, and Washington still opposed direct negotiations between Israel and the Arabs.⁷²

**Figure 1** 'Anyhow, thank you' by Kariel Gardosh (Dosh), October 1, 1962. The text by Nasser's cigar says 'offensive missile,' while that above Kennedy's ice cream says 'Hawk missile.'

71  ICAB, December 16, 1962, ISA.
72  ICAB, December 23, 1962, ISA.

# 10

## Was Kennedy the 'father' of the US–Israeli alliance? (1962–63)

During the Kennedy era, Israel managed to obtain Hawk anti-aircraft missiles, adjust the balance of power, increase economic aid and get US support for diverting the waters of the Jordan River. The United States, motivated by its desire to prevent the Soviet Union from taking over the Middle East, recognized the pro-Nasser regime in Yemen,[1] and hoped that Nasser's visit to the United States would bring him closer to the West.[2] The Americans did not believe that Nasser would attack Israel, but the Hawk affair had taught them that making generous gestures in advance was not worthwhile, because by selling Israel the missiles they had effectively sabotaged the Joseph Johnson Plan for resolving the refugee problem.[3]

Robert W. Komer was determined to force Israel's leaders to accommodate to US policy.[4] The United States needed, he believed, to make Israel understand it was the client and that the United States was the patron. In December 27, 1962, Golda Meir told Kennedy that Israel's concern was the arms race, not annexing territories, and that Egypt was secretly preparing for 'radiological war.' In addition, huge numbers of Arab refugees engulfing the state would change its demographics and it would cease to be a Jewish state, for which the US administration would bear the blame. Kennedy promised the balance of power would be maintained, adding that the United States had a 'special relationship' with Israel: 'We made it clear to the Arabs repeatedly that those special relationship [sic] are not negotiable.' Although it had no official alliance with Israel, it felt like its 'most

---

1 FRUS, 1961–1963, XVIII: 260–2.
2 FRUS, 1961–1963, XVIII: 267–8.
3 Don C. Bergus to William R. Crawford, December 8, 1962, Secret, NARA, NEA/NE, Box 6; Beeley to the Earl of Home, February 14, 1963, Secret and Guard, NA, FO 371/172869/10640/63G.
4 FRUS, 1961–1963, XVIII: 272–3.

intimate' ally, similar to the alliance she had had with Britain during World War II and beyond. The United States was not demanding that Israel ignore its own interests, he said. The President emphasized: 'It is quite clear that in the case of an invasion the United States would come to the support of Israel. We have that capacity and it is growing.' Granted, Israel could not absorb massive numbers of Arab refugees, who were preparing an 'Algerization' of the Palestine problem, as Meir explained, meaning fighting a guerilla war against Israel. Kennedy warned that if nothing were done to resolve the refugee issue, within two years the tension with the Arabs would escalate, as in Kashmir. Finally, Kennedy mentioned the reactor in Dimona and his opposition to nuclear proliferation.[5]

However, the meeting had no effect on US priorities. Egypt was a bigger problem for the United States than Israel.[6] John Badeau, the US ambassador to Egypt, warned that punishing Egypt would lead it to strengthen its ties with the Soviet Union. Guaranteeing Israel's existence was only fourth on the US list of Middle East priorities, after reducing Soviet influence, increasing its own influence and protecting the flow of oil to Western Europe.[7] The State Department set policy and the President accepted it, and ending aid to Egypt was regarded as a catastrophic error because Nasser was liable to fall into the arms of the Soviet Union.[8] The dynamics of the conflict were stronger than the State Department. Pentagon intelligence reported that Egypt had received missile boats, missiles and fighter planes from the Soviets.[9] Despite the possible upset of the balance of power, the United States trusted Israel and its strong army to prevent Nasser's involvement in Syria.[10] In the meantime, Walt W. Rostow, new Special Assistant to the President for National Security, fostered along with Komer the illusion that supervision of nonconventional weapons was possible.[11] US intelligence noted that the Soviets wanted to turn the Middle East into Eastern European-like 'people's

---

5 FRUS, 1961–1963, XVIII: 276–83; ICAB, 30 December, 1962, ISA.
6 FRUS, 1961–1963, XVIII: 292.
7 Bar-Haim to USD Director, 'Principles of US Policy in the Middle East, Conversation with Rodger Davis, Deputy Director for the Middle East, 15 January, 1963,' ISA, 3378/13; FRUS, 1961–1963, XVIII: 301–3.
8 Gazit, 'Middle Eastern Affairs in the Eyes of the State Department,' January 18, 1963, ISA 3378/13.
9 FRUS, 1961–1963, XVIII: 319–20.
10 Gazit to USD, 'Yemen and Its Significance, Conversation with Strong, January 24, 1963,' Restricted, ISA 3378/14.
11 FRUS, 1961–1963, XVIII: 345–6.

democracies' and to exploit Arab fears, and were spreading false rumors about IDF maneuvers.[12]

Ben-Gurion felt that Israel was a long way from a genuine special relationship with the United States. Despite Kennedy's promises, Ben-Gurion knew that Israel could rely only on itself.[13] Reflecting on this state of affairs, William Crawford, who was in charge of the Israel–Lebanon desk, observed that Israel was like a person living in a nice well-defended air-conditioned house in the middle of a jungle.[14]

In January 1963, US Secretary of Defense Robert McNamara announced that the United States would parallel military aid to Israel with future Soviet arms shipments to Egypt and Syria, and would not accept Soviet arming of the Arabs without compensating Israel.[15] The United States wanted to make it clear to the Arab countries that it had a vested interest in Israel's security and right to exist.[16]

The issue of the nuclear reactor in Dimona resurfaced to test the special relationship. The CIA was told by the Board of National Estimates that the reactor would damage the West's image in the Arab world and escalate East–West tensions. Nasser would be tempted to attack Dimona, but it was hard to believe that the Soviet Union would supply the Arabs with nuclear weapons; they had not even given them to their own satellites.[17] Kennedy agreed to improve intelligence gathering and ordered an immediate inspection of the reactor, and also tried to convince Israel to abandon its plans for an atomic weapon.[18] If Israel were to prevail on the question of the refugees, it was reasoned, they would assume that the United States could be overruled on other matters as well,[19] thus the State Department advocated the return of some of the Arab refugees to Israeli territory based on UN Resolution 194 (11).

Ben-Gurion did not make light of Kennedy's promises regarding Israel's security, but feared the Arabs' increasing strength and preferred

12 Roger Hilsman to the Secretary, INR: Bureau of Intelligence and Research, Research Memorandum, 'Soviet Objectives and Strategy in the Middle East', February 8, 1963, Secret, NARA, NEA/NE, 1962–1963, Box 4.
13 FRUS, 1961–1963, XVIII: 317.
14 Gazit to USD, 'Security Problems and Nasser,' January 31, 1963, Secret, ISA 3377/5II.
15 Gazit to USD, 'McNamara Announcement before the Congress Armed Forces Committee,' January 30, 1963, Secret, ISA 3379/3.
16 FRUS, 1961–1963, XVIII: 389.
17 FRUS, 1961–1963, XVIII: 398–401.
18 National Security Action Memorandum, in FRUS, 1962–1963, XVIII: 436–7 (March 26, 1963).
19 FRUS, 1961–1963, XVIII: 437–41.

deterrence to war.[20] He sent Peres to Washington again to meet with Kennedy to discuss the danger of Soviet missiles in Egypt. Kennedy pointed out that a nuclear missile was more dangerous, but Peres said it was far in the future and Israel would not be the first to introduce nuclear weapons into the region. Peres noted the connection between the regional and the East–West conflicts. The initial move for the Soviets, he said, would be arming Egypt with missiles.[21] Peres said that the United States should present Nasser with an ultimatum, either to fight Israel and the United States, or to cooperate with the US administration; the State Department remained unconvinced.[22]

Kennedy praised Nasser for establishing a reconstituted UAR with a trilateral federation with Syria and Iraq on April 17, 1963, but expressed concern over the arms race with Israel.[23] The State Department did not regard the article on Palestinian liberation in the federation's covenant as dangerous as long as the Arabs were preoccupied with internal problems.[24] However, Ben-Gurion told Kennedy that the federation would have a detrimental influence on regional stability, and that even the Hawk missiles the Americans were selling to Israel would not deter the Egyptians.[25] If Nasser gained control over Jordan, Ben-Gurion said, Israel could be cut in two, and Jordan was problematic because King Hussein was in constant danger of assassination. Nasser wanted to unite the Arab states in preparation for a war on Israel. Ben-Gurion rejected the idea of annexation of the West Bank and relied on the increasing number of Mirage fighter jets to seventy.[26]

Kennedy's promise to Golda Meir that the United States would assist Israel if it were attacked was useless, because US military action required the consent of both houses of Congress. Ben-Gurion, Minister of Labor Yigal Allon and Chief of Staff Zvi Tzur did not believe Nasser was headed for war. However, Allon argued that contingency plans should include measures to induce part of the West Bank's Arabs to flee eastward. Ben-Gurion warned against panic. He said he preferred an alliance with the United States or France, or deterrent weapons, to

20  KFADC, March 27, 1963, ISA.
21  Gazit, 'Peres Conversation with U. Alexis Johnson, Deputy Secretary of State for Political Affairs,' April 3, 1963, Top Secret and Personal, ISA 4326/26.
22  Peres–Talbot, April 4, 1963, Top Secret, April 4, 1963, ISA 4326/26.
23  FRUS, 1961–1963, XVIII: 469–70.
24  FRUS, 1961–1963, XVIII: 476.
25  FRUS, 1961–1963, XVIII: 481–2, 528–9.
26  KFADC, April 26, 1963, ISA.

war.[27] Eban suggested a mutual defense pact with the United States, noting his concerns for the next decade. In ten years, he said, the population of the Arab countries would be 150 million, as opposed to 90 million in 1963, Egypt was building a nuclear reactor and economic trends also favored the Arabs. Ben-Gurion was more optimistic, arguing that immigration was more important than military superiority.[28]

Komer suggested that a defense treaty could be conditioned on Israel's forfeiting its nuclear weapons program. He argued that aircraft carriers from the Sixth Fleet (*Enterprize* and *Saratoga*) could be moved into the Eastern Mediterranean. Nasser needed to understand that, because of its security needs, Israel could not be restrained.[29] Ben-Gurion told Kennedy that Israel's chief security problem was the Egypt–Syria unification and that the United States had to take steps to counter it and also to insist on the complete demilitarization of the West Bank. The provision in the revived UAR's charter calling for the liberation of Palestine also remained controversial. Under Secretary of State George Ball said that 'the liberation of Palestine' was just a slogan, but if put into practice the United States would take it very seriously. On the Cold War level, Komer was convinced that increasing Arab Nationalism was the main obstacle to regional Soviet expansion.[30]

Ben-Gurion suggested that to prevent aggression from the UAR, Israel again ask for a Soviet–US statement of respect for regional sovereignty and that Israel seek a military alliance with one of the powers, proposing France, the United States and NATO. With the United States there would have to be an open alliance, and, while joining NATO would serve as a deterrent, there were serious obstacles. Even if the UAR dissolved, Egypt alone would present a significant threat with its population of 27 million Israel-hating people.[31] Israel found itself trapped by US interests. Avraham Harman, Israel's ambassador to the United States, warned the government that 'friends,' namely the Americans, could not be relied on to supply political results.[32] In addition, the State Department feared that Israel would occupy the West Bank and that in response Nasser would blow up the oil pipelines, block the Suez Canal, strengthen his ties with

27 ICAB, April 25, May 5, 1963, ISA; cf. Peres–de Murville: DDF, 1963, 2: 631.
28 ICAB, May 5, 1963, ISA.
29 FRUS, 1961–1963, XVIII: 484–8.
30 Robert Komer, 'Memorandum for Record Conversation with Roland Evans, New York Herald Tribune,' May 2, 1963, Confidential, JFKL, NSF Countries, Box 322.
31 ICAB, April 30, 1963, ISA.
32 Harman to Yachil, May 14, 1963, Top Secret and Highly Personal, ISA 3377/9; FRUS, 1961–1963, XVIII: 516; Chase and Lerman, 1965: 437–8.

the Soviet Union and blame the United States.[33] Moreover, the political and psychological impact of a nuclear bomb would be greater than its strategic value and send Nasser to seek support from the Soviets.[34] In May 1963, in the name of regional stability, the United States requested biannual inspections of the reactor in Dimona, fearing that if nuclear weapons were detected the Soviet Union might supply them to Egypt.[35]

Kennedy sought a compromise.[36] His advisors recommended that a US security commitment be conditioned on Israel's not developing missiles or nuclear weapons. If supervision of the arms race succeeded, Israel's security would improve and the United States would stop flirting with Nasser.[37] Harman was of the opinion that the State Department's influence had to be limited by the President and his advisors. The United States had to provide the essence of the settlement, not its form: it needed to state its readiness to respond if Israel were attacked, to include Israel in military consultations and to cooperate politically. On May 8, 1963, Kennedy promised to preserve the territorial integrity of the states of the region as a whole, including Israel, which was the most that could be expected as long as there was no change for the worse in the balance of power.[38] Israel found that insufficient as it did not guarantee military aid. While the US administration was sensitive to any small change in the balance of power, it still refused be Israel's primary arms supplier.

Harman took at face value Khrushchev's statement that there would be no world war because Communism would triumph by other means. There would be no significant development in the next two years, but the danger was in the long term. He said the Americans were neither stupid, anti-Semitic nor anti-Israeli, but they were also not omnipotent. A defense treaty had not been obtained because of cold political considerations.[39]

Komer reevaluated relations with Israel, concluding that the United States should in fact enter into secret negotiations with Israel, conditioned on its ceasing to pressure the United States, not invading the West Bank and agreeing to the oversight of its nuclear facilities. Writing to Ben-Gurion, Kennedy again focused on supervision of the reactor

---

33 Gazit to Meir, 'The West Bank,' May 13, 1963, Top Secret and Personal, ISA 4314/10.
34 FRUS, 1961–1963, XVIII: 517–18.
35 FRUS, 1961–1963, XVIII: 525–6.
36 FRUS, 1961–1963, XVIII: 526–7.
37 FRUS, 1961–1963, XVIII: 529–35.
38 Harman to Yachil, May 14, 1963, Top Secret and Highly Personal, ISA 3377/9.
39 KFADC, May 15, 1963, ISA.

in Dimona. Given the military and political developments in Egypt, he said, he understood Israel's concern, but no one was threatening Israel with nuclear weapons. The commitment to Israel would be endangered if Israel failed to supply information about its nuclear program.[40]

The US administration wanted to dictate regional rules. Israel was important to it, but not a key country. Kennedy told Badeau that there was no imminent danger, but that there was a long-term threat. Israel had to give firm assurances, not disturb the peace or manufacture nuclear weapons, consult with the United States before acquiring or producing weapons, cooperate with the UN and find a positive solution to the problem of the refugees. If within six months Egypt had not limited its arms, the United States would hold unilateral talks with Israel regarding a security guarantee. If Israel did not limit its arms, the United States would exert more pressure and reconsider aid to the Arab countries.[41]

Ben-Gurion was to retire from politics on June 16, 1963. In principle, for the short term he focused on national security, believing it necessary to have deterrence sufficient to prevent war, but also sufficient force to win a war. However, his long-term goal was peace. It was not clear if time was on Israel's side. Its enemies were becoming more numerous, powerful and advanced. Even if immigration increased fourfold it would be impossible to match the natural population increase of the Arab countries, and Israel's qualitative advantage would dwindle. However, Israel's international standing was improving. Ben-Gurion predicted that the Cold War would end when the two sides had no choice but to find common ground, perhaps in ten or fifteen years.[42] He was disappointed by the lack of American and British commitment to Israel and so pinned his hopes on France.[43]

Under Kennedy's direction, Talbot consulted with US diplomats in the Arab world about what would be required for negotiating a security guarantee for Israel. Most of them warned that, if one were in fact negotiated, the Soviets would give the Arab countries a similar guarantee. They also raised questions about the dilemma of US policy toward Israel and the definition of the special relationship. Despite the fact that in principle Walworth Barbour, the US ambassador to Israel, was pro-Israel, he was not thrilled with the idea of granting Israel a security guarantee. In his

---

40  FRUS, 1961–1963, XVIII: 543–4; A. Cohen, 1998: 123–34; Bass, 2003: 216; Barbour to Rusk, 15 May, 1963, Secret, Eys Only, JFKL, NSF, Countries, Box 119.
41  FRUS, 1961–1963, XVIII: 536–7, 542–5.
42  MPC, June 6, 1963, LPA.
43  John Beith to FO, May 22, 1963, Confidential, NA, FO 371/170531/ER1051/5.

opinion, the President had already expressed concern for Israel's security, and a reaffirmation in a different format would not bolster Israel's sense of security. To actually strengthen Israel would necessitate adding cooperative military planning and intelligence exchanges, and access to the US arsenal. For the Arabs, there would be no problem because they believed that such a partnership already existed. Barbour asked Talbot whether the United States could risk giving Israel a free hand with its borders. In addition, Israel's claim that the Arab states should absorb Palestinian refugees was highly doubtful. Israel would never agree to arms control before its security situation had improved. Finally, Barbour favored joint military planning and intelligence cooperation with Israel, as well as access to US weapons, instead of a 'reaffirmation' of a guarantee.[44]

Badeau advised against granting Israel a security guarantee, which would place US–Israeli relations in the same category as Soviet–Cuban relations and create substantial problems with regard to the border issue, preventing US freedom of action in the region. Moreover, a guarantee would remove any possibility of pressuring Israel for more concessions on arms inspections. In his opinion, Israel had done nothing to mitigate the conflict. A security guarantee would only make effective supervision of Israel more difficult and clearly have a catastrophic influence on the Arab world, increase the antagonism toward Israel and induce the Arabs to coordinate their military planning. It would also be detrimental to US oil interests, as well as present the Soviet Union with a golden opportunity to renew its influence, now at its lowest point since the Suez War. Instead he proposed close regional arms supervision with no security guarantees at all, and an aid plan.[45]

Parker Hart, the US ambassador to Saudi Arabia, agreed with Badeau. He maintained that a guarantee for Israel would undermine Washington's special relationship with King Faisal and jeopardize US interests. Cairo would claim that Saudi Arabia had made a secret pact with Israel, not just with the United States. King Faisal of Saudi Arabia might nationalize the ARAMCO oil company and turn down US aid for training and equipping his army and ask Egypt, indirectly meaning the Soviets, to step in instead. Hart warned against giving Egypt an excuse to attack pro-US Arab countries which, despite the guarantee, would leave Israel as insecure as before. Better, in Hart's view, was mutual Israeli–Egyptian deterrence than disarmament or a security guarantee. It would also be

---

44 Barbour, Tel-Aviv, to Talbot, June 6, 1963, NARA, Official-Informal, Top Secret, POL-ARAB-ISR.
45 Badeau, Cairo, to Talbot, June 5, 1963, NARA, Eyes Only, Official-Informal Personal. POL-ARAB-ISR.

better to sell Israel the occasional Hawk missiles than to grant it a formal defense treaty. The United States should remind all the parties to the conflict that East and West were engaging in marathon efforts to achieve disarmament.[46]

The chargé d'affaires in Kuwait, Dayton Mak, was the only US diplomat to address the nuclear question. Given the Arab threats to destroy Israel, he could hardly blame the Israelis for concern over their security. He saw no reason to doubt that the Arabs would go to war with Israel the moment they were strong enough. It would therefore be remiss on the part of the United States not to do 'something' to prevent war from breaking out. Given the threats to its existence, it would be unreasonable to expect Israel not to develop nuclear capabilities, and in the long run it was unlikely that Israel would agree to a security guarantee as a substitute for independent nuclear capability.[47]

Robert Stookey, the chargé d'affaires in Yemen, claimed that if Israel had not existed the United States would have had to create it as a bridgehead against the Arabs. For the Arab-Muslim world, he said, all nations are either Muslims in 'The House of Islam' (*Dar al-Islam*) or non-Muslims in 'The House of War' (*Dar al-Harb*). It was an Islamic imperative to conquer non-Muslim countries, he said, and for that reason the Arabs would only sign armistices with infidels, not peace treaties, making final and lasting peace with them inconceivable. However, a defense treaty with Israel would do serious damage to US standing. Far preferable would be a presidential declaration of a US commitment to Israel's defense. It did not have to be ratified by the Senate and would cause only a brief flare-up in US–Arab relations. The United States had two options: either to accommodate extremist extortion to appease the sensitivities of the Arabs or to risk a direct regional conflict between the blocs.[48]

The most extreme reaction came from Armin Meyer, US ambassador to Lebanon. He said it was a Newtonian law of physics that every action had an equal and opposite reaction, and a treaty for Israel would mean a renewed Arab–Soviet embrace. The President, he claimed, was helpless in the face of Zionist influence and there was only the slightest hope for Israel's future as long as its policy was based on a 'fortress' mindset. An

---

46 Parker T. Hart, Jidda, to Talbot, July 1, 1963, NARA, Secret and Personal, POL-ARAB-ISR.
47 Dayton S. Mak, Kuwait, June 13, 1963, NARA, Official-Informal, Secret, For Talbot from Chargé d'Affaires, POL-ARAB-ISR.
48 Robert W. Stookey, Chargé d'Affaires, Taiz, Yemen, to Talbot, June 8, 1963, Secret, NARA, RG 59, NEA/NE, Box 1.

open pact between the United States and Israel would reduce the pressure on Ben-Gurion to accommodate the Arabs. The idea made Meyer furious and he said he sometimes wondered 'whether history is not repeating itself in that Israel, having made its exodus from Egypt, having won its Joshuan triumphs militarily, and having had its David slay the Philistines, may not now be entering into the period of Jeremiah-like lamentations, bewailing a future diaspora which its very policies tend to assure. I hope it does not seem facetious but it seems to me that a touch of Christian brotherhood might avert the doom.'[49] Nonetheless, he recognized the long-term threat to Israel and agreed that perhaps only a US security guarantee could help. In 1948, all State Department officials had predicted that Israel would be a 'permanent thorn in the flesh of American policy in the Middle East.' Now it was too late and they had to ensure Israel's survival. US support for diverting the Jordan River and its provision of Hawk missiles left the administration only minimal room to maneuver and had whetted Israel's appetite for additional demands. If the United States gave in to Israel's demands, the administration would be unable to complain when the Soviets responded by placing troops. Such a situation would create another dangerous flashpoint.

John McCloy, the President's Special Emissary for Near East Arms Limitation, objected to a pact on the grounds that they were coming too close to Israel. Talbot warned once again that a guarantee for Israel would invite a Soviet guarantee for the Arabs.[50] Surely, the recommendations of the American diplomats in the Middle East blocked the idea of an official security guarantee for Israel for a long time to come.

The time for a decision had come. Kennedy discussed with his advisors what kind of guarantee there might be needed to grant to Israel in order to avoid a conflagration in Jordan and to stop the race for nuclear capabilities. Talbot was in favor of making promises to both sides in order to avoid a bilateral agreement which would lead to problems with the Arabs. Kennedy suggested offering Israel what had already been offered: sensible promises in exchange for not crossing into Jordan, not developing nuclear weapons and not getting entangled in the problems of the region. Talbot and Komer noted that Israel would not be satisfied with a unilateral security guarantee. Israel's goals were a full defense treaty, cooperative planning for the hour of need and large quantities of military equipment. Kennedy encouraged low-level military dialogue.

49 Armin H. Meyer for Assistant Secretary of State Talbot, June 2, 1963. Secret, POL-ARAB-ISR. No less critical on the proposed security guarantees were the ambassadors in Damascus and Amman: POL-ARAB-ISR (June 10, 11) 1963.
50 FRUS, 1961–1963, XVIII: 589–92.

Israel's leaders still had demands and grievances. They wanted more aid because of the high cost of weapons and were worried by the United States' cultivation of Nasser. They claimed that the Dimona reactor was Israel's bargaining chip and would not give it up without concrete compensation. The reactor was a deterrent postponing the danger of war for many years to come.[51] Harman demanded a clear deterrent power and bilateral security arrangements, including formal mechanisms for bilateral treaties and a mutual analysis of conventional arms escalation. US policy should be definitive like in Berlin. The US administration was concerned that a guarantee would bind the United States. A guarantee meant a pact, for which Israel would have to relinquish its nuclear weapons and Nasser would be warned that Israel would receive weapons whenever Egypt did.[52] Rusk and Talbot told Kennedy a distinction had to be made between the issue of Dimona and the security guarantee so that Israel did not benefit from a connection between them. The guarantee should be limited to cases of tangible aggression and, if Israel engaged in provocation, assistance would be denied; only secret, low-level talks would be held.[53]

The JCS backed Kennedy's opposition to a security guarantee and cooperative military planning on the grounds that granting them would open a new Cold War front. However, they also claimed that land, sea and air forces could intervene within thirty to seventy-two hours of an attack. Should Israel be attacked, the most effective assistance the United States would be able to give would be to destroy Arab airfields.[54]

Israel claimed that Arab first strikes would cost many lives and that the upset in the balance of power needed to be repaired through a US guarantee and arms.[55] The Arab threat required that Israel strengthen its deterrent capabilities and the United States had to become its primary arms supplier, providing weapons free of charge and increasing its annual financial aid. Nevertheless, Chief of Staff Tzur maintained that the IDF was strong enough to respond in the event of war. Harman was optimistic, saying that the promise of Hawk missiles meant the United States was treating Israel as an ally. Additionally, Israel received $46 million in 1963, $25 million of which was indirect military assistance.

51 'Discussion on US–Israeli Relations headed by Meir,' June 13, 1963, ISA 4320/27.
52 FRUS, 1961–1963, XVIII: 648, 653–6.
53 [Dean Rusk,] Memorandum for the President, 'Israel's Desire for a United States Security Guarantee,' [July 22, 1963,] Enclosure No. 1, NARA, NEA/NE, Box 3.
54 FRUS, 1961–1963, XVIII: 658–61, 667–9.
55 Memorandum of Conversation, 'Israel's Requirement for a Security Guarantee,' July 26, 1963, Participants: Gazit, Harrison M. Symmes, Confidential, Box 7.

Eventually, it would be possible to sign a treaty with the United States, but not currently because there was no immediate threat. Levy Eshkol, Ben-Gurion's successor as prime minister, understood that Israel could make do with funding for arms purchases in Europe and evade US supervision of the Dimona facility.[56]

The Nuclear Test Ban Treaty was signed in Moscow on July 25, 1963, by the United States, the Soviet Union and Britain. Other countries were invited to sign and Israel announced its agreement on July 31. While the danger of a world war had not passed, the treaty brought new hope. The general assessment was that the superpowers had agreed to the treaty out of a fear of nuclear proliferation. Harman claimed that Kennedy had a spiritual and historical worldview. Kennedy, he said, recognized Israel's historical right to exist, adding that the United States was in control of the situation and, if the situation exploded because of the Arabs, they would stand by Israel.[57] The reactor in Dimona was not a cause for concern. Eshkol had agreed to oversight in August 19, 1963, and Kennedy was satisfied with Israel's cooperation with the Nuclear Test Ban Treaty.[58] Nevertheless, the Kennedy administration was concerned that Israel would force a security guarantee, arms, and cooperative planning and intelligence, and that in the end the United States would station troops on Israeli soil, as had happened in Berlin.[59]

Rusk believed the potential threat to Israel had evaporated along with the UAR. Nasser had been disabused of his illusions and his economy was faltering, creating the opportunity to bring him in line with weapons oversight.[60] However, Eshkol and his advisors worried about possible emergency situations, such as an Egyptian army incursion into the Sinai Peninsula, and the debate raged. Eshkol feared that Washington would test Israel's consent to inspection in Dimona. Eban warned that the US commitment lacked everything an alliance required, which was automatic and public commitment to assistance, as if the United States itself were under attack. Not surprisingly, his model was the special relationship between the United States and Britain.

Dayan stressed the importance of the nuclear reactor and opposed any alliance or guarantee that would prohibit Israel from taking over the West Bank if necessary, and said the Kennedy administration

56 'Consultation with IFM and Defense Ministry,' July 30, 1963, ISA 7935/5a.
57 KFADC, August 13, 1963, ISA.
58 FRUS, 1961–1963, XVIII: 691–2.
59 William R. Polk to Grant, 'Near Eastern Arms,' September 2, 1963, Top Secret, NARA, RG 59, NEA/NE, Box 1.
60 FRUS, 1961–1963, XVIII: 701–3.

should offer Israel larger, long-range Pershing surface-to-surface missiles. Eshkol suggested that Israel not develop a nuclear bomb if the United States offered a different deterrent weapon. Peres feared a sudden escalation with Syria, in which case Nasser would come to Syria's aid, war would break out, Washington would demand a ceasefire and the Sixth Fleet would disappear. In the final analysis, the United States maintained alliances only with countries whose enemies were the Communists.[61]

Eshkol renewed the struggle for a bilateral anti-aggression defense treaty based on intelligence of accelerated Egyptian armament, including the assembly of an array of hundreds of surface-to-surface missiles, the development of chemical and biological weapons, a plan for a 100 megawatt nuclear reactor and the production of plutonium.[62] However, the US position remained the same: a commitment to Israel's security and superiority without acceding to Israel's demands threatening US interests; both Britain and France had also vetoed security guarantees.[63]

However, Israel was concerned about the US rapprochement with Egypt, despite Egypt's involvement in Yemen, which included the use of mustard gas, and despite the German scientists in Egypt.[64] As for new tanks, Rusk claimed the tank was no longer relevant because an individual soldier could destroy one with a handheld anti-tank missile.[65] Eshkol's basic concern was that the Arabs would conclude that the United States had no treaty with Israel and that the lack of open commitment and cooperative planning was liable to cause the Arabs to miscalculate, while a defense treaty might make them more pragmatic.[66] However, Eshkol failed to convince Kennedy to grant a security guarantee. On October 2, 1963, Kennedy claimed that the current arrangements were sufficient to control the situation. The United States had forces for rapid response in the Mediterranean and could defend any country in the region. A security guarantee would offer the Soviet Union an opportunity to 'fish in murky waters.' Nevertheless, Kennedy promised constant attention to

---

61 'Consultation Regarding Correspondence with Kennedy,' September 6, 1963, ISA 3377/10.
62 Eshkol to Harman and Gazit, September 10, 1963, Top Secret and Personal, ISA 3377/6.
63 FRUS, 1961–1963, XVIII: 705–8.
64 On July 21, 1962, Egypt publicly and successfully tested surface-to-surface missiles with the assistance of German scientists, something which created panic in Israel.
65 FRUS, 1961–1963, XVIII: 717–19.
66 Draft Reply to President Kennedy's Letter, October 3, 1963, ISA 3370/10.

Israel's security situation, while the United States would consider how to deal with a renewed Arab threat.[67]

Global considerations dictated that the United States could not renege on its commitments, and the concept of 'flexible response' could not enter into a contractual obligation with Israel, and Kennedy's adoption of an 'aggressive' policy did not improve the situation. The reinforcements sent to the Middle East (two air force squadrons and an aircraft carrier for the Sixth Fleet) were intended primarily to strengthen Saudi Arabia.[68] Eshkol was dissatisfied. Nasser had about 200 missiles, three times the planes of Israel and did not need provocation to go to war. Eshkol added that only missiles or the knowledge that Israel could counterstrike could deter him.[69] He was told the United States did not want war and wanted to maintain the balance of power and that it did not want to bring the Cold War to the Middle East by assisting Israel against a Soviet–Arab enemy. In any event, US intelligence was highly developed and would not be surprised.[70] Eshkol was not reassured, but was however convinced that, despite the quantitative disparity, Israel was stronger than the Arabs.[71] The State Department stressed that, even with their state-of-the-art weapons, Arab capabilities were not impressive and the Sixth Fleet could respond within 24–72 hours if Israel were attacked; in addition, it did agree that Israel needed new tanks.

Moreover, the Kennedy administration was disabused of its illusions regarding Nasser. He was involved in Algeria, had introduced Soviet arms into Egypt and refused to withdraw from Yemen. However, they decided, it was better to try to influence him than to argue with him. US Under Secretary of State Averell Harriman was warned that, if Eshkol did not obtain guarantees for the future, he would be replaced by someone younger and less cooperative like Shimon Peres.[72]

The Israeli embassy in Washington was confident, but the possibility of a surprise attack gave Eshkol no peace. Ambassador Barbour claimed that investigations had shown Nasser to be aware of the US commitment to Israel, in itself a deterrent. Eshkol feared that the intervention of

---

67 FRUS, 1961–1963, XVIII: 720–2.
68 FRUS, 1961–1963, XVIII: 726–7.
69 Arad to IMUN and IMW, October 4, 1963, Top Secret and Personal, ISA 3377/10.
70 Harman to Yachil, 'Conversation with Feldman,' October 14, 1963, ISA 3377/10.
71 Consultation Concerning Alliances with the USA, Ministry of Defense, October 30, 1963, ISA 7935/5a.
72 Jacob Blaustein, Governor Harriman, et al., 'Israel's Security,' October 31, 1963, Secret, Limit Distribution, NARA, RG 59, NEA/NE, Box 3.

the Sixth Fleet would come too late. If Israel did not receive surface-to-surface missiles and other military equipment, it would have no deterrent capability. The Kennedy administration still insisted that supplying surface-to-surface missiles would lead the Soviets to supply them to the UAR, leading to Israel's destruction, and the Americans refused Israel's requests for joint planning, regular consultation and heavy weapons.[73] The State Department refused to capitulate, claiming that disagreements among allies were normal. Israel had already received a substantial commitment and it did not have to be put in writing. However, Israel asked how, in the hour of need, would the Sixth Fleet be 'activated?'[74]

The State Department feared the missile race would end in war and that the Cold War would worsen the threat to Israel. Israel noted that it required a minimum of security, and needed to replace outdated equipment and reinforce its navy.[75] In November 1963, Eshkol sent Deputy Chief of Staff Yitzhak Rabin and Head of Military Intelligence Aharon Yariv to meet Komer and discuss the Egyptian threat. Rabin acknowledged that military disparity was a psychological problem, but Nasser's overweening self-confidence would induce him to wage a surprise attack. Komer answered that US help was close in Turkey, the air base in Adana and the Six Fleet as well as the British RAF Bomber Command in Cyprus, and wondered why Israel always questioned US capabilities. Rabin, however, knew that open treaties with allies made for more powerful deterrence and asked what would happen if American and Israeli planes appeared at the same target at the same time without recognizing each other.

Komer claimed that superpower support on both sides of the conflict would turn Israel into a garrison state. After years of significant economic assistance and regular declarations, there was no reason for Israel to doubt US reliability. Rabin said that, because of the US arms embargo of 1948, Israel had won its War of Independence thanks only to Czech (that is, Soviet) weapons, proving that it could not rely on vague declarations which bore less weight than an official alliance. Komer said that Nasser understood US determination to defend Israel as clearly as if there were a formal alliance, and asked Rabin if Israel planned to purchase solid-fuel rockets from France or produce its own missiles. The reactor in Dimona would provide Israel with a genuine deterrent, but would open a Pandora's box and set off a new arms race, and the US administration

73 Arad to IMW, November 4, 1963, ISA 3377/10.
74 Arad, Yachil–Jernegan Conversation, October 30, 1963, ISA 3378/1.
75 FRUS, 1961–1963, XVIII: 777–9.

wanted more information about Israel's plans. Rabin said that even the missiles were only a psychological threat, and the political leadership needed to assure the populace that it had adequate measures for deterrence.[76] Informally, the State Department's legal advisor said that the US commitment was the equivalent of a signed treaty and would bind future presidents. The President would activate the army if Israel were attacked. Even the support for diverting the Jordan River was absolute and the United States understood Israel's need to defend it vigilantly.[77]

The day before Kennedy's assassination, Komer accused Israel of trying to destroy the middle-ground position that the United States had adopted in the Middle East, warning that the Soviets would be delighted. He wondered why Israel was so cautious about revealing its defense plans to the United States, which was guaranteeing Israel's existence, serving as Israel's banker and was Israel's most powerful friend. If Israel were in trouble, it was the United States that would come to its aid, not France or West Germany. He complained that Israel was evasive, raising suspicions about the Dimona reactor. The United States had to know if Israel was acquiring weapons that would lead to an arms race and a serious upsetting of the balance of deterrence. An operation in Jordan could lead to a war involving the United States. Israel was using its foreign currency reserves to purchase missiles from France costing hundreds of millions of dollars, while at the same time demanding hundreds of tanks from the United States.

The US administration's position was that even a thousand Egyptian missiles had only psychological value. Israel did not understand US policy, claimed the administration, and the two sides were like ships passing in the night.[78] However, Israel faced a genuine threat. On July 29, 1963, Nasser announced that he had no choice but to restore to the Palestinian people their lost rights. The Syrian chief of staff made a similar statement in August, as did the Iraqi foreign minister at the UN General Assembly in October. Following a debate at the General Assembly, the refugee issue became a public concern in Israel, with the government's position remaining that Arab refugees should be resettled in the Arab countries.[79]

---

76 FRUS, 1961–1963, XVIII: 779–86, 788, 792–5; on the problems related to France's control on supply of uranium and plutonium for the Dimona reactor: DDF, 1963, 2: 61–53, 103–4.
77 Gazit, Rabin–Chayes Meeting, A. Chayes, November 15, 1963, ISA 7935/5a.
78 FRUS, 1961–1963, XVIII: 139–40, cf. 798–801; Bass, 2003: 139–40.
79 KR 35: 93–116, 126–41.

President Kennedy was assassinated on November 22, 1963, and succeeded by Vice-President Lyndon Johnson. Komer told McGeorge Bundy, Special Assistant to the President on National Security Affairs, he was concerned that the new Ba'ath regime in Syria would be more militant than Nasser and would drag him into aggression, and that the crisis over Israel's diversion of the Jordan River would worsen during the presidential election campaigns. US Middle East policy seemed to be succeeding only in Iran. The United States, he explained, did not always have leverage and the short and long terms usually conflicted. The new president acknowledged that it was important to maintain relations with Nasser and the other neutralists, such as Nehru, because, if the West lost them, the balance of power could swing against it.[80]

The intelligence community supported the State Department and rejected Israel's claim that Egyptian missiles were a threat to morale. France's intention to supply Israel with 250 surface-to-surface missiles would increase the risk of war.[81] They could not punish Nasser by cutting off all assistance lest they lose him to the Soviets.[82] Moreover, the State Department foresaw that Israel would occupy the Golan Heights and that the Soviet Union would only become involved on Syria's behalf at a diplomatic level, without entering an inter-bloc conflict.[83]

Initially, Israel felt no less distress under the Johnson administration. Israel could purchase state-of-the-art American M60 tanks, but only at full price. The Israeli defense budget was 10–12 percent of its GNP and it was inconceivable that Johnson could not find $10–15 million for aid when Khrushchev was assisting Egypt. Peres suggested West Germany grant Israel $50 million a year over the course of five years; according to the Israeli military intelligence directorate, Egypt was receiving more than $200 million a year from the Soviet Union.[84]

The director of the State Department's Intelligence and Research Bureau was concerned by a speech given by Nasser (on December 23, 1963), who had increased his anti-imperialist rhetoric for the ears of Soviet Deputy Prime Minister Alexander Shelepin and had received an

---

80 FRUS, 1961–1963, XVIII: 820–1.
81 Special National Intelligence Estimate, FRUS, 1961–1963, XVIII: 825–6 (December 4, 1963).
82 FRUS, 1961–1963, XVIII: 848.
83 William R. Crawford, Lucien L. Kinsolving to Rodger Davies, 'Memorandum, Contingency Planning for Jordan Waters: A Possible USSR View,' December 17, 1963.
84 Meeting (Eskol, Eban, Peres et al.), 'Arms Deals Affairs,' December 16, 1963, ISA 7935/5a.

interest-free loan from China. The director expected extreme polarization, with an Arab–Soviet axis confronting a US–Israeli one. Nasser would not go to war with Israel, but would cause trouble in Cyprus, the Persian Gulf and Algeria.[85] Peres assured the United States that Israel did not want the national water carrier to cause a war, but acts of sabotage and infiltration against Israel were always a possibility.[86]

The improvement of US–Israeli relations that occurred during the Kennedy era can only be understood in the context of the inter-bloc conflict. The main issue was whether the United States should grant a security guarantee to Israel. The overriding concern in the US administration was that Egyptian alienation would lead it directly into a military alliance with the Soviet Union, which would mean global escalation and the likelihood of war. It has been claimed that Kennedy fathered a de facto alliance with Israel at the end of his presidency and that the friction between US national interests and the special relationship had ended, assertions which are baseless and unsubstantiated.[87] Contemporary documents in various archives show that at the time Israel was profoundly disappointed with US commitments. At the time of Kennedy's death, Israel was disappointed at how its relations with the United States had been upgraded only in the face of an increasing Arab threat. Israel had not obtained a formal defense pact or a regular supply of weapons. Israel's leaders willy-nilly realized that US policy in the Middle East was dictated by US interests. A change in policy could be effected only by a significant change in Soviet policy, a coup in Egypt or a radical change in the balance of military power, such as the introduction of nuclear weapons.[88]

Kennedy's initial and final positions regarding Israel were identical. Early on in his presidency, he had said that Khrushchev did not want to resolve controversial international problems, calling him wild and unreasonable, an impression he made on other visitors from the West.[89] Thus, there is no foundation for the claim that Kennedy was the author of the alliance between the two countries simply because he sold Israel Hawk missiles. His administration refused to grant Israel a security

---

85 Thomas L. Hughes to the Secretary, Nasser's Speech and its Implications for US Policy, December 24, 1963, Secret, NARA, NEA/NE, Box 3.
86 KFADC, December 17, 1963, ISA.
87 Little, 1993: 176; Ben-Zvi, 1993: 83; Bass, 2003: 246.
88 Arad, USD Director to Levavi, 'Plan of Action in the US,' November 28, 1963, ISA 3378/1.
89 Amos Elon Interview with Kennedy (August 11, 1961), *Haaretz*, November 24, 1963.

guarantee or to sell it heavy weapons, although the United States was a generous economic patron. Given the circumstances of the time, perhaps nothing more was possible, but it was sufficient to maintain Israel's qualitative advantage. Kennedy opened the way to adjusting the balance of power and Johnson widened it to parallel Soviet penetration, but he also refused to grant Israel a security guarantee.[90] Iran, not Israel, was regarded as the country most vulnerable to Soviet attack in the Middle East.[91]

90  Gazit, 2002: 173–85.
91  FRUS, 1961–1963, XVIII: 576.

# 11

# Khrushchev, Israel and Soviet Jewry (1961–64)

Following the Kremlin, the Soviet press published articles attacking Zionism and accusing Israel of manufacturing nuclear weapons in the interests of Middle Eastern imperialism.[1] Nevertheless, Israel's foreign ministry was optimistic because the Kremlin also attacked Nasser.[2] While the Soviet Union did call for the return of the Arab refugees and recognized only the partition borders of 1947, it did not support the Arab demand to destroy Israel. The Kremlin wanted both a neutral Israel[3] and to obviate any manifestation of a Jewish national revival on its own territory. An international conference in support of Soviet Jewry was held in Paris in mid-September 1960, which an angry Kremlin called an anti-Soviet plot to aggravate the Cold War. Soviet Jews, it claimed, enjoyed full rights and many had received national decorations.[4] Israel's ambassador to Moscow, suggested Israel have Kennedy ask the Soviet Union to allow at least the reunification of families. Despite unceasing efforts to suppress Jewish nationalist sentiments, large numbers of Soviet Jews longed to emigrate to Israel.[5]

Harel claimed that Khrushchev sought détente and that the Kremlin's political position would be determined by a pragmatic evaluation of the country's interests, thus Israel could take steps to improve relations. Newly opened scientific and cultural ties could be exploited to encourage restlessness among Soviet Jews. The Soviet public opposed the assimilation of the Jews and that would make it easier to promote emigration.[6] He continued advocating neutrality, insisting that Khrushchev's goal

---

1 Observer, 'The Bankrupts' Congress,' *Trud*, January 6, 1961: 3.
2 Dagan to Harel, January 18, 1961, ISA 33321/1.
3 IFM, Survey No. 4, Confidential (February 1961): 12, 3332/11.
4 IMM to DEE, January 20, 1961, Confidential, ISA 2337/8; Z. Sheinis, 'International Zionism,' *Novoye Vremya* 4, January 1961: 9–12.
5 Harel to Meir, February 6, 1961, ISA 4308/13.
6 KFADC, March 8–9, 1961, ISA.

was to create a neutral buffer zone from Southeast Asia through India, the Middle East and Central Europe to Finland. If Kennedy advocated the neutrality of countries like Laos instead of pursuing a doctrine of nuclear bases, Soviet attitudes would change. The Soviet Union would consider Israel's demands for regional disarmament and might not supply Nasser with advanced weapons.[7]

However, Israeli–Soviet relations were damaged by a series of espionage incidents and Isser Harel, chief of the Israel Security Agency (Shin Bet), worried about Israelis spying for the Soviet Union (the Israel Baer affair),[8] the attempt of the Communist Party in Israel for the 'Algerization' of Israeli Arabs and the cutting off the Galilee from Israel.[9] The Soviet minister of culture had told Ambassador Aryeh Harel that the Kremlin would not reestablish cultural ties with Israel because culture and politics were directly connected. She claimed there was no problem concerning Soviet Jewish emigration, the Kremlin had permitted thousands of Jews to reach Israel through Poland and had created an autonomous Jewish region in Birobidzhan. The Soviet Union, Harel countered, had helped forty small ethnic groups foster their languages and culture, but not the Jews, and later told the foreign ministry he doubted that the Soviets had any interest in improving relations.[10]

The diplomatic impasse worsened. The Kremlin rejected the idea that the Arab refugee problem resulted from the Arabs' desire to destroy Israel and claimed to support repatriation because of the refugees' suffering and the Arab struggle against imperialism. Israel answered that history taught that no refugee problem had ever been solved by returning the displaced people to their homes, including White Russians exiled from the Soviet Union after the Bolshevik Revolution.[11] *Pravda* then attacked Israel's judicial system, claiming a conspiracy with the German government to stage the Eichmann trial.[12] Israel's image as a servant of US interests was so much a part of Soviet policy that it made it pointless for Israel to abstain in votes on issues such as admitting Communist China

---

7 Harel to Dagan, 'Soviet Middle Eastern Policy,' April 5, 1961, ISA 3322/19.
8 Israel Baer was a former officer in the IDF who was also a Soviet spy and was arrested in 1961, and who died in prison.
9 KFADC, June 29, 1961, ISA.
10 Harel to Dagan, 'Meeting with Minister of Culture Furtseva,' April 24, 1961, ISA 3332/1.
11 Bar-Haim to USD, 'Conversation with Borisov,' Soviet Embassy, Washington, May 1, 1961, Secret, ISA 3332/19.
12 Harel to Yahil and Dagan, June 30, 1961, Secret, ISA 2327/8. Adolf Eichmann was a Gestapo officer in charge of the expulsion of European Jews to their extermination. He was caught by Mossad, tried in Jerusalem and hanged in 1961.

to the UN. It was obvious that, as long as the Cold War continued, Jews would not be allowed to leave the Soviet Union.[13] Increasingly close ties between Israel and West Germany greatly worsened Israeli–Soviet relations.[14] Aryeh Levavi, the Israeli foreign ministry's Soviet expert, argued that the deterioration was caused by a clear and unambiguous Soviet analysis of the Cold War. Nasser might not turn into a Communist, he said, but he could still promote a socialist revolution.

The Soviets were trying to Russify their myriad ethnic groups. Its position was clear: coexistence, that is, peaceful competition, until the victory of Communism.[15] When a Yiddish-language Soviet journal, *Sovietish Heimland*, made its first appearance, Eshkol said there was not a trace of Jewish content in it.[16] Ambassador Harel, who had visited Birobidzhan, reported that Khrushchev had complained that Soviet Jews did not want to settle there and become farmers. Harel said it was not farming that repelled the Jews, there were tens of thousands of Jewish farmers in Israel.[17] However, he remained optimistic, believing that relations with the Soviets could improve through commercial and cultural exchanges. He claimed the Soviets were certain they would ultimately be victorious against the West, but felt the Communist regime would eventually metamorphose into a socialist welfare state. The differences between the two superpowers, he argued, would grow progressively smaller as long as war did not break out.[18]

Yakov Malik, the Soviet deputy foreign minister, warned Harel that relations would not improve because of demonstrations in Israel and the West in support of Soviet Jewry, anti-Soviet propaganda in synagogues and Ben-Gurion's declaration that the Kremlin feared that it would lose Arab support if Jews were allowed to emigrate to Israel. In addition, the director of the Near East desk of the Soviet Foreign Ministry warned that commercial and cultural relations with Israel would cause untold damage to the Soviet Union's relations with the Arabs.[19] The situation worsened after the arrest and trial of a group of Zionist activists in the summer of 1961. Levavi maintained that the Kremlin wanted to

13  B. Eliav to S. Avigur, N. Levanon and Z. Netser, November 3, 1961, ISA 4316/9.
14  Y. Herzog (Ottawa) to Levavi, October 18, 1961, Top Secret and Personal, ISA 4316/9.
15  Convention of Heads of Israeli Diplomats in Western Europe, Zurich, August 28, August 31, 1961, ISA 3420/17.
16  Israel Press Bureau, Information for the Press, Prime Minister's Reply to a Question by Hanna Zemer of Davar, December 2, 1961, ISA 5188/2.
17  Harel to Dagan, December 7, 1961, Confidential, Immediate, ISA 3349/1.
18  Harel to Bendor, 'Ideology in Brief,' December 4, 1061, ISA 3349/1.
19  Kissilev to Malik, December 13, 1961, in SDMEC 2: 372–4.

assimilate the Jews because Communist ideology denied the existence of a Jewish nation. In addition, the publication of Yevgeny Yevtushenko's poem 'Babi Yar,' which contradicted the official line and identified the victims of the Holocaust as Jews rather than Soviets, had not helped matters and was attacked at Communist Youth Movement rallies.[20]

Harel persevered, hoping against hope. Gromyko told him there were no real disputes between the two countries and Harel complained that there were no cultural and commercial relations.[21] Despite supporting the Arab states, he said, the Soviet Union had been moderate on the refugee question at the UN General Assembly. His optimism kept the foreign ministry from angering the Soviet Union by establishing diplomatic relations with maverick Albania. One foreign ministry official argued that the Sino-Soviet rupture had huge importance and would affect world history.[22] However, Israel had to face the truth. In early 1962, the Soviet labor union newspaper *Trud* accused the Israeli ambassador of spying for the United States. The article, 'Zionism: A Cover for Spies,' charged that three Israeli envoys had recruited twenty agents to spy on Arab countries.[23]

Israel was promised better relations with the Soviet Union on condition that Israel not vote against it in the UN or cooperate with the United States in rehabilitating West Germany. In return, the Soviet Union would keep the Arabs from attacking Israel. Once the Cold War ended, the Soviet Union might help solve Israel's dispute with the Arabs and allow its Jews to emigrate.[24] However, as far as the Israeli foreign ministry was concerned, the Soviet attitude was ambiguous and antagonistic to Zionism, although the Kremlin did seem to want correct relations with the Jewish state. Thus, some foreign ministry members maintained, Israel should respond in kind, advocating ties while urging Jews throughout the world to challenge the Soviet Union for its treatment of the Jews.[25]

Ben-Gurion saw any improvement in relations with the Soviet Union as overbalanced by its increasing support for Egypt. Not only did he reject advice to weaken Israel's ties with West Germany, he wanted

---

20 Y. Berger-Barzilai, 'Survey,' December, 11, 1961, ISA, 311/5.
21 Harel to Yahil and Dagan, January 3, 1962, ISA 3427/23.
22 Avidan to Eytan, 'Albania and the Deciphering of the Etruscan Language,' January 11, 1962, ISA 945/24.
23 KFADC, January 23, 1962, January 30, 1962, ISA (Yachil).
24 Avidan to the Chargé (Moscow), 'Sneh-Abramov Conversation, Soviet-Israeli Relations,' February 2, 1962, ISA 3427/23.
25 Avidan[?] to Sattath, February 15, 1962, ISA.

closer relations with it. Khrushchev, Harel insisted, wanted an East–West accommodation. The Soviets, he said, should not be faulted for annexing other regions because every great power sought to expand its sphere of influence. The article in *Trud* had been intended to frighten the Jews with no connection to relations with Israel. While official Soviet policy might oppose a Jewish national culture, the country's laws recognized a Jewish nationality, using it to mark its passports. Israel should be careful not to link the Soviet Jewry problem to the Cold War, Harel said.[26]

The Soviets accused Israel of not promoting East–West coexistence despite its global connections. Israel, they claimed, based its foreign policy on the assumption that restored colonialism would ensure its security and that war with the Arabs was inevitable. In addition, Israel overreacted to every instance of anti-Semitism in the Soviet Union – such as the crusade in the Israeli press against the 'pogrom' in Malakhovka in October 1959 (see Chapter 7), which the Soviets claimed had never occurred – because it did not want improved relations; mob attacks on American synagogues had been far worse.[27]

Returning to Israel, Harel proposed measures to improve relations with the Soviet Union, including recruiting wealthy American Jews to expand their commercial ties to the Soviet Union to end the boycott on trade, opposing arming West Germany with nuclear weapons and not using the Jewish issue against the Soviet Union during the Cold War.[28] However, as a member of the left-wing party (LeAhdut HaAvodah) he did not consider that such measures could only be taken with US support and the State Department encouraged only individuals and groups to protest Soviet activities against Jews and members of other nations.[29] He also disregarded the East–West disagreement over nuclear disarmament, in which the Soviets claimed the West would not disarm because the production of nuclear weapons was a mainstay of the capitalist economy.[30] In addition, he ignored the fundamental Soviet position of supporting Arab countries striving to shake off the shackles of imperialism and gain independence. Finally, he denied the principal bone of contention between Israel and the Soviet Union, that Zionism contradicted the fundamentals of Soviet ideology.

26  KFADC, March 15, 1962, March 19, 1962, ISA.
27  Conversation between MK S. Z. Abramov and Soviet Consul Abdinko, April 5, 1962, ISA 3427/23.
28  Harel to Meir, August 5, 1962, ISA 3427/23.
29  FRUS, 1961–1963, V: 456–9.
30  Tekoah to Levavi, 'Conversation with Tsarapkin,' August 28, 1962, Secret, ISA 3427/23.

Yosef Tekoah, the new Israeli ambassador to the Soviet Union, claimed the Soviets had a 'Jewish question complex.' He told Soviet leaders that the long-suffering Jewish people were sensitive to the fate of their fellow Jews.[31] The major obstacle was Nasser, who as a Soviet lackey was trying to expel the West from the Middle East.[32] Soviet support for national liberation movements in the Third World was then at its height and it gradually became clear that there was little chance for a change in the Soviet position.[33] Despite the urgency of the Soviet Jewry question, the arms race continued as the core issue between Israel and the Soviet Union. Radio Moscow termed the shipments of Hawk missiles to Israel a dangerous and provocative act. *Izvestia* reported that, at the height of the Cuban Missile Crisis, American experts had gone to Israel to oversee twelve missile bases.[34] On December 13, 1962, Khrushchev had boasted that the Cuban crisis had ended with a Communist victory, as Soviet officials and the Communist press continued attacking Israel.[35]

Even as the United States and the Soviet Union faced a stalemate, the campaign for Soviet Jewry scored a success. In February 1963, *Izvestia* published correspondence between Khrushchev and Bertrand Russell, who raised the issue of Soviet treatment of the Jews. Khrushchev denied there was anti-Semitism in the Soviet Union and continued claiming they had offered the Jews an opportunity to switch to productive professions and even to have their own country, but they had refused.[36]

Ben-Gurion perceived that preventing Jewish immigration to Israel meant continued Arab support for the Soviets. The Soviet Union sold arms to Nasser to keep him dependent on them for spare parts and ammunition, and that in itself would help the Kremlin destroy Israel if and when it was ready to do so.[37] The reconstituted UAR of Egypt, Syria and Iraq was announced on April 17, 1963. Ben-Gurion wrote to Khrushchev that, while it was an internal Arab matter, the founding charter of the federation included an article on the 'liberation of Palestine,' which was equivalent to the destruction of Israel. The Soviet Union's commitment to peaceful coexistence had to apply to

---

31  Tekoah to DEE, September 3, 1962, Secret, ISA 3427/23.
32  Levavi at Convention of Israeli Diplomats in Western Europe, Zurich, Second Session, September 15, 1962, ISA 3420/17.
33  KFADC, January 1, 1963, January 8, 1963.
34  Meir-Bodrov Conversation, December 28, 1962, Secret, SDMEC 2: 392–3.
35  Tekoah to Yachil, December 20, 1962, Secret, 3427/21, ISA.
36  A. Eshel (Rio de Janeiro) to LAD Director, Conversation with the Soviet Ambassador in Brazil, Andrei A. Fomin, May 10, 1963, ISA 3426/23.
37  KFADC, March 27, 1963, ISA.

the Middle East as well, Ben-Gurion argued. Khrushchev ignored the letter.[38]

In May 1963, Khrushchev wrote to the heads of the Mediterranean states to propose a nuclear-free region with the United States and the Soviet Union granting joint security guarantees. The West regarded the move as an attempt to weaken the United States and NATO, while Ben-Gurion felt that Khrushchev was retreating into Stalinism and the letter was another example of Soviet hypocrisy. He hoped Israel could establish ties with China, which, he predicted, would become the world's major power in fifteen years.[39] He told the Knesset that he hoped the superpowers would guarantee regional nuclear disarmament. At a secret cabinet meeting, he called Khrushchev hypocritical and deceitful because the Soviet Union demanded disarmament from everyone except itself. It was futile to ask Khrushchev why he provided Egypt with bombers that could reach Tel Aviv with ten tons of explosives in three and half minutes. The key to Soviet relations with Israel, he said, was its Cold War interests.[40] In the larger context, there was no chance that the Kremlin would stop supplying Egypt with Soviet weapons, it was just doing business, no different from Israel supplying arms and uniforms to West Germany's army.[41]

Golda Meir acknowledged that Israel had nothing to gain from East–West tensions because it had no nuisance value,[42] but détente did not mean ignoring Soviet Jewry. On the contrary, it should be considered one of the world's three largest issues, along with racism in the United States and the last vestiges of colonialism. Israel should not, however, give even the slightest impression that it wanted the issue of Soviet Jewry on the international agenda to sabotage détente. Israel remained disappointed with the State Department, which claimed that reports were greatly exaggerated and the situation of the Jews was satisfactory. If the Jews were suffering, it was because of local issues, not official policy, which was to erase ethnic and religious distinctions by assimilating all its minorities into the Soviet Communist majority.[43]

---

38  Ben-Gurion to Soviet Prime Minister [May 9, 1963], May 13, 1963, ISA 3427/23.
39  ICAB, May 26, 1963, June 2, 1963, ISA.
40  KR 37: 1822–4 (May 13, 1963).
41  Hanan Gior, Military Attaché (Rangoon) to DEE Director, Meeting with Military Attaché, Soviet Embassy, Tokyo, May 25, 1963 [May 17, 1963], Confidential, ISA 3427/23.
42  KFADC, August 6, 1963, ISA.
43  Yahil to Heads of IDF, Soviet Jews, September 1, 1963, Secret, ISA 750/20.

Nonetheless, the Middle East arms race remained Israel's worst headache. Gromyko told Michael Comay, Israel's ambassador to the UN, that the Arabs needed Soviet arms to ward off imperialism. His excuse for the Soviet veto of a Security Council resolution condemning the murder of two unarmed Israeli farmers in Almagor by Syrian soldiers (August 20) was that 'in border incidents justice is not only with those who are killed.'[44]

The Israeli cabinet was skeptical of the possibility of improving relations with the Soviet Union because Israel would continue pressing the Kremlin about Soviet Jewry. Eban claimed that, as long as the Arab–Israeli conflict continued, the Soviet position would remain unchanged. It was also generally feared that the longer Soviet Jews remained in the Soviet Union, the greater the danger they would assimilate. Eshkol suggested voting with rather than against the Soviet Union at the UN, but Eban said there had been very few such opportunities, only the Hungarian revolution and the admission of Communist China into the UN, neither of which had softened the Soviet position toward Israel. Shaul Avigur, the head of Nativ (the Israeli secret agency in charge of emigration from Eastern Europe), insisted that, as long as the Cold War continued, there was no solution to the issue of Soviet Jewry.[45]

Israel's relations with the Soviet Union improved superficially. Israeli musicians visited the Soviet Union and Israel imported Russian furs, and the two countries exchanged technical expertise and delegations from the diamond industry. In addition, Israeli ships were allowed to anchor at Russian ports and tourism increased. Some families were reunited and a new Israeli embassy was built in Moscow. The cabinet believed, however, that the complete assimilation of the Jews was still part of Kremlin policy and that votes at the UN made no difference, only a global demand would make it allow its Jews to emigrate.[46] The issue was considered crucial for the future of Israel because, except for in the United States, there were no large reservoirs of Jews. Avigur desired that Israel's population should reach a critical mass of 4–5 million. However, the Kremlin was placing enormous pressure on Soviet Jews to assimilate, with attendant demoralization. The Soviet goal was to make its Jews hate everything Jewish, including the State of Israel.

44 Comay (New York) to Y. Herzog and Levavi, October 3, 1963, Secret and Personal, ISA 3427/23.
45 Sareinu (Mapai Ministers' Caucus), October 31, 1953, 7921/9/1.
46 Tekoah to Meir et al., 'Israel-Soviet Union, Summary,' December 6, 1963, ISA 3427/23.

The Kremlin had not restrained anti-Semitism in the local press, especially in the Ukraine, shocking public figures like Bertrand Russell and Jean-Paul Sartre. Jewish immigration would have to be fought for and it was uncertain whether détente would help. The Soviet Union's failing economy could lead to chaos, where the Jews would become the victims of a bloodbath.[47]

After the signing of the Nuclear Test Ban Treaty, Khushchev proposed an agreement for resolving urgent international crises. The imperialists, he claimed, fomented territorial disputes, while the use of force was the sacred right of peoples liberating themselves from colonial rule. The enormous changes in the international order had instilled the idea of coexistence in countries with different social regimes and Leninist foreign policy had adopted it as well.[48] Meir, meanwhile, noted that he made no reference to Israel. She said Israel had no illusions that world leaders would convene, commit to throwing down their arms, and the Messiah would arrive. What if Israel disarmed and there was a pro-Nasser coup in Jordan or Syria? If the Arabs attacked Israel, Khrushchev would simply say that his proposal did not apply to Israel because the Soviet Union recognized only the 1947 partition borders.[49]

The Arab summit conference in Cairo (January 13–16, 1964) introduced a new dynamic into the Arab–Israeli conflict by voting to promote an alternative to Israel's proposed national water carrier. Nasser told the summit that there would be no immediate war with Israel, but nevertheless a joint command was set up, headed by an Egyptian general. The Palestinian problem now became the pan-Arab strategic focus.[50] The Soviet embassy in Israel sought to reassure the Israeli leadership that Soviet policy supported the status quo, and Radio Moscow's Arabic-language program had warned the summit participants not to undertake hostile acts. The Israeli foreign ministry instructed Israeli diplomats merely to express hope that the Soviet Union would not aid Arab aggression.[51]

However, deterioration in Israeli–Soviet relations seemed unavoidable. The Soviet embassy told Israel that if it wanted better relations it should

---

47 KFADC, December 31, 1963, January 7, 1964, ISA (Avigur and Eliav).
48 Avidan to IMM, 'Khrushchev–Eshkol Letters,' January 3, 1964 [5], Confidential, ISA 7228/6a.
49 KFADC, January 14, 1964, January 20, 1964, ISA.
50 Sela, 1982: 26–37.
51 Avidan to Tekoah and IDEEM, Eshkol's Reply to Khrushchev's Letter, January 24, 1964, ISA 311/5; Govrin, 1998: 230–2; on the Cairo summit, see Rabin in KFADC, 28 January, 1964, ISA.

stop disseminating anti-Soviet propaganda. The anti-Jewish activities in the Soviet Union were explained as part of the regime's general campaign against religion, including Islam and Christianity.[52] The Israeli foreign ministry claimed that even though 310 Soviet Jews had emigrated to Israel in 1963, as opposed to seven in 1959, official discrimination in the Soviet Union had become worse. The Jews were slandered in the Soviet press as parasites who worshiped the golden calf and hatched nefarious plots. The solution would be to have the two blocs remove the Middle East from the Cold War.[53]

Israel decided to increase pressure on the Kremlin. It released a series of news items about religious discrimination, including the desecration of Jewish cemeteries.[54] The Israeli embassy in Moscow pressed the US embassy to declare that the prohibition against baking *matzot* (unleavened bread) for Passover was not an internal Soviet matter. The US position, which Israel wanted to change, was that any US involvement in the issue of the Soviet Jews would only harm them because they were already suspected of being American agents.[55]

Israel reckoned that the position of Soviet Jews had worsened in the wake of the appearance of Trofim Kichko's violently anti-Semitic book 'Judaism Without Embellishment,' published in Kiev by the Ukrainian Academy for Science in 1963, and withdrawn from circulation by Khrushchev. Meir said that the cartoons it contained were worse than those that appeared in the notorious Nazi tabloid *Der Stürmer*. One showed Ben-Gurion erasing the 'Thou Shall Not Kill' from the Ten Commandments.[56]

Eshkol feared that, given the current poor relations, Khrushchev might send missiles and military personnel to Egypt. The Kremlin applauded when Nasser and the Algerian leader Ahmed Ben Bella supported the 'liberation of Palestine,' so Israel's preparations for deterrence and possibly a war should not have surprised Khrushchev.[57]

Khrushchev visited Egypt for three weeks in May, during which he attended the inauguration of the Aswan Dam. He promised Nasser a loan, agricultural equipment, continued military assistance and support

---

52 Levavi to Avidan, 'S. Z. Abramov-Lichachev Conversation,' March 18, 1964, ISA 3573/19.
53 Avidan in DEE, March 19, 1964, ISA 3573/19.
54 Cable from IMM, April 5, 1964, ISA 7228/7.
55 Agmon (Moscow) to DEE, 'USA Position Concerning the Soviet Jewry Problem,' April 6, 1964, Secret, ISA 3575/4.
56 KFADC, 18 February, 1964, ISA; Ben-Gurion, 16 June, 1964, ISA.
57 Eshkol in KFADC, April 20, 1964, ISA.

for the Arab struggle against imperialism, using the Arab refugee issue to increase tension. Meir asked the Soviet ambassador, Mikhail Bodrov, if that were consistent with the Soviet claim that it supplied arms only for self-defense.[58] Bodrov answered that she was exaggerating the significance of Khrushchev's visit.[59]

The Soviets also defended Egypt's employment of German scientists, claiming the Soviet Union did not intervene in the internal affairs of other countries. Given Israel's aggression and receipt of Hawk missiles, the Soviets maintained, the Arabs needed defensive weapons. Furthermore, it claimed, the Cairo summit proved that the Arab countries sought peace and that the Soviet Union would support Israel's national water carrier only within an international framework and with Arab consent.[60] Soviet reports of Khrushchev's visit were ambiguous. Nasser, they claimed, would enjoy Soviet support if he restricted the West's reach into the Arab world. The Soviet Union would be the first to stop Egypt if it attacked Israel, which had a powerful military and could be certain of US support.[61] Returning from Egypt, Khrushchev told the Soviet leadership that Nasser was a true progressive and the Arabs should be offered additional weapons.[62]

Khrushchev's visit unsettled the Israeli government and convinced it that the time had come to put the issue of Soviet Jewry on the international agenda. There was a severe economic crisis in the Soviet Union, a rupture between the Soviets and China, and Communist parties in the West were rebelling against Soviet control. Khrushchev should be told to allow more family reunification and to grant his country's Jews more autonomy.[63] Avigur proposed that Israel openly link the issue of Soviet Jews to the Cold War as part of strengthening détente. What was needed, he said, was criticism that could be translated into political strength.[64] The issue of Soviet Jewry was currently being discussed in

58 Avidan to IMM, 'Meir-Bodrov Conversation,' May 13, 1964, ISA, 7936/1a; SDMEC 2: 426–7; Beeley (Cairo) to Butler, 'Visit of the Soviet Prime Minister to the UAR,' June 4, 1964, Confidential, NA FO371/178589/VG103138/19.
59 Eliezer Livneh to Eshkol, 'Conversation with Counselor Lichachev,' [21] May 25, 1964, Top Secret, ISA 7936/1a.
60 Agmon to DEE, 'Meeting with Acting Head of the Near East Department in the Soviet Foreign Ministry,' May 19, 1964, ISA 3574/9.
61 H. Bar-On, Counselor, Washington to Levavi, 'Conversation with Counselor Lukianov,' June 23, 1964, Secret, ISA 7936/1a; cf. G. Meir in ICAB, May 18, 1964, May 31, ISA.
62 Fursenko and Naftali, 1997: 531.
63 Netzer (Bar) to Peled (London), 'Soviet Jewry Problem,' May 14, 1964, ISA 750/20.
64 Tekoah to Yahil, June 1, 1964, ISA 5373/19.

the UN and Western governments were aware of its importance. During a visit to Denmark, Khrushchev continued to deny that there was a Jewish problem in the Soviet Union. Half of his friends were Jews, he declared, and he had never heard of any Jewish problem. He also said that Nasser had not listened to him in the past and had been defeated, and he was certain the Egyptian leaders would be more cautious in the future. When asked whether he had conditioned the supply of arms on Egypt not using them against Israel, he answered that the sale had been commercial, not political. Asked whether his warning that force not be used to resolve conflicts also applied to Israel, he said no, Israel's leaders were Zionist nationalists and American lackeys.[65] According to one source, Khrushchev's visit to Egypt had redoubled the anti-Semitism in the Soviet Union, increasing the fears of Soviet Jews and their desires to emigrate. Jews from Kiev remembered Khrushchev's hatred of them after World War II when he was Communist Party Secretary in the Ukraine, and called him a pig.[66]

About to return from the Soviet Union, Tekoah said the issue of Soviet Jewry was far greater than the Arab–Israeli conflict and that the situation of the Jews in the Soviet Union was tragic. The regime wanted to deprive them of their religious identity, and anti-Semitism and discrimination, particularly academic discrimination, were rampant and increasing, and Kremlin policy was designed to eliminate the Jewish people in the Soviet Union as a collective body. However, there were encouraging signs. Every appearance by an Israeli performer turned into a huge Jewish demonstration, and a Russian–Hebrew dictionary and an anthology of Hebrew poetry had been published. Furthermore, he noted, the Sino-Soviet conflict was worsening and the Kremlin might seek a long-term alliance with the West. East–West détente might not include a solution to Israel's problems or those of Soviet Jews, but the issues should not be ignored. Kremlin policies were founded on practical and pragmatic rather than ideological considerations, Tekoah maintained, including its policies toward Nasser. A more flexible Israeli policy could lead to a satisfactory solution for the Jewish issue and, if the gates were opened, the 750,000 Jews in the Baltic States, western Ukraine and Moldova would emigrate to Israel.[67]

65 Levin (Copenhagen) to Levavi and Bar, June 26, 1964, ISA 4094/14; KFADC, 30 June, 1964, ISA (Meir).
66 Yaakov Yanai, 'Conversation with MK A. Goldstein on his Visit to the Soviet Union,' July 14, 1964, ISA 7228/7a.
67 KFADC, August 17, 1964, ISA.

In point of fact, the Soviet leadership's main concern was not the Jews but the fear that NATO would deploy nuclear weapons in West Germany. Bodrov, for example, argued that the German threat against the Soviet Union was no less serious than Nasser's threat to Israel. Yet it was still not clear whether Khrushchev meant to include the Middle East in his proposal to resolve all border disputes by peaceful means.[68] Meir, optimistically for a while, believed that the Soviet Union would support the Arabs openly, even if Khrushchev did not seek to destroy Israel.[69]

From Israel's point of view, the test of improved relations remained a solution for Soviet Jews. Israel needed a fundamental change in Soviet policy toward the Jews as part of the US negotiations with the Kremlin. US Supreme Court Justice Arthur Goldberg called for unrelenting public pressure, but noted that the American Jewish public was paralyzed, divided as it was among twenty-four different organizations. Tekoah argued that Israel could help the Soviets through an exchange of scientific knowledge and could offer economic support. Eshkol opposed, saying the Arabs would object and Khrushchev would prevent Jews from leaving. The issue had to be moved from Israel to the international diplomatic stage.[70] Khrushchev should recognize that the Jewish issue was delicate and important, and that he had to address it personally. Israel's ambassador to Washington said that President Johnson should tell Khrushchev that the issue was detrimental to détente.[71] Meanwhile, Bodrov continued to maintain that Soviet Jews had voluntarily chosen Russian culture and intermarriage.[72]

When Khrushchev was ousted in October 1964, decision-makers in Israel found themselves at a dead end. So far 460 Soviet Jews had come to Israel, compared with 72 in 1963. The cabinet ministers differed over how much pressure should be placed on the Kremlin, deciding in the end that Israel emphasize the fact that the Soviet constitution explicitly outlawed anti-Semitism. In the short term, raising the issue of Soviet Jewry in moral terms would not change Soviet policy. Hope lay only in improved relations between the superpower blocs. The focus should be on family reunification, using the slogan 'let my people go.' Eshkol agreed without hesitation.[73]

68 Eliezer Doron, DEE Director to Tekoah, 'Conversation with the Soviet Ambassador and his Adviser,' August 5, 1964, Secret, ISA 7227/7a.
69 KFADC, September 22, 1964, ISA.
70 [Session on] 'Soviet Jewry,' Eshkol, Meir, Avigur et al., September 2, 1964, ISA 7938/5a.
71 Harman to Levavi, September 9, 1964, ISA 3566/28.
72 Eshkol–Namir Conversation, October 5, 1964, ISA 7933/4a; SDMEC 2: 441–3.
73 [Session on] Soviet Jewry, October 14, 1964, Eshkol, Meir, B. Eliav, etc., ISA 7938/5a.

During the last four years of Khrushchev's tenure, Israel focused its diplomacy with the Soviet Union largely on the issue of Soviet Jewry rather than on Soviet involvement in the Middle East. Israel, small and isolated, could not change US foreign policy once the Soviets had made it clear that there could be no resolution of the Arab–Israeli conflict that did not include Turkey and Iran. Trapped, Israel directed its efforts toward promoting the religious and cultural equality of Soviet Jews and accelerating the pace at which Soviet Jews were allowed to emigrate to Israel. It was clear that only East–West détente could thaw the Jewish issue, which motivated Israel's pressure on Presidents Kennedy and Johnson. The Israeli government, despite its desire not to get entangled in the Cold War, had no choice but to use it to promote the issue of Soviet Jewry.

# 12

# Was Johnson the 'father' of the US–Israeli alliance?: the Memorandum of Understanding (1964–65)

President Johnson wrote to Prime Minister Eshkol in January 1964 extolling the close relations between the two countries and expressing hope for continued mutual understanding. He also mentioned issues on which they differed, including Israel's security, regional stability and the Arab refugees.[1] Israel replied that the balance of power was its number one priority and had prompted its request for military aid. Israel's ambassador to Washington, Harman, said that Israel had to replace at least 300 of its tanks with more advanced models to keep its deterrent edge. Rusk repeated his previous claim that anti-tank weapons had rendered tanks irrelevant, as happened to the cavalry. The State Department was concerned that an escalating missile race in the Middle East would threaten US security.[2] Komer, the NSC senior staff member in charge of the Middle East, rejected Israel's requests for modern weapons, claiming it had no real reason to fear Egypt because even with Soviet tanks Nasser had no realistic military option and his army was still inferior to Israel's.[3]

John Badeau, the US ambassador to Cairo, worked energetically to sabotage closer American relations with Israel, noting that Egypt was vital to US interests. A dramatic American step taken in Israel's favor, such as imposing a solution on the Arab–Israeli conflict or halting aid to Egypt would not be effective. Egypt was refraining from becoming a Soviet satellite because of its cognizance of Western interests and economic aid it was receiving from the United States.[4]

1 FRUS, 1964–1968, XVIII: 1–2.
2 FRUS, 1964–1968, XVIII: 3–6; Gazit, Rodger Davies, 'Israel Request for Tanks, Missiles and Naval Equipment,' January 3, 1964, Secret, NARA, NEA/Ne RG 59, Box 6.
3 FRUS, 1964–1968, XVIII: 6–7.
4 John Badeau to the President, Group 3 – Downgraded at 12-year Intervals, January 3, 1964, Secret, NARA, RG 84, NEA/NE, Box 6.

Badeau was quite influential in Washington, but not exclusively. National Security Advisor McGeorge Bundy emphasized the low quality of Egypt's anti-tank weapons. Israel needed new tanks, he said, but why give them away ('grant in aid') when Israel was buying surface-to-surface missiles from France?[5]

Moreover, the State Department feared that the Arab reaction to Israel's nuclear potential, the diversion of the Jordan River and the Kremlin's exploitation of the refugee issue would be detrimental to the US position in the Middle East. Rusk thought it would be best to give Israel tanks to stop it from pressing for security guarantees. The State Department, intransigent, felt that the 'special partnership' Israel was seeking would promote stronger Arab–Soviet ties and reduce the United States' ability to work for peace. Cold War tensions in the Middle East had been reduced only because the United States had balanced its own interests with those of Israel's security. The Arabs might not be capable of confronting Israel, but they were liable to bring catastrophe on themselves. The State Department also believed that the United States could oversee the Israeli nuclear program.

The Johnson administration had strategic reservations regarding Israel because its appetite appeared greater than its needs. Rusk claimed the United States had to stop the arms race, declare again that it would defend any country that was attacked and receive assurance from Israel that in exchange for the tanks it would not waste money on sophisticated missiles or nuclear weapons. The United States, he said, should also reconsider the refugee question and persuade Nasser to keep his conflict with Israel in low gear.[6]

On January 13–16, 1964, the Arab summit meeting in Cairo had decided to establish a joint military command and threaten an economic boycott of countries supporting aggression. Displeased and worried, Israel's leaders assumed that they could depend on the United States, particularly on the Sixth Fleet.[7] The damage would be enormous if even half of Egypt's 500 surface-to-surface missiles hit their targets, but only at the outbreak of a war, otherwise they were mainly a deterrent. The Cairo summit's threat to act against the diversion of the Jordan River reflected the Soviet threat, but Israel feared the world would view it as incitement to war.[8]

---

5 FRUS, 1964–1968, XVIII: 11–16; Harman to Eshkol and Meir, January, 10, 1964, Top Secret, ISA 7935/5a.
6 FRUS, 1964–1968, XVIII: 18–23.
7 ICAB, December 29, 1963 (Meir), ISA; KFADC, January 20, 1964 (Meir), ISA.
8 Rabin in KFADC, January 28, 1964, ISA.

The State Department, however, was not concerned about the Cairo summit, it was more worried by Israel's missiles and nuclear development. It was also unmoved by the American Jewish community's criticism of US policy toward Israel, which argued that the United States should unreservedly support the Jewish state because they shared values of democracy, humanitarianism and progress. More important was Nasser's declaration that Israel's nuclear weapons were a casus belli for Egypt, even if a war were suicidal, and he needed reassurance to dissuade him from purchasing Soviet weapons.[9] Americans inspected the Dimona facility in January 1964 and reported it was currently not capable of producing weapons. Komer, however, maintained that long-term Middle East escalation was inevitable because of the danger inherent in the missiles France was selling to Israel, which, he implied, could carry nuclear warheads.[10]

The Johnson administration had to decide whether to supply Israel with new tanks. US officials believed it would be preferable to postpone the decision to shortly before the presidential election to ensure that Israel, having obtained the tanks, not make further demands when the President would find it politically inexpedient to refuse. President Johnson was convinced that Israel needed new tanks and authorized their sale.[11] Predictably, Badeau asked that the decision be reconsidered. Egypt, he felt, would not respond to the tank sale with the same restraint it had shown regarding the Hawk missiles, because tanks were offensive weapons. Supplying Israel with tanks would give the Soviet Union an excuse to penetrate Libya, Jordan and Saudi Arabia, exploiting the conflict as a tactical tool in the East–West conflict. The sale of tanks was tantamount to a US military commitment to Israel and endangered US regional interests.[12] The United States would lose standing in the Arab world if the tanks were sold simultaneously with the diversion of the Jordan River, and the ensuing crisis would be more severe than Nasser's nationalizing of the Suez Canal.[13]

---

9 Rodger Davies to Phillips Talbot and John Jernegan, 'Speech before American Jewish Committee,' February 10, 1964, Confidential, NARA, RG 59, NE/NEA.
10 FRUS, 1964–1968, XVIII: 29–31; Komer to Jernegan, 'The UAR Israeli Missile Problem,' February 13, 1964, Secret, NARA, RG 59, NE/NEA.
11 FRUS, 1964–1968, XVIII: 31–6.
12 Badeau to Department of State, 'The United Arab Republic and American Tanks for Israel,' February 20, 1964, Secret, NARA, RG 59, NEA/NE, POL 1, ISR, UAR.
13 Dean Rusk, Memorandum for the President, March 4, 1964, NARA, RG 59, NEA/NE, Box 6.

Eban told Rusk that the tank sale would be symbolic rather than practical, since the tanks would not actually be supplied in the near future. The sale would show the United States' determination to counter aggression. Rusk told him that no treaty obligated automatic US support of its allies, and Eban answered that was exactly why Israel needed an independent military force. Bundy, also present, rejected Eban's suggestion for joint planning. The US goal, he said, was to keep nuclear weapons out of the Middle East.[14]

Myer Feldman, Deputy Special Counsel to the President, was sent to persuade Israel to cancel the purchase of French surface-to-surface missiles and help it find an alternative supplier of tanks. He was chosen because he was the closest person in the administration to both Israel and the Jewish community, but was first and foremost loyal to the President. If he were unsuccessful, the Arabs might launch an anti-Israeli, anti-American propaganda campaign, pressure Western oil companies working in the Middle East to renegotiate their concessions and revoke Western commercial flights and military privileges in the Arab world. He recommended to President Johnson that the United States ensure that Israel received the tanks it needed. Israel had already purchased ninety tanks from Britain, but American tanks were the best available and they needed to be supplied before the balance of forces was altered.[15]

The US administration dismissed Nasser's anti-Israel speech on February 22, claiming that Arab leaders had to verbally attack Israel to stay in power. The Cairo summit had shown that Nasser was realistic and moderate, the administration claimed, and, while Israel's security depended on the United States' ability and willingness to halt aggression, there was no such thing as total security, not even Americans enjoyed that.[16] Intelligence had shown that the Egyptian missiles were not operational and that Israel was exaggerating their potential damage. Komer complained to Johnson that Israel ignored the fact that the French missiles were hugely expensive and ineffective. There could be no doubt that the United States was determined to prevent the destruction of the Jewish state, but a formal guarantee would send the Arabs to Moscow for help, eventually leading to a situation more threatening to Israel. US–Israeli relations could not be unilateral, he warned. US responsibility for Israel's security gave it a legitimate voice in determining Israeli policy.

14 FRUS, 1964–1968, XVIII: 50–2, 61–4; cf. ICAB, March 22, 1964 (Eban), ISA.
15 FRUS, 1964–1968, XVIII: 66–72; Dean Rusk, 'Memorandum for the President, Mr. Feldman's Mission to Israel,' March 4, 1964, NARA, NEA/NE, Box 6.
16 FRUS, 1964–1968, XVIII: 73–5, 114–21.

With the exception of the Suez Crisis in 1956, the United States had systematically taken a pro-Israel stance. The Israelis were aware of that and expressed doubts solely to bargain. Israel had no reason to complain about US aid. So far it had received about a billion dollars, in comparison to Egypt's $880 million. A public commitment would not offer any more of a deterrent than already existed, he told Johnson.[17]

Israel warned Feldman that deterrents were necessary in the fact of a growing Arab threat. Feldman responded that missiles would have no effect, Israel would not receive tanks for free and should buy them from West Germany. Eshkol told him that Egypt's fighter bombers, navy and armored corps gave it military superiority, and its missiles could be improved. In an Egyptian offensive, Eshkol predicted, the United States would submit a complaint to the UN and wait for a Soviet response as Israelis died. Eshkol acknowledged that the United States had the best of intentions, but that Nasser had not abandoned belligerence. Komer regarded Eshkol's determination to acquire missiles as confirmation of Israel's desire for a nuclear deterrent. Five hundred new tanks in Israel, he said, would increase Arab suspicions and offer the Soviets new openings.[18]

The US embassy in Israel told the Soviets that the United States had no proof Israel intended to develop atomic weapons, but that matters could change if Egypt persisted in making threats. The Soviets responded with global demands. They wanted Germany neutralized, criticized the American Polaris missile program, because the submarines could carry nuclear missiles, and noted US military superiority. Furthermore, general disarmament was preferable to regional weapons control, because the United States itself believed that hostilities might break out before Washington and Moscow could reach an agreement.[19] According to the State Department, the Egyptian missiles made Israel anxious because of the East–West stalemate on arms control. The Israelis asserted that the Soviet Union was pampering Nasser, the United States was giving him aid, he had three to four times as many tanks and airfields as Israel, and was rumored to have ordered material to construct a dirty nuclear bomb.[20]

Yitzhak Rabin, Israel's new chief of staff, warned that the Arabs could easily start a war with a Middle Eastern Pearl Harbor. While the Israeli

17 FRUS, 1964–1968, XVIII: 76–8.
18 FRUS, 1964–1968, XVIII: 89–90.
19 Stephen Palmer to Earl Russell, Officer in Charge, Lebanon-Israel Affairs, (1), April 12, 1964, Secret, NARA, RG 59, NEA/NE, Box 8.
20 ICAB, April 18, 1964 (Eshkol); KFADC, April 20, 1964 (Meir), ISA.

air force would be the determining factor in the war, Israel still needed a deterrent. Little wonder that Eshkol exclaimed, 'Let me die with Philistines!', while Dayan observed that the cabinet was 'melancholic.'[21] However, the United States was afraid Nasser would panic over the nuclear issue and ask the Soviets to install nuclear missiles on Egyptian soil operated by Soviet personnel. That would leave the United States with no option, making it essential to prevent the Middle East arms race from escalating to the nuclear level.[22]

The US ambassador to Beirut, Armin Meyer, warned against an all-out arms race that could lead to a US–Soviet confrontation. He also proposed that Israel accept Joseph Johnson's plan for resolving the refugee problem, which would ensure that Israel did not have to absorb a large number. If Israel wanted to survive in the Middle East, he said, the plan was preferable to the 'fortress' concept because the refugee problem was the largest factor in the Arab–Israeli conflict.[23]

The US administration tried to achieve a stable regional balance. King Hussein of Jordan complained that the diversion of the Jordan River would enable Israel to absorb more immigrants, threatening the Arabs. President Johnson responded that the current allocation of the Jordan's waters, according to Johnston's plan was fair. Hussein also failed to persuade McNamara that the Soviet Union had offered him both diplomatic relations and an opportunity to purchase combat jets inexpensively.[24] The administration knew Jordan had nothing to bargain with, but it understood the Arab fear that more immigration would induce Israel to seek to annex further territory.[25]

Feldman, accompanied by Deputy Assistant Secretary of Defense Frank Sloan, was sent to Israel to inform the Israeli government that the tank deal had been canceled. Komer told Feldman that the Arabs knew the United States would help Israel if it were attacked, but that its policies had to appear balanced. The United States would help Israel purchase tanks from Britain and Germany and would supply artillery and new engines for the German tanks. The Jewish lobby unsuccessfully tried

21 KFADC, April 21, 1964 (Rabin), ISA; ICAB, 10 May 1964 (Eshkol), ISA.
22 William Polk to Walt Rostow, Department of State, Policy Planning Council, 'Our Policy Toward the UAR,' April 7, 1964, Secret, in Rostow, Memorandum for the President, April 14, 1964, Secret, NARA, RG 59, NEA/NE, Box 1.
23 Meyer to Secretary of State, 'U.S. Arms to Israel,' April 9, 1964 Secret, LBJL, NSF, Box 138.
24 FRUS, 1964–1968, XVIII: 90–101.
25 Bar-Haim (Washington) to USD Director, 'Levavi-Talbot Conversation,' [21] April 22, 1964, ISA 3502/1.

to convince the US administration to supply American tanks directly to Israel.[26] Feldman met with Eshkol, Meir and Peres and told them that the deal had been canceled in anticipation of the Arab response to the Jordan River diversion project and an Arab demand for Soviet arms.

The two most sensitive points in US–Israeli relations remained the French surface-to-surface missiles and Israel's alleged nuclear arms program. The Americans were worried that the combination of the missiles and possible nuclear weapons could lead Nasser to launch a preemptive attack with unfortunate consequences for US–Israeli relations. Komer claimed that Israel felt it was under siege, which created a 'fortress' mentality.[27] The US administration, understanding Israel's need for reassurance after Khrushchev's visit to Egypt, granted $10 million a year for the purchase of tanks from West Germany.[28] The United States could not accede to every Israeli request, doing so would endanger US interests and its covert initiatives for weapons inspections, resulting in further East–West polarization.[29] The State Department maintained that Egypt bore most of the responsibility for the escalation, but that Israel had also contributed by purchasing missiles. If Soviet missiles were deployed in Egypt, the US military burden in the region would be greater. A regional balance of power was essential to obviate the acquisition of more missiles and nuclear weapons.[30]

President Johnson invited Eshkol officially to visit the United States (June 1–3, 1964). He told Eshkol that he was unreservedly committed to Israel's security and that the United States would be a presence wherever it was needed. The United States, he said, would help Israel obtain tanks through a third party. The JCS maintained that Israel was militarily superior to Egypt, which would not be a threat until 1970. However, Johnson asked why Israel refused to allow inspection by the IAEA, which would reassure Nasser. Eshkol, he said, could rest assured that the United States had both a moral and a financial obligation to Israel. Eshkol answered that Khrushchev's visit had granted Nasser prestige, arms and money. Nasser could easily attack without Khrushchev's consent and against

26 McGeorge Bundy to the President, 'Special Heads for the States,' February 5, 1965, Secret, LBJL, NSF, Box 26.
27 FRUS, 1964–1968, XVIII: 124–39, 147–51.
28 Russell, Memorandum for the President, 'Visit of Israeli Prime Minister Eshkol,' May 27, 1964, Secret, NARA, RG 59, NEA/NE, Box 6.
29 Background Paper, 'Israel's Security Concerns,' Secret, May 28, 1964, NARA, RG 59, NEA/NE.
30 Background Paper, 'Near East Arms Race,' Secret, May 28, 1964, Drafted by Russell, NARA, RG 59, NEA/NE.

American wishes, and wreak extensive damage in a matter of days. He said that Nasser intended to produce hundreds of missiles and would be able to attack within two to three years. Israel, he emphasized, could not allow itself to lose a war and the Jewish people would not permit the rise of another Hitler. He asked Johnson to offer public support for Israel, as Khrushchev had done for Egypt. Nasser did not need to know what was going on in Dimona. Did he tell Johnson about his missiles? However, Eshkol was pleased by his meeting with the President. He felt that a lasting connection and true mutual trust had been established.[31] Feldman remarked that Johnson's position derived from his instinctive feeling that Israel was a Western democracy. He had an aversion to anti-Western Arab countries and to the term 'neutralism.'[32]

Peres conferred with US Air Force Chief of Staff General Curtis LeMay and Assistant Secretary of Defense Cyrus Vance. Eshkol noted the psychological importance of joint planning, but LeMay maintained that there was no need for it. Israel could choose the targets and the United States would hit them. The United States distrusted and feared ambiguous situations and was carefully monitoring events in the Middle East. Vance promised speedy action in case of attack with plans for every eventuality.[33]

Conversing privately with Peres, who had accompanied Eshkol, Komer dismissed what he called 'myths.' One was the Israeli claim of a US bias in the Arab–Israeli conflict. The fact was, he said, that since 1947 the United States had supported Israel by deterring an Arab attack. It needed to maintain the appearance of pursuing a balanced policy to prevent the Arabs from shifting completely toward Moscow, but in fact it stood behind Israel against the Arabs. Another myth was that the United States, by supporting Nasser, had arrested his policy of territorial expansion. That was not the case, Komer said, and subsequently the United States would foster relations with Egypt only when there were clear mutual interests, providing him with an alternative to dependence on the Soviet Union. The third myth was that the United States would not defend Israel in an emergency. Frankly, he said, the claim had become annoying. Given the US commitment to Israel, it did not need a nuclear force. The more important thing, Komer said, was not what might actually happen in a crisis but rather what potential aggressors thought

---

31 FRUS, 1964–1968, XVIII: 152–9; ICAB, June 18, 1964, ISA; KFADC, 22 June, 1964.
32 Harman to Meir, August 24, 1964, Top Secret and Personal, ISA 7226/11.
33 'Israel's Security Concerns,' June 2, 1964, Secret, Participants: Eshkol, Peres, Vance, LeMay et al., NARA, RG 59, NEA/NE, Box 6.

would happen. Komer added that Israel was being evasive about the Dimona reactor. Were not US–Israeli relations, he asked, close enough to allow more candor?[34]

Indeed, two American academics, both from Harvard University, in the fields of foreign affairs and national security offered moral advice to Israel. Thomas Schelling argued that Israel had to exploit its ability to develop nuclear arms because it was her strongest bargaining card. Henry Kissinger maintained that Israel's strategic position required it to have a first-strike capability. Only nuclear weapons could provide it with a response to missile development in Egypt.[35]

Israel held its ace, the Dimona reactor, close to its chest. Nasser would not allow any oversight of his missiles and in such a situation the United States was powerless to achieve a modus vivendi in the regional arms race. The Johnson administration assumed that only an East–West understanding could prevent dangerous developments, and the chiefs of staff did not believe such an accord could be reached because the Soviets' main objective was to eject the West from the Arab world.[36] Indeed, Rusk claimed that détente was an illusion. The big issues – Berlin, Cuba and Vietnam – remained 'dangerous sours.' It could well be, he suggested to Eban, that the internal situation in the United States and the Cuban crisis had had a calming effect on the Kremlin, but this was not the case with secondary issues that were erupting in the world's new states.[37]

The State Department admitted its evaluation of the ramifications of the Cairo summit and the significance of a united Arab command had been mistaken, the result of Arab threats regarding the diversion of the Jordan River and incitement to establish a separate Palestinian entity in contradiction of Arab promises to put both issues on hold.[38] In addition, there was no sign that the Soviet Union meant to stop pouring arms into the Middle East.[39] Eshkol was pleased with the change in the US position, believing that, if Nasser took over Jordan, Israel could seize the West Bank with US sanction and demand its demilitarization. After the US presidential elections, Johnson and Khrushchev might institute talks

34 FRUS, 1964–1968, XVIII: 164–7, cf. 176–8, 199–200, 205–6.
35 Colonel Dan Hiram (Washington) to Peres, 14 July, 1964. Top Secret, ISA 7935/11a.
36 FRUS, 1964–1968, XVIII: 173–5, cf. 204–5; FRUS, 1964–1968, X: 122.
37 Rusk-Eban, Memorandum of Conversation, 'Soviet–U.S. Détente,' March 4, 1964 Secret, LBJL, NSF, Box 138.
38 FRUS, 1964–1968, X: 178–88, 206–10, 212–14.
39 Harman to Uri Lubrani, 'Meeting of Harman with Deputy Under Secretary of State Thompson in Washington,' April [25]24, 1964, Secret, ISA 7226/11a.

to end the global arms race and in the meantime Israel could legitimately ask for guarantees that the reactor Nasser wanted to build would be used, as promised, to desalinate water.[40] In addition, the US administration was under pressure to stop aid to Egypt.[41]

Israel had completed work on the National Water Carrier and began pumping water from the Jordan River on May 28, 1964, worsening the conflict with the Arabs. A second Arab summit was held in Alexandria in September with the stated goal of improving Arab defensive capabilities.[42] To Israel, two Arab summits in a single year seemed fraught with danger. Golda Meir thought it showed Israel needed stronger ties with the United States, France and West Germany. The world should not be indifferent when thirteen UN members resolved to destroy another member and US humanitarian aid to Egypt was helping it prepare for war with Israel.[43]

A State Department forecast for 1968 called Israel a stable country with a flourishing economy. Its economic growth was 9 percent and foreign currency reserve $1.3 billion. Israel itself was less optimistic. According to a State Department report, if the United States were to grant Israel a formal security guarantee and 100 Pershing nuclear missiles, it would stop developing its own nuclear capability. However, in the meantime the US administration learned that Israel had upgraded the Dimona reactor to produce plutonium, meaning it could produce a nuclear weapon within nine months. Polarization was growing, the Soviet Union and the Arabs on the one side and the United States and Israel on the other. Washington could compel Israel to agree to its policies, the report maintained, especially when reparations payments from Germany should end in 1966, but the administration refused to do so for internal reasons.[44]

A State Department forecast for 1972 predicted that Israel's GNP and industry would develop more rapidly than the Arab states'. Nevertheless, regarding the middle class, ultimately it would lose out to Egypt, which was expanding its educational system. Israel would have a nuclear bomb by 1972, and Soviet expansion in the region would be blocked, according

---

40 Eshkol–Gazit Conversation, September 1, 1964, ISA 7933/4a.
41 Phillips Talbot to Governor Harriman, 'Growing Pro-Israel, Anti-U.A.R., Campaign for Action,' September 10, 1964 Confidential, NARA, RG 59, NEA/NE, Box 1.
42 Sela, 1982: 38–49.
43 ICAB, May 3, 1964 (Eshkol), ISA; ICAB, September 13, 1964, ISA; KFADC, September 22, 1964, ISA.
44 Memorandum, 'Israel: 1968 – You Are There,' October 5, 1964, Secret, NARA, RG 59, NEA/NE, Box 7.

to the report.[45] Generally speaking, it was predicted that no political or military volcano was about to erupt in the Middle East. Nasser and the other Arab leaders realized that military action against Israel would be useless and King Hussein was a stabilizing factor. According to the forecast, only Syria seemed to be confrontational and unwilling to accept the Arab consensus. The Alexandria summit had not recommended the use of force, reflecting the fact that the Arabs appreciated the IDF's strength and that it was backed by US power. Israel's security was assured, which provided an opportunity to progress toward a solution to the conflict, despite the issues of the arms race and the refugees.[46]

The Soviet Union remained concerned about Israel's refusal to allow the Dimona reactor to be inspected. In State Department assessment, Eshkol had still not decided if he wanted an independent or external (namely, American) deterrent. He might yield to domestic pressure, because many Israelis viewed nuclear weapons as vital to the survival of the state. The United States' main leverage was a threat to cut off military and economic aid, but Eshkol was unimpressed. Israel would not need further military assistance until November 1965, by which time it would have developed nuclear arms. The most important US consideration was to prevent Israel from developing an atomic bomb. The price would be high, Israel would ask for jet planes or Pershing missiles, and the United States would be drawn into the arms race.[47] However, the US administration preferred to trust the Pentagon's assessment that Israel's military superiority, along with the unrivaled capabilities of the Sixth Fleet, were deterrent enough; surface-to-surface missiles were unnecessary. However, US officials believed that Israel would be able to manufacture two or three nuclear devices by the end of 1965.[48] It seemed necessary to demonstrate to Israel's leaders just how powerful the American deterrent was. To that end, Peres, Rabin, IDF intelligence chief Aharon Yariv, Air Force Commander Ezer Weizman and Navy Commander Yohai Ben-Nun were invited to tour the Sixth Fleet's most powerful aircraft carrier, the *Forrestal*.[49]

\* \* \*

45 William R. Polk to Walt Rostow, Policy Planning Staff, 'The US in the Middle East: 1965–72,' October 26, 1964, Limited Official Use, NARA, RG 59, NEA/NE, Box 7.
46 Rodger Davies to Phillips Talbot, 'Meeting with Conference of Presidents,' October 19, New York City, 'Talking Points for Meeting with Conference of Major American Jewish Organizations,' Confidential, October 16, 1964, NARA, RG 59, NEA/NE, Box 3.
47 FRUS, 1964–1968, XVIII: 231–5.
48 Russell, Nineteenth General Assembly, Position Paper, 'Israel's Security Concerns,' New York, December 1964, November 18, 1964, Secret, NARA, NEA/NE, Box 7.
49 Rabin, 1979: 127–8 (November 11, 1964).

On Thanksgiving Day, November 26, 1964, African students set fire to the American library in Cairo, an incident considered particularly worrying because it was a symptom of what US Ambassador Lucius D. Battle called 'dissonance in US–Egyptian relations.' Egypt was increasingly critical of US foreign policy, and President Johnson responded that Congress might not vote to supply wheat to Egypt. On December 19, an American civilian aircraft was shot down over Egyptian territory and its crew was killed. Battle informed Nasser that he would receive no more aid. On December 23, Nasser gave a speech at Port Said, with Soviet Deputy Prime Minister Alexander Shelepin standing beside him, in which he said that anyone who was not pleased could 'drink from the sea,' an Arab insult, adding that Egypt would not accept 'gangsterism from a cowboy,'[50] namely, President Johnson. Rusk ruled every American initiative halted until Egypt made an overture to the United States.[51] With Egypt clearly in the Soviet camp, Israel should have benefited. Rusk did not deny that relations with Egypt had deteriorated, but he did not think the situation helped Israel. Eban, however, said that the Americans defined Israel as a US ally even if no written treaty existed.[52]

Meanwhile Syrian attempts to rechannel some of the Jordan River's headwaters led to firefights with the IDF. On November 13, following a heavy Syrian barrage targeting two northern Israeli settlements, Eshkol and Rabin decided to respond, for the first time, with air strikes against Syria, angering the cabinet, which had not been consulted. The State Department refused to sever relations with Nasser because the Egyptian ambassador to Washington claimed that without economic aid his country would fall into the arms of Communism.[53] The Americans were worried that talks with the Israelis would be detrimental to US relations with the Arabs[54] and, under the circumstances, Eshkol was prepared to accept a visit from American nuclear experts, but not an inspection. They would be guests, he said, not inspectors, and would be expected to arrive without equipment.[55]

On January 21, 1965, the President received a report from the Gilpatric Committee on Nuclear Proliferation. The Committee recommended giving Israel the same assurances as it had regarding US support in the case of an Egyptian invasion. The promise should be revoked if

50 FRUS, 1964–1968, XIX: 242–54; Little, 1994: 161–2.
51 FRUS, 1964–1968, XVIII: 252–5.
52 KFADC, December 15, 1964, ISA.
53 ICAB, November 15, 1964, ISA; FRUS, 1964–1968, XVIII: 264–9.
54 FRUS, 1964–1968, XVIII: 261–2.
55 FRUS, 1964–1968, XVIII: 262–4, 304–5.

Israel acquired nuclear arms and Egypt should also be warned against acquiring nuclear arms. Without such steps, no effective policy that would keep Israel from developing an independent nuclear force could be implemented.[56]

The State Department eventually realized that the Alexandria summit had not contributed to regional stability. Jordan wanted American planes, tanks and artillery, and the United States feared that providing them would escalate the arms race and that Israel would also ask for more military aid. The State Department told Jordan what it had told Israel, to purchase the materiel in Britain and France. Washington feared that if Jordan acquired Soviet arms Israel would find itself nearly surrounded by Soviet client states, bringing the East–West confrontation in the Middle East to a critical point.[57] On the other hand, the State Department knew that Egypt had received weapons from the Soviet Union as well as the promise of a loan. The United States feared that Nasser would eject the UN force in the Sinai and Gaza, threaten Eilat and confront Israel directly. According to Rusk, the United States had to compete with the Soviets by offering arms to Jordan, Lebanon and Saudi Arabia.[58] The decision was made to supply twenty planes to Jordan in the hope that Israel would understand that the alternative, Soviets arms in Jordan, would be far worse. The Arab–Israeli balance in the air would be kept (475:175).

Israel would now receive weapons and Eshkol should have been pleased, but he cabled President Johnson that, in the absence of Israeli geographic depth, he feared that the Jordanian army would inevitably turn aggressor and that the United States would lose control of the events. The United States responded that Israel needed to understand that the Western deterrent to an attack was very real.[59] Even Komer acknowledged that the United States would have to supply Israel with more arms, planes included. The Soviet Union had to be prevented from gaining ground but without harming US relations with the Arabs. President Johnson ruled that limited arms would be supplied to both Jordan and Israel because the alternative, a security guarantee for and joint military planning with Israel, would have worse consequences.[60] The Israeli embassy in the United States told the Israeli leadership that premature unreserved US support of Israel was not in the interests of

56 FRUS, 1964–1968, XI: 172–8.
57 FRUS, 1964–1968, XVIII: 269–71, 274–7.
58 FRUS, 1964–1968, XVIII: 283–7.
59 Eshkol to Harman, February 4, 1965, Confidential and Immediate, ISA 7935/12a.
60 FRUS, 1964–1968, XVIII: 308–18.

either country, because any deviation from the status quo was liable to lead to further East–West polarization.[61]

Averell Harriman, Under Secretary of State for Political Affairs, and Komer were sent to Israel to persuade its government that the American arms in Jordan would not undermine Israel's deterrent capabilities. Eshkol argued that giving arms to Jordan would be a psychological gain for the Arabs, who had already been encouraged when West Germany announced it would not sell tanks to Israel.[62] Komer concluded that Israel was preparing itself psychologically for a preemptive strike and, if the West Germans did in fact renege on selling tanks to Israel, the United States would have to supply them.[63]

Rabin warned that the US plan to arm Jordan was dangerous for Israel. The West Bank, he said, had to be demilitarized. Komer told him that the United States was keeping Arab states from becoming Soviet clients. If the United States did not supply arms, the Arabs might initiate a preemptive attack, which would indicate to Israel that conventional arms could no longer serve as a deterrent, leading it to commence the production of nuclear weapons. Komer recommended that the United States provide Israel with tanks, asking in return that it consent to the US arms deal with Jordan and for restraint in dealing with the border tensions resulting from the diversion of the Jordan River.[64] Israel would receive arms only if it agreed, in writing, not to develop nuclear weapons and not to take action against the Arabs' Jordan River diversion project.[65]

Meir told Harriman that there was a terrible sense of foreboding in Israel. He replied that the new Kremlin leadership was active in international affairs and that he was aware of the surge in the Soviet supply of weapons to the Arabs. The unified Arab command was a real threat, he acknowledged, but the Sixth Fleet served as its most important deterrent. Now, with Israel in its seventeenth year and its situation precarious, the United States was determining a new policy toward the Jewish state. Rabin told Harriman and Komer that the Arabs possessed enormous quantities of military hardware and that Egypt alone could drop 810 tons of bombs a day on Israel. Eshkol, who wanted Phantoms, was asked instead to buy Mirage IV and B-66 planes. He also agreed to

---

61 Gazit to Bitan, February 7, 1965, Top Secret, ISA 3504/4.
62 ICAB, February 14, 1965, ISA; ICAB, February 28, 1965, ISA; AAPBRD, 1965: 363–6; Jelinek, 2004: 413–29, 451–67; Hindenburg, 2007: *passim*.
63 FRUS, 1964–1968, XVIII: 324–30, 332–3; ICAB, March 21, 1965, ISA.
64 Bitan to Harman, 'Visit of Achiasaf [Komer],' to Harman and Gazit, February 16, 1965, ISA 7935/12a.
65 FRUS, 1964–1968, XVIII: 343–7.

commit to pursuing all avenues to peace except in the UN, where the Soviet Union would quash its initiatives. Harriman recommended that the US administration give Israel what it requested, but the administration was not willing to supply bombers, although it was prepared to be flexible on the issue of the oversight of Israel's nuclear program.[66]

On March 1, 1965, the US administration decided to supply arms to both Jordan and Israel, fearing that with Soviet approval Egypt could station MiGs in Jordan, but refused to commit to supplying planes to Israel. The United States, Rusk said, would not stand an Israeli flirt with nuclear weapons. Israel, he said, was acting in cold blood. Eshkol defended his position by stating that Israel needed nuclear weapons to counter Nasser's threat to destroy Israel, that many US promises had not been kept and that Israel needed clearer commitments. The State Department realized that the United States had no means of overseeing Israel's nuclear program. The US embassy's science attaché in Tel Aviv, Dr. Robert Webber, claimed that Israel was misleading the United States, and that the American team of experts had not been given full access to the facility in Dimona.[67] Komer hoped that Israel would accept the administration's dictate without making further demands, claiming that the Americans had reached the limit of their capabilities, because additional aid for Israel would mean abandoning other US interests in the Middle East. If the United States sold arms to Israel, it had to be certain that Israel would not launch a preemptive war or develop nuclear weapons. However, he also realized that sooner or later the United States would have to sell Israel not only tanks, but fighter jets.[68]

The same month, after news of a new Soviet–Egyptian weapons deal, the establishment of a unified Arab military command and the final cancelation of West Germany's sale of tanks to Israel, Eshkol and Komer drafted a top secret memorandum of understanding (March 10, 1965). According to its terms, the United States reiterated its promise to preserve Israel's security, independence and territorial integrity and to firmly oppose all regional aggression. The United States also reaffirmed

66 Report on Harriman Mission, Three Sessions and Internal Consultations, February 24–7, 1965, Top Secret, ISA 7935/1a.
67 FRUS, 1964–1968, XVIII: 382–4; Yigal Allon, Minister of Labor, stated that Dimona was a 'great bargaining-card' in the negotiations with the United States, cf. ICAB, February 28, 1965, ISA; also Peres to Prof. Ernst D. Bergmann, claiming that Dimona 'changed our position in the political map,' Peres Correspondence, 1955–65, LPA.
68 FRUS, 1964–1968, XVIII: 387–9.

that Israel's deterrent capability prevented Arab aggression and that it would be attentive to Israel's demands and problems. Jordan would not deploy the tanks it received in the West Bank, and the administration would supply Israel with tanks. On the nuclear issue, Israel promised not to be the first country to introduce nuclear arms into the region. Israel opposed the section in the memorandum, calling for Israel to defend its water interests peacefully; Komer conceded the point.[69] Israel, he said optimistically, would see the light at the end of the strategic superiority tunnel in five, ten, fifteen years. Eshkol was less enthusiastic.[70]

In the end, it was the memorandum of understanding that formed the basis for the US–Israel alliance. Levy Eshkol called it an 'historical turning point.' The memorandum had been expedited by the United Arab Command's demand that Jordan refurbish its military. The US agreement with Jordan, signed on March 18, was an achievement for the United States and Israel in that Hussein committed himself to deploying American tanks only in the East Bank.[71] However, US intelligence warned that escalation in the Middle East increased the danger of inter-bloc polarization. Israel was liable to disrupt the Jordan River diversion project in Jordan and Syria, leading to large-scale hostilities. Israel would have surface-to-surface missiles and nuclear bombs in two to four years. Eshkol promised to take American fears into account and subdue those in Israel who were pushing for war.[72]

Finally, Israel had secured the United States as a de facto ally and would receive preferential treatment on the issues of the diversion of the Jordan River and nuclear capabilities. Israel now had greater bargaining power because there was no real chance for a US agreement with either Egypt or the Soviets. Israel had to agree to IAEA supervision, but it was not a condition for continuing US aid.[73] For Nasser, the Johnson administration feigned a balanced policy and the US ambassadors in the Arab countries had no choice but to fall into line. The Johnson administration presumed it could, to a certain extent, control the Arab–Israeli conflict

---

69 Memorandum of Conversation at Residence of Ambassador Barbour, Tuesday, March 9, 1964, ISA 7935/2.
70 Meeting held at the Ministry of Defense, Tel Aviv, March 10, 1965, ISA 3501/17; however, Eshkol stated that the coming understanding was important as much as the Balfour Declaration, cf. ICAB, March 3, 1965, ISA.
71 FRUS, 1964–1968, XVIII: 404–5; ICAB, February 28, 1965 (Meir), ISA.
72 CIA, NIE, 'The Arab–Israeli Problem'; FRUS, 1964–1968, XVIII: 402–3 (March 10, 1965).
73 FRUS, 1964–1968, XVIII: 420; W. Cohen, 1994: 294; Ben-Zvi, 2004: 1–85.

and that it could contain the Middle East and keep it from becoming a Cold War arena.[74]

The United States was Israel's only hope, and, even with the memorandum, it seemed to be facing an uncertain future. France and Britain had grown lukewarm and Israel demanded real guarantees, not platitudes.[75] According to Willy Morris, head of the British Foreign Office's Middle East department, Israel was a foreign element in the Middle East and its continued survival depended on Western support and the largesse of the international community. The Foreign Office also did not think that the return of the Palestinian refugees was an eventuality. Britain believed that three factors prevented an Arab war of liberation: Israel's military might, the American Sixth Fleet and the lack of Arab unity. The Arab fear of Israeli territorial expansion could be placated by persuading the Arabs that immigration to Israel would be limited – unless the Soviets opened their gates – and the Arabs should be told that the Negev was no great prize for Israel.[76] Apparently, the United States and Britain did not actually understand the danger inherent in the Arab–Israeli conflict and the role that the Soviet Union played in fanning the flames. Two years before the outbreak of the Six Day War, the West had not yet fully appreciated the threat. Israel needed full Western support and only by providing it could the West have gained the influence necessary to prevent the war.[77]

---

74　Little, 1994: 145–67.
75　Morris, April 29, 1956, Secret, NA, FO 371/180874/ER1074/2.
76　Morris to Sir George Middleton, Cairo, May 21, 1965, Confidential, NA, FO 371/180668/E1421/108; British intelligence assessment was that Israel could produce enough plutonium within two years to manufacture a few nuclear weapons. Meanwhile, it could defeat the Arabs without it: J.I.C. (65)25(Final), Cabinet, The Development of Nuclear Weapons by Additional Countries, 1965–1967, July 19, 1965, Top Secret, NA, CAB158/58.
77　Mr. Beith's Valedictory Dispatch, October 27, 1965, Confidential, NA, FO 371/180847/ER1015/26; Heimann, 2010: 69–88; cf. Israel's cabinet sessions since the first Arab Summit in Cairo.

# 13

# Johnson, Israel and the Cold War: testing the Memorandum of Understanding (1965–67)

The Memorandum of Understanding turned Israel into a US client state, but its implementation had to be negotiated. In April 1965, Israel submitted a formal application for tanks and planes which was rejected by the Americans, who feared they would be used for unprovoked offensive military actions.[1] However, the State Department did not readily accept Israel as a client, interpreting the Memorandum in the most limited way possible, restricting the supply of arms with only rare exceptions. President Johnson demanded that Israel agree to IAEA oversight. Eshkol replied that the United States should prioritize conventional disarmament because the conventional arms race was the most liable to lead to war. He promised, however, that Israel would not stage a full-scale preemptive attack over the Jordan River diversion, but would open fire in response to provocation.

The Memorandum of Understanding did not resolve the issue of the nuclear facility at Dimona. Eshkol acknowledged, for the first time, that Israel was seeking nuclear weapons capability because it had no US security guarantee. US officials were furious with Israel for having deliberately misled them. They suspected Israel of planning to bomb the Aswan Dam to flood the Nile Delta and maintained that the United States should impose its policies on Israel. Israel had, after all, signed the Nuclear Test Ban Treaty and it had to allow international inspections of Dimona.[2] Johnson warned Eshkol that, if Nasser believed that Israel was developing nuclear arms, the result might be Soviet deployment of missiles in Egypt. Agreeing to IAEA oversight was thus in Israel's own interests, he said, it would gain by demonstrating its peaceful intentions.[3]

The United States and Israel disagreed on the interpretation of the special relationship. Israel maintained they shared common goals, such

1 Bitan to Meir, 'Points for Discussion with Talbot,' April 18, 1965, ISA 7230/1a.
2 FRUS, 1964–1968, XVIII: 454–6.
3 FRUS, 1964–1968, XVIII: 463–4.

as regional peace, but the problem was achieving them. Things would be different, Israel said, if it belonged to NATO or had a security guarantee or deterrent weapons. The US administration argued that Israel was exaggerating the dangers. The United States wanted to keep the special relationship from becoming exclusive, which could have led to the Soviets being granted exclusive influence in the Arab countries. Now Israel was capable of withstanding an Arab attack, but what would the situation be twenty-five years on when it had to face modern Arab societies? The administration expected Israel, a stable democracy, to have a higher capability for self-restraint than it was currently displaying. Israel claimed that, in view of Arab threats, it was vitally important for the United States to announce publicly that it was supplying the Jewish state with arms.[4]

The State Department ignored the fact that Nasser was prepared to accept Israel only as another version of Lebanon, with a population that was 40 percent Arab. Nasser had also stated explicitly that he expected the superpowers to intervene to prevent war.[5] However, the superpower détente was weak, with mutual suspicion because of the war in Vietnam. Furthermore, new Soviet Premier Alexei Kosygin was concerned that the United States might deploy nuclear weapons in West Germany, which might fall into the hands of another Hitler. He was terrified by the possibility, he said, despite assurances from Averell Harriman, the US ambassador-at-large, that the United States would not allow West Germany to become a nuclear power.[6]

The disagreements between the United States and Israel worsened with the appearance of Fatah, the Palestinian national liberation movement. Fatah staged terrorist attacks against Israel from Jordan, leading to retaliatory Israeli strikes which the Americans severely criticized. The IDF's operations against the Syrian project to divert the Jordan River and in the West Bank were perfect examples of the limited use of power to maintain peace, Israel declared.[7] The State Department did not accept Israel's claim that attacking the Syrian water project was self-defense. Komer proposed to President Johnson that he condition the supply of planes and tanks to Israel on its ending its threats against the Arab water diversion project. The issue of inspecting Dimona remained, however,

4 Meeting between Mr Talbot and Mr Bitan, 18 April, 1965, Secret, ISA 7920/21/a.
5 Gazit, 'Conversation with Bergus, Egypt,' Top Secret and Personal, August 6, 1965, ISA 3502/9.
6 FRUS, 1964–1968, XI: 219–21.
7 ICAB, May 30, 1965, ISA; KFADC, June 1, 1965 (Rabin), ISA.

and Rusk warned Israel that continued rejection of IAEA oversight would cast a pall over relations between the two countries.[8]

The Johnson administration took a narrow view of the memorandum. The United States would help Israel purchase planes in Europe, but American aircraft would not be sold because jets capable of carrying nuclear weapons would be a major step toward polarization.[9] Rusk told Meir that the Middle East was like the Indian subcontinent, India versus Pakistan. She rejected the comparison, saying that Israel, unlike either India or Pakistan, faced the constant threat of annihilation. For example, she said, the September 13–17, 1965, Casablanca summit had discussed plans and budgets for a war to destroy the Jewish state. Rusk disagreed, saying Nasser would become more moderate and claiming his rhetoric was shaped by pan-Arab ideology and meant for consumption by the Arab world. Like the doctrine of jihad, it would remain theoretical.[10] What the United States feared was that the Soviet Union would exploit Nasser's weakness to force him to accept Soviet missile and submarine bases. Komer emphasized the US commitment to aid Israel if it were attacked. The United States had made it very clear to Nasser that, if he attacked Israel, he would have to fight them as well.[11]

Science attaché Dr. Robert Webber reported that the Dimona reactor was in fact a nuclear weapons project in which Israel had invested half of its research and development budget for 1959–64. He said that Israel was not currently planning to mount nuclear warheads on missiles, but was concerned about a nuclear threat a decade hence, and did not rely on superpower efforts to prevent nuclear proliferation.[12]

In October 1965, US administration officials rejected the Israeli request for 210 airplanes, but held out hope for the following year. The administration retained the position that the United States should not become the Middle East's principal arms supplier.[13] Israel continued to remind

8 FRUS, 1964–1968, XVIII: 476–8, 483–5.
9 Harrison M. Symmes to Ambassador Raymond Hare, 'Your Meeting with Ambassador Bohlen on September 29 at 9:30 a.m.,' September 28, 1965, Secret, Exidis, NARA, RG 59, NEA/NE Files.
10 FRUS, 1964–1968, XVIII: 522; 'Rusk-Meir Meeting,' September 29, 1965, ISA 4328/1.
11 Meir–Komer Discussion, October 2, 1965, ISA 7230/21a.
12 Debriefing of Dr. R. T. Webber, Science Attaché, American Embassy, Tel Aviv, November 18, 1965, Secret, Limdis, NARA, RG 59, NEA/NE Files, Box 7.
13 Townsend Hoopes, Deputy Assistant Secretary of Defense for International Security Affairs to Senator Stuart Symington, November 20, 1965, Confidential, NARA, RG 59, NEA/NE Files, Box 1.

the United States that its very existence was in jeopardy. Eshkol rejected the Western position on the Arab summit conference and Israeli military superiority. Egypt was leading an Arab plot to destroy Israel, he declared, it had cut its domestic civilian programs in order to purchase planes, helicopters and tanks. Eshkol said the Arabs would be encouraged to start a war because the Johnson Doctrine did not clearly state US intentions regarding Israel. Eshkol warned that if the great powers did not halt the arms race Israel would take steps to ensure that Nasser could not attack.[14]

At the same time, the escalating Vietnam War cast its shadow over the Cold War. Johnson needed to be persuaded, Israel suggested, that trust between the two countries had to be restored, perhaps in the form of the sale of Intruder planes.[15] Rodger Davies, Talbot's deputy, admitted that only assurances of Israel's security, with Egyptian acceptance, could persuade Israel to agree to a nuclear-free zone in the Middle East. Israel noted that Nasser had announced at Helwan that the Egyptian military budget was being increased by £150 million sterling, to £350 million.[16] The US administration could not ignore the Helwan speech and, in January 1966, Rusk and McNamara agreed to supply Israel with twenty-four Skyhawk planes, which, however, could hardly prevent East–West polarization. With the Soviets arming Egypt, Syria, and Iraq, Rusk proposed to Gromyko that they reach an understanding on curbing arms supplies to Egypt and Israel. Gromyko answered that first the superpowers had to reduce their own forces.[17]

Eban, newly appointed as Israeli foreign minister, stated that while the memorandum of understanding included a commitment to supply planes, it would be a problem for the United States. As for the Dimona reactor, the US administration hesitated to demand stricter inspections because of the stalemate at the Geneva arms control talks. The United States did not want to escalate the Cold War. Perhaps, Eban suggested, the Johnson administration would realize that it would be easier to accept the Dimona reactor than to provide security guarantees.[18] Komer said that inspection of the reactor, not the planes, was the first item of business. He made no commitment to economic aid because, he said, the cost of the Vietnam War and the President's Great Society programs

14  FRUS, 1964–1968, XVIII: 530–2.
15  Bitan to Harman and Evron, January 14, 1966, ISA 3975/15.
16  Gazit to Harman, 'Conversation with Rostow,' January 16, 1966, Top Secret, ISA 3975/16.
17  FRUS, 1964–1968, XVIII: 534–6; FRUS, 1964–1968, XI: 245–9.
18  KFADC, January 18, 1966 (Eban) ISA.

had drained the budget, and demanded a more moderate line from Israel as a precondition for a US–Israeli compromise. Eshkol felt it was not a threat, but rather that the Americans thought that new arms would diminish Israel's incentive to develop nuclear capabilities.[19]

Despite the disagreement, State Department officials described US–Israeli relations as 'unusually' close. The two countries, they said, had similar goals, while the disputes were over emphasis rather than substance. The main problem was Israel's desire for an even closer relationship, which the US administration wanted to avoid. Relations, however, were based on full candor, with the exception of the missile and nuclear programs. Komer warned that the United States had little room to maneuver. Its commitment to Israel's defense almost predicated intervention in an Arab–Israeli war, so it was in US interests that Israel have a deterrent advantage. The more secure Israel felt, the less risk there was it would attack first, providing it with arms would reduce the possibility of eventual US intervention, and a judicious supply of arms would keep Israel from developing atomic bombs.[20]

The State Department was optimistic before Eban's first visit to Washington as foreign minister; changes in the government had marginalized hardliners like Ben-Gurion, Meir and Peres.[21] President Johnson sought to use Eban's visit to Washington to promote trust and explain that US aid to South Vietnam proved the United States kept its promises to its friends, no matter how small. Eban replied that, if the Soviets were not supplying arms to Israel's enemies, Israel would not need US aid. Unlike South Vietnam, he said, Israel had a stable government and independent defense capabilities. He suggested that Johnson focus on small countries whose self-defense capabilities reduced their dependence on the United States. The source of the crises of the 1960s in Panama, Laos, Cyprus, Congo, the Dominican Republic and Vietnam, he said, was internal instability and the lack of defensive capabilities.

Johnson promised that, subject to US national interests, he would do everything in his power for Israel. Eban called him a 'political artist,' saying he had entirely changed the atmosphere between the two countries.[22] Eban sought to convince the United States to accept the vague declaration that Israel would not be the first country to introduce nuclear arms into the

---

19 FRUS, 1964–1968, XVIII: 536–8; Eshkol in KFADC, February 1, 1966, ISA.
20 FRUS, 1964–1968, XVIII: 543–7.
21 Harrison M. Symmes to Raymond Hare, Memorandum, 'Your Meeting with Foreign Minister Abba Eban,' Monday, February 7, 3:00 p.m., February 4, 1966, NARA, RG 59, NEA/NE Files, 1964–66, Box 2.
22 FRUS, 1964–1968, XVIII: 547–9.

Middle East, but also to convince the United States that the Soviet Union was the main problem. He would, he said, remain optimistic in view of Gromyko's promise to try to solve the Middle East conflict peacefully.[23]

Johnson and McNamara decided that Israel should not be sold state-of-the-art fighter jets because that could set off a new Middle East arms race and because the planes were needed in Vietnam. Furthermore, in return for the secret sale of Skyhawks, Israel had to state firmly that it would not be the first country to introduce nuclear weapons into the Middle East, would consent to oversight of the Dimona reactor and would have to promise not to arm the planes with nuclear weapons. In other words, the Johnson administration had changed its attitude toward Israel. Eban noted that, having once refused in principle to become Israel's principal arms supplier, the Johnson administration was now exactly that, and attributed the change to public pressure.[24] Yitzhak Rabin and Ezer Weizman, the Israeli Air Force commander, said that Israel's defensive capabilities would now be far superior to those of Jordan and Saudi Arabia. The Israeli leadership credited Secretary of Defense Robert McNamara as being the prime mover behind the new approach. He had declared that the stronger Israel was, the greater the chance it would not be attacked.[25]

Israel hoped that a stronger Washington–Moscow détente would improve Israel's relations with the Kremlin. Israel did not want to be compelled to cast its UN votes solely in accordance with US interests, preferring to maintain some neutrality so it could lobby the Soviet Union on the status of its Jews.[26] Johnson and his associates were skeptical about the future of détente, which was becoming less attractive to the Soviets. The State Department suggested that tensions within the Soviet regime might lead it toward moderation and coexistence, but in the meantime the Kremlin was prepared to enter into negotiations only on its own terms, which included an accord in Vietnam based on Hanoi's conditions, abandoning NATO's nuclear program, keeping Germany divided indefinitely, and a stop to what it called 'the export of counterrevolution.' Détente could not be achieved only by superior military strength, true détente could thrive only if ideological hostility ended.[27]

\* \* \*

23 Memorandum of Conversation, 'Current U.S.-Israeli Issues,' February 8, 1965, NARA, RG 59, POL ARAB-ISR, Box 2.
24 FRUS, 1964–1968, XVIII: 547–9, cf. 550–4, 556–7; ICAB, May 22, 1965, ISA.
25 FRUS, 1964–1968, XVIII: 581–2; KFADC, January 8, 1966 (Eban), ISA.
26 FRUS, 1964–1968, XVIII: 555–6, 567, 589–90.
27 FRUS, 1964–1968, XIV: 384–7 (March 23, 1966), 'Prospects for Détente with USSR.'

Israel's refusal to support the war in Vietnam annoyed the US administration, as did its refusal to send a military unit, which Israel feared would damage its standing in the UN with the Third World and the Soviet Union. Instead, it said it would send a small medical or agricultural team, while the United States wanted an engineering corps unit to rebuild roads and bridges. Most important for the Americans was so see the Israeli flag flying alongside those of the other nations fighting Communism. Eshkol preferred to have fifteen South Vietnamese sent to Israel to learn how to grow potatoes.[28] US officials tried to persuade Israel to recognize South Vietnam before the planned elections there. Eban equivocated, saying that the United States had to understand Israel's delicate efforts to reach an understanding with the Soviet Union regarding its Jews and the Arab–Israeli conflict. Eban also argued that political instability in the United States made Israel reluctant to get involved in Vietnam. There would be no Knesset majority for such a move, he said, and Israeli public opinion would not support it. The State Department argued that only a small minority of Americans opposed the war.[29]

According to the Pentagon, Eshkol's refusal to sign the agreement for inspection in Dimona in exchange for supply of forty-eight planes was motivated by his not wanting to be remembered as abandoning Israel's nuclear capabilities or as exposing the Dimona reactor to inspections in exchange for planes. The United States felt that it should be receptive to the sensitivities of a small nation like Israel and do without an official agreement. More pressing was the US preoccupation with deterring or providing a response to a military attack on the United States and with defending and promoting its global interests. The JCS were concerned that the Communists did not view arms control in the same way that the West did.[30] A year before the Six Day War, the US intelligence community was focused on the Soviet effort to end its strategic inferiority.[31]

Israel's diplomats considered Johnson's approach to Israel fundamentally positive, but he was a politician conditioned to power and personal benefit.[32] The public announcement of economic aid to Israel ($72 million), followed by the announcement of the plane sale, gave, according to Walt W. Rostow, unimpeachable testimony of Johnson's

28 Argov to Bitan, February 16, 1966, Secret, ISA 4023/33.
29 Hadow to Rose, April 28, 1966, Secret, Guard, NA, FO 371/186813/ER103145/5 [Hare–Eshkol Conversation].
30 FRUS, 1964–1968, X: 364 (March 7, 1966).
31 FRUS, 1964–1968, X: 406–8 (June 16, 1966).
32 Evron to Bitan, April 8, 1966, ISA 3975/13.

support for Israel. Israel viewed the Skyhawks deal as a turning point,[33] but the US administration viewed the deal as a calculated and unique occurrence.[34]

However, the issue of inspections of Dimona remained unresolved. The Egyptians threatened that Israel's development of nuclear weapons would be met with the establishment of Soviet bases in Egypt,[35] so American nuclear experts visited Israel at the beginning of April 1966. They reported that, based on the evidence, Israel was not manufacturing nuclear weapons, but that it was not impossible that they had been misled. Nothing was known about uranium Israel had bought from Argentina and Israel might have a chemical separation facility in another location. Rusk demanded regular biannual visits.[36]

With Israel and Syria clashing over the Arabs' project to divert the Jordan River, the Soviet Union warned Israel not to concentrate forces on its northern borders. The State Department claimed the Soviets were trying to defuse the situation,[37] but Israel took a different view of the Soviet Union's increased activity in Syria.[38] The prevailing opinion in the State Department was that Israel would initiate a war sometime in the coming years, but that the Kremlin's cautious behavior in Vietnam and elsewhere indicated it would not intervene even if Israel penetrated deep into Arab territory.[39]

Vietnam became a dilemma for Israel. As Lyndon Johnson's popularity waned, he sought to leverage his support for Israel into support for his position on Vietnam. Perhaps Johnson did not fully understand why it was difficult for Israel to back the United States on Vietnam. Harold Saunders, who replaced Komer as the NSC's Middle East expert, claimed Israel should be kept out of the Vietnam War because its problems would create too much of a mess. However, Israel's position, such as it was, with the Soviet Union would not be mortally wounded if it sent a few agricultural advisors to South Vietnam. Vietnam could, he said, be an excellent card for the United States to play in its ongoing

33  FRUS, 1964–1968, XVIII: 576–7.
34  Informal Visit of President Z. Shazar of Israel, Background Paper, 'U.S. Arms to Israel,' July 26, 1966, Secret, NARA, NEA/NE Files, Box 2.
35  FRUS, 1964–1968, XVIII: 614.
36  Shalom, 2004: 210–11; FRUS, 1964–1968, XVIII: 582–3.
37  Bitan to Harman, May 27, 1966, Top Secret, Immediate, ISA 3975/12.
38  Bitan to Harman and Evron, Eban–Barbour Conversation, June 15, 1966, Top Secret, Immediate, ISA 3975/12.
39  Stephen J. Campbell, UNP, to William Wolle, Memorandum, 'Politico-Military Contingency Planning for Arab-Israel Dispute,' May 2, 1966, NARA, RG 59, NEA/NE Files, Box 8.

negotiations with Israel.[40] Israel feared that unreserved identification with the US involvement in Vietnam would worsen its Cold War problems. American soldiers were being killed every day in Vietnam, which was why the United States would not undertake an unqualified obligation to Israel, there was too much danger of a war in the Middle East.[41] In reality, Israel's recognizing South Vietnam was not sufficiently important to cause the Americans to condition the delivery of the Skyhawks on it.[42] The United States needed to understand that Israel had to act cautiously not to provoke a sharp Soviet reaction, which was why the foreign ministry had reservations about Moshe Dayan's visit to Vietnam (he went up as a war correspondent for the Israeli newspaper *Ma'ariv*).[43]

The Israeli foreign ministry maintained that Israel should support the United States in Vietnam, because the outcome of the war would demonstrate the force of US security guarantees. Harman demanded restraint. If Israel were to get involved on the side of the United States in Vietnam, he declared, the Soviet Union would increase its support for the Arabs.[44] Johnson was furious. What would a US commitment to Israel be worth, he said, if 14 million people in South Vietnam were abandoned?[45] Israel, however, remained skeptical about American promises. The United States was not pleased with Israel's equivocation regarding Vietnam, while Israel claimed its relations with the United States were based on mutual understanding and not on a quid pro quo.[46]

Saunders was optimistic, stating that a new Middle East could be created to block the Soviet Union and that, following a declaration by Tunisia's President Habib Bourguiba that Arab–Jewish coexistence was not impossible, the seeds of Arab–Israeli détente had been sown, if not yet sprouted.[47] The nuclear reactor in Dimona remained the main bone of contention. Israel argued that inspections would not eliminate the conventional arms race; Rusk threatened that the United States would withdraw its support. Eban argued that Israel needed assurance that the United States would not give Egypt information about Israel's nuclear

---

40 Hal Saunders to WWR [Rostow], June 3, 1966, Secret, LBJL, NSF, Names File, Saunders Memoranda, Box 7.
41 Raphael to Bitan, June 20, 1966, Secret, ISA 3975/12.
42 KFADC, June 21, 1966 (Dinstein), ISA.
43 [Eytan]USD, WED to IMW, June 21, 1966, Top Secret and Personal, ISA 4023/31.
44 Bitan to Harman, 'Vietnam,' July 6, 1966, Top Secret, ISA 3975/14.
45 Harman to Bitan, 'Dinner with President Johnson on the Sequoia,' July 14, 1966, Secret, ISA 7230/21.
46 Argov to Harman and Evron, November 4, 1966, Secret, ISA 3975/2.
47 FRUS, 1964–1968, XXI: 29–31.

program; Ambassador Barbour proposed compromise of third-party verification.[48] The moderated US position was prompted by the anti-Western position taken by Nasser, who was threatening open support of the Vietcong if the United States halted economic aid. Regardless, the US administration refused to sell Israel advanced weapons, fearing Arab reactions.[49] Eban, as usual, remained optimistic. Nasser's remarks about the dissolution of Egyptian–Syrian unification and the recognition of the legitimacy of Middle Eastern sovereign states showed possible future Egyptian readiness for coexistence with Israel in a matter of three to four years, like India and Pakistan. Young people were sick of the slogan about the 'liberation of Palestine.' The situation in the Middle East had changed, Eban said.[50]

The State Department was optimistic as well. It expected no worsening of the Middle East conflict in the near future, but the danger was nuclear weapons. Israel's economy was thriving, it had the largest GNP of any developing country and its annual rate of growth was at 10 percent. Its imports exceeded its exports, but the gap was shrinking.[51] The Soviet Union was careful not to provoke a crisis that could lead to an East–West confrontation and had not committed itself to supporting the shaky regime in Syria.[52] The CIA followed the State Department. Israel, it said, preserved its qualitative superiority in the face of Arab quantitative superiority. The Arab countries taken together had twice as many tanks, their navies were three times as large and they had ten times as many bombers, but neither Israel nor Egypt would have nuclear weapons before 1970, the CIA predicted.[53]

However, on November 13, 1966, Israel conducted a military operation in the West Bank village of Samu near Hebron in retaliation for Fatah raids in Israel. Just before the operation, the State Department had termed US–Israeli relations 'excellent.'[54] Israel complained that the Vietnam War had paralyzed the United States in the Middle East, keeping

48 FRUS, 1964–1968, XVIII: 654–6.
49 FRUS, 1964–1968, XVIII: 630.
50 Eban's Lecture at the Bern Convention [of Israeli Diplomats], July 31, 1966, 4031/10.
51 William D. Wolle to Raymond Hare, 'Briefing of House Members,' on August 10, 1966, August 5, 1966, NARA, RG 59, NEA/NE Files, Box 3.
52 FRUS, 1964–1968, XXI: 32–4.
53 'Arab-Israeli Arms Survey. Study Prepared in the CIA,' in FRUS, 1964–1968, XVIII: 633–4 (September 1, 1966).
54 Hare to Acting Secretary, 'Briefing Memorandum: Courtesy Call on You by Ambassador of Israel,' October 26, 1966, October 25, 1966, NARA, RG 59, NEA/NE Files, Box 5.

it from responding to new Soviet moves.[55] The operation infuriated the US administration, claiming Israel was endangering Jordan's stability. Eshkol apologized but protested that he had no other way to protect his citizens.[56] The administration warned that if Israel had used Patton tanks in the operation, further shipments would be postponed and aid and credit to Israel might be suspended or canceled. Since border incidents had as usual occurred on the Syrian border, the United States was concerned Israel would attack Syria, not Jordan.[57] Rostow claimed the United States advocated accommodation and that Israel was leading the Americans down a blind alley.[58] Eshkol promised to examine the option of static defense but was concerned that not responding actively to terrorism would demoralize the Israeli public. Rusk proposed self-restraint. Harman objected that Arab terrorism had reached Israel's doorstep and created a siege mentality. The State Department abandoned the idea of suspending arms shipments, asking in return that Israel not retaliate. It recommended that Eban calm tempers at home rather than pour oil on troubled waters.[59]

The Johnson administration assumed that the situation in the Middle East was not as bad as in Vietnam, the Arab summit had failed and the Syrian regime would eventually collapse. The response to future Arab terrorism had to be diplomatic. The United States depended on the Soviet Union to restrain Syria, even though Israel claimed Soviet influence on Damascus was negligible.[60] Eshkol admitted that the balance of forces favored Israel, but that the doubling of Egyptian military strength over the previous decade could not be ignored. He warned, however, that the Jews in Israel were liable to remain a minority in the region, like the Maronites in Lebanon and the Copts in Egypt. Eban noted the US administration's apathetic reaction to the Soviet penetration of Syria.[61] The United States, however, was far more concerned about the escalating situation in Vietnam.[62] The NSC decided that relations with Egypt had reached a watershed, with Nasser subverting the Arab monarchies, identifying with the Soviet Union[63] and warning that if food shipments

---

55 Harman to Eban, November 9, 1966, Top Secret and Personal, ISA 7939/2a.
56 FRUS, 1964–1968, XVIII: 663–4; ICAB, November 13, 20, 1966, ISA.
57 FRUS, 1964–1968, XVIII: 664–8.
58 FRUS, 1964–1968, XVIII: 669–72.
59 FRUS, 1964–1968, XVIII: 677–86.
60 Harman to Eban, November 18, 1966, ISA 3975/2.
61 KFADC, December 20, 1966 (Eban), ISA.
62 FRUS, 1964–1968, X: 500–1.
63 FRUS, 1964–1968, XVIII: 689–90, 694–6.

were not resumed he would abandon his position of neutrality. Egypt's ambassador to Washington, Mustafa Kamel, argued that the Near East was more dangerous and important than Vietnam, claiming that Soviet pressure on Egypt might become intolerable. Rusk gave in and aid was resumed, although he acknowledged that a confrontation with Nasser was inevitable.[64] The administration's immediate concern was that Syria would turn into a Soviet offensive base, like Cuba.[65]

Now Eban feared a turn for the worse. While Israel's military advantage and deterrent capabilities had proved themselves, the Arabs had launched a guerrilla war. Komer claimed that the American public was preoccupied by Vietnam and domestic issues, and would not stand for greater US involvement in the Middle East.[66] Israel managed to get through the West Bank reprisal unscathed. The US concern that Israel was tossing lit matches into tinder had abated, but not entirely.[67] The administration feared that Israel in fact wanted an East–West confrontation in the Middle East.[68] Eshkol announced publicly that the situation was serious because the Syrians had declared that terrorism against Israel was legal and that they would encourage it.[69]

Once calm had been restored, the US administration wanted to give its status as Israel's patron a firmer foundation. First, it wanted to inspect the Dimona reactor in a way that would not affect Israel's security. In February 1967, US intelligence estimated that Israel was closer to producing nuclear weapons than had previously been thought and Eshkol was asked to permit an urgent visit to Dimona.[70] The Cold War context was clear. The United States found itself continuously having to calm Soviet tempers, but did not manage to persuade them that it had no intention of arming West Germany with nuclear missiles.[71] The United States also feared that, despite Eshkol's promise of restraint, Israel might attack

64 Argov, 'Don Bergus,' February 5, 1967, Top Secret, 3977/21.
65 'Four Sessions with Bergus, Director Egypt Section, and Atherton, Director Lebanon, Syria, Jordan, Iraq,' November 29–30, 1966, ISA 3977/20.
66 Evron to Bitan, 'Eban-Katzenbach Conversation,' December 12, 1966, Top Secret, ISA 3977/20.
67 Harman to Bitan, December 20, 1966, ISA 3975/2; ICAB, December 4, 1966, ISA 3977/20.
68 Evron to Biran and Gazit, 'Conversation with Thomas Hughes, Director of Research and Intelligence in the State Department,' January 10, 1967, Top Secret, ISA 3975/17.
69 KR 47: 916–17 (January 17, 1967).
70 FRUS, 1964–1968, XVIII: 734–7, 766.
71 FRUS, 1964–1968, XI: 297–300.

Syria.[72] Despite continuing tensions on the Syrian front, the Pentagon did not recommend supplying Israel with more arms. Granting its request for 200 APCs would strain the situation with Jordan and turn the United States into Israel's major arms supplier. Rostow agreed, saying that Israel would not receive free military equipment and that after the Samu operation no one in the administration thought it should. Congress opposed increasing aid because Israel's per capita GNP exceeded that of several European countries.[73]

The Johnson administration worried about its problematic status as a regional patron. The United States was obliged to Saudi Arabia because of its oil concessions, and the survival of the Hashemite monarchy was also an important goal. Johnson and Vice-President Humphrey had unequivocally reaffirmed Kennedy's obligation to Israel's existence (May 8, 1963), a fact known by all the countries in the region. However, the Middle East was a gray area and difficult to analyze. Perhaps the United States should retreat from its current obligations. Alternatives were examined, but the decision was made to continue the current policy, consider each case on its merits and then decide how to support the United States' principal clients. The West would continue to depend on Arab crude oil for the coming decade. The Middle East contained two-thirds of the free world's known oil reserves and provided a third of the West's needs, costing only about a tenth of the oil pumped in the United States itself. In addition, Arab oil supplied more than a half of Western Europe's needs, 85 percent of Japan's.[74]

Israel believed that the United States would not test its patronage if it believed there was no danger of an Arab offensive against Israel, and the Americans had told Israel that war was unlikely: Israel's position was sound and that its deterrence was effective. The United States opposed actions against Syria because it did not want a new Cold War front, was uneasy about its existing obligations and favored non-intervention in regional crises. Rather, it preferred not to seek fundamental solutions to regional conflicts. The Vietnam War and the deep divisions it caused within the American public had made the administration leery of involvement in another armed conflict. The US goal in the Middle East was not to fan the flames, and only a serious Syrian provocation

72 FRUS, 1964–1968, XVIII: 742–3, 746–8; ICAB, December 18, 1966, ISA.
73 Evron to Bitan, 'Conversation with Saunders,' February 13, 1967, Secret, ISA 3977/21.
74 'The United States Government Commitments in the Near East; Near East Oil: How Important is it?,' FRUS, 1964–1968, XXI: 41–3 (February 8, 1967).

with large numbers of casualties would justify military action, the State Department maintained.[75]

The United States feared that Israel would resume its reprisals,[76] dragging the Americans into further strategic commitments. Israel's leaders were defensive, declaring that the Soviet threat also extended to US air bases in the Indian Ocean participating in the war effort in Vietnam. There would be no US–Soviet détente as long as there were no clear spheres of influence.[77] Where they did exist, the United States did not intervene, such as in the Soviet bloc in Eastern Europe, which was hardly the case in the Middle East. As US–Egyptian relations grew more strained the US–Israel patron–client relationship should have strengthened. Rostow took a tough line against Nasser, but avoided a final rift because he remained the most important Arab leader, was not a Communist tool and was prepared to continue a moratorium on the conflict with Israel.[78] Nevertheless, relations were not easy. The State Department agreed to sell Israel 100 APCs to patrol its borders and to grant credit for the purchase of spare parts, but it also imposed restrictions which would be in place until Israel allowed inspections of the Dimona reactor, stating that Israel would not receive maintenance equipment or a loan.[79]

Saunders claimed he knew of no relationship the United States had with any other country as complex as the one with Israel, calling it a sincere, profound friendship, but he was referring to its character and not its substance. Instead of frank dialogue, there were long exhausting negotiations and Israel was not prepared to acknowledge its errors (Samu), he said. Israel answered that a sincere, profound friendship did not mean total agreement. The United States, Israeli diplomats claimed, had trouble understanding Israel's considerations and mindset, and essentially how concerned Israel was about Soviet penetration of the Middle East, despite the move toward détente in other regions.[80]

Johnson told the Jewish lobbyist David Ginsburg that he knew that 95 percent of the American Jews had voted for him and asked in complete secrecy to receive a detailed program of what he could do for Israel. However, he found himself in an awkward position when McNamara

---

75  Harman to Bitan, February 7, 1967, Secret, ISA 3997/21.
76  FRUS, 1964–1968, XVIII: 758–60.
77  Argov to Bitan, 'Soviet Penetration in the Middle East: Making the US Government Properly Aware,' February 9, 1967, Top Secret, ISA 3977/21.
78  FRUS, 1964–1968, XVIII: 763–5, 767–73, 780–2.
79  FRUS, 1964–1968, XVIII: 774–5, 778.
80  Argov to Evron, 'Israel-US Relations,' March 15, 1967, Top Secret, ISA 3977/21.

and Nicholas Katzenbach, new Under Secretary of State, opposed Israel's requests.[81] Harman advocated playing the American Jewish card to demand spare parts for tanks and Hawk missiles, and economic aid in view of the security burden, which cost her 11 percent of her GNP. He also said that Israel should demand US recognition of Israel's right to pursue an active defense. The United States had to tell both the Soviet Union and the Arabs that fomenting a Palestinian war of 'liberation' put the entire region in jeopardy. The US administration also had to recognize that the return of Arab refugees would mean the destruction of Israel. Israel wanted to discuss the Kremlin's attitude toward Israel, and the inspection visits to Dimona.[82] Where Israel failed completely was in persuading the administration to take action on the issue of the Soviet Jews. Joseph Sisco, Assistant Secretary of State for International Organization Affairs, said that, since the Soviets had agreed to sign a ban on testing nuclear weapons in space, they should not be pestered on other issues.[83]

Israel continued to measure the reliability of its newly-established understanding with the United States in terms of the amount of aid received. The State Department and Pentagon agreed to $48 million, but refused a development loan on the grounds that Israel's economy was progressing. Supplying APCs was liable to be interpreted by the Arabs and the Soviets as a shift toward the United States becoming Israel's major supplier of heavy weapons; the United States preferred to put its efforts into restraining the arms race. Rostow tried to strengthen the US administration's new understanding with Israel by taking a tough position on the Dimona reactor. American technicians had been invited to visit (on April 22), but only when their report came out would it be possible to determine if biannual inspections were necessary. If Israel signed the nuclear non-proliferation treaty, the Soviets might eventually agree to restraining the arms race.[84] However, conversations between the United States and Britain made clear the extent to which the administration did not control Israel, neither on the nuclear issue nor the French supply of missiles, nor on the matter of Israel's deterrence capability.[85]

In April 1967, Syrian artillery opened fire on Israeli farmers working the land in the demilitarized zone at the foot of the Golan Heights (Kibbutz Ha'on). Eshkol approved an Israeli Air Force action and six

---

81 Evron to Bitan, March 17, 1967, Top Secret and Personal, ISA 7938/10.
82 Harman to Bitan, March 18, 1967, ISA 7938/10a.
83 Harman to Bitan, October 4, 1966, Top Secret and Personal, ISA 3977/20.
84 FRUS, 1964–1968, XVIII: 786–9.
85 Everret to Moberly, April 6, 1967, Secret, NA, FCO 17/110/119133G.

Syrian planes were shot down. President Johnson's response was that Israel had taught the Syrians a lesson. Lobbyist Abraham Feinberg protested, asking why the President could not do for Israel what de Gaulle was doing. Johnson now agreed to a compromise on the APCs, while the State Department demanded that Israel refrain from cultivating fields in the demilitarized zone.[86] The general feeling in the US administration was that matters were under control, and the CIA did not regard the incident as particularly serious. Inter-Arab rivalry weakened the Arabs' fighting capabilities, although it furthered crises that could catalyze an armed conflict; the Soviets were promoting their own interests without pushing for war. The most serious eventuality would be Israel's deploying of strategic missiles. The Soviets were committed to helping the Arabs in case of attack and might supply them with missiles, but without nuclear warheads. Chances were good that the threat of superpower intervention would avert an attempt by either side to use force to solve the conflict.[87] McNamara ruled that Israel did not need the APCs because its forces were superior in all combat areas. Israel's security would be increased by supplying US arms to the moderate Arab states, preventing regional polarization.[88] The State Department believed that Syria was isolated in the Arab world and noted that the Soviets had not reacted strongly to the April incident.[89] The State Department assumed that the Soviet Union was only supplying arms to the Arabs to gain more influence in the region, not to destroy Israel.[90] Rostow said the principal problem was Israel's desire to gain a US security guarantee, while building a military force if the guarantee were not activated quickly in the case of a surprise attack. The United States would be in an intolerable situation if Israel had both a US guarantee and nuclear capabilities. It was, therefore, necessary to reach a profound understanding on the nuclear question which would enable an open and unapologetic continuation of the friendship between the two countries.[91]

US intelligence suspected that Israel was constructing a facility to extract plutonium and Rostow wanted the delivery of the APCs delayed

---

86 Evron to Bitan, April 8, 1967, Top Secret and Personal ISA, 7938/10a.
87 National Intelligence Estimate, in FRUS, 1964–1968, XVIII: 791–2 (April 13, 1967).
88 FRUS, 1964–1968, XVIII: 792–3.
89 Yaish to USD, Syria, April 24, 1967, Secret, ISA 3977/15.
90 Harold W. Glidden RNA/NEA to Alfred L. Atherton, NEA/IAI, Memorandum, 'Comments on NEA's Draft Memcon of April 5, 1967 on Near East Arms Control,' April 20, 1967, Secret, NARA, RG 59, NEA/NE Files, Box 9.
91 FRUS, 1964–1968, XVIII: 798–9.

until it became clear whether the team visiting the reactor had received full cooperation. Additionally, the increase of the PL 480 to $28 million should be postponed. The American Jewish community, with its liberal leanings, would certainly agree to Israel joining the nuclear Non-Proliferation Treaty (NPT). US intelligence suspected that Israel was constructing a facility for extraction of plutonium, and was also investing a great deal of money in French surface-to-surface missiles that could carry nuclear warheads.[92] Israel's nuclear activity was not the only problem, and the State Department and Pentagon complained that US–Israeli relations were a one-way street, where Israel asked and the United States gave. Israel argued that only its own presence represented the free world in the Middle East. Without it the UAR, now effectively defunct, would still exist, Lebanon and Jordan would have disappeared and the Soviet Union's position would be much stronger. The President's consent was vital for obtaining engines for tanks and planes, but it was also needed in order to change the atmosphere at the State Department and Pentagon.[93] Arthur Goldberg, the US ambassador to the UN, recommended reaching a reasonable compromise with Israel on military and economic aid which would not be detrimental to US relations with the Arab states.[94] However, Israel remained concerned that the Vietnam War would prevent the United States from intervening directly in a regional Middle East conflict, while Harman tried to persuade the US administration that indirect intervention was possible.[95]

Two weeks before the outbreak of the Six Day War, Katzenbach determined that the IDF was superior to any combination of Arab forces and would retain its advantage for at least five years. However, for long-term reasons, Israel would not accept restrictions on sophisticated weapons, even in the absence of inspections of Arab conventional weapons. The United States wanted to persuade both Israel and Egypt to sign the NPT. Katzenbach accused Israel of insincerity and of hiding its nuclear activity and plans. The State Department hoped that within a year it could create a link between arms inspections and Israel's requests for military and economic aid. In the meantime, the US intelligence need to track Israel's arms programs had high priority.[96]

92 FRUS, 1964–1968, XVIII: 794–7.
93 Bitan to Harman and Evron, 'Eshkol's Conversation with Feinberg and Ginsberg,' April 28, 1967, Top Secret, Personal, ISA 3977/22.
94 FRUS, 1964–1968, XVIII: 812–14.
95 Harman to Bitan, May 12, 1967, Secret, ISA 3975/17.
96 FRUS, 1964–1968, XVIII: 814–17.

On May 1, 1967, Townsend Hoopes, the Deputy Assistant Secretary of Defense for International Security Affairs, warned that Israel was requesting military aid to obtain a greater identification with the United States. There was a danger that further steps in that direction would worsen East–West tensions in the Middle East. Israel's enemies viewed its deterrent force as unchallengeable and therefore none of Israel's requests required attention as matters of military necessity. Nevertheless, he recommended allowing Israel to replace the gasoline engines of its British Centurion tanks with diesel engines, doubling their range. Israel, he suggested, should also be allowed to manufacture parts for its Skyhawks.[97] Rostow said that the United States had granted most of Israel's demands. Like Hoopes, he too opined that the problem was US identification with it, given Israel's nuclear intentions and US interests in the Arab world. He backed the President's desire to support Israel, but was concerned that its intention was to maneuver the United States into closer identification. Many problems remained without solutions, such as Middle East oil ($2.75 billion in investments and $750 million in yearly profit), and the Arab belief that the Zionists controlled US Middle East policy.[98]

On the eve of the Six Day War, the East–West confrontation and the toxicity of the Arab–Israeli conflict dictated the measure of control that the US patron had over its Israeli client. On the one hand, the United States could not allow itself to enter into a military alliance with Israel, which would have destroyed the delicate, tenuous relations it had with the pro-Western Arab states. On the other, it was inconceivable that the superpowers would reach an agreement on the Middle East if the Kremlin continued to insist on the dismantling of US bases in Turkey and Iran, which the United States could not afford to sacrifice, in exchange for stopping the flow of Soviet arms to Egypt.

Israel's main point of dispute with its US patron, oversight of its nuclear program, had not been resolved, but it was far from destroying relations between the two countries. The United States believed it was in control of the situation in the Middle East, despite Soviet maneuvering. As long as a war did not break out, the United States would not be persuaded that Israel was a victim of the Cold War.[99] The United States remained equivocal, and both the State Department and Pentagon admitted that they were moving slowly on Israel because of their concern about the

---

97 Townsend Hoopes to Walt W. Rostow, May 1, 1967, Secret, LBJL, NSF, Box 139(2).
98 FRUS, 1964–1968, XVIII: 817–19.
99 David Ginsberg, 'Memorandum for the President,' in Bitan to Eshkol and Eban, April 27, 1967, Top Secret and Personal, ISA 3977/22.

full range of US interests in the Middle East. The United States was committed to Israel's survival, but the government and private sector had invested billions of dollars into the oil industry and earned billions in profits from it each year, thus there was no choice but to keep channels open to both camps. Israel wanted the United States to warn the Soviet Union and the Arabs not to support a Palestinian war of national liberation, but Israel had not taken the stand that the Americans wanted on the Vietnam War.[100]

A meeting of NATO experts agreed unanimously that Israel should not be abandoned and that a balance of forces had to be maintained between Israel and the Arab states. However, other Western interests in the region also had to be attended to. The border incidents with Syria, which originated in Arab terrorism, were liable to ignite flares, but no one worried they could spiral into full-scale combat. The United States thought that the Soviet Union did not want a Middle East war, although it did not seem to want to prevent one either.[101] Confidence in Israel's military superiority persuaded the US intelligence community that no real war was in the offing. However, if war broke out, it would engulf the entire Middle East in flames, and both superpowers wanted to prevent such an eventuality. Arab military inferiority was so obvious that there was no chance that other Arab countries would come to Egypt's aid if it decided to go to war,[102] and the nuclear reactor at Dimona clearly was a deterrent, at least in Israel's eyes.[103]

---

100 Hal Saunders to Walt W. Rostow, April 20, 1967, Secret, LBJL, NSF, Box 139(2).
101 'NATO Expert Working Group on the Middle East. United Kingdom Contribution,' April 4–7, 1967, Confidential, NA, FCO 17/12.
102 J.I.C. (67)26(Final), 'A Comparison of Certain Arab States up to the End of 1967,' Report by the Joint Intelligence Committee, April 17, 1967, Secret, NA, CAB 158/66.
103 Peres to Prof. Ernst D. Bergmann, May 4, 1967 S. Peres, Correspondence, 1955–65, Peres Files, LPA.

# 14

# The Soviet Union, Israel and Soviet Jewry (1964–67)

When Khrushchev was ousted in October 1964, Israel wondered how Soviet policies would change. Regarding the Jews, there were no changes. Ivan Dedioulia, first secretary of the Soviet embassy in Israel, claimed there was no anti-Jewish discrimination in the Soviet Union. Nasser's threats, he stated, were 'idle.' The Alexandria summit proved that confrontation with Israel was put off forever.[1] Israel, he said, was irrational about the refugee and water issues, and should allow the Dimona reactor to operate under IAEA oversight; he did not understand how Israel could exert so much influence over the United States.[2]

Talks between the Soviet Union and Israel focused on Soviet Jewry and trade, not the nuclear issue. The Soviet ambassador-designate, Dmitri Chuvakhin, said that Soviet Jews were not refugees and there was no reason for them to emigrate to Israel. Nevertheless, relations between the two countries improved in the post-Khrushchev era. In October 1964, Israel and the Soviet Union reached an agreement on Russian property in Israel, which seemed to herald a possible resumption of trade. Chuvakhin warned that it was important that neither side interfere in the internal affairs of the other.[3] He accused Israel of waging a campaign in the West. By contract Israel was calling for an end to anti-Jewish discrimination and anti-Semitism, with family reunification in Israel on humanitarian grounds.[4]

---

1 [Shlomo Levav,] Deputy Director DEE to IMM, 'Conversation with Russians,' October 22, 1964, Confidential, ISA 3574/9.
2 Stephen Palmer to Rusk, 'Are the Soviets Seriously Concerned that Israel Might Opt for Nuclear Weapons?,' February 22, 1965, Confidential, NARA, RG 59, NEA/NE, Box 2.
3 Katz to Eban, Levavi, Doron, October 26, 1964, Secret, ISA 3574/1; Bialer, 2005: 160–7.
4 Levavi to IDM, 'Presenting the Soviet Jewry Problem at the Coming UN Session,' November 1, 1964, Secret, ISA 3575/2.

Israel's policymakers decided that the consciousness of the international community regarding the issue of Soviet Jewry should be raised and suggested activating Communist parties abroad. Transition to a new regime in the Kremlin offered a window of opportunity, but activity would focus on the United States; in April 1964, an umbrella organization was established to lead the campaign. It shortly became apparent that early optimism had been misplaced. Eban saw no significant follow-up to Gromyko's declaration that, in principle, the Soviet Union supported the territorial integrity of all the countries in the region.[5]

Globally, the major question was whether the United States and Soviet Union could reach an agreement on regional arms control.[6] More important was the Kremlin's rejection of the Israeli proposal for negotiations with the Arabs without preconditions, and its criticism of the skirmish between Israeli and Syrian forces in the north in November, which ended with an Israeli air attack on Syrian artillery posts on November 13.[7] When Chuvakhin claimed that the world would not allow Nasser to destroy Israel, Eshkol replied that at the UN the Soviet Union always sided with the Arabs and that *Pravda* published cartoons equating Zionism with Nazism.

The main Israeli–Soviet issue was the Soviet Jews and their emigration to Israel. Chuvakhin argued that it would be contrary to the Soviet national interest, but nevertheless recommended to Gromyko that the Soviets try to improve relations with Israel in fields like trade and culture, which could be done without damaging relations with the Arabs. The Kremlin rejected his advice. Golda Meir, then foreign minister, opined that the Kremlin did not genuinely want to improve relations with Israel. It might not want to see Israel wiped off the map but that did not prevent it from encouraging and arming the Arabs.[8] The general zeitgeist made Israel focus more intently on redeeming the Soviet Jews, leading to a campaign launched with the help of the United States and its Jewish community. The State Department, however, insisted that the Soviets regarded Soviet Jews as an internal matter, just as civil rights for American blacks was an internal matter.[9] The Soviet Union claimed the

---

5 'Secretary's Delegation to the Nineteenth Session of the UNGA, New York, December 5, 1964', NARA, RG 59, NEA/NE, Box 9.
6 Savir (Cologne) to MED, October 26, 1964, 'The Situation in the Middle East,' Secret, ISA 3535/16.
7 [Bartov] to DEE, December 2, 1964, December 27, 1964, ISA, 3574/1.
8 Meir-Chuvakhin Conversation,' January 14, 1965, ISA 3573/23; ICAB, January 17, 1965, ISA.
9 Rosen to Bar [B. Eliav], 'Report on the Meeting with Tyler and Kohler,' December 9, 1964, Top Secret and Personal, ISA 3575/2.

campaign was anti-Soviet Cold War propaganda, insisting that incidents of anti-Semitism were isolated.[10]

Gromyko told Eban that the objective of Soviet policy was to reduce tensions and prevent imperialist intervention in the Middle East. Relations between the two countries were normal and correct, he said, adding that the goals should be to lessen tension between Israel and the Arabs and to prevent outside interference.[11] The Soviets claimed their Middle Eastern policy was a by-product of their relations with the West. US interest in détente offered hope to the Middle East, Gromyko said, but the Kremlin demanded that US Polaris missiles be taken out of commission. Israel said that it was threatened more by conventional arms than by nuclear weapons, and Gromyko claimed in response that the Kremlin intended to limit arms shipments to Egypt.[12] However, the Israeli foreign ministry was pessimistic.[13] On November 23, Shelepin visited Cairo, signaling closer relations between the Soviet Union and Egypt, a gesture of Soviet support important in light of Egypt's worsening economic situation.[14] Meir feared that in the absence of an East–West agreement the Cold War was approaching the Middle East. She saw Nasser as the major beneficiary, considering him an expert international blackmailer.[15]

Now it became clear that the new Soviet leadership did not intend to improve relations with Israel. The Israeli leadership resolved to increase its efforts on behalf of Soviet Jewry. Moscow's official policy continued to be the compulsory assimilation of the Jews. Meir said she hoped the issue of Soviet Jews would be on the agenda of superpower negotiations, but Israel, not wanting to endanger its own relations with the Eastern bloc, waited futilely for the United States, Britain and France to make the case for Soviet Jewry at international events.[16] The State Department still refused to exert official pressure on the Kremlin regarding its treatment of Soviet Jews.[17]

---

10  Ram Nirgad (New York) to Doron, December 14, 1964, ISA 3575/2.
11  IMUN (Comay) to IFM, Y. Herzog, 'Minutes of Conversation between Eban and Gromyko, at the USSR Mission,' December 18, 1964, ISA 3571/1.
12  Gazit to Doron, 'Conversation with the Senior Adviser in Soviet Embassy Washington, Alexander I. Zinchuk,' December 28 [24], 1964, ISA 3573/24.
13  Doron to Gazit, January 4, 1965, ISA 3573/24.
14  IMM (Tekoah) to IFM, Avriel and Doron, December 30, 1964, Personal, ISA 2573/24.
15  KR 42: 1698 (Meir).
16  '"Sareinu" Session in Meir's House,' January 26, 1965, ISA 7934/1a.
17  Eliav (New York) to Netzer, February 10, 1965, ISA 4092/2.

In the meantime, Kosygin called the Arabs the Soviet Union's natural allies[18] and publicly supported wars of national liberation.[19] Its disappointment with the new Soviet regime caused the Israeli government to allow Nativ to encourage Soviet Jews to emigrate to Israel, knowing that whatever Israel did would be perceived in the context of the Cold War. There was a rise in immigration from the Soviet Union, with 531 Soviet Jews allowed to leave for Israel in 1964 as opposed to only seven in 1959, a fact kept secret lest it arouse Arab anger.

Nativ's head, Avigur, was encouraged when, in August 1964, Khrushchev granted official recognition to the national rights of the Soviet Union's 1.6 million ethnic Germans and Armenians.[20] However, the Soviets claimed the Jews were not a national group but rather a privileged, elite class of professionals. When the Soviets forbade raising the issue of the Jews at international forums, Israel regarded it as tacit acknowledgment that whether they were a national group or a special class, they constituted a problem.[21] Chuvakhin claimed that the Vietnam War and Israel's position on Soviet Jews prevented improved relations. The Israeli foreign ministry argued that the Marxist doctrine of historical materialism required the Soviet Union to recognize that Israel's political weight was greater than its population would indicate. Chuvakhin agreed, but complained that Israel had tied its fate to the West.[22] Israel rejected Soviet criticism of its decision to establish diplomatic relations with West Germany, noting that the Soviets dealt with the German industrial firm Krupp despite its pro-Nazi past, yet Israel had to apologize for buying arms from West Germany. The arms the West was providing to West Germany and Israel were defensive. The Arab countries severed their relations with West Germany after it established diplomatic relations with Israel in May 1965. The Soviet Union hardened its line against Israel, believing West Germany was a full partner in NATO's nuclear arms program.[23]

As Israeli–Soviet relations worsened an official protest was lodged with Israel's ambassador to Moscow, in which the Soviets charged an

18 DEE Diary (4), DEE Bulletin No. 16, September 30, 1965, ISA 3013/6.
19 Kosygin was interviewed by James Reston in the *New York Times* on December 8, 1965.
20 KFADC, March 9, 1965 (Doron, Avigur), ISA.
21 Report by Marmor, IMUN, 'Soviet Representative on Russian Jewry Problem,' DEE Bulletin No. 15, Secret and Personal, September 3, 1965, ISA 3013/6.
22 Palmer, Embassy Tel Aviv to Department of State, March 22, 1965, Secret, NARA, RG 84, NEA/NE Files, POL ISRA-USSR, Box 2.
23 IMM [Govrin], 'Conversation with Vladimir Mayorov, in Charge of Israel in the Soviet Foreign Office,' May 12, 1965, ISA 3574/1.

IDF build-up along the Syrian border. Imperialist forces in the Middle East, they claimed, were ignoring the UN General Assembly resolution to prohibit interference in the internal affairs of member states. The Soviet Union blamed the United States for the lack of Middle East disarmament negotiations,[24] while *Pravda* attacked what it called Israeli provocations, such as its reprisals in Jordanian territory.[25] Israel asked Poland to help mend fences with the Soviet Union; Poland refused, saying the Soviet Union viewed Israel as a Western state in every respect.[26]

Before his return to Israel, Ambassador Yosef Tekoah expressed hope that the Soviet Union would eventually recognize the full significance of Israel's rebirth, but Moscow's threats were distressing, he said, because of the arms race. Gromyko equivocated, arguing that relations between the two countries were fairly normal and correct.[27] However, Nasser's visit to Moscow (August 27–September 1) revealed the Kremlin's real intentions. In a joint declaration issued on September 1, the Soviet Union stated its full support for the anti-imperialist struggle of the Arab peoples. The declaration did, however, note the principles of peaceful coexistence and respect for the sovereignty and territorial integrity of all the countries in the region.[28]

There was no progress on either the regional conflict or the issue of Soviet Jewry. There were small gestures, such as the opening of a *yeshiva* (Talmudic college) in Moscow and promises that Jews would be allowed to bake *matzot* for Passover. While Israel did not consider the gestures particularly significant, they did mark a small retreat by the Kremlin, the result of pressure. Perhaps, Israeli leaders thought, the Soviet ramparts could finally be breached.[29] Katriel Katz, Israel's new ambassador to Moscow, sought to thaw relations through cultural and commercial exchanges. He complained to Jerusalem that Soviet–Israeli relations were a function of Soviet–Arab relations. He was told that the Arabs did in fact demand that the Soviets treat Israel as a pariah state,

24 Aba Gefen (Buenos Aires) to DEE, 'Conversation with the Soviet Adviser,' June 20, 1965, ISA 3573/22.
25 Levavi to IMM, 'Eban-Chuvakhin Discussion,' May 31, 1965, [June 3, 1965], ISA, 3573/22.
26 'Doron's Journey in East Europe,' DEE Bulletin No. 13, from DEE Diary, June 28, 1965, Secret, Personal, ISA 3013/6.
27 DEE Bulletin No. 14, DEE Diary, (1) 'Soviet Union' (2) 'The Ambassador in Moscow Leaves His Post,' July 21, 1965, ISA 3013/6.
28 Bartov to Doron, August 29, 1965, ISA 3574/9; Doron to Foreign Minister [Meir], September 2, 1965, ISA 3574/9; Heikal, 1978: 143–7.
29 Doron to IDM, 'Interim Summary,' September 6, 1965, ISA 3013/6; cf. ICAB, October 24, 1965 (Meir), ISA.

but the fact that it still had diplomatic relations with Israel showed it had rejected the demand. Israel did not believe a real change was likely to occur because the new Kremlin leadership was weak and the war in Vietnam was eroding peaceful coexistence. Israel could only maneuver through the situation using cultural, tourist and commercial ties. The Soviet Union wanted to keep Israel as a card to play against the Arabs, it was argued, and thus refused to grant them the means to destroy Israel, nuclear weapons for example.

Israel was certain that eventually there would be a change in the official Soviet line. The Kremlin regarded Israel's importance as worthy of consideration, given its influence and international ties, but Alexander Shchiborin, the director of the Middle East department in the Soviet foreign ministry, hinted that the 'Elders of Zion' were steering world events.[30] Israel said that while the Soviet constitution forbade anti-Semitism, Jews were constrained in all areas of life by a high-level order amounting to official anti-Semitism, while Katz said that there was but a narrow gap between Nazi and Soviet anti-Semitic propaganda.[31] However, the Israeli foreign ministry saw signs of moderation in the Soviet press and *Novoye Vremya* published a letter from the Moscow correspondent of the Israeli Communist Party's newspaper defending Israel's water rights in the Jordan River basin.[32]

Katz argued that the only solution for Soviet Jews was emigration to Israel and not only for family reunification. It was an illusion, he said, to believe that a change in the Kremlin's rhetoric indicated an upcoming policy change. Such a decision would not be made in the Soviet foreign ministry, only through Communist Party institutions, which determined the Soviet Union's foreign policy.[33] Israel's Communist leaders were told that that the Soviet Union did not challenge Israel's right to exist, but that the rights of the country's Arab minority and the Palestinian diaspora had to be defended, although there were indications that the Soviets had little respect for the doctrines of Arab socialism and unity.[34]

Eshkol tried to establish better relations with the Soviet Union, rejecting claims that Israel supported the West in the Cold War. On the contrary,

---

30  Katz to Doron, 'Conversation with Shchiborin,' December 1, 1965, ISA 3573/22.
31  Doron to Eytan, 'Impressions,' December 9, 1965, ISA 3563/20.
32  Doron to Meir, 'Positive Revelations in the Soviet Press,' December 7, 1965, ISA 961/25.
33  Doron, 'Impressions from a Journey to East European Countries (May-June 1965),' October 5, 1965, Secret, ISA 3563/20.
34  'The Soviet Communist Party and the Split in Maki,' DEE Bulletin No. 20, DEE Diary, January 26, 1966, ISA 5968/19.

he said, Israel was doing its utmost to end the Cold War, for example, by endorsing the Soviet principle of resolving territorial disputes without resorting to force. In the Knesset, however, he sharply criticized the Soviet Union for its treatment of the Jews. In response, Chuvakhin accused Eshkol of asking for international pressure to be exerted on the Soviet Union. He was particularly angry with Eshkol for his use of the phrase 'forced assimilation.' Gromyko's speech supporting the creation of the Jewish state in 1947, Chuvakhin claimed, had been intended to cover only those Jews already living in Palestine.[35]

Levavi, now director general of the Israeli foreign ministry, said that Israel found itself trapped between hope for immigration from the Soviet Union and dependence on the West, which forbade its taking an anti-US position in the Vietnam War. He admitted that Israel had very little international influence.[36] Eban concluded that the Soviet Union wanted to increase regional tensions, such as in Yemen, but only that.[37] The Kremlin's official position was that they had made it clear to the Arabs not to rely on the Soviet Union if they attacked Israel. Israel rejected the claim because the Kremlin refused to halt or even curb its arms shipments to the Arab states.[38]

Chuvakhin told Gromyko what he wanted to hear, that Israel was important to the West's strategic program and served as a link between NATO and CENTO (Central Treaty Organization, originally the Baghdad Pact), but economically, he said, Israel was barely eking out. Surprisingly, he proposed that the Soviet Union launch a peace initiative in the four-power forum and the UN. The provisions, he suggested, should be a cessation of arms shipments, a nuclear-free zone (even if it did not include the removal of the US Sixth Fleet from the Mediterranean) and a reinforcement of progressive forces in the entire area to achieve neutrality and curb the Arab extremists calling for Israel's destruction. Finally, he warned that a local conflagration could lead to a world war.[39] Eban acknowledged that Israel relied on the United States, but insisted that it sought a four-way agreement, even an informal one, to slow down the arms race. The Arabs, he said, accepted

---

35 Meroz (Paris) to Avner (Ottawa), February 2, 1966, ISA 7935/9/a.
36 DEE Bulletin No. 21, DEE Diary, '(1) The Soviet Union,' February 25, 1966, Secret, Personal, ISA 3013/6.
37 Doron to IMM, [9] March 13, 1966, Secret, ISA 4048/28.
38 Evron (Washington) to Bitan, 'Conversation with the Minister in the Soviet Embassy, Alexander Zinchuk,' March 22, 1966, Secret, ISA 4048/28; cf. Peres detailed list of the arms supplied by the Soviets to the Arabs: KFADC, March 9, 1965.
39 Chuvakhin to Gromyko, in SDMEC 2: 491–9 (March 21, 1966).

Israel's diversion of the Jordan River because they did not want an outbreak of hostilities.[40]

Eshkol told Chuvakhin that Israel needed immigration for its development. With immigration, its population would reach three million by the end of the decade and five million by the end of the century. He cautioned that the lull in the conflict with the Arabs was temporary and that the situation could deteriorate. Chuvakhin argued that the Soviet Union had a duty to aid peoples fighting colonialism, and that included the Arabs.[41] Relations between the two countries continued to be correct, but cool. At most there was a marginal improvement and Soviet consent to allow more family reunification and to restrain anti-Israel propaganda.[42] However, when the neo-Ba'ath party seized power in Syria in February 1966, the new Syrian prime minister visited Moscow and a joint communiqué was issued. It declared Soviet support for the Palestinian struggle against Zionism and gave Soviet legitimization to Syria's support for the Palestine Liberation Organization's (PLO) terrorist campaign.[43] In addition, Kosygin visited Cairo in May (10–19), where he said that a certain country possessed nuclear arms and declared his support for the Palestinian people's struggle for their rights.[44]

The principal Soviet concern was the United States' intention to deploy nuclear weapons in German territory, which the Soviet Union connected with ex-Chancellor Konrad Adenauer's visit to Israel and his evasive attitude to the Oder–Neisse border.[45] Levavi acknowledged that European security was a matter of life and death for the Soviet Union and the entire world, but to achieve peace in Europe it was necessary to prevent hostilities in other areas.[46] Israel defended its reprisals in Jordan and Syria, saying it would not turn the other cheek when attacked. That

---

40 Doron to IMM, March 29 [30], 1966, Secret, ISA 4048/28.
41 Doron to IMM, April 22, 1966, Secret, ISA, 4048/28.
42 Doron to Eban, 'Our Relations with East European Countries,' April 26, 1966, ISA 4048/29.
43 Communiqué of Syrian Prime Minister in the Soviet Union, April 26, 1966, Confidential, ISA.
44 MBR to the Ambassador (Ottawa), 'Tekoah's Evaluation,' May 22, 1966, ISA 4049/5.
45 The Potsdam summit had established the Oder–Neisse border between Poland and East Germany. However, West Germany refused to recognise it. Israel was aware of the political repercussions of the Oder–Neisse border on her unrecognized borders with her Arab neighbors, which where agreed upon only as armistice agreements in Rhodes in 1949. These borders were recognized as international borders by the UN only after the Six Day War.
46 Tekoah to IMM, Warsaw, May 23 [11], 1966, Secret, ISA 4048/29.

might have been what the Jews did in the ghettoes, but not in the Jewish state.[47] Eban still believed it was possible to curb the deterioration of Israeli–Soviet relations, claiming that the international situation determined the Soviet position. Any change in relations would require the Soviets to regard Israel not as an underestimated force and to realize they gave too much emphasis to the positions of the Arabs.[48]

About a year before the Six Day War, the Kremlin began heightening the tension in Israel's north. Vladimir Semyonov, the Soviet deputy foreign minister, warned of concentrations of Israeli forces along the northern border, claiming it was part of an imperialist offensive.[49] Eban said that Israel was acting with restraint on the Syrian border and did not retaliate when a Fatah mine laid with tacit Syrian consent killed two civilians on May 16, near Elmagor. Israel, he emphasized, was the victim of Syrian aggression. Levavi quoted to Chuvakhin speeches made by the Syrian president calling for a war of annihilation against Israel.[50]

Eban refused to surrender. He wanted East–West détente and hoped for a pragmatic Arab approach to Israel. It was unclear what was motivating the Kremlin, possibly the reactor in Dimona, possibly its own Jewish problem, possibly both on the backdrop of the East–West conflict, perhaps a desire to create a 'new Cuba' on the Syrian border.[51] For whatever reason, they were acting against Israel, which in turn was supporting Soviet Jewry. The Soviet Union had the means to punish Israel, it could recognize PLO chief Ahmad Shukeiry and withdraw its support for the territorial status quo. However, Israel's real fear was Soviet involvement in Syria. Meir Amit, the director of Mossad, was worried by the arms display the Soviets put on during Egypt's Revolution Day; Eshkol claimed the Soviets did not frighten him.[52]

Israel had few illusions, but it had not properly appreciated the significance and importance of Syrian Communist Party participation in the Ba'ath government. It became apparent that Soviet support of the new Ba'ath regime was not just propaganda. The Soviet Union now wanted Syria to act as a bridgehead in the Middle East. Israel felt that diplomacy

---

47 Katz to DEE, 'Conversation with Shchiborin,' May 17, 1966, Secret, ISA 4048/24.
48 'Eban to the Heads of Departments in IFM on His Visit to Poland,' May 24, 1966, Secret, ISA 1387/10.
49 'Letter Given by the Soviet Foreign Ministry to Ambassador Katz,' May 25, 1966, ISA 7935/9; ICAB, May 29, 1966 (Eban), ISA.
50 Doron to IMM, April 26, 1966, Secret, ISA 4048/24.
51 KFADC, May 31, 1966 (Eban and Namir), ISA.
52 'Raphael and Evron Conversation with Rusk,' July 27, 1966, Secret, ISA 3977/16/3; KFADC, July 12, 1966 (Amit), ISA; July 19, 1966 (Eshkol), ISA 3977/16/3.

should be used to improve relations, but overt acts of hostility should be responded to forcefully. However, the US ambassador to Israel, Walworth Barbour, was not particularly concerned by Soviet declarations about preparing for war with Israel, regarding them as propaganda resulting from the loss of global Soviet influence and the weakness of the Syrian regime. Nevertheless, Israel pursued a cautious path and did not establish diplomatic relations with South Vietnam, fearing the Kremlin would exploit the move to further worsen relations.[53]

It was not only the Soviet Union's expansionism in the Middle East that caused Israeli–Soviet relations to deteriorate, but also the international campaign for Soviet Jewry. The Soviets declared David Gavish, the second secretary in Israel's embassy in Moscow, persona non grata and expelled him from the country, theoretically on charges of espionage, but in fact because of his involvement in a local Zionist circle.[54] Clearly, Israel could not respond by expelling Soviet diplomats. Israel was active in the Soviet Union not only because of its Zionist ideological obligations and demographic plight, but also because of Soviet anti-Semitism. Anti-Semitic incitement was rife in Soviet scientific institutions and other places where Jews were generally employed, and propaganda depicted Israel as an agent of Western espionage, carried out in the Soviet Union by the Jewish minority. The West, the Soviets thought, needed Soviet Jewish spies because having failed to spy on the Soviet Union on its own. Israel was also regarded by the Soviets as a bridgehead for Western subversion in the Arab countries.

On October 3, *Pravda* accused Israel of concentrating forces on the Syrian border with the eventual objective of overthrowing the Syrian regime ('General Rabin is Polishing his Sabers'). Israel's military preparations, the article claimed, were accompanied by a highly visible visit by the Sixth Fleet's flagship, the *Springfield*, to Beirut and the cessation of negotiations between the Syrian government and the British oil company Iraq Petroleum. Moreover, the United States and Saudi Arabia had allotted $250 million to the plot to overthrow the Syrian leadership, *Pravda* continued. Eshkol denied the accusations, stating that Israel did not interfere in the internal affairs of other countries and wanted peace, although it knew how to defend itself against aggression.[55]

---

53 Shek to IDM, Paris, Rome, Brussels, Bonn, June 19, 1966, Top Secret, Personal, ISA 3975/12.
54 Katz to Nativ Director General, August 1, 1966, Top Secret, Urgent, ISA 7935/9a; ICAB, August 14, 1966 (Eshkol), ISA.
55 Bartov to DEE, 'Anti-Israeli Incitement among Jews in Moscow,' September 26, 1966, ISA 4059/9; Katz to DEE, October 30, 1966, ISA 4048/23 (after Rabin's interview in IDF weekly *Bamahaneh*, September 12, 1966).

Gromyko demanded that Israel condemn US involvement in Vietnam and denounced Israel's activities in Africa, which he claimed were being guided by the West. Eban responded that the Soviet Union did not recognize the armistice lines between Israel and its neighbors. According to Gromyko, the staff of the Israeli embassy in Moscow was disseminating propaganda and meeting with Soviet Jews.[56] The Kremlin claimed it was trying to curb Syria, but that it did not always listen to Moscow.[57]

By March 1966, with the Soviets increasing their ties to the new regime in Damascus, relations between Moscow and Jerusalem were rapidly deteriorating.[58] Israel reasoned that the Middle East was an ideal arena for the Soviet Union to pursue its interests while the United States was tied down in Vietnam. The Kremlin again employed brinksmanship and warned Israel that the USSR was taking all necessary measures to prevent a violation of Middle East peace and regional security, accusing Israel of fanning the flames in coordination with the West. Katz took a bleak view of the way the Soviets linked the incidents on the Israel–Syria border with the Cold War. Chuvakhin claimed that Moscow was doing everything it could to rein in the Syrians while accusing Eshkol of having lost control of his militaristic machine. Gromyko reported to the Central Committee that Israel was responsible for the tension on the Syrian border, while the Soviet ambassador in Damascus asked the Syrian prime minister to curb Fatah, which enjoyed support from China.[59] Despite its public support for the Syrian position, the Soviet Union acknowledged that the situation on the Israel–Syria border was volatile. At the same time, the West feared that if the UN Security Council did not explicitly condemn Syria for its support of terrorism, Israel would carry out a reprisal.[60]

Israel might have unlinked the issue of Soviet Jewry from the Kremlin's support for the radical Arab states, but it is doubtful whether such a strategy would have helped. On December 3, Kosygin held a press conference in Paris where he claimed that his government was doing everything in its power to enable family reunification. The

---

56 IMUN to IFM, Levavi, October 1, 1966, Secret, Immediate, ISA 4048/23.
57 Evron to Bitan, October 4, 1966, Top Secret, Personal, ISA 4048/23.
58 Zak, 1988: 305–8.
59 Katz to Eban, November 9, 1966, Secret, Urgent, ISA 4049/27; ICAB, October, 8 1966 (Eban), ISA; SDMEC 2: 526–36.
60 Caradon to Brown, 'The Security Council: Consideration of the Israeli Complaint Against Syria,' November 15, 1966, Confidential, NA, FO 371/186839/ER1091/253.

announcement, Israel said, would have to be judged by its implementation.⁶¹ However, Israeli policy toward the Soviet Union was a gamble because the internal workings of the Kremlin remained a mystery. The only indication of the Kremlin's decision-making process was a combination of vitriolic attacks on Israel in the Soviet press and the careful protocol followed by Soviet diplomats in their conversations with their Israeli counterparts. Chuvakhin pointed out the contradiction between Eban's conciliatory language and the extremist statements made by Minister of Labor Yigal Allon, who had warned of the consequences of the entry of the Egyptian army into Jordan or the West Bank. Eban said that Allon was expressing his personal opinion and that Israel was committed to the ceasefire agreements and had no interest in occupying the West Bank in the event of Hussein's assassination.⁶²

Tekoah remained optimistic. Cultural, academic and commercial ties with the Soviet Union could be expanded and Israel could participate in a future East–West détente. There was a clear contradiction in Soviet policy, in that the Kremlin did not want hostilities it might have to become involved in, but tension in the region helped it realize its ambitions. The Soviet Union was restraining the Arabs, but at the same time tightening its hold on them. The benefit to Israel would come if an East–West accommodation were achieved, which was possible because of the growing rift between Peking and Moscow.⁶³

The United States, and Israel to a certain extent, assumed that the Kremlin had the Arab–Israeli conflict under control. However, the Soviet embassy in Washington claimed that the Syrians refused to take Soviet advice to avoid war and turn its attention to internal development. The solution, according to the Soviets, was for all the countries in the region to take a neutral position in the East–West conflict.⁶⁴ Increasingly, there were signs that the Kremlin was linking domestic Jewish issues to its Middle East policy, and had no compunction about vilifying both Judaism and Zionism.⁶⁵

---

61 B. Eliav to Friends in the US, 'Our Reaction to Kosygin Announcement in Paris,' December 11, 1966, Secret, ISA 7938/6a.
62 Ilan to IDEEM, 'Eban-Chuvakhin Conversation,' December 21, 1966, Secret, ISA 312/2.
63 Tekoah to Eban, Levavi, 'Israel-Soviet Union: Suggestions for Summary,' December 29, 1966, Secret, Personal, ISA 4049/23.
64 Evron to IFM, 'Conversation with Soviet Chargé Zinchuk,' December 20, 1966, ISA 4097/1.
65 [No author, no date], 'Israel and the Soviet Union,' ISA 63823–4/a.

Israel put the Soviet Jewish issue at the top of its priorities, even though it was harmful to Israeli–Soviet relations, justifying itself as motivated by its responsibility for the fate of the Jewish nation. Thus, despite the overwhelming importance of the Cold War, Israel was committed to the ingathering of the Jewish Diaspora and was completely open and sincere in its position.[66] Soviet policy was fixed and anti-Israeli, but only up to a certain point. The Soviets no longer mentioned Israel's right to exist lest it upset the global balance of power. Moscow's restraint in the face of Israel's reprisal on July 14, and August 19, indicated that it would not intervene in the future.[67]

According to Israeli analysis, the Soviet Union would not seek additional arenas for expansion because of its problems with China, Romania and East Germany. Yet the situation in the Middle East seemed to invite the realization of the old Russian dream to isolate Turkey and take control of the sea lanes between the Mediterranean and the Indian Ocean. In the meantime, Israel relied on the United States, expecting that Soviet conditions for ending the Vietnam War would include the reduction of tensions in other areas. Israel's foreign ministry believed that negotiations to end the war would soon begin, with a tactical advantage for the United States, enabling a package deal that would include the Middle East and Southeast Asia.[68]

Even if Israel did not expect direct Soviet involvement in a future Middle East war, it became more worried. The Sixth Fleet, the United States insisted, provided Israel with a military advantage. Eban told Harold Wilson, the British prime minister, that in any case Israel felt besieged ('we have a Cuban attitude'), and complained that the Kremlin wanted to preserve tension without causing an explosion. However, if it did not curb the Arabs, there could easily be a war. Only fear of China, Eban maintained, would impel the Soviet Union to move closer to the West, which would give the West new bargaining power in the Middle East.[69]

---

66 M. Yuval, 'Israel and the Soviet Union,' Information for IDM, January 13, 1967, ISA 1396/19.
67 IDF General Headquaters, Intelligence Department, Special Intelligence Survey, 16/67, January 25, 1967, Secret, ISA 7935/9a.
68 Karmil to Tekoah, February 12, 1967, ISA 4049/6.
69 'Eban-Wilson Conversation,' February 20, 1967, ISA 3977/21; Record of Meeting between the Foreign Secretary and the Foreign Minister of Israel Mr Abba Eban, February 21, 1967, NA, PREM 13/1582/ER3/3.

The Soviets, said the Israeli leadership, were increasing their penetration of Syria and southern Arabia and, while there was cause for concern, the situation was not yet critical. The United States was aware of the situation and was exercising vigilance. What worried Israel was the danger of the establishment of an East European Communist-style popular democracy in Syria. However, on April 7, 1967, Israel downed seven Syrian planes, and the situation changed dramatically: the region was now hurtling toward the Six Day War. The Soviets attributed the incident to the forces of imperialism and extremist Israeli militarists. They quoted Rabin as having promised an Israeli response. The Kremlin warned Israel that it had to examine the existing situation carefully and not turn their country into a pawn in the hands of hostile foreign powers.[70]

At a cabinet meeting on April 17, Eshkol voiced his concern about the Soviet Union's accusation that Israel was acting on behalf of imperialist interests. He also worried about the closing of the qualitative gap in military capability between Israel and the Arabs. However, he took comfort in the severe economic situation in Egypt. NATO's experts reportedly believed that the rivalry between Nasser and King Faisal of Saudi Arabia had marginalized the conflict with Israel on the Syrian border.[71] In the meantime, Soviet threats grew stronger. Semyonov condemned both the United States and Israel, saying that local conflicts near the Soviet Union were especially dangerous.[72]

In his final conversations with Levavi just prior to the crisis of May 1967, Chuvakhin disregarded UN Secretary General U Thant's censure of Fatah operations and asserted that Israel was solely responsible for terrorist acts on its territory and would bear the consequences. It had to consider the connection, he said, between the frequency of border incidents and the internal situation in Syria. Border tensions resulted from disputes between the West and Syria. Levavi responded that Syria and Fatah acknowledged their responsibility for the incidents. The Soviet Union, he said, should use its influence with Syria to prevent border clashes. Chuvakhin blamed 'Israeli organizations.' Israel, he said, was not permitted to cultivate fields located in the demilitarized zones on its

---

70 'Communique by the Soviet Foreign Ministry,' April 21, 1967, as read to Katz by Deputy Foreign Minister Malik, Top Secret, ISA 7226/6.
71 'Meeting of NATO Experts on the Middle East,' April 4–7, 1967, 'German Contribution,' Paris, March 28, 1967, NA, FCO 17/12.
72 Katz to Tekoah, April 27, 1967, Confidential, Immediate, ISA 4048/30.

border with Syria and it was unfortunate that it had no explicit plans for achieving peace with its neighbors.⁷³

Worsening relations between the Soviet Union and Israel were exacerbated by Israel's increasing international pressure regarding the issue of Soviet Jewry, but its importance should not be exaggerated. As long as the issue was not part of East–West détente negotiations, Israel had no chance of success. Moreover, the Arab–Israeli conflict was not independent of the Cold War, but was subject to its dynamics. The Soviets sought

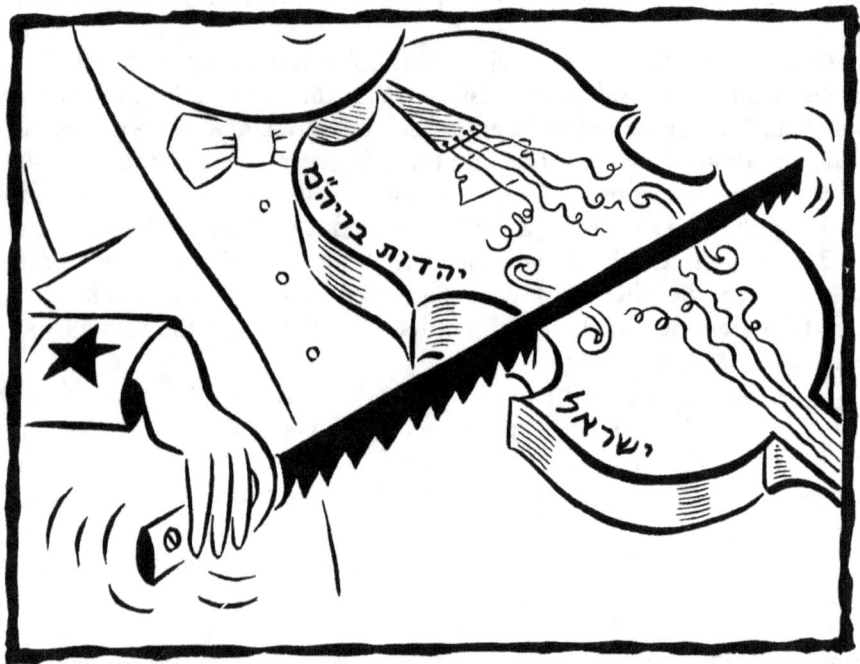

**Figure 2** 'The Soviet government cancels the exchange of orchestras with Israel' by Yaakov Farkash (Ze'ev), September 26, 1966. The text on the left says 'Soviet Jewry,' while the text on the right says 'Israel.'

73 Ilan to Katz, 'Levavi-Chuvakhin Conversation,' May 12, 1967, Top Secret, Immediate, ISA 3977/22.

The Soviet Union, Israel and Soviet Jewry

**Figure 3** 'Moscow is ready to send its football team to Israel' by Yaakov Farkash (Ze'ev), September 27, 1966. The original caption says, 'Do you have a headache? Take a ball [pill]!'

to break through US containment and viewed the Arab states as effective tools for achieving their goal. The cost did not seem particularly high, especially since the Kremlin believed that it was in control of the situation. In fact, the crisis that led to the Six Day War proved the extent to which the Soviets had in fact failed to control its Arab clients.

# 15

# The United States and the crisis of the Six Day War (May 14–June 5, 1967)

The United States was entirely unprepared for the Six Day War despite the warnings Israel had sent to Washington. In May 1967, an American research group presented Walt Rostow with possible scenarios for a Middle East emergency, but too late, as the United States had not prepared itself for such an eventuality. On May 22, when contingency plans were reviewed, it became apparent that, aside from 1,400 Marines in Naples, there was no large force that could easily be deployed.[1] Prime Minister Eshkol, the IDF command and the Israeli government knew local tensions could easily deteriorate into war, and the IDF demanded Israel stage a preemptive attack. One potential site was the Syrian border. Israel had conducted raids in response to attacks by Arab terrorists and regarded Syria's project to divert the headwaters of the Jordan River as an act of war. Eshkol, concerned about the danger and hoping for a diplomatic solution, warned against a new operation involving Syria ('Will we live on our sword all our life?').[2] Allon warned Syria not to instigate a 'popular war' by the Palestinians, because it could be the target of a 'devastating offensive' by Israel.[3]

Temporarily, Eshkol prevailed and no action was taken. Israel continued to warn of an imminent escalation, but in Washington the warnings fell on deaf ears, while US officials complained Israel did not update them on its military planning. However, in mid-May Nasser had expelled the UN observers and the Egyptian army entered the Sinai Peninsula. Rusk maintained that the Soviets were the key factor, conducting a policy of brinksmanship and not avoiding risk the way the United States did. For Israel, the US position on regional Soviet penetration did not provide sufficient security. Soviet aggression was obvious and it was unclear how

---

1 Thomas Enders to Mr. Rostow, White House, Draft, Arab–Israeli Contingency Paper, Attachments 4–5 to follow, May 22, 1967, LBJL, NSF Country, Box 105.
2 Eshkol, *Lamerchav*, Headline, May 12, 1967.
3 Interview with Minister of Labor Yigal Allon, *Lamerchav*, May 14, 1967: 2.

far the Soviet Union would go to risk war. US ambiguity in the Middle East encouraged the Kremlin, Israel maintained, and the United States needed to decide how deep its commitment to the region was, taking into consideration that its resources were being drained by the Vietnam War.[4] There was a significant discrepancy between Israel's priorities and those of the Johnson administration. Walt Rostow felt the various Ba'ath factions were vying for power, bringing anarchy to the regime, and Egypt would not go to war without Syria. Thus, it was difficult for the US administration to understand what made Nasser aggressive, because Egypt apparently did not want to anger the United States, especially since President Johnson had granted all of its requests.[5] The US chargé d'affaires in Cairo had informed Egypt's government that Israel was not calling up its reserves and that the United States would not tolerate an Egyptian attack on Israel unless it was provoked. If necessary, he said, the United States would take forceful action as it had done in 1956. Egypt promised not to take the initiative, but would defend itself if attacked.[6] Visiting the region, Harold Saunders, the NSC's Middle East expert, did not see evidence of an impending war. He told Rostow that the President had to display warmth toward Israel, but to consider the state of the dollar and the positive US balance of payments in the Middle East, where it had a surplus of hundreds of millions of dollars, as opposed to a worldwide deficit of over a billion. Israel, however, felt that the West needed to be convinced that the Middle East was part of the Cold War. It claimed that the United States and the Soviet Union had drawn global de facto borders in which Communist expansion would be allowed and the time had come to limit it in the Middle East. The State Department, taking its cue from *Pravda* and *Izvestia*, was certain that the Kremlin did not want a Middle East war. Vietnam and Germany, they said, were the real obstacles to an East–West accord. The Soviets did not want détente in the Middle East because tension helped increase its influence, so although it might continue fomenting dissention, that did not mean it wanted war.[7]

The Johnson administration realized how serious the situation was on May 17, when it learned that Egypt's chief of staff had demanded the evacuation of UNEF from the Sinai Peninsula. The administration was worried by reports of Syrian and Egyptian confidence that the Soviet

---

4 Shlomo Argov, Deputy Director of USD, to Tekoah, May 14, 1967, Top Secret, ISA 4078/4.
5 Evron to Bitan and Peres, May 16, 1967, Top Secret, Personal, ISA 7938/10a.
6 FRUS, 1964–1968, XIX: 6–7.
7 Levanon to Bitan, May 17, 1967, ISA 3975/17.

Union would aid them in a war. The United States supported the Israeli claim that in international law an attack on a country was an attack by a country,[8] that is, Israel's neighbors could not shirk responsibility for terrorist attacks. Rostow cautioned that the Egyptian army deployment in the Sinai Peninsula was an exercise in brinkmanship. Unfortunately, Israel's threats merely confirmed Syria's claims about its mobilization. Johnson warned Eshkol not to worsen the situation. He said he could not be responsible for actions taken by Israel without consulting with the United States. The United States wanted to defuse the situation, he said, and was sensitive to the Soviet–Arab lie that the Americans and Israelis were plotting together.[9]

Eshkol was disappointed because Johnson had not mentioned the US promise to defend Israel even as Syria and Egypt were being promised Soviet support. There were developments urgently requiring the reassertion of US commitment, not only Soviet support for the Arabs, but also the enormous military force Egypt had deployed close to the Israeli border (four divisions and 600 tanks) and its support for terrorist attacks against northern Israel.[10] In point of fact, the United States and the Soviet Union were not in control of the situation. The Soviet ambassador to Washington, Anatoly Dobrynin, promised Eugene Rostow, Deputy Secretary of State for Political Affairs, that the Soviet government was trying to calm the situation. Washington warned Israel that the test would be the blocking of the Straits of Tiran.[11]

Walt Rostow suggested that if Israel commenced hostilities the US administration should check with the Pentagon for a military response, and only then reaffirm the US commitment. On May 19, Johnson consulted with Rusk, Rostow and McNamara. The Middle East crisis, they believed, required nothing more than repeating the guarantee of the regional status quo (the Tripartite Declaration). The Pentagon, however, recommended that on short notice part of the Sixth Fleet could be sent from Italy to the Eastern Mediterranean.[12] The US commitment was conditioned on Israel not initiating military action without advance US approval. Israel assigned a major part of responsibility for the crisis to the administration, believing that the feeble US response to Soviet and Egyptian actions over the previous year had led to the current impasse.[13]

8   Evron to Bitan and Raphael, May 17, 1967, ISA 4078/4.
9   Harman to Levavi, May 18, 1967, Top Secret, Personal, Urgent, ISA, 4078/4.
10  FRUS, 1964–1968, XIX: 19–23.
11  FRUS, 1964–1968, XIX: 24–6.
12  FRUS, 1964–1968, XIX: 30–4.
13  Harman to Eban, May 20, 1967, Secret, Urgent, ISA 4078/4.

The US administration said that it stood by the 1957 agreements guaranteeing Israeli vessels free navigation through the Straits of Tiran. The commitment was conditional on Israel's not taking military action without first consulting Washington. Israel was not satisfied and tried to persuade the State Department to send a US destroyer to Eilat to test the blockade, a request rejected on the grounds that it would be regarded as provocation. The United States would act only under UN auspices, and the only US aid offered to Israel was the immediate supply of 20,000 gas masks.[14] Particularly worrying was the American claim that it was not the right time to respond to Israel's security needs. However, the greatest disappointment was the US failure to counter Soviet policy. Eban called for the administration to demand that the Egyptian army withdraw from Sinai, ensure that part of UNEF remain in place and demand talks on freedom of navigation.[15]

The Arabs continued their military build-up and rhetoric. Syria talked about 'defeating the Crusaders' while Egypt, US officials reported, hoped that Israel would start a war so that the Arabs could defeat it. The Americans warned Egypt's leaders not to assess the situation based on information received from Moscow and Damascus. The Soviet and Syrian leaderships claimed that Israel was preparing to attack Syria, but had no real evidence.[16] On May 21, Johnson told a disappointed Eshkol that Israel had to trust UN Secretary General U Thant to defuse the situation.[17] Israel said a war could break out because of a Soviet miscalculation, but it was not entirely clear if the Kremlin had promised Syrians backing, and Johnson would not make a formal commitment.[18]

On May 23, Nasser closed the Straits of Tiran. The United States, pleading for time, requested that Israel not send ships to test the blockade, and the United States would inform Moscow that it was an act of aggression. Johnson sent a halfhearted letter to Nasser stating that any illegal crossing of borders in the Middle East could lead to war, but that US–Egyptian friendship remained firm. He praised Nasser for his development and modernization efforts and said that he hoped to continue working with him, but that it was vital to save the Middle East, and all of humanity, from war. At the same time, Eugene Rostow repeated

---

14 Harman to Levavi, Bitan, Raphael, May 20, 1967, Immediate, Urgent, ISA 4078/4.
15 Eban to Harman, Raphael, May 20, 1967, Top Secret, Personal, Urgent, ISA 4078/4.
16 FRUS, 1964–1968, XIX: 36–42, 49–54.
17 FRUS, 1964–1968, XIX: 46–7.
18 Evron to Bitan, Raphael, May 21, 1967, Secret, Urgent, ISA 4078/4.

the President's warning that Israel should not undertake any action that might lead to war.[19]

Eban was not pleased with US administration's handling of the crisis. He tried to persuade the Americans that what was at stake was not only Israel's existence, but all US global commitments. The White House needed to understand that, if the United States did not meet its commitments in the Gulf of Aqaba, the reliability of its NATO and CENTO commitments, and Berlin's status, would be called into question. By keeping promises to Israel, the President would make political capital with those who were challenging his policies on Vietnam. The Middle East crisis did not require him to send in hundreds of thousands of soldiers. If Nasser won a war, world security would be catastrophic. Eban told the President that the US opportunity in the Middle East was easier and less dangerous than Cuba, but that failure to meet its obligations would be more humiliating.[20]

The US administration submitted the crisis to the UN Security Council. The President would not take action before consulting congressional leaders, who were very sensitive to international involvement; Rusk asserted that the US commitment to Israel was applicable only within the framework of the UN Charter.[21] A typical example of the administration's weakness was Johnson's May 22 letter to Kosygin, which neither warned nor insinuated, merely referring to the events that had brought the region to the brink of war. The time had come, Johnson wrote, for both the United States and the Soviet Union to exert their influence to defuse the crisis.[22]

Rusk realized that closing the Straits had worsened the conflict. While the Israeli government promised not to take action without consulting the United States, he admitted that Israel could not be restrained for long. The State Department sent a fairly explicit communiqué to Moscow, noting that Egypt had deployed large forces in Sinai without Israeli provocation. The United States believed that the Soviet Union did not want war and was aware of the US commitment to territorial integrity and political sovereignty and its opposition to using aggression and force to resolve disputes.[23] The statement by Richard Nolte, the US ambassador in Cairo, that the blockade of the Straits of Tiran was an

19 FRUS, 1964–1968, XIX: 58–63.
20 Eban to Harman, Raphael, IFM, May 23, 1967, Top Secret, Personal, Urgent, ISA 4078/4.
21 Evron to Levavi, Bitan, May 23, 1967, Secret, Urgent, ISA 4078/4.
22 FRUS, 1964–1968, XIX: 68.
23 FRUS, 1964–1968, XIX: 65, 72–3.

act of aggression, made no impression on Egypt. The Egyptian foreign minister said in response that the United States was now in direct conflict with his country.[24]

Gromyko blamed Israel for everything. Its claims regarding terrorist attacks were baseless, he said. The Soviet Union sided with Syria and the United States should influence Israel. The US ambassador in Moscow, Llewellyn Thompson, told the State Department he was concerned the Soviets would not hesitate to worsen the Middle East crisis as a lever to mitigate the US bombing of Hanoi.[25] However, the Western leader who most disappointed Israel was de Gaulle, who wanted to conduct an independent policy in the Middle East at Israel's expense. Seeking gains for France in the Arab world, he opposed military and diplomatic action against them, solicited closer relations with the Soviet Union and avoided cooperation with the United States and Britain outside the framework of the UN.[26]

CIA Director Richard Helms told the President that Israel was capable of defending itself and could launch limited strikes or a major offensive. It enjoyed a qualitative military advantage despite quantitative inferiority in manpower and equipment, although in terms of air power it actually had a small advantage. However, if he were wrong, he cautioned, the Arabs' numerical superiority would make them victorious. Within the first forty-eight hours, Israel could deploy a maximum of 280,000 troops against 117,000 Arabs, but the Arab deployment would soon grow to half a million. Helms acknowledged that the crisis had worsened since the blocking of the Straits of Tiran, but thought that neither side wanted war. Nasser knew that Israel would view the blockade as a casus belli, but was confident of Soviet support. No one was in control of the situation, Helms said.[27] Israel tried to persuade Washington that the Soviets would not stop Nasser until they understood that supporting him meant a direct confrontation with the United States. The Soviet ambassador to the UN claimed that the Straits of Tiran were sovereign Egyptian territory and not an international waterway.[28]

24 FRUS, 1964–1968, XIX: 66–7.
25 Moscow to State, Incoming Telegram, May 23, 1967 (5085) Secret, NARA, RG 59, Central Files 1967–69.
26 Sir Patrick Reilly to FO, May 25, 1967, Secret, Immediate, NA, FCO 17/483/ER/5; cf. 'De Gaulle-Wilson Conversation,' June 19, 1967: DDF, 1967: 749–59; Heiman, 2010:69–88.
27 FRUS, 1964–1968, XIX: 73–6.
28 FRUS, 1964–1968, XIX: 83–4.

The Americans turned to the British government, which thought the West had to offer a naval escort to ships sailing through the Straits to or from Eilat. Rusk insisted that the United States could participate in such an escort only with congressional approval.[29] Walt Rostow tried, on May 23, to push for a more resolute response. He argued that the main issue was whether Nasser and his Soviet backers were going to dominate the area, and asked if the United States was going to back down in the Middle East. The United States, he said, had to back the pro-Western countries and end Egyptian and Soviet encroachment.[30] The call for action, however, was left unanswered.

At an NSC meeting on May 24, Johnson suggested that UN and multilateral moves were likely to fail, but lessons had been learned from Congress's support for the Gulf of Tonkin Resolution (August 7, 1964).[31] Senators Stuart Symington and William Fulbright said the United States could not manage two crises and had to choose between Israel and Vietnam; McNamara disagreed. General Wheeler, Chairman of the JCS, said that while the United States had a powerful fleet in the Mediterranean, its land forces in the region were small. Johnson asked what would happen if diplomatic efforts failed and Wheeler answered that Israel would have to receive military help in both the short and long run, even if the US administration was persuaded that Israel could handle the Arabs.

The key issue was whether the Soviets had deliberately initiated a crisis in the Middle East to divert US attention from Vietnam. Wheeler and Helms thought it had not. Johnson asked what he needed to do. Wheeler said that, since a long war would wreak havoc on Israel's economy, they had to consider whether to send an army to confront Nasser. Johnson asked if the Soviet Union would intervene and Wheeler told him that, if Nasser lost, the Soviets might simply leave the region. McNamara said he expected that in a war each side would try to achieve aerial superiority, and the Soviets might supply the Arabs with manned aircraft. According to Helms, the Kremlin was seeking a propaganda victory by portraying itself as the savior of the Arabs. In such a scenario, the Arabs would reject the United States as a regional power. Lucius D. Battle, new Assistant Secretary of State for Near Eastern and South Asian Affairs, suggested that the Kremlin had promised Nasser additional support, or

29 FRUS, 1964–1968, XIX: 85–7.
30 FRUS, 1964–1968, XXI: 210; May 23, 1967, Secret, Immediate, ISA 4078/4.
31 The Gulf of Tonkin Resolution of 1964 signified the beginning of US military intervention in Vietnam. Congress granted, by overwhelming majority, the President the use of approriate force to repel any attack on US forces.

that perhaps he had gone a little off the rails. Still, while he wanted to reassert himself as a leader of the Arab world and a player on the global stage, his economy was in ruins; perhaps that was why he was leaving a political door open to resolving the crisis.[32]

The US administration was reluctant to take action and the CIA agreed, claiming Nasser did not want war. He had exploited the crisis to improve his image as a leader and losing a war would destroy his gains. He wanted to pressure Israel but not to attack it, he could provoke, not destroy. The Soviets' goal was to damage US standing in the Arab world. Once it felt it had done so, it would not worsen the crisis, fearing Israel would decimate the Arabs and damage the Soviet position. It would not openly support the Arabs because it did not want a direct confrontation with the United States.[33] Britain was also unwilling to endorse an aggressive policy. At most, it would send a small force of frigates and minesweepers, but it far preferred to support the French initiative for a diplomatic effort.[34]

Israel remained pessimistic and the United States believed Israel could deter a war. Eshkol said the mission of Shams Badran, the Egyptian minister of war, to Moscow showed Egypt and Syria were not only on the road to war but that they were coordinating with the Soviet Union. Eban was sent to Washington to request a commitment from the administration for aid if Israel were attacked. Eshkol warned the government that Israel could not conduct a preemptive strike while Eban was there, lest Israel be accused of trying to trick the administration, as Japan did in Pearl Harbor.[35] The Americans continued to insist that diplomacy could resolve the crisis, and, meeting with Eban on May 25, Rusk said that US intelligence was of the opinion that Nasser would act irrationally if Israel attacked before U Thant had submitted his report to the Security Council. The President, he said, was not authorized to consider an attack on Israel as an attack on the United States. For that, he would require approval from Congress, and in such an event the United States might find itself having to choose between the Middle East and Vietnam.

Eban said that the most important thing was for the United States, as the leader of the Free World, to take effective deterrent measures. For the Americans, however, the issue of who started the war was critical, Rusk claimed. Eban warned that the situation was 'apocalyptic.' Israel, Eban maintained, could no longer delay and would have to decide between

32  FRUS, 1964–1968, XIX: 87–91.
33  FRUS, 1964–1968, XIX: 96–9, 103–5.
34  Cabinet, May 25, 1967, NA, CAB/128/42, Part 2.
35  KFADC, May 26, 1967 (Eshkol), ISA.

military action and surrender. He reiterated that the US administration had to declare that an attack on Israel was the same as an attack on the United States, and to coordinate the two countries' armies in preparation for a possible offensive.[36] Eban stood fast, telling the Americans that Israel preferred war to surrender. It had delayed making a decision because President Johnson had asked for time, and Eban had been sent to Washington see if that meant an armed challenge. Israel believed that the United States could open the Straits of Tiran with no danger simply by deploying a few escort ships.

Eban gave the Pentagon documents dated back to 1957 of US commitment to defend freedom of navigation in the Straits of Tiran. McNamara said Israel could trust the American will and ability to keep its commitments, but warned that the United States would not support a preemptive Israeli attack. The goal was to prevent war, and the UN option should be exhausted and congressional and American public support ensured for any necessary action. Eban replied that Soviet extremism doomed any UN initiative to failure, and that Israeli military intelligence had confirmed that a joint Egyptian–Syrian attack was expected soon. McNamara told him that, according to US intelligence, the Egyptian army was prepared for defensive, not offensive, action. In despair, Eban responded that the US commitment was not only for defeat and that there had to be a joint operational plan.[37] However, the administration had to make a decision and Rusk presented Johnson with the options of allowing Israel to decide how best to defend its national interests or sending a naval force to keep Egypt from interfering with free navigation in the Gulf of Aqaba. The State Department supported the latter.[38]

On the afternoon of May 26, the upper echelons of the Johnson administration met. General Wheeler reported that Israel had mobilized about two-thirds of its ground forces. Its air force and navy were at full deployment, but Israel could not keep its reserves mobilized for more than two months without debilitating economic consequences. Its military strategy was based on achieving a tactical surprise by first attacking enemy airfields, so there was no need to marshal the US army. Battle argued that the Soviet Union was trying to turn the crisis into a confrontation between the Americans and the Arabs, and whatever the United States did would lead to trouble. If it did not support Israel, the radical Arab states would call the United States a paper tiger. If it did support Israel, its standing in the Arab world would be severely damaged.

36  FRUS, 1964–1968, XIX: 109–14.
37  FRUS, 1964–1968, XIX: 118–22.
38  FRUS, 1964–1968, XIX: 123–6.

The only figure in the State Department who supported Israel's view was Joseph Sisco, who said that the sea passage to Eilat was vital to Israel. If Israel conceded that, it would be the beginning of the end. Israel had no confidence in the UN, where any decision would be to Israel's detriment and U Thant himself was hostile. Israel's fear was that the UN would accept the current status quo, including the blockade. The US position had not changed, Rusk told Eban, 'Israel would not be alone unless it chose to be alone.'[39] American public and congressional opinion required that every effort be made to avert war. On a military level, General Wheeler was ready to take action to open the Straits of Tiran with a non-Israeli test ship, or an Israeli ship with a naval escort. If it were attacked, the United States or its allies could respond by bombing. Egypt would back down if the Western naval powers brought together an impressive force.

At a loss, the President consulted with his close advisors. McNamara said that the United States could not promise Israel free navigation in the Gulf of Aqaba. Clark Clifford, chairman of the President's Foreign Intelligence Advisory Board, however, maintained that Israel's future was at risk and that the United States had to guarantee free shipping to Eilat, without making any commitment to Israel. George Ball, former Under Secretary of State, warned of a severe oil crisis, while Supreme Court Justice Abe Fortas advocated using force to break the blockade to keep Israel from having to make the decision.

The President rejected Fortas's proposal. It would be impossible, he said, to promise Eban everything he wanted. Congress was pressuring him to find a solution to the crisis under UN auspices. McNamara demanded a final decision to warn Israel that if it attacked it would be alone, and to reassure it that, following a UN debate, the President would take action to ensure free navigation. Fortas opposed telling Israel that it would remain alone in the crisis. However, Israel's fate was sealed by Rusk and McNamara.[40] The CIA claimed that if it attacked first Israel could win on its own, achieving air superiority within twenty-four hours. If Egypt attacked first, Israel would achieve air superiority within two to three days, while at the same time repelling attacks from Syria and Jordan.[41] Everyone in the administration was aware of the oil issue: a third of the Free World oil and 70 percent of Western European oil came from the Arab world. Saudi Arabia and Bahrain alone supplied all the oil needed for Vietnam War. However, if cut off demand

39 FRUS, 1964–1968, XIX: 132–3.
40 FRUS, 1964–1968, XIX: 127–36.
41 FRUS, 1964–1968, XIX: 138–9.

could be fulfilled by increasing production in California and the Gulf of Mexico. The Soviet Union could not compensate the Arabs for their loss of income if they imposed an oil embargo on the West.[42]

Johnson stood his ground with Eban. He did not accept the claim that Israel had to choose between surrender or resistance, and Eban agreed to examine the option of an international solution. The question was whether the United States would honor its commitment to free navigation. Eban suggested the commanders of the US and Israeli armies meet to plan a joint response. Johnson said his position was clear: he supported free navigation and opposed aggression, timing was another matter. Israel's should not be hasty, better to give the UN a chance, even if it was no more likely to solve the Middle East crisis than the Vietnam War. While Johnson rejected the Israeli proposal for a joint command, he ordered McNamara to consult with Israel. The administration also had to consider Egypt's reactions. Nasser asked the US government not to take military action, claiming the closing of the Straits of Tiran was a return to the status quo ante of 1956.[43] The following day, however, Mohamed Hassanein Heikal, editor of *Al-Ahram* and Nasser's close friend, wrote that war with Israel was unavoidable.[44]

The CIA supported the administration. Nasser had no military capabilities, it maintained, and the Soviet Union would prevent it from starting a war. It was unreasonable to think the Soviets had planned together with Egypt to close the Straits. The Soviet goal was to persuade the Arabs that the United States was their enemy. If Nasser were defeated, the Soviets would do more than make threats. They apparently were counting on great power intervention before Nasser took a mortal blow.[45] Barbour advised the State Department to send an American officer to Israel for talks to alleviate its anxiety.[46]

Rusk claimed the United States and Britain were preparing an international naval escort, and that unilateral Israeli action would be irresponsible and a catastrophe. Eugene Rostow, Rusk's deputy, told Eshkol the Soviet Union had assured the United States that Egypt was not preparing

42 [No author,] 'Oil,' [no date,] Secret, LBJL, NSF Countries, Box 105. For a different assessment of the Director of the Office of Fuels and Energy, May 23, 1967: 'The loss of Saudi Arabia and Kuwait together would create serious disturbances. Loss of more would cause disruptions in Europe (and Japan) commensurate to the size of the loss.' Cf. FRUS, 1964–1968, XXXIV: 416–19.
43 FRUS, 1964–1968, XIX: 146–7.
44 Nolte to State, 'Middle East Crisis,' May 26, 1967, Confidential, NARA, Central Files, 1967–1969, Box 15.
45 Board of National Estimates, in FRUS, 1964–1968, XIX: 148–51 (May 26, 1967).
46 FRUS, 1964–1968, XIX: 155–6, 186–7.

an attack. Israel, however, believed that the Soviet Union was heightening the tension.[47] Johnson asked Kosygin to influence Egypt to end the blockade and expressed hope that the UN would resolve the crisis. The desire to avoid involvement in a war was greater than the US commitment to Israel. The following day, Rusk assured Gromyko that Israel was not preparing to attack. The JCS also worked to alleviate tensions. The Soviets, they said, had learned their lesson in the Cuban Missile Crisis. They would increase their aid to the Arabs, but not supply nuclear weapons and missiles.[48]

Frustrated by American spinelessness, Eshkol told Johnson that an international escort should operate in the Gulf of Aqaba within a week or two. Nasser's speeches were growing more extreme and he had signed a defense pact with King Hussein of Jordan on May 30. The time had come for a confrontation. However, the decision-making processes in Washington were defensive and bordered on appeasement. Rusk and McNamara were prepared only to send an Israeli-owned ship through the Straits, one containing no oil and not flying an Israeli flag. If it passed without incident, they would try one with a strategic cargo. Many congressmen were reluctant to grant the executive branch powers enabling it to embroil the United States in an unnecessary war. The reason was the Gulf of Tonkin incident of August 1964, which had involved the United States in the Vietnam War.[49] Israel was more disappointed by Britain, which resolved to avoid military intervention contrary to its interests at any price, despite the similarity between the current situation and the European crisis of 1938, and 1956.[50]

Israel was anxious about US sluggishness. Nasser was talking about returning to the status quo ante of 1948 and Iraqi forces were being airlifted to Jordan, yet Israel's defense had not been coordinated with the military forces of its most important and powerful ally. The two countries' air forces were not using a common code and the IDF had no contact with the Sixth Fleet. Israel asked for the immediate delivery of missiles, tanks and combat planes.[51] On May 28, the Israeli cabinet debated a preemptive attack, but the votes were tied (nine–nine). It

---

47 FRUS, 1964–1968, XIX: 159–60.
48 FRUS, 1964–1968, XIX: 167–72.
49 FRUS, 1964–1968, XIX: 190–5.
50 Cabinet, 'Middle East Memorandum by the Secretary of State for Foreign Affairs,' Appendix: Memorandum by Foreign Affairs Officials, C(67)88, May 29, 1967, Confidential, NA, FCO 17/496/ER2/5; Crossman, 1976, 2: 354–8; Castle, 1984; 257–8; Brenchley, 2005: 129–34.
51 FRUS, 1964–1968, XIX: 198–200, 221 note 5.

approved a first strike in principle but did not set a date. Rabin warned that a decision not to attack Egypt would mean fighting a war later on much less favorable terms. Eban still opposed an attack, saying that Johnson would organize an international show of force in the Straits.[52]

On May 28, the US administration received a memorandum predicting an immediate war, which Israel would win. An unqualified Israeli victory over the Arabs was expected and, while the Soviet Union would help the Arabs and seek to end the war, it would not intervene directly. In the end, the Soviets would demonstrate their dissatisfaction with US policy in the region, but would not walk out of nuclear non-proliferation negotiations, just as they had not done as a result of the Vietnam and Berlin crises.[53]

The administration hesitated to organize an international flotilla for the Straits of Tiran, and American diplomats serving in the Arab countries were pessimistic about the regional response since, they claimed, such an action would set the United States on a collision course with the Arabs. The US ambassador to Damascus, Hugh Smyth, warned that Israel was an unviable client state and that its connection and value to the United States was largely emotional, and could not compare to the larger range of vital US interests in the Arab world.[54] However, a clear majority in the House of Representatives supported Israel and at least a hundred congressmen were concerned about the concentration of Egyptian forces in the Sinai Peninsula and the damage the crisis was causing to the Israeli economy. The United States had to take action to open the Straits of Tiran, according to Congressman Emanuel Celler. They did not believe that the Soviet Union would confront the United States directly.[55]

Eban's trip to Washington disappointed the Israeli government, which had expected to be given if not a green light, then at least massive economic and military aid. On June 1, the cabinet sent Mossad chief Meir Amit to meet McNamara. Amit told him that the Soviets, seeking to control the entire region (Iran included), were considering a 'grand plan' which would have a 'domino effect' on the Middle East and which would be a long-term threat to US interests. The United States had to prove its determination to protect those interests by granting Israel military aid and unambiguous political support, which would avert Soviet

---

52  ICAB, May 28, 1967 (502) (Eban), ISA; Haber, 1987: 192–3; Gluska, 2004: 321–5.
53  Contingency Paper, 'Immediate Arab-Israeli War,' May 28, 1967, Secret, Middle East Crisis, II, LBJL, NSF Countries, Box 107.
54  FRUS, 1964–1968, XIX: 214–15.
55  FRUS, 1964–1968, XIX: 219–20.

involvement. If Israel's airfields were destroyed, the United States would have to employ extreme measures, Amit warned.[56]

Meeting with CIA Director Helms, Amit revealed that Israel was on the brink of war and could not wait more than a few days. He said that Israel believed it would win within three to four weeks with losses of 4,000: 'it was better to die fighting than starving,' he told Helms. The Middle East offered the United States an opportunity to demonstrate its commitments far more cheaply than Vietnam. Helms reported to Johnson that Eshkol's appointment of Moshe Dayan as minister of defense was ominous.[57] Helms said that US policy would be decided by the President, McNamara and Rusk. The only US official who could have told Amit that Israel should wage a preemptive attack was James Angleton, the CIA's counterintelligence chief, who was not authorized to do so.[58]

US intelligence was pessimistic. The damage to US standing in the Arab world had already been done and opening the Straits of Tiran would not make much of a difference. Jordan and Saudi Arabia were reevaluating their relations with the United States. The reactions of the non-Arab Muslim countries would be less severe, but eventually they would join Nasser and the Soviets. If the United States used force to open the Straits, Egypt would close the Suez Canal and the supply of oil to the United States would be disrupted. The IDF maintained that, without a preemptive Israeli attack, Nasser would win a huge psychological-political victory.[59] According to State Department intelligence, nuclear arms would not factor into the current crisis.[60]

There were three prominent instances of the US administration's rejection of Israel's position on the crisis. First, Clifford rejected the claim that Nasser presented a vital threat to US interests. All the United States could do, he argued, was to escort a ship flying an Israeli flag through the Straits and let Egypt fire the first shot. He had no clear idea of where the

---

56 FRUS, 1964–1968, XIX: 223–5.
57 CIA, Office of the Director, Sensitive, Memorandum for the President, June 2, 1967, Secret, Sensitive, Attachment 1: Views of General Meir Amit, Head of the Israeli Intelligence Service on the Crisis in the Middle East, National Security Archives, George Washington University.
58 Meir Amit, Report on Trip to the US, May 31–June 2, 1967, Meir Amit Archives, Tel Aviv. Copy in possession of Tom Segev.
59 Sherman Kent, Implications in the Moslem World of forcing the Straits of Tiran, in FRUS, 1964–1968, XIX: 228–30 (June 1, 1967).
60 INR – George C. Denney, Jr. to the Secretary, 'French Military Transactions with Israel,' Annex, 'Major Items of French Origin in Israeli Arms Inventory as of 1967,' May 31, 1967, LBJL, NSF Countries, Box 105.

Soviet Union was headed. The constant fear was that a failure to resolve the crisis would lead to an East–West confrontation, and a confrontation with the Soviets would be a very serious matter involving vital US interests.[61]

Second, Charles Yost, the President's special envoy to Nasser, was pessimistic and maintained that an action by the naval powers could succeed only if it were coupled with military action, otherwise the United States would find itself at a dead end like Britain and France did in 1956. Israel needed assurances that it would receive assistance if its existence were threatened. Pressure, such as cutting off Egyptian access to the International Monetary Fund, would not make Nasser back down, it would push him further into the arms of the Soviets.

Third, at a meeting with veteran US envoy Robert Anderson, Nasser told him that war was inevitable. He refused to accept the existence of Israel and demanded the return of a million Arab refugees to their homes. He wanted the friendship of the United States, but its policies were influenced by the Jewish vote. Anderson believed Nasser was ready for war.[62]

Israel told the Americans that time was running out. Nasser was getting stronger and the political and psychological pressure in Israel was intensifying. Action had to be taken in the Gulf of Aqaba using an Israeli ship, not with an international flotilla. If the Egyptians fired first, would the United States stand by its position that Israel had a legitimate right to self-defense? Would it brake Soviet involvement?[63] Israel wanted a timetable for a blockade-breaking task force, but Rusk still lacked multilateral backing. Walt Rostow's inclination was to accept the Israeli solution, but Rusk disagreed. He was worried because the Soviets had not yet reacted to the blockade. He continued to evade a commitment to backing Israel in a preemptive strike, claiming that the question of who started the war was of great concern to Congress.

Harman, Israel's ambassador to Washington, stressed that the Israeli government would not accept a Munich-style surrender and did not want to sacrifice 10,000 lives to American waffling. Rusk claimed Egypt had promised not to attack, and a similar commitment from the Soviets would prevent a clash. Harman told him that the Soviets were trying to gain time to change the status quo to prevent a direct confrontation

---

61 Evron to Eban, Bitan, June 1, 1967, Top Secret, Personal, Immediate, ISA 7919/2a.
62 FRUS, 1964–1968, XIX: 185, 217–18, 222–3, 231–7; Yost, 1968: 304–26.
63 FRUS, 1964–1968, XIX: 244–6.

with the United States. The Pentagon's claim, rejected by Israel, was that the Jewish state could absorb a first strike. Harman pushed for a test run through the Straits by a vessel flying an Israeli flag. Rusk foisted him off with the claim it could lead to confrontation with the Soviets and required rethinking.[64] The Pentagon was the first to admit the administration had failed to resolve the crisis. France, Canada and Britain in particular were patently weak and the United States remained Israel's only refuge, while, according to the Pentagon, the only option was compromise.[65]

On June 3, Johnson told Eshkol he had confidence in the powers of the UN, concealing from him the administration's common opinion that the chances for a peaceful resolution to the crisis were weak. He was franker with Harold Wilson, repeating what he had said to Eban: 'You will be alone if you go it alone.' Johnson told him that he was not a dictator and that he required the agreement of Congress to act. Vietnam had made the House and the Senate far more cautious and they would not give him a free hand the Middle East. Johnson feared that if Moshe Dayan, Israel's new and hawkish defense minister, were in charge, Israel would start a war that would lead to a Cuba-style eyeball-to-eyeball confrontation between the United States and the Soviet Union. The difference was that this time the parties would not be just the superpowers, which were strong and self-controlled, but their agents, whom the superpowers could not completely control.[66]

Rusk, McNamara and their staffs met in Washington on June 2 with the British cabinet secretary and the British ambassador to Washington, Sir Patrick Dean. US reservations surfaced over sharing proposals for possible solutions in the Middle East. Rusk said that if Nasser left the blockade of the Straits of Tiran in place nothing could stop Israel, especially with Dayan as minister of defense. McNamara reported that Israel was prepared to attack and win, now or in a week. Rusk, unlike McNamara, feared that Israel would lose. The real question was whether the Soviets would come to Egypt's aid if it faced defeat. Rusk's principal concern was an Arab oil boycott, and both he and McNamara said that the United States would use force only with congressional approval. Dean claimed future joint planning on political and military issues was

---

64 FRUS, 1964–1968, XIX: 247–51.
65 FRUS, 1964–1968, XIX: 259–62.
66 'Record of Conversation between the Prime Minister and the President of the United States at the White House,' 2 June, 1967, Secret, NA, FCO17/496/ER/2/5; Extract from a Note of a Meeting at the White House, June 2, 1967, Top Secret, NA, FCO 17/510/ER2/10.

necessary, to which Rusk and McNamara responded that the time was not yet ripe.[67]

The US administration was helpless. Rusk admitted that the United States could not command Israel not to fight, and while thus far the administration had managed to stop it, the calls for jihad in the Arab world reinforced Israel's apocalyptic psychology. Neither Israel nor the Arabs were deterred by the possibility of war and both were certain of victory. The United States was committed to the independence and territorial integrity of all the countries in the region and to international naval law, and could not prevent Israel from sending vessels through the Straits of Tiran. Israel would fight for free navigation and the United States could not restrain it. The United States could not ignore its commitments to Israel and tell it to fight while remaining neutral.[68]

Meanwhile, terrorist attacks started in Saudi Arabia, oil supply from Kuwait was in danger, and so was the air base in Libya. A younger generation of Arabs was reaching maturity after having been brainwashed by propaganda that the United States was responsible for the existence of the State of Israel. Whereas, in Israel, the United States was being accused of selling out the Jewish state by not letting it go to war.[69]

Fewer than twenty-four hours before war broke out, Walt Rostow told Johnson what he wanted to hear: the United States had to achieve its goals in the Middle East without war. Nasser, he noted, was belligerent but below the surface there was potential for moderation, regional economic development and recognition of Israel, all hinging on the resolution of the refugee problem. The question was whether it would be possible to survive the current crisis and find a solution that would prevent the destruction of Israel. Israel believed that there was little chance that the Soviet Union would intervene militarily if Nasser were attacked, he noted. He suggested that US–Arab relations would best be served by an Israeli military victory without US military intervention. Nasser should be told that the United States would honor its commitments, that UN observers should be placed on both sides of the Israel–Egypt border and that a solution for the Arab refugee problem should be sought. It was also be necessary to ask Congress to approve the use of force to protect the passage of non-Israeli ships. The United States would acknowledge Israel's right to secure the passage of its own ships and to defend itself if

67 FRUS, 1964–1968, XIX: 237–44.
68 FRUS, 1964–1968, XIX: 266–8.
69 'The Current Focus of the Near East Crisis,' in FRUS, 1964–1968, XIX: 270–2 (June 3, 1967).

it encountered resistance. If the United States pursued such a program, Rostow told the President, Israel could be kept at bay until June 18. In the intervening period, the Kremlin should be pressured to end the blockade. It was in both Israel's and the United States' interest to act like a sheriff at 'high noon.'

Rostow claimed that the Soviet Union would exert pressure on Nasser to accept a pragmatic deal if the Soviet command could be convinced Israel was capable of defeating the Arabs. The Kremlin made no commitments about the Straits of Tiran, but the crisis should end with oil flowing into Eilat, the contending armies should draw back, the UN observers should be redeployed and talks on the refugee question development should resume.[70]

However, strategy A, the idea of a flotilla ('regatta') accompanied by the US navy, was buried out of fear of it having severe political and economic consequences, even if the Egyptians did not use force. It would create a state of war and lessen the Kremlin's ability to restrain itself. Not only would that not serve US interests, it would worsen East–West polarization in the Middle East. Strategy B, taking an Israeli ship through the Straits of Tiran, would almost certainly lead to war, and an unaccompanied ship would be turned back. If it resisted, the Egyptians would attack it, Israel would respond and war would break out. Nevertheless, the plan had the advantage of not directly involving the United States or the Soviet Union. Both would want to end the war and support a peaceful accommodation.

There was a third strategy: a political compromise. Egypt would consent to the passage of non-Israeli oil tankers and Israel would make no further demands. If that could be accomplished, it was important for the United States not to take action that would commit it to the flotilla, and Israel had to be persuaded not to take action in the Gulf of Aqaba as long as efforts to achieve a peaceful resolution were being made.[71] It was recognized that the United States wielded only limited control over Israel, and thus the UN would be asked to find a solution and a multinational force should be established if all political efforts failed. The basic objective was to gain time, while it was clear to the administration that Israel had very little time left. The fear of damage to US interests made the administration follow a non-involvement policy of waiting for the regional forces to play out. To avoid US involvement, the United States could not give Israel a green or even an amber light.[72]

70  FRUS, 1964–1968, XIX: 272–7.
71  FRUS, 1964–1968, XIX: 280–3.
72  Quandt, 1992: 197–228.

On June 5, Israel's air force staged the long-delayed preemptive strike on Egypt's airfields. Eshkol informed Johnson that Israel had gone to war to repel Nasser's aggression because Israel's integrity and very existence were menaced by the five Egyptian infantry and two armored divisions in Sinai. Egypt intended, Eshkol charged, to cut the Negev off from Israel. Egypt had instituted an illegal blockade in the Straits of Tiran and Nasser had declared total war against Israel. The UN had shown itself to be ineffective when Israel's existence was threatened. Eshkol told Johnson he hoped that the United States would do everything in its power to prevent the Soviet Union from exploiting and expanding the conflict.[73] Deputy Assistant Secretary of State for Public Affairs and Director of Office of News, Robert McCloskey, claimed across-the-board US neutrality ('in thought, word and deed'), to which special presidential assistant Joseph Califano complained that the State Department's position was 'killing us with the Jews in this country.' Rusk said that, by neutrality, he meant the United States insisted that the rights of American citizens in the Middle East should not be compromised, not that it was unconcerned.[74] McCloskey had accurately portrayed the administration's unwillingness to take a clear stance. Rusk's principal concern was to convey to the Soviets that the United States had not been involved in Israel's decision to go to war.[75] Johnson later claimed that he had sided with Israel during the crisis and sought to distance himself from McCloskey's declaration.[76] Ben Wattenberg, a speechwriter and aide to the President, did not dare tell Johnson that Rusk's declaration of neutrality had damaged the President's standing in the Jewish community.[77]

From the Israeli point of view, the United States did not do enough to prevent the war, primarily because of its fear of turning the Middle East into another Cold War theater. Johnson later tried to atone for his mistakes. On June 19, he presented the conditions necessary for peace in the Middle East: each nation had a fundamental right to exist, which its neighbors should respect; the issue of the refugees had to be solved; naval rights had to be respected; the UN Security Council had to ask its members to report on arms shipments; and the political independence and territorial integrity of all the countries in the region had to be

---

73 FRUS, 1964–1968, XIX: 302–3.
74 FRUS, 1964–1968, XIX: 311–12.
75 Johnson, 2008: 45.
76 Califano, 1991: 204–6.
77 Ben Wattenberg, Memorandum for the President, 11 p.m., June 5, 1967, Middle East Crisis, III, LBJL, NSF Countries, Box 107.

**Figure 4** 'The chef's specialty' by Kariel Gardosh (Dosh), May 15, 1967.

respected. The United States would act to achieve peace, but the principal responsibility lay with the people of the region and their leaders.[78]

Johnson told William Fulbright, chairman of the Senate's Foreign Relations Committee, that he had done everything he could to keep Israel from going to war, winning him condemnation in Israel. If Israel acted irresponsibly, Johnson said, it would cause an outbreak of emotion, that is, anti-Semitism, in the United States.[79] Johnson's attitude toward Israel during the crisis was problematic. After the war, however, his position was unambiguously pro-Israeli, demanding the resolution of the problems that had led to the war rather than a unilateral Israeli withdrawal from the territories it had occupied, as the Soviet Union demanded. De Gaulle and Wilson had despaired of achieving a US–Soviet agreement in the Middle East.[80]

78 FRUS, 1964–1968, XIV: 520–1 (composed by Walt Rostow).
79 Johnson, 2008: 51–2.
80 Record of a Discussion [De Gaulle–Wilson] Held at the Grand Trianon, June [19]20, 1967, Secret, PREM 13/162; DDF, 1967: 749–59.

**Figure 5** 'Did you say something?' by Kariel Gardosh (Dosh), May 25, 1967.

The roots of the Six Day War lay in the flimsy arrangements imposed on Israel in February 1957, which did not obligate the United States to use force to defend the rights of Israeli ships in the Straits of Tiran. While Johnson deviated from the policy of his predecessors to become, de facto, the supplier of Israel's arms, he carried on their policies by not codifying Soviet relations with Israel and the Arab countries into a framework that would prevent war. Free passage for Israeli shipping in the Gulf of Aqaba and the demilitarization of the Sinai Peninsula and Gaza Strip remained critical issues, and there is no doubt that the US and Soviet ambivalence toward their clients laid the groundwork for the outbreak of war.

The United States could not have prevented the war by using force to open the Straits of Tiran because Johnson did not want to get involved in another theater of war. Unambiguous warnings to the Soviets and Nasser might or might not have averted war, because the Middle East was a no-man's-land between the two superpowers. The sources do not support the claim that Israel received an amber light from the United States to start a war, and it certainly did not receive a green light.[81] The United States was not a helpless power, but found itself in a strategic trap created by the Cold War.

81  Quandt, 1992; Parker, 1997: 132–5; Raviv, 1998: 105–6.

# 16

# The Soviet Union and the Six Day War (May 14–June 5, 1967)

The archives of the Soviet Union's two decision-making bodies, the Communist Party Central Committee and the Politburo, cannot be accessed, so a reliable account cannot be given of Soviet Union's role in the crisis. However, selected documents have been published and the issue can be discussed, at least, on the diplomatic level.[1] The Kremlin's view was that since early 1966 (with the neo-Ba'ath coup in Damascus) the Middle East was on the brink of crisis but that it would be possible to prevent a slide into war. The Syrian regime's backing of the Arab terrorist organizations forced the Kremlin leadership to increase its warnings to Israel. However, unable to fully control its Arab allies, the Soviets could not halt the escalation in the Sinai Peninsula and the Straits of Tiran that eventually led to war.[2]

On May 13, just before the onset of the crisis, Anwar Sadat, then speaker of the Egyptian National Assembly, met in Moscow with Minister of Foreign Affairs Gromyko and his deputy Semyonov. Gromyko warned that the imperialists were exploiting Israel and using it for subversion in the Middle East. Sadat told him that those who wanted to destroy Israel should talk less and act more. Gromyko and Sadat agreed that the West's imperialist struggle against Syria was a battle against the entire Arab people, and that both their countries, sharing common interests, needed to stand firm against the plot.[3]

According to Nasser's mouthpiece, Mohamed Hassanein Heikal, editor of *Al-Ahram*, Semyonov warned Sadat that the situation in the Middle East was dangerous because Israel was concentrating forces on the Syrian border in preparation for an attack during the third week of May.[4] Syria had previously received similar information from the Soviets,

---

1 SDMEC, see Naumkin, 2003.
2 Ben-Tsur, 1976: 26–153.
3 SDMEC 2: 551–3.
4 Heikal, 1978: 174–5.

but Egypt's leadership was initially skeptical when hearing it from the Syrians. Sadat took it seriously only when he received the information from top Soviet figures, and he immediately transmitted the message to Nasser, who then sent his forces into Sinai.

On May 16, *Pravda* criticized the Israeli government for threatening the security of its neighbors. It cited an interview in which Rabin had said that Israel was training special military detachments to fight Syria. *Izvestia* repeated the Kremlin's warning to what it called 'ruling cliques' in Israel which continued to play with fire. The United States and Britain, it claimed, were forming a coalition to fight the anti-imperialists defending the Damascus regime. The US–Israeli alliance extended beyond the Middle East and, in exchange for US aid, Israel was transporting equipment and fuel from the United States and Japan to South Vietnamese ports. Eshkol was quoted as saying that Israel would grant the request of the puppet regime in Saigon for technical assistance. Eban had visited US bases in Asia and had intervened not only in Vietnam and Syria, but in Aden as well.[5]

Katriel Katz, Israel's ambassador to Moscow, protested the articles in the Soviet papers. There were no IDF force concentrations on the Syrian border, he said, and Rabin had been speaking of the training of special units to prevent terrorist infiltration and attacks. If Syrian aggression continued, Israel would defend itself. Katz then asked the Soviet government to restrain Syria, which he maintained was responsible for the critical border situation.[6] In Israel, Ya'akov Herzog, director-general of the prime minister's office, assumed that the Soviet Union would support Egypt and that, if the Soviet navy moved toward Syria and the Sinai Peninsula, the US Sixth Fleet would redeploy in the region. Given the ensuing risk of world war, he believed the UN Security Council would act to ensure the cessation of hostilities.[7]

Eban protested to the Soviet ambassador about Egyptian forces concentrated in the Sinai Peninsula. The UN observer force had reported to Egypt that there were no Israeli force concentrations in the north. Israel felt that war could be averted if Egypt could be convinced not to attack or interfere with free navigation. In principle, the problem should have been brought before the Security Council. However, Chuvakhin, Soviet ambassador to Israel, declared wholehearted support for Syrian and Egyptian policy. The cause of the current situation, he claimed, was the Israeli government's hostile propaganda. Although the situation was serious, Egypt's expulsion of UNEF had been justified, and in any case its presence depended on the consent of the country where it was deployed.

5 IMM to DEE, May 16, 1967, ISA 4048/27.
6 Tekoah to Katz, May 17, 1967, Secret, Immediate, ISA 4048/3.
7 'Session Summoned by Eshkol,' June 3–4, 1967, ISA 4512/3a.

Eban denied that Israel had threatened to attack Syria and only required it to respect Israel's territorial integrity, he told Chuvakhin. Eban asked: what did the Soviet Union intend to do to prevent a further deterioration toward war? The ambassador replied that the Soviet Union intended to do very little and that Israel's leaders should stop making bellicose declarations. Eban said that would hardly be sufficient, since the Arabs would have to stop their terrorist attacks, such as shelling Kibbutz Manarah on the Lebanese border and mining the road to the northern town of Rosh Pina, to say nothing of the Egyptian deployment in the Sinai Peninsula. Chuvakhin was not impressed, claiming there was no proof that Syria was responsible for the terrorist attacks and that both events had most likely been staged by the CIA.[8]

In the meantime, Deputy Prime Minister Yigal Allon spoke in Moscow with Semyonov, who charged that foreign elements were using Israel as a tool to topple the Syrian regime. Allon agreed that foreign interests were clashing in the Middle East, but maintained that Israel was not participating in the superpower contest and was not anyone's tool. It had no choice but to pursue a policy of self-defense, even if it displeased the United States and the Soviet Union.[9]

All Katz could do was challenge the distorted reports in the Soviet press. *Krasnaya Zvezda* (Red Star) had emasculated U Thant's report, he charged. He also warned the Soviets that the rest of the world understood the situation and that in the end Syria, Egypt and the Soviet Union would be held responsible. In response, a Soviet Middle East official said that Israel was creating a warlike atmosphere and seeking to topple the Syrian regime. Katz invited him to Israel to see the Syrian terrorists that Israel had captured. One Hitler was enough, he said.[10] *Pravda* published an article accusing the United States of goading Israel into invading Syrian territory. The US leadership's adventurism, it claimed, was in line with its new crimes in Vietnam and provocations over Cuba. US imperialism, the article charged, followed a doctrine of local conflicts and small wars to support its position in different parts of the world. The article included a map showing Israel's borders as those of the UN partition resolution of 1947.[11]

Katz warned Llewellyn Thompson, US ambassador to Moscow, that the Soviets had begun executing a comprehensive plan to eject the West from the Middle East. They had allowed Nasser to deploy forces in the Sinai Peninsula and block entry to the Gulf of Aqaba as a test of publicly stated Western determination to prevent a change in the status quo south

8 Tekoah to Katz, May 19, 1967, Top Secret, Immediate, ISA 4983/3.
9 Allon to Eban, in IMM to IFM, May 21, 1967, Secret, ISA 4048/3.
10 Katz to DEE, Visit to Shchiborin, May [23] 22, 1967, Secret, ISA 4048/27.
11 IMM to DEE, May 22, 1967, ISA 4048/3.

of Iran and Turkey. Dmitri Pozhidaev, the Soviet ambassador to Cairo, had spoken with Nasser twice, but on neither occasion did he make any serious effort to restrain him.[12]

The Johnson administration, which wanted to promote détente in Europe and Southeast Asia, but not in the Middle East, refused to confront the Soviet Union. Johnson wrote to Kosygin that 'elements' in Syria were provoking Israel and sending the region down a path of ever greater violence. The two superpowers had to use their influence to defuse the situation. Johnson's letter made no impression on the Kremlin, which regarded the appeal as a maneuver to justify Israeli aggression.[13] According to US intelligence, the Soviet Union did not want war, but the report was skeptical of Soviet sincerity about its attempts to alleviate tensions in the Middle East. There was no evidence that it was doing anything to restrain the Arabs, preferring to let the current crisis fade away, because a defeat of Nasser would greatly embarrass the Soviet Union and the Soviets believed that they could rely on other countries to resolve the crisis.[14] US intelligence was not aware that on May 25 Semyonov had officially endorsed Egyptian and Syrian policy, citing Israel's 'plots' and US actions in Vietnam and the Dominican Republic, promising the Arabs that the Soviet Union would support them 'at the highest level.'[15]

Israel felt the declaration was propaganda and did not commit the Soviet Union to military intervention. The Kremlin had sided with Nasser, the aggressor, and disregarded the UN Secretary General's accusation that PLO was responsible for regional tension. Israel feared that Nasser would regard the Soviet position as encouragement for belligerence.[16] Katz recommended that Israel urge friendly countries to protest to the Kremlin even though the Soviet response was a foregone conclusion. Moreover, public opinion in the Free World had to be involved. The Soviets, he said, were sensitive to demonstrations and to charges of supporting aggression.[17]

12  Katz to Eban, May 23, 1967, Secret, Personal, Immediate, ISA 4078/4; SDMEC 2: 561–3.
13  FRUS, 1964–1968, XIV: 485–7 (May 19, 1967).
14  INR – Thomas L. Hughes, Director of Intelligence and Research, 'Soviet Letting Middle East Crisis Take its Course,' May 23, 1967, NARA, RG 59, Central Files, 1967–1969, Box 11.
15  'Semyonov Discussion with Lebanese Ambassador,' May 25, 1967, SDMEC 2: 566–8.
16  Tekoah to IMW etc., May 25, 1967, Immediate, Secret, ISA 4083/3, ISA.
17  Katz to Levavi, May 24, 1967, Secret, Immediate, ISA 4083/3.

The Soviets may or may not have known that Israel's neighboring Arab states planned to initiate a crisis, and, while Israel was convinced that the Soviets were behind it, there was no proof of Soviet–Syrian collusion.[18] United Press International (UPI) reported that Communist diplomats wanted a package deal linking de-escalation in Vietnam to peace in the Middle East, leading the State Department to ask why the Soviet Union would assume that the United States, which had refused to stop its bombing of North Vietnam without a parallel move on Hanoi's part, would agree to prevent the Egyptian navy from halting ships on their way to Eilat. Hanoi feared that shipments of supplies would not be able to reach North Vietnam if the Suez Canal were closed, thus Hanoi's declaration of support for the Arabs was no more than lip service.[19] Israeli leaders also feared that the two regions might be linked. An Israeli diplomat said that the Kremlin did not fear a conventional war in the Middle East, and that Soviet leaders believed they could help the Arabs more than the United States could help Israel because of its constraints in Vietnam.[20]

On May 26, Kosygin warned Eshkol that it would be an 'enormous' error if warmongers in Israel were to get the upper hand. A military confrontation had to be prevented for the sake of global peace and security. The conflict had to be resolved without resorting to war, he said. Responsibility would lie with the aggressor.[21] Katz maintained that the Soviets were trying to create the impression that the Kremlin was restraining the Arabs, while their real intention was to sabotage the Western initiative to open the Straits of Tiran.[22] At first, the Soviets waffled as to whether the Straits were Egyptian territorial waters or an international sea lane. They offered only the vague information that their position was determined by global Soviet policies. Trying to blame the United States for the crisis, Kosygin wrote to Johnson on May 27 that, according to information received, Israel was planning to attack its neighbors and the outcome would depend largely on the US government, because Israel would not dare attack without US backing. All measures should

---

18 KFADC, May 26, 1967 (Eshkol and Yariv), ISA.
19 Thomas L. Hughes, Director of Intelligence and Research (INR), U.S. Department of State, to the Secretary, Intelligence Note, 'The Inevitable Middle East-Vietnam "Package Deal," But Contents Unknown,' May 25, 1967, Confidential, NARA, Central Files, 1967–1969, Box 7; George C. Denny to the Secretary, 'Hanoi Supports Arabs But Perhaps Unhappily,' June 2, 1967, Confidential, NARA, Central Files, 1967–1969; Z. Brezezinski, 'Sinai and Saigon, Should the Two Be Linked?,' June 7, 1967, Secret, Middle East Crisis. IV, LBJL, SNF.
20 Eshel (Vienna) to Tekoah, Ilan, May 26, 1967, ISA 4083/3.
21 Kosygin to Eshkol, May 26, 1967, Top Secret, ISA 4083/3.
22 Katz to DEE, May 26, 1967, Secret, Immediate, ISA 4083/3.

be taken to prevent war, but not at the Arabs' expense. If Israel started a war, Kosygin warned, the Soviet Union would come to the aid of the countries under attack. Neither side wanted conflict, he said, and the two superpowers had to use every means at their disposal to prevent it.[23]

Vietnam continued casting its shadow over the Middle East. Valerian Zorin, Soviet ambassador to Paris, rejected a French proposal for talks between the United States, the Soviet Union, Britain and France, claiming his country could not negotiate with the United States while it was bombing Vietnam. The Arabs needed arms, he said, because they feared the United States and its friends. Furthermore, Middle East stability required the Americans to sail the Sixth Fleet out of the Mediterranean.[24] State Department intelligence was certain the Soviet Union would benefit from the blockade of the Straits of Tiran, as it had done in 1956.[25] The backing the Kremlin gave to Nasser after the expulsion of UNEF made it likely that the Soviet leadership had advance knowledge of Egypt's intention to close the Straits. US ambassador Thompson asked a Soviet official the question directly and was told that Nasser had acted alone.[26] He reasoned that the Soviets had given Nasser a blank check without knowing specifically what he was planning, and he had trouble reconciling it with the Soviet claim that they wanted to avoid war.[27] The Soviet Union's unswerving support for the blockade indicated probable Soviet knowledge about Nasser's intentions. However, in a State Department intelligence assessment, the crisis began after Eshkol's warning to Syria until which, the intelligence agency maintained, Saudi Arabia had been the major target of Soviet Middle East penetration.[28]

Shams Badran, the Egyptian minister of war, visited Moscow on May 24, where he received Kosygin's support for the blockade. According to *Pravda*, Soviet military leaders advised Egypt to prevent the situation from deteriorating. Gromyko also advised restraint. However, Marshal Grechko, the Soviet minister of defense, told Badran to be firm and not to

23 FRUS, 1964–1968, XIX: 159–60.
24 Charles E. Bohlen, Paris to Department of State, 'Soviet Comments,' May 27, 1967, Confidential, NARA, RG59NEA/NE.
25 Thompson to Rusk, May 31, 1967, Confidential, NARA, RG 59, Central Files, 1967–1968, Box 7 (Conversation with Mikhail Voslenski).
26 Thompson to Rusk, May 27, 1967, Secret, NARA, RG 59, Central Files, 1967–1968, Box 7.
27 On the weekly meeting of the Western ambassadors in Moscow, see Harrison to FO, May 31, 1967, Confidential, NA, FCO 17/483/ER/5.
28 George C. Denny, Director of Intelligence and Research, US Department of State, to the Secretary, Research Memorandum, 'Pattern of Soviet Propaganda Preceding Near East Crisis,' June 1, 1967, NARA, RG 59, NEA/NE.

allow the United States to blackmail him, because the Soviet Union would support Egypt. Nevertheless, Badran wrote to Nasser that Grechko's promises should not be taken literally, a letter which, unfortunately for Egypt, arrived after the war had begun. Had it arrived it time, the situation might have been different. Whether or not the Soviet leadership knew of the blockade in advance is moot, but what is certain is that they worsened the crisis by supporting the blockade as soon as it was imposed.[29]

Katz accused the Kremlin of planning the crisis. The Soviets, he said, deliberately ignored Arab aggression and it was clear that the Soviets intended to buy the sympathy of the Arabs and mobilize left-leaning world public opinion. Soviet hints to the staff of the Israeli embassy claiming they were moderating the Arabs were meant to conceal joint planning with Syria, Egypt, Iraq and Algeria, whose objective was to distance the West from Middle Eastern oil and end its influence over Turkey and Iran. Israel was the intended victim, on the Soviet assumptions that war would inspire the Arab world's revolutionary regimes, UN intervention would be prevented by a Soviet veto and the Western powers, fearing direct Soviet involvement, would hesitate to intervene.[30]

The State Department's intelligence unit maintained that the Soviet Union did not intend to start a war, but rather wanted to restrain all parties involved. In actual fact, US intelligence knew little about decision-making in the Kremlin. Israel tried to enlist the support of progressive elements in the West, asking them to condemn Soviet support of Arab aggression. If Nasser were not compelled to retreat, there would be war and history would hold responsible those who claimed to head the peace camp.[31]

To Kosygin, Eshkol accused Syria of worsening the crisis, reminding him that the Security Council had condemned Syria on May 19, 1967. The decisive factor had not been the evacuation of UNEF, Eshkol wrote, but rather Egypt's declaration of its willingness to battle Israel, climaxing in the blockade of the Straits of Tiran, an act of war violating international law. Egypt was provoking war and on May 26 Eshkol referred to the blockade as the beginning of a campaign to destroy Israel. Accusing Israel of being a cat's paw for foreign elements was an insult to a country that was acting solely in self-defense. Eshkol called on the

---

29 Heikal, 1978: 179–80; Govrin, 1998: 259–62; Primakov, 2004: 187.
30 Katz to Levavi, May 27, 1967, Top Secret, Personal, Immediate, No. 88, ISA 4083/3.
31 Eliashiv Ben-Horin to Israeli Embassy, Mexico etc., May 30, 1967, Immediate, 'Instructions Not to Mix in the Soviet Jewry Problem,' ISA 4083/3; George C. Denny, to the Secretary, 'Soviet Reaction to Maritime Nations' Declaration,' May 30, 1967, Secret, Exidis, NARA, RG 59, Central Files, 1967–1969, Box 11.

Soviet Union to join forces with the other powers to work for a permanent peace according to the principles of territorial integrity, abstention from hostilities and non-intervention in internal affairs. The Soviets told Israel to be optimistic,[32] while the same day Gromyko told the Central Committee of the Communist Party of the Soviet Union that Israel had completed a general mobilization of its forces and that a protest should be lodged with the Israeli ambassador in Moscow.[33]

On May 27, Gromyko warned Katz that hawkish Israeli leaders were endangering their country. Katz told him that Cairo and Damascus were inciting war hysteria and that the Egyptians were declaring that the time had come to turn the clock back to 1948, and were planning an offensive in the spirit of Hitler's Final Solution. Gromyko replied that the critical question was: who would start a war?[34] On June 2, the leading article in *Novoya Vremya* claimed that the imperialist forces were exploiting the IDF as a strike force against the Arab liberation movement. The source of international tensions, it continued, was Vietnam and any attempt to divert attention from it was to play into the hands of imperialism.[35]

The question remained as to what the Soviet Union's intentions in the Middle East really were. They were always interested, but it was only at the beginning of 1966, with the second coup of the leftist Ba'ath regime in Syria, the pending British evacuation of Aden and the ambiguity of US policy, that the stars had aligned for the Soviets. It was a rare opportunity and the Kremlin was not about to let it slip away; the Soviet leaders were prepared to risk their relations with the West and Israel if they could succeed. Nasser scored the Kremlin a victory by uniting regional pro-Soviet forces and, instead of direct military intervention in Syria, the Kremlin used Egypt.[36]

The day the war broke out, Kosygin sent a cable to Eshkol condemning Israel's attack on Egypt, accusing Israel of violating the UN Charter and claiming that if the bloodshed were not stopped Israel would be responsible for the consequences.[37] The Soviet threat was unambiguous, but Israel, which had to grapple with life and death issues, paid only partial attention to it. Israel's leaders were cautious regarding Syria because it

32  Tekoah to IMM, June 1, 1967, Secret, Immediate, ISA 4083/3.
33  SDMEC 2: 571.
34  Katz to Levavi, June 2, 1967, Secret, Urgent, ISA 4083/3.
35  Observer, 'The Middle East Situation,' New Times, 23, June 7, 1967 (Russian edition: *Novoya Vremya*, June 2).
36  Ilan to Tekoah, June 3, 1967, Secret, ISA 4083/3; Raviv to Washington (Shimoni), June 18, 1967, ISA 4083/3.
37  Tekoah to IMM etc., June 6, 1967, Secret, Urgent, ISA 4083/3.

was a Soviet client. The State Department intelligence, however, gave the Soviet threat its full attention. Soviet support for the Arabs, the State Department maintained, was vocal but restrained, and there had been no change in Soviet troop deployments. The Soviet fleet in the Middle East had been reinforced but its strength was still acceptable. The Arab leaders acted irresponsibly, yet the Kremlin fanned their fears, encouraged them and provided arms. Moscow may not have sought a war in the Middle East because one would probably bring on Western aggression, making the Soviets have to choose between abandoning the Arabs or intervening directly. The balance between the Soviets' fear of an all-out war and their desire to play the role of the Arabs' defender could be established only by the war itself. Washington was incapable of understanding the Kremlin's motives. However, China had no hesitation in granting the Arabs full support. On June 6, Peking accused the Soviets of betraying the Arabs by agreeing to a ceasefire, and Chinese Prime Minister Zhou Enlai compared the Palestinian struggle to that of the Vietcong.[38]

The CIA believed that the Kremlin had not participated in planning the crisis, that Nasser had decided to close the Straits of Tiran without consulting the Soviet Union and that the Kremlin had been surprised by the rapid pace of Nasser's actions, and informed Washington it was interested in peace.[39]

The Soviet Union broke off diplomatic relations with Israel on June 10, not a surprise considering the blow that Israel had just dealt to Egypt. Chuvakhin asked when the IDF intended to prove it sought peace by withdrawing from Syria. The Soviet ambassador warned that if Israel did not withdraw it would bear the consequences.[40] Israeli representatives in the West were advised to announce that the Soviets had broken off relations because they could not force Israel into a Munich-style surrender. The Soviet Union, the foreign ministry said, had goaded the Arabs by offering full public support for terrorist attacks and the destruction of Israel. Soviet diplomats had deceived their Western colleagues when they said that the Soviet Union was restraining the hotheads in Damascus and Cairo.[41] With the exception of Romania, the Soviet satellites in Eastern Europe also

---

38 Thomas L. Hughes to the Secretary, 'International Reactions to Mid-East Hostilities,' June 6, 1967, Secret, Central Files, 1967–1969, Box 15; Thomas L. Hughes to the Secretary, Intelligence Note, 'China Finds Profit in Arab Losses,' June 9, 1967, Confidential, NARA, RG 59, Central Files, 1967–1969, Box 14.
39 'Current Soviet Attitudes and Intentions in the Middle East,' FRUS, 1964–1968, XIV (June 9, 1967): 403–5.
40 Eban–Chuvakhin Conversation, June 10, 1967, ISA 1698/7.
41 Ilan to Israel Embassy, London etc., June 10, 1967, Secret, Urgent, ISA 4083/3.

broke off diplomatic relations.[42] Israel was concerned that the Soviet leadership had played a Machiavellian role in fomenting the war, following a master plan for achieving its interests at the expense of both Israel and the Arabs. The objective was to bring the region to the brink of war because the Soviets wanted to perpetuate the Arab–Israeli conflict.

The bogus report that Israel was concentrating forces on the Syrian border had played a decisive role in starting the war, and it had originated with the Soviet leadership. When the Israeli ambassador to the UN tried to persuade the Soviet ambassador of Israel's desire to avoid war, he was greeted with scorn and asked: who needed facts? Israel's suspicion that the Kremlin was following a master plan was reinforced by the $2 billion worth of arms the Soviet Union had supplied to the Arab countries since 1955, most of which had gone to Egypt, and included tanks, fighter planes, submarines, destroyers and artillery.[43]

Realizing that it had failed to recognize Soviet intentions, the United States adopted a new policy, although it did not satisfy Israel's expectations. On the one hand, Rusk refused to accept the Soviet demand that Israel withdraw unconditionally from the territories it had occupied, without receiving in exchange Arab recognition of Israel's right to exist.[44] On the other, the United States was concerned that the Middle East would go nuclear. The West's worst fear was that Israel would develop nuclear weapons and that China would provide them to the Arabs, and the two superpowers genuinely feared a nuclear confrontation in the Middle East.[45]

Israel could claim to have improved its position. Still, Kosygin vilified Israel before the UN General Assembly, although he did recognize its right to exist. In theory, the advisor to the Soviet embassy in Washington also asserted that the Arab doctrine of the right to destroy Israel was nonsense. However, the Soviets said, the United States had to persuade Israel to be more flexible toward the Arabs and consider Arab pride, and to act in 'the spirit of Tashkent' (namely, the Tashkent summit which ended the war between India and Pakistan in January 1966, mediated by the Soviet Union).[46] In practice, the Kremlin leadership took a tougher

42 DEE Bulletin, Nos. 36–7, July 6, 1967, ISA 4095/20.
43 Raviv to Shimoni IMUN, Soviet Conspiracy in the Middle East, September 18, 1967, ISA 4083/2.
44 FRUS, 1964–1968, XIV: 506; A. Cohen, 1998: 273–6.
45 'Development of Nuclear Weapons by Additional Countries 1967–1976,' Report by the Joint Intelligence Committee, JIC(67) 25 (Final), June 5, 1967, Top Secret, UK/US Eyes Only, NA, CAB 158/66; A. Cohen, 1998: *passim*.
46 FRUS, 1964–1968, XIX: 522–4; George C. Denny to the Secretary, 'Kosygin Opens with Maximum Demands,' June 19, 1967, Confidential, NARA, INR, Note 502.

line. The Communist Party Central Committee claimed that the United States had known in advance of the Israeli attack. Gromyko argued that the United States must have had advance warning and could have done more to avert war. The claim was denied by Arthur Goldberg, US ambassador to the UN, and countered with the assertion that the US administration had received assurances from both sides that they would not initiate hostilities. Israel, said the Americans, was not their puppet.[47]

At the opening of the Glassboro Summit (June 23), Kosygin claimed that the Soviet Union had curbed the Arab intention to go to war, whereas the United States had failed to do the same with Israel. Johnson replied that the failure had been mutual. The Arabs had blocked the Straits of Tiran, he noted, and war could have been prevented had the flow of arms to the Middle East been stopped. The United States sought to limit the development of anti-ballistic missiles, he said, for the sake of peace in both the Middle East and Vietnam. Kosygin declared that the Soviet Union supported only economic development, such as the Aswan and the Euphrates dams, to improve the quality of life of poor populations in the Middle East.

The Middle East had now become the most important item on the East–West agenda. Kosygin insisted Israel withdraw to the June 5 lines, but did not threaten a new war. The US President, he said, had to understand that the Arabs were an 'explosive people,' and Nasser had to be supported to prevent the situation from deteriorating further. The Arabs would fight with their hands, fists and hunting rifles, he cautioned.[48] Disarmament talks could not begin while the Vietnam War dragged on and until a permanent solution had been achieved in the Middle East. He claimed there would be no peace without an Israeli withdrawal from the territories it had captured. Johnson responded that the problem was a matter of justice, reminding Kosygin that he himself had publicly supported Israel's right to exist at the UN. Israel, Kosygin insisted, had to be compelled to retreat, after which the Straits of Tiran would be opened.

Johnson, now clearly supporting Israel, told Kosygin that Israel should not be expected to pull back its forces before the dangers which had initially caused the conflict had been eliminated. Israel, he reminded him, had not gone to war until after Nasser had blocked the Straits of Tiran.[49] Kosygin said the Soviet Union demanded the US acknowledge Israel as the aggressor, that Israel withdraw from the territories it had occupied and compensate the refugees. Israeli withdrawal had to be

---

47 FRUS, 1964–1968, XIX: 535.
48 FRUS, 1964–1968, XIV: 514–25.
49 FRUS, 1964–1968, XIV: 538–43.

the first step, not the last. Kosygin stressed the severity of the refugee problem. Even if the United States agreed to take in 5,000 refugees, they might not accept the offer and would continue to demand to return to their original homes. Kosygin claimed that Israel sought to annex the West Bank and Gaza Strip, to demilitarize the Sinai Peninsula and the Golan Heights, and to maintain control over Jerusalem. Johnson responded that, while an Israeli withdrawal could assuage some of the fears, it would not solve the fundamental problems. Kosygin said he had hoped the President would support an Israeli withdrawal, but he now realized that the United States was endorsing Israeli aggression and was influenced by the ubiquitous Zionist forces. The time was long past when a country could capture foreign territory, Kosygin maintained. The President said the situation could have been controlled if Nasser had not threatened to destroy Israel, moved his troops into the Sinai Peninsula and closed the Gulf of Aqaba, so that Nasser was obviously the aggressor. Kosygin said that if the United States did not agree to a peace accord it would bring upon itself the wrath of millions of Arabs. Johnson asserted that the United States wanted peace, but warned that, if the Soviets sent arms to the Middle East, the Americans would consider doing the same, despite its interest in regional development. Kosygin expressed his regret that no accommodation had been reached on the Middle East. He hoped, he said, that the United States would exert its influence over Israel.[50]

The Americans felt that the Soviet Union would not take risks in the Middle East in the near future. It would, however, keep tensions high, even though it did not particularly want to destroy Israel. Israel believed that there was no immediate threat and that the Soviet Union would not violate the understanding that the two superpowers not send their own troops to fight in the region. Soviet sources indicate that Chairman of Supreme Soviet Nikolai Podgorny refused to grant Nasser an official defense pact and told him that arming Egypt was no substitute for a political solution.[51]

To understand the Kremlin's actions, it is necessary to analyze Soviet Cold War strategy. It supported the Arabs against Israel to sabotage the West's position in the Middle East, to impede the US war effort in Vietnam and to jeopardize the economies of Western Europe by cutting them off their principal oil supply. It also wanted to retaliate against Israel for its interference in internal Soviet affairs. The Israeli campaign

---

50  FRUS, 1964–1968, XIV: 544–56; Farid, 1994: 13–15; Johnson, 2008: 60, 62–3.
51  Levanon–Toon discussion, June 21, 1967, ISA 4083/2.

for the right of Soviet Jews to emigrate to Israel endangered the multinational character of the Soviet state. The rapid escalation of the crisis of May–June 1967 meant that war could not have been prevented and the conditions for armed conflict were already in place. The Soviet Union could have prevented war by exerting pressure on Egypt, but with the United States bogged down in Vietnam and the US administration facing increasing domestic unrest, the opportunity was too tempting. The hawks in the Soviet leadership, Brezhnev and Grechko, prevailed over Kosygin and Gromyko and did not fear that fanning the flames in the Middle East would endanger détente, since in any case they did not advocate it. Israel warned the United States that the Kremlin would seek escalation, although it did not seek war. The two superpowers did not prevent their clients from drifting into the crisis, while the Soviet Union was also dragged by its clients into deeper involvement than it had originally intended. In practice, the Soviet leadership led the region into war, while the United States did not do enough to curb the Soviets or to restrain the Arabs.

Newly available documents illuminate to some extent the Soviet leadership's confusion on the eve of the Six Day War and afterward. The most telling Communist confession came in an amazingly candid speech by Leonid Brezhnev, the Secretary of the Communist Party of the Soviet Union, before the Central Committee. He repeated his mantra that Israeli aggression was merely a link in a chain of aggressive international imperialism headed by the United States. Brezhnev maintained that Egypt had surprised the Soviets by demanding the evacuation of UNEF. He claimed that the Arabs had been warned that their bellicose rhetoric and their calling for a war of destruction against Israel would set off a wildfire in the Middle East. Nasser was warned on May 26 to do everything to avert a confrontation with Israel.

Brezhnev astounded his audience when he declared that it had not been the Soviet military that had failed, but rather the Arabs' inadequate combat skills and their low morale.[52] He stressed that, while the Arabs did not recognize Israel, the Soviet Union did. But it opposed the bellicosity of the Arab leaders. The Arab goal of destroying Israel would have led to even more serious consequences had their armies indeed succeeded in conquering the Jewish state. The United States and Britain would almost certainly have become involved in the war had it reached

---

52 Brezhnev to the Plenum of Central Committee of the Soviet Communist Party, June 20, 1967, in Ro'i and Morozov, 2008: 302–36.

that point. Since the Soviets would have had to respond, this would have brought the globe close to a third world war.[53]

The amount of risk that the Soviet Union was ready to take is evidenced by the massive military aid that it granted to the Arabs despite their defeat. Brezhnev notified a meeting of the Communist states in Budapest that Israel was devoid of any economic power and depended on foreign aid. It lacked oil and other mineral resources and the United States was using her as a 'puppet' against the Arab states. If the United States stopped its aid, it would quickly disappear. However, he criticized the Arabs for their lack of unity, except in their opposition to Israel. Nasser consistently stressed Egypt's alliance with the Soviet Union in order to compel the Soviets to fight Israel. But, the Soviet Union had no interest in a war with Israel. The conflict could not be decided by war, Brezhnev emphasized. The Arabs refused to accept the principle of ending the war, although it was not tantamount to recognizing Israel, as Tito, the Yugoslav leader, explained. Tito also opined that Nasser was under pressure from Algeria not to end the war with Israel. Wladyslaw Gomulka, the Polish leader, exclaimed that Israel could not be defeated by Algerian or Chinese methods. The Bulgarian Communist leader, Todor Zhivkov, warned against exposing the Soviet bloc to a nuclear strike.[54]

Brezhnev noted with satisfaction that Egypt, Syria and Algeria had come close to adopting the ideology of the Soviet bloc and that the United States was aware of this. Nevertheless, he severely criticized the Arab defeat, which he said resulted from neglect, lack of understanding of the nature of a modern army and incompetence. The Arab states, he said, were feudal societies. Men who operated modern weapons needed high-school educations and at least two years of training. Nasser might have been flagellating himself, but Brezhnev did not feel any better. He acknowledged that the Soviet Union had suffered a blow to its morale and prestige, but he placed the blame squarely on the Arabs, and on Nasser in particular. No one in the Soviet Union understood how two million Israelis were able to beat so many Arabs equipped with Soviet weapons. He complained that the Arabs had intended to drag the Soviet Union into war when it was

---

53 'Record of Conversation between the Polish Politburo Member Zemon Kliszko and Soviet Leader Leonid Brezhnev,' Moscow, in Ro'i and Morozov, 2008: 336–9 (24 June, 1967).

54 Polish Record of Meeting of Soviet Bloc leaders (and Tito) in Budapest (Excerpts), June 11, 1967, Secret, CWIHP; Gomulka reported to the Polish Politburo on June 27, 1967: 'Nuclear war was in the air at the Moscow summit since the situation is inching toward war' (in Stola, 2006: 166).

already involved in Vietnam. The Soviet position was that the destruction of Israel was not an acceptable war goal. The Soviet Union was fully capable of destroying Tel Aviv with conventional missiles, but that would mean a world war, something the Soviet bloc sought to avoid at any price, and he was almost certain that the United States did not want one either. The problem was to persuade Nasser that to survive he had to agree to a political accommodation.

The Soviet Union proposed to Nasser that, following an Israeli withdrawal, he announce his support for freedom of navigation in the Gulf of Aqaba and the Suez Canal. He was mistaken if he thought that closing the Suez Canal would have an effect on the United States. The United States could survive without the Canal, but Nasser could not. It was symptomatic of Arab Nationalism, he said, to avoid the search for a solution. The Soviet Union was helping Nasser with arms and advisors, but they could only defend his country. Brezhnev praised himself for sending military aid to the Arabs on the second day of the war. The Soviet Union was especially angry over the fact that some of its new planes and missiles had fallen into US hands and that West Germany was now in possession of Soviet tanks. Kosygin also warned the Arabs against resuming hostilities. They were deluded if they thought that fifty Soviet pilots and 1,000 advisors could produce an Arab victory. If the Soviet Union were to send in its own troops, Kosygin warned, the United States and Britain would do the same. The Arabs had to think carefully before starting another war. They would be smarter to exploit Johnson's fear of losing the Arab world and Africa and use it as leverage to achieve a favorable compromise.[55]

Brezhnev was furious that the Arabs were opposing an end to the war. They were setting themselves up for another defeat and the end of the progressive Arab regimes. The Soviet bloc could not allow this to happen. It would mean a nuclear war with the West and the consequences could not even be guessed at. Despite his anger with the Arabs for allowing themselves to be beaten, he remained committed to them and would send $258 million worth of arms without conditions, he said. Marshal Grechko said that the Egyptian army did not have the capability to operate the weapons it had received. It was not prepared for defense, much less for an offensive war. He consoled himself by saying that leadership required knowing not only how to win, but also how to lose.[56] Israel had clearly proven its military superiority. That would be called into doubt in 1973, during the Yom Kippur War, but it would also open a door to a partial peace.

55 'Polish Record of a Meeting of Soviet-Bloc Leaders,' 11 July, 1967, CWIHP.
56 Farid, 1994: 21–40, 42–7 (discussion with Aref, President of Iraq, and Boumedienne, President of Algeria).

**Figure 6** 'The chicken refused to be sacrificed' by Yaakov Farkash (Ze'ev), October 13, 1967.

**Figure 7** 'No withdrawal without peace' by Yaakov Farkash (Ze'ev), October 17, 1967.

**Figure 8** 'Five points' by Yaakov Farkash (Ze'ev), October 20, 1967.

**Figure 9** 'The Israeli scorpion in the Sinai Desert,' *Krokodil*, 18 (1967).

**Figure 10** 'We are determined', *Krokodil*, 18 (1967).

# Conclusions

## Israel in the regional and international arenas: asset or liability?

Israel's initial status in the international arena was unique. It was a country under siege, its neighbors on all sides rejected its existence and the superpowers were skeptical of its ability to survive. The Soviet Union had played a key role in its establishment by voting in favor of the UN Partition Plan, but was opposed to its Zionist ideology. Since mass immigration was at the top of Israel's agenda, it was unlikely that Israel could maintain correct diplomatic relations with the Soviets because immigration would undermine the image of the Soviet Union's multinational structure. In addition, Israel had openly supported the United States during the Korean War, shattering its pretense of non-alignment, necessary more for domestic than for foreign policy maneuvers.

However, the Soviet Union could not be maneuvered, and the first US loan to Israel was enough to convince the Soviets that Israel's policy of non-alignment was a fiction. It therefore rejected Israel's request for military and financial aid, claiming that Israel was a US satellite, and it regarded Israel as a liability almost from its inception. Repeated attempts to base relations with the Soviet Union on trade and culture were fruitless because the Kremlin's considerations were strategic and centered on the Cold War. Eventually, Israel understood that there would be no change in relations with the Soviet Union before an East–West détente.

The United States had also played a key role in Israel's establishment and, once the state had been founded, it was completely dependent on US financial aid, despite the arms embargo. Had Israel really been non-aligned and neutral, the United States would never have been as generous with its aid. Nevertheless, throughout the 1950s and early 1960s, the United States also regarded Israel as a liability, both political and financial, and as endangering Western interests. Unlike the Soviet Union, however, US motives were not only related to the Cold War. It did genuinely want to find a solution to the Arab–Israeli conflict,[1] but trial and error taught the Americans that the conflict had an independent existence and its own dynamic. The various US plans and programs – the Johnston Plan for resolving water issues, the Johnson Plan for resolving the Palestinian refugee problem and Project Alpha for territorial concessions in favor of Israel's Arab neighbors – all failed and were not replaced by new initiatives.[2]

The East–West global confrontation also had its own dynamic but for geostrategic reasons was linked to the Middle East in concentric circles, Turkey and Iran on the outside and Israel and the Arab states in the center. By the 1950s, the objections of all the Arab states to the West's position on Israel forced Washington to lower Israel's status, which was raised again in the mid-1960s, however, after the United States' bitter experiences with Arab Nationalism. Because of their strategic importance, the United States had to favor the moderate Arab states, but that did not mean it had abandoned Israel. According to conventional wisdom, the tactical change in Israel's position vis-à-vis the United States came during the Kennedy administration (the supply of Hawk missiles), but there was still the US dilemma of how to categorize Israel, as liability or asset, and while the dilemma weakened under Johnson, it did not disappear. Israel became less of a liability, but not more of an asset, and it did not get the defense treaty it wanted. The United States could not step in and solve the Arab–Israeli confrontation at Israel's expense while the radical Arab states followed anti-Western and pro-Soviet policies, and in any case the moderate Arab states were equally anti-Israel, with none of them willing to accept a solution which included Israel's existence.

Since the Soviets still threatened Western positions in the Middle East, the United States abandoned its attempts to solve the Arab–Israeli confrontation and focused instead on the Eisenhower Doctrine of intervening in any country which felt itself threatened or endangered by the Communists. The Doctrine did not change US status in the Middle East, but it did indirectly help Israel in that it allowed the use of US financial aid to purchase arms in Europe. When Iraq left the Western camp for the Soviets, Israel became a partial asset which could help keep Jordan from falling prey to Nasser, which would have endangered US interests. Regardless, the United States still refused to sign a defense treaty with Israel.

Even at the beginning of the 1950s, US regional interests had no influence on Israel's need for a genuine patron, despite its willingness to

---

1 Hahn, 2004: 279.
2 See Allen, 1961: 1, 3.

accept client status. The United States would assure its continued financial survival, that was all. Israel was considered an even worse liability because it demanded arms to balance what the Arabs possessed. Thus, paradoxically, the United States evaded its responsibilities for the fate of the only country in the Middle East which completely identified with the West. Israel's tactical error was not realizing in time that not only did the United States have influence in the Middle East, but the Soviet Union could become a regional hostile factor overnight.

Israel was trapped by both superpowers. The Soviet Union would not agree to any solution to the Arab–Israeli conflict without the removal of US bases from Iran and Turkey, which would have meant the end of the Western alliances. That was unrealistic because it would have meant a complete Western surrender to the Soviet Union and a Soviet victory in the Cold War in the Middle East, with serious implications for other regions. Thus, Israel's Western orientation would be necessary until the fall of the Soviet empire. The Kremlin called Israel a tool of imperialism and a Western strategic base, and exploited the Arab–Israeli conflict for its own ends. By supporting national liberation movements, the Soviet Union could build strategic bases in the radical Arab states, but those turned out to be both a financial and a military drain, and did not prevent the Soviets from losing the Cold War.

Israel, despite its democratic government and identification with the West, was considered a liability and was marginalized, although the United States did realize that the core of the problem was the lack of a solution to the Arab–Israeli conflict and not the arms race. However, no solution was readily available, not only because Israel refused to have its borders altered, but because, and more to the point, Nasser demanded that the entire Negev be returned to Egypt and that all the Arab refugees be returned to Israel, which would have changed Israel's demographics to the point where it ceased to be a Jewish state.

Israel's status changed during Johnson administration – the Memorandum of Understanding – despite the fact that the Middle Eastern dynamic remained the same, under the influence of three factors. The first was Egypt's attempted subversion of the pro-Western Arab regimes and its threatened intervention in the war in Yemen; the second was the Soviets' increasing involvement in Egypt, Syria and Yemen; and the third was Israel's increased stature demographically, financially and militarily as a component of the West, inducing the United States to include it in its regional interests.

The military capabilities demonstrated by Israel during the Suez War and the nuclear reactor in Dimona improved considerably Israel's bargaining power. The reactor angered the United States because, despite the so-called 'special relationship,' it came as a surprise. The reactor was particularly valuable to Israel, allowing it to ignore the dictates of its patron regarding its security in the face of the military build-up of its enemies. Only two years before the Six Day War, following Soviet attempts to deepen Soviet involvement in the Middle East, was the United States convinced to shift from being a suspicious economic patron to an active arms supplier, through its European allies.

Under Truman, the United States' refusal to sign a defense pact with Israel was not based on ideological grounds, because the United States never doubted Israel's democracy or its identification with the West. It was a matter of preserving Western strategic superiority in the Middle East. The main issue was that Israel did not share a border with the Soviet bloc. Another issue was the ongoing, escalating conflict between Israel and its neighboring Arab states, which prevented it from being a full client. During the 1960s, Washington was afraid that Israel would drag it into a regional then global conflict. While the Memorandum of Understanding allowing for the provision of offensive weapons signaled a change, the conditions were not yet ripe for patron–client relations of the type given to strategic assets. The US administration was afraid of involvement in another Cold War front, and in addition it could not fully control Israel in the way that it could its other clients.

One key question still outstanding is why the United States accepted the construction of the reactor in Dimona, which diminished its influence on Israel. In all probability it was because Israel could not be punished without endangering the balance of power and tipping the scales in favor of the Soviets and their regional allies, especially Nasser, who was regarded as particularly dangerous. Israel's nuclear potential and the threat of reprisals against Arab terrorist attacks forced the United States to make significant improvements in Israel's strategic deterrent capabilities despite the danger of a regional superpower confrontation. The State Department, which had no choice but to agree, distanced itself from the decision to supply Israel with arms. On the eve of the Six Day War, Israel was still considered a liability, its official situation still vague and unacceptable to the US government. The gap between Israel and the United States regarding each other's capabilities to deter Arab aggression remained large and not only was the war not prevented, but Israel was extremely disappointed by the Sixth Fleet's inaction.[3] Israel achieved both its conventional and non-conventional deterrence owing

---

3 See Isenberg, 2005. Isenberg claims that the Sixth Fleet was not meant to solve regional conflicts, only to constitute 'preparation for a worst-case Soviet-centered scenario' (717).

to French vital assistance because of Nasser's support for the Front de Libération Nationale in the Algerian War, although de Gaulle distanced himself from Israel after the Evian Conference.

### Israel's image as a victim

At first glance, Israel, regarded by the United States as a liability, would be expected to accept its image as a victim of both the Cold War and the unresolvable Arab–Israeli conflict, both of which kept it from receiving full US support. Israel was trapped, not only surrounded on all sides by enemies, but begging for financial and economic favors as well. The idea that Ben-Gurion was responsible for the image of Israel as a victim, the result of his demonizing the Arabs and their leaders, has no basis in fact. Rather, the image was forced on Israel, demonized by Nasser in his desire to make it a state of 'all its citizens,' and, if his conditions were not met, he would initiate a war to destroy it. Soviet propaganda turned Israel into an enemy of Communism and the obstacle to complete Arab national liberation and the Kremlin was quick to provide Nasser with weapons.

Israel's image as victim was the result of the majority of the country's strong aversion to Communist theory and practice. Ben-Gurion's unequivocal adherence to Western culture and ideology, even if it endangered the Soviet Union's Jews and alienated its government, was the result of the concept that the fate of the country would be decided in a confrontation with an enemy that would never compromise, combined with Western assistance. In practical terms, the Soviet Union would not let its Jews emigrate to Israel and would not maintain even minimal commercial or cultural ties with Israel, the result of its long-standing heritage of anti-Semitism and its hostility to Zionism.

Israel's image as a victim was strongest during the Eisenhower administration, which categorically denied Zionist ideology and wanted to solve the problems of the Middle East at the expense of Israel's interests. Its efforts failed because it did not appreciate the importance of the Arab–Israeli conflict in the Cold War. Khrushchev – perhaps somewhat less anti-Semitic than Stalin, but not above using anti-Semitism as a tool – exploited the United States' alienation from Israel and did not hesitate to threaten to destroy Israel during the Suez War, increasing Israel's self-image as victim. Israel could not dream of eliminating Nasser's regime, although it knew he might initiate war. However, Israel never accepted its status as victim, as demonstrated by its ongoing campaign for Soviet immigration, the Suez War, and the Six Day War. Ben-Gurion was certain that another war would follow Suez, and his objective was to strengthen Israel with immigration, deterrent capabilities and preparations for war. While the Soviet Union was Machiavellian in its plotting against Israel, the United States was not. The US administrations from Truman to Johnson had one iron-clad rule, dictated by the State Department: no policies regarding Israel could be divorced from US regional and global strategies. Thus, the 'special relationship' of the Kennedy era conflicted with the US realpolitik and was meant to satisfy both American Jews and Israel, and keep Israel from feeling that it was being sacrificed on the altar of Western Cold War interests.

The term 'special relationship,' never wholly bilateral, has to be examined in light of the costs and benefits during the Cold War. In fact, the United States did cease to be apathetic to Israel's fate, but it would be an exaggeration to call Kennedy the 'father' of a US–Israeli alliance.[4] Given the constraints of Arab oil and containing Communism, the most the Kennedy administration could do was issue a declaration in May 8, 1963, which did little or nothing to free Israel from its image as victim and had only psychological value. The receipt of Hawk missiles, defensive weapons, did not help because the United States refused to be Israel's main supplier of offensive arms, and the image of victim remained.

However, its image was dramatically strengthened by the nuclear reactor in Dimona and the purchase of French surface-to-surface missiles and Mirage fighter planes. Within ten years, Israel went from victim to strategic factor, but the core problems of Arab hostility and Arab unwillingness to accept Israel's deterrent power remained. The West gradually abandoned the image of Israel as victim, replacing it with one of perennial troublemaker that had to be restrained, but whose deterrent power had to be reinforced to guard such a moderate Arab state as Jordan. Even by the eve of the Six Day War, Israel had not convinced the West that its deterrence was not effective and that the situation would deteriorate into war.

## Patrons and clients

The root of the evil in the Middle East during the Cold War was the lack of a regional agreement between the superpowers, making it a region devoid of rule where the patron superpowers had no control over their clients, a situation which deteriorated into the Six Day War. The tail

---

4 Ben-Zvi, 1993, 2002; Bass, 2003.

indeed wagged the dog, and the dog was sleeping. The increased supplies of arms to Israel under Johnson, to match Soviet arms supplied to the Arabs, did not deter the Arabs because the basic conflict was a zero-sum game, and nurtured by their denial of the State of Israel, and a superpower agreement would have been possible only if one of the sides, or both, had capitulated.

US strategic global constraints kept it from fully controlling Israel. The lack of a mutual defense pact enabled the client, at least partially, to dictate terms to its patron. The Soviet Union did not demonstrate any particular desire to control its Arab clients even before the outbreak of the Suez War. It did not meet the Arabs' demands for sophisticated weapons or to use them to start a war. The Kremlin, as much as the United States, without clear superiority over the West in the Middle East, did not want to open up a new Cold War front that might lead to a shooting war.

Generally speaking, US and Soviet patron–client relations differed. While the United States attempted to convince both sides to restrain themselves, the Soviet Union did not, although its ability to do so was perhaps greater. It is unlikely that a client's dependence on its patron will keep it from going to war. The patrons in this case could have been firmer, but were not, probably because firmness would have weakened their hold. Trying to restrain Israel would have had to involve sanctions, which would have cost the United States any leverage it might have had regarding Israel, and the Soviets did not want to lose the leverage the Arabs gave them. Thus, de facto, unbeknownst to them, by 1967 both patrons had lost control of their clients. When the dogs lunged at each other, it turned out that their leashes were too weak to hold them at bay.[5]

Since the Arab–Israeli conflict had no obvious solution in any event, the two superpowers abandoned the issue and turned their attention to détente beyond the borders of the Middle East, leading, eventually, to the War of Attrition which presaged the Yom Kippur War. The patrons realized too late that the conflict was so dangerously great that they had lost control over their clients. Nasser held the key and, although he did not want the war, he became its victim because of his pan-Arab, pan-Islamic and pan-African ideology, his desire for revenge and his belief that the Soviet Union would support him, without taking the deterrent capabilities of Israel and the United States into consideration.

---

5 The image is taken from Secretary of State Dulles's conversation with Eban (August 7, 1954): 'Man seeing ferocious looking dog being assured by owner dog is not biting variety, replying you know that, I know that, but does the dog know it' (DFPI, 9: 530).

Actually, both sides were victims of the Cold War. Nasser thought he could overcome Israel, if not in a shooting war then by strangulation, without having to tell the Soviets. Israel thought one stunning victory would be sufficient to inaugurate a new order in the Middle East, one Israel could live in. Neither side understood that the two superpowers were more interested in détente in Europe and the Far East than in dealing with a local conflict with no prospect of resolution. Israel could not convince the United States in time that the Soviet Union's penetration of the Middle East was part of its global program. Even on the eve of the Six Day War, the United States regarded Israel as endangering its Middle Eastern interests and also regarded its neighbors as inviting a regional crisis, but it was too involved in Vietnam to consider the issue in depth.

The United States was also extremely concerned and wary of what the global consequences might be of massive military involvement in the Arab–Israeli conflict. In effect, neither patron acceded to its clients' demands for formal alliances and cutting-edge weapons lest they themselves become involved in a war. The more Israel and the Arabs demanded and received, the less willing they became to accept weapons oversight. After the Six Day War, the Soviets realized how great and misguided their expectations had been. Suddenly, Brezhnev discovered that the Arabs had neither the technical knowledge nor the intellectual foundation to operate the modern weapons they had been given for 'self-defense.' An abashed Kremlin recognized Israel's 1949, rather than its 1947, borders and claimed that talk of destroying it had been an empty threat.

### Soviet Jews as a star in the Cold War constellation

Not only geopolitics and strategic interests determined Israel's fate, but also its ideology of the ingathering of the exiles, that is, massive immigration, and demographic considerations. As early as 1948, it was obvious to Ben-Gurion that 700,000 Jews were not enough to maintain a country surrounded by millions of Arab enemies. The Jewish population of the Soviet Union was particularly attractive as an object of immigration. Not only was their current situation uncertain and insecure, but they had made an enormous contribution to founding Zionism. The Kremlin objected instinctively to Jewish emigration and to a certain degree that objection was integrated into its Cold War strategy. However, with or without Israeli pressure for Soviet Jewish emigration, the Soviets would have pursued a policy of infiltrating the

Middle East as part of their long-range strategy to overcome the West. Traditional Russian anti-Semitism also played a part, as evidenced by various Soviet publications, which increased in number and viciousness after Israel won the Six Day War.[6]

Israel's Cold War pessimism turned out to be accurate. The Soviet leadership was trapped by its failed attempts to resolve its Jewish issue either by massive assimilation or with a territorial solution, and after the post-1967 détente had no choice but to allow immigration. The main obstacle had been the refusal of the United States, until the Six Day War, to officially support Soviet Jewish immigration for fear of sabotaging détente. Only after the Six Day War did the United States recognize the depth of Soviet Jewish identification and solidarity with Israel, and become convinced that it could be used for leverage.[7]

## The test of leadership

It is doubtful whether Johnson could have prevented the Six Day War. His severest critic claims that had he been blessed with independent thought and an analytic mind, he would have been able to respond to the crisis more successfully. He read nearly nothing and thus his understanding of foreign policy was superficial and he fell victim to clichés and stereotypes.[8] He has also been defended on the grounds that he did not have the tools to prevent the war, although he and his advisors made every effort to do so.[9] He might also have been a pawn in the hands of his White House, Pentagon and State Department advisors, who had no new initiatives to suggest. Perhaps Truman or Kennedy would have been more assertive in dealing with the Soviets and Nasser, perhaps at the last minute Khrushchev could have restrained Nasser and Syria, perhaps Eshkol could have used his charisma to curb the military. The problem was probably less one of personality and more one of statesmanship, and had the West or Israel been able to show significant deterrent capabilities, political, military or even nuclear, the war might have been prevented.

---

6 Kalugin, 1994: 52–3.
7 [No author, no date], 'The Six Day War and Soviet Jews,' ISA 4050/2.
8 Heinrichs, 1994: 26, 30.
9 Dallek, 1999: 15–16; Woods, 2006: 77.

## The failure of the Jewish lobby

The Jewish lobby in Washington was unable to prevent two of Israel's most difficult situations: the withdrawal from the Sinai Peninsula and the Six Day War. Both were the direct result of its basic inability to achieve what Israel wanted most of all, a mutual defense pact. The lobby's only conspicuous success was in helping to acquire economic aid for Israel despite the Arab boycott. Fearing the possibly negative consequences of the Cold War, it did not demand strongly enough that the US administration take a firmer stand against the Soviet Union and Egypt. However, it must be said that it did help to prevent, under Kennedy and Johnson, the conditioning Israel's receipt of weapons and economic aid on Israel's making concessions on the issues of the refugees, territories within the Green Line and the oversight of conventional and nuclear weapons.

In addition, the term 'special relationship' was not a creation of the Jewish lobby, but rather of Kennedy's difficulty to persuade his advisors to sign a defense pact with Israel which would not have promoted US interests. The term was primarily a slogan to improve morale during a crisis, both in Israel and within the American Jewish community, because the relationship lacked what Israel needed most of all. The Jewish lobby could work only within the framework of US interests. It could, in certain instances, prevent erosion of the administration's positions on Israel because of the potential Jewish vote, which could influence public opinion and Congress, but not the White House itself.[10] Eventually, the position of the State Department changed and Israel was no longer regarded as a liability, however not yet an asset, and after the Six Day War its existence was accepted.

Realpolitik, the desire to use détente to minimize the damage done by the Cold War, influenced the two superpowers to pursue policies that were detrimental to Israel. Israel, however, preserved the local balance of power although it did not have sufficient deterrent capabilities, and managed to survive the Cold War in the Middle East.

---

10 See Brands, 1995: 184–5.

# Bibliography

Akten zur Auswärtigen Politik der Bundesrepublik Deutschland, 1963–1967 (Munich, 1994–98).
Allen, George (1961). 'Are the Soviets Winning?' *American Academy of Political and Social Science* 336 (July 1961): 1–11.
Alteras, Isaac (1993). *Eisenhower and Israel: U.S.–Israeli Relations, 1953–1960*. Gainesville.
Aronson, Shlomo (1999). *The Politics and Strategy of Nuclear Weapons in the Middle East*. Albany.
Ashton, Nigel J. (1996) *Eisenhower, Macmillan and the Problem of Nasser: Anglo-American Relations and Arab-Nationalism, 1955–1959*. New York.
Badeau, John (1983). *The Middle East Remembered*. Washington.
Barak, Eitan (2007). 'Between Reality and Secrecy: Israel's Freedom of Navigation through the Straits of Tiran, 1957–1967.' *Middle East Journal* 61(4): 657–79.
Bar-On, Mordechai (1994). *The Gates of Gaza: Israel's Road to Suez and Back 1955–1957*. New York.
Barrett, Roby Carol (2007). *The Greater Middle East and the Cold War: United States Foreign Policy Under Eisenhower and Kennedy*. London and New York.
Bass, Warren (2003). *Support Any Friend: Kennedy's Middle East and the Making of the U.S.–Israeli Alliance*. Oxford and New York.
Ben-Gurion, David (1954). *Vision and Road* vol, V. Tel Aviv (Hebrew).
Ben-Gurion, David (1972). *Israel: A Personal History*. London.
Ben-Gurion, David (1993). *Like Stars and Dust: Essays from Israel's Government Year Book*. Sede Boqer.
Ben-Tsur, Abraham (1976). *Soviet Factors and the Six Day War: Struggles in the Kremlin and Implications for Our Region*. Tel Aviv (Hebrew).
Ben-Zvi, Abraham (1993). *The United States and Israel: The Limits of the Special Relationship*. New York.
Ben-Zvi, Abraham (1998) *A Decade of Transition: Eisenhower, Kennedy, and the Origins of Israeli–American Alliance*. New York.
Ben-Zvi, Abraham (2002). *John F. Kennedy and the Politics of Arms Sales to Israel*. London.
Ben-Zvi, Abraham (2004). *Lyndon B. Johnson and the Politics of Arms Sale to Israel: In the Shadow of the Hawk*. London.

Bialer, Uri (1990). *Between East and West: Israel's Foreign Policy Orientation, 1948–1956*. Cambridge.
Bialer, Uri (2005). *The Christian World in Israel's Foreign Policy, 1948–1956*. Bloomington.
Bohlen, Charles E. (1973). *Witness to History, 1929–1969*. New York.
Boyle, Peter G. (2005). *The Eden–Eisenhower Correspondence, 1955–1957*. Chapel Hill and London.
Brands, Henry W. (1995). *The Wages of Globalism: Lyndon Johnson and the Limits of American Power*. New York and Oxford.
Brands, Henry W. (1989) *The Specter of Nationalism*. New York.
Brenchley, Frank (2005). *Britain, the Six Day War and its Aftermath*. London.
Brent, Jonathan, and Vladimir P. Naumov (2003). *Stalin's Last Crime: The Plot against the Jewish Doctors*. New York.
Byroade, Henry A. (1954). *The Middle East*. Reprinted from the Department of State Bulletins of April 26 and May 10, 1954. Publication 5469. Near and Middle East Series 16. Washington.
Califano, Joseph A. (1991). *The Triumph and Tragedy of Lyndon Johnson: The White House Years*. New York.
Castle, Barbara (1984). *The Castle Diaries, 1964–1970*. London.
Catterall, Peter, ed. (2003). *Macmillan Diaries: The Cabinet Years, 1950–1957*. London.
Chase, Howard W., and Allen H. Lerman, eds. (1965). *Kennedy and the Press: The News Conferences*. New York.
Clifford, Clark (1991). *Counsel to the President: A Memoir*. New York.
Cohen, Avner (1998). *Israel and the Bomb*. New York.
Cohen, Michael (1982). *Palestine and the Great Powers, 1945–1948*. New Jersey.
Cohen, Michael (1997). *Fighting World War Three from the Middle East: Allied Contingency Plans, 1945–1954*. London.
Cohen, Michael (2005). *Strategy and Politics in the Middle East, 1954–1960*. Abingdon.
Cohen, Warren I. (1994). 'Balancing American Interests in the Middle East: Lyndon Baines Johnson vs. Gamal Abdul Nasser.' In: Warren I. Cohen and Nancy Bernkopf Tucker, eds., *Lyndon Johnson Confronts the World: American Foreign Policy, 1963–1968*. New York, pp. 270–309.
Copeland, Miles (1969). *The Game of Nations: The Amorality of Power Politics*. London.
Copeland, Miles (1974). *Without Cloak or Dagger: The Truth about the New Espionage*. New York.
Costigliola, Frank, ed. (2014). *The Kennan Diaries*. New York.
Crossman, Richard (1976). *The Crossman Diaries: The Diaries of a Cabinet Minister, 1964–1970, II*. London.
Cumings, Bruce (1995). 'Revising Revisionism' or 'The Poverty of Theory in Diplomatic History.' In: Michael J. Hogan, ed., *America in the World: The Historiography of American Foreign Relations Since 1941*. Cambridge, pp. 52–59.

Dagan, Avigdor (1970). *Moscow and Jerusalem: Twenty Years of Relations between Israel and the Soviet Union.* London.
Dallek, Robert (1998). *Flawed Giant: Lyndon B. Johnson and His Times, 1961–1967.* New York.
Dallek, Robert (1999). 'Lyndon Johnson as a World Leader.' In: Henry W. Brands, ed., *The Foreign Policies of Lyndon Johnson Beyond Vietnam.* College Station, pp. 6–48.
Dallek, Robert (2003). *John F. Kennedy: An Unfinished Life, 1917–1963.* London.
Danchev, Alex (1999). 'Special Pleading.' In: Kathleen Burk and Melvyn Stokes, eds., *The United States and the European Alliance Since 1945.* Oxford, pp. 271–88.
DDF (1987–2008). Documents diplomatiques français. 1962–1967. Paris
Decter, Moshe (1963). 'The Status of Jews in the Soviet Union.' *Foreign Affairs* 42(1): 420–30.
DFPI 1 (1981). *May 14, 1948–September 30, 1948.* Jerusalem.
DFPI 2 (1984). *October 1948–September 1949.* Jerusalem.
DFPI 3 (1983). *Armistice Negotiations with the Arab States: December 1948–July 1949.* Jerusalem.
DFPI 4 (1986). *May–December 1949.* Jerusalem.
DFPI 5 (1988). *1950.* Jerusalem.
DFPI 6 (1991). *1951.* Jerusalem.
DFPI 7 (1992). *1952.* Jerusalem.
DFPI 8 (1996). *1953.* Jerusalem.
DFPI 9 (2004). *1954.* Jerusalem.
DFPI 11 (2001). *January–October 1956.* Jerusalem.
DFPI 12 (2009). *October 1956–March 1957.* Jerusalem.
DFPI 13 (2008). *1958–1959.* Jerusalem.
DFPI 14 (1997). *1960.* Jerusalem.
Dobrynin, Anatoly (1995). *In Confidence: Moscow's Ambassador to Six Cold War Presidents.* London and Seattle.
Eban, Abba (1977). *An Autobiography.* New York.
Evensen, Bruce J. (1992). 'Truman, Palestine and the Cold War.' *Middle Eastern Studies,* 28(1): 120–56.
Farid, Abdel Majid (1994). *Nasser: The Final Years.* Reading.
Ferrell, Robert H., ed. (1991). *Truman in the White House: The Diary of Eben A. Ayers.* Missouri.
Frankel, Jonathan (1991). 'The Soviet Regime and Anti–Zionism: An Analysis.' In: Yaacov Ro'i and Avi Beker, eds., *Jewish Culture and Identity in the Soviet Union.* New York and London, pp. 310–54.
Frankland, Noble, ed. (1957). *Documents on International Affairs, 1955.* London.
FRUS, 1946, VI (1969). *Eastern Europe; the Soviet Union.* Washington.
FRUS, 1946, VII (1969). *The Near East and Africa.* Washington.
FRUS, 1947, IV (1972). *Eastern Europe; the Soviet Union.* Washington.

FRUS, 1947, V (1971). *The Near East and Africa*. Washington.
FRUS, 1947, VI (1972). *The Far East*. Washington.
FRUS, 1948, I (1) (1975). *General; United Nations, Part 1*. Washington.
FRUS, 1948, I (2) (1976). *General; United Nations, Part 2*. Washington.
FRUS, 1948, IV (1974). *Eastern Europe; The Soviet Union*. Washington.
FRUS, 1948, V (1) (1975). *The Near East, South Asia, and Africa, Part 1*. Washington.
FRUS, 1948, V (2) (1976). *Eastern Europe, the Soviet Union*. Washington.
FRUS, 1949, I (1976). *National Security Affairs, Foreign Economic Policy*. Washington.
FRUS, 1949, V (1978). *Eastern Europe, The Soviet Union*. Washington.
FRUS, 1949, VI (1977). *The Near East, South Asia, and Africa*. Washington.
FRUS, 1950, I (1977). *National Security Affairs; Foreign Economic Policy*. Washington.
FRUS, 1950, V (1978). *The Near East, South Asia, and Africa*. Washington.
FRUS, 1951, I (1980). *National Security Affairs; Foreign Economic Policy*. Washington.
FRUS, 1951, V (1982). *The Near East and Africa*. Washington.
FRUS, 1952–1954, II (1984). *National Security Affairs*. Washington.
FRUS, 1952–1954, III (1979). *United Nations Affairs*. Washington.
FRUS, 1952–1954, IX, Part 1 (1986). *The Near and Middle East*. Washington.
FRUS, 1952–1954, VIII (1988). *Eastern Europe; Soviet Union; Eastern Mediterranean*. Washington.
FRUS, 1955–1957, V (1988). *Austrian State Treaty; Summit Meetings; V The Foreign Ministers Meetings*. Washington.
FRUS, 1955–1957, XII (1992). *Near East Region: Iran; Iraq*. Washington.
FRUS, 1955–1957, XIII (1989). *Near East: Jordan–Yemen*. Washington.
FRUS, 1955–1957, XIV (1988). *Arab–Israeli Dispute, 1955*. Washington.
FRUS, 1955–1957, XV (1989). *Arab-Israeli Dispute, January 1-July 26, 1956*, Washington.
FRUS, 1955–1957, XIX (1990). *National Security Policy*. Washington.
FRUS, 1955–1957, XVI (1990). *Suez Canal Crisis, July 26 –December 31*, Washington.
FRUS, 1955–1957, XVII (1990). *Arab–Israeli Dispute, 1957*. Washington.
FRUS, 1955–1957: XXV (1990). *Eastern Europe*. Washington.
FRUS, 1955–1957, XXVII (1992). *Western Europe and Canada*. Washington.
FRUS, 1958–1960, II (1991). *United Nations and General International Matters*. Washington.
FRUS, 1958–1960, XI (1992). *Lebanon and Jordan*. Washington.
FRUS, 1958–1960, XII (1993). *Near East Region: Iraq, Iran, Arabian Peninsula*. Washington.
FRUS, 1958–1960, XIII (1992). *Arab–Israeli–Dispute; United Arab Republic; North Africa*. Washington.
FRUS, 1961–1963, V (1998). *The Soviet Union*. Washington.

FRUS, 1961–1963, VII (1995). *Arms Control and Disarmaments.* Washington.
FRUS, 1961–1963, XIII (1994). *Western Europe and Canada.* Washington.
FRUS, 1961–1963, XVII (1994). *Near East, 1961–1962.* Washington.
FRUS, 1961–1963, XVIII (1995). *Near East, 1962–1963.* Washington.
FRUS, 1964–1968, IV (1998). *Vietnam, 1966.* Washington.
FRUS, 1964–1968, V (2001). *Vietnam, 1967.* Washington.
FRUS, 1964–1968, X (2002). *National Security Policy.* Washington.
FRUS, 1964–1968, XI (1997). *Arms Control and Disarmament.* Washington.
FRUS, 1964–1968, XIV (2001). *Soviet Union.* Washington.
FRUS, 1964–1968, XIX (2004). *Arab–Israeli Crisis and War, 1967.* Washington.
FRUS, 1964–1968, XVIII (2000). *Arab–Israeli–Dispute, 1964–1967.* Washington.
FRUS, 1964–1968, XX (2001). *Arab–Israeli Dispute, 1967–1968.* Washington.
FRUS, 1964–1968, XXI (2000). *Near East Region; Arab Peninsula.* Washington.
FRUS, 1964–1968, XXII (1999). *Iran.* Washington.
FRUS, 1964–1968, XXX (1998). *China.* Washington.
FRUS, 1964–1968, XXXIV (1999). *Energy Diplomacy and Global Issues.* Washington.
Fursenko, Aleksander, and Timothy Naftali (2006). *Khrushchev's Cold War: The Inside Story of an American Adversary.* New York and London.
Fursenko, Aleksander, and Timothy Naftali (1997). *'One Hell of a Gamble': Khrushchev, Castro, and Kennedy, 1958–1964.* New York.
Gaddis, John L. (1997). *We Now Know: Rethinking Cold War History.* Oxford.
Gaddis, John L. (2011). *George F. Kennan: An American Life.* New York.
Gaiduk, Ilya V. (1996). *The Soviet Union and the Vietnam War.* Chicago.
Ganin, Zvi (1979). *Truman, American Jewry, and Israel, 1945–1948.* New York and London.
Ganin, Zvi (2005). *An Uneasy Relationship: American Jewish Leadership and Israel, 1948–1957.* Syracuse.
Gazit, Mordechai (1984). *President Kennedy's Policy toward the Arab States and Israel.* Tel Aviv.
Gazit, Mordechai (2002). *Israeli Diplomacy and the Quest for Peace.* London.
Gendzier, Irene (1997). *Notes from the Minefield: U. S. Intervention in Lebanon and the Middle East, 1945–1958.* New York.
Gerges, Fervez (1994). *The Superpowers and the Middle East: Regional and International Politics, 1955–1967.* Boulder.
Ginat, Rami (2001). 'Origins of the Czech–Egyptian Arms Deal: A Reappraisal.' In: David Tal, ed., *The 1956 War: Collusion and Rivalry in the Middle East.* London, pp. 145–67.
Ginor, Isabela, and Gideon Remez (2007). *Foxbats Over Dimona: The Soviet Nuclear Gamble in the Six Day War.* New Haven.
Gluska, Ami (2004). *Give the Order! Israel's Political Leadership on the Road to the Six Day War, 1963–1967.* Tel Aviv (Hebrew). An abridged English-language version was published in 2007: *The Israeli Military and the Origins*

*of the 1967 War: Government, Armed Forces, and Defense Policy, 1963–1967*. London.
Golan, Galia (1990). *Soviet Policies in the Middle East*. Cambridge.
Golan, Galia (2006). 'The Soviet Union and the Outbreak of the June 1967 Six Day War.' *Journal of Cold War Studies* 8(1): 3–19.
Golani, Moti (1998). *Israel in Search of a War: The Sinai Campaign, 1955–1957*. Brighton. I used the fuller Hebrew version: *There Will be War Next Summer*, 1997.
Gorlizki, Yoram, and Oleg Khlevniuk (2004). *Cold Peace: Stalin and the Soviet Ruling Circle*. Oxford.
Gorodetsky, Gabriel (2003). 'The Soviet Union's Role in the Creation of the State of Israel.' *Journal of Israeli History* 22(1): 4–20.
Govrin, Yosef (1998). *Israeli–Soviet Relations, 1953–1967*. London.
Haber, Eitan (1987). *'Today War will Break Out': The Reminiscences of Brig. Gen. Israel Lior, Military Attaché to Prime Ministers Levi Eshkol and Golda Meir*. Tel Aviv (Hebrew).
Hahn, Peter L. (1993). *The United States, Great Britain, and Egypt, 1945–1956: Strategy and Diplomacy in the Early Cold War*. Chapel Hill and London.
Hahn, Peter L. (2004). *Caught in the Middle East: U.S. Policy toward the Arab–Israeli Conflict, 1945–1961*. Chapel Hill.
Hahn, Peter L. (2007). 'The Cold War and the Six Day War: US Policy Toward the Arab–Israeli Crisis of June 1967.' In: Nigel G. Ashton, ed., *The Cold War in the Middle East: Regional Conflict and the Superpowers, 1967–1973*. London, pp. 16–34.
Harel, Isser (1987). *Soviet Espionage: Communism in Israel*. Tel Aviv (Hebrew).
Heikal, Mohamed (1972). *Nasser: The Cairo Documents*. London.
Heikal, Mohamed (1975). *The Road to Ramadan*. London.
Heikal, Mohamed (1978). *The Sphinx and the Commissar: The Rise and Fall of Soviet Influence in the Middle East*. New York.
Heimann, Gadi (2008). 'France–Israel Relations Under De Gaulle's Presidency, 1958–1967.' PhD dissertation, The Hebrew University of Jerusalem.
Heimann, Gadi (2010). 'In Search of a Route to World Power: General De Gaulle, the Soviet Union, and Israel in the Middle Eastern Crisis of 1967.' *International History Review* 32(1): 69–88.
Heinrichs, Waldo (1994). 'Lyndon B. Johnson: Change and Continuity.' In: Warren I. Cohen and Nancy Bernkopf Tucker, eds., *Lyndon Johnson Confronts the World: American Foreign Policy, 1963–1969*. New York, pp. 9–30.
Heller, Joseph (2000). *The Birth of Israel, 1945–1949: Ben-Gurion and His Critics*. Gainesville.
Helms, Richard, and William Hood (2003). *A Look Over My Shoulder: A Life in the Central Intelligence Agency*. New York.
Herring, George (2008). *From Colony to Superpower: United States Foreign Policy since 1776*. London and New York.
Herzog, Jacob David (1975). *A People that Dwells Alone: The Speeches and Writings of Yaacov Herzog*. Ed. Misha Louvish. London.
Hilsman, Roger (1967). *To Move a Nation: The Politics of Foreign Policy in the Administration of John F. Kennedy*. New York.

Hindenburg, Hannfried von (2007). *Demonstrating Reconciliation: State and Society in West German Foreign Policy toward Israel, 1952–1965.* New York.
Holloway, David (1987). *The Soviet Union and the Arms Race.* New Haven and London.
Hoopes, Townsend, and Douglas Brinkley (1992). *Driven Patriot: The Life and Times of James Forrestal.* New York.
Hunt, Michael (1997). *Crises in U. S. Foreign Policy: An International Reader.* New Haven and London.
Hunt, Michael (2007). *The American Ascendancy: How the United States Gained and Wielded Global Dominance.* Chapel Hill and London.
Immerman, Richard H., ed. (1990). *John Foster Dulles and the Diplomacy of the Cold War.* Princeton.
Isenberg, Michael T. (2005) *The United States Navy in the Era of the Cold War and Violent Peace,* Vol. 1. New York.
Israelian, Victor (2003). *On the Battlefields of the Cold War: A Soviet Ambassador's Confession.* University Park, Pennsylvania.
James, Laura M. (2006). *Nasser at War: Arab Images of the Enemy.* New York.
Jefferys–Jones, Rhodri (1998). *The CIA and American Democracy* (2nd edition). New Haven and London.
Jelinek, Yeshayahu (2002). 'Konrad Adenauer and the State of Israel: Between Friendship and Realpolitik, 1953–1963.' *Orient* 43 (1): 47–52.
Jelinek, Yeshayahu (2004). *Deutschland und Israel 1945–1965: Eine neurotisches Verhaeltnis.* Oldenburg.
Johnson, Robert David (2008). *Lyndon Johnson and Israel: The Secret Presidential Recordings.* Research Paper No. 3 (July 2008). Ramat Aviv.
Kalugin, Oleg (1994). *The First Directorate: My 32 Years in Intelligence and Espionage Against the West.* New York.
Karabell, Zachary (1999). *Architects of Intervention: The United States, The Third World and the Cold War, 1946–1962.* Baton Rouge.
Kenen, Isaiah L. (1981). *Israel's Defense Line: Her Friends and Foes in Washington.* Buffalo.
Kent, John, ed. (1995). *Egypt and the Defence of the Middle East, Vol. III: 1953–1956.* London.
Keren, Michael (1983). *Ben-Gurion and the Intellectuals: Power, Knowledge and Charisma.* De Kalb.
Kerr, Malcolm (1971). *The Arab Cold War: Gamal Abd Al–Nasir and his Rivals, 1958–1970.* London.
Khrushchev, Sergei, ed. (2000). *Nikita Khrushchev and the Creation of a Superpower.* University Park, Pennsylvania.
Khrushchev, Sergei, ed. (2006). *Memoirs of Nikita Khrushchev, II: Reformer, 1945–1958.* University Park, Pennsylvania.
Khrushchev, Sergei, ed. (2007). *Memoirs of Nikita Khrushchev, III: Statesman, 1953–1964.* University Park, Pennsylvania.
Kissinger, Henry (1994). *Diplomacy.* New York.
Klantsching, Gernot (2003). 'Oil, the Suez Canal, and Sterling Reserves: Economic Factors Determining British Decision Making During the 1967 Arab–Israeli Crisis.' *Diplomacy & Statecraft* 14(3): 131–50.

Kostrychenko, Gennadi (1995). *Out of the Red Shadow: Anti-Semitism in Stalin's Russia*. New York.
Kramer, Mark (1998). 'The Soviet Union and the 1956 Crisis in Hungary and Poland: Reassessment and New Findings.' *Journal of Contemporary History* 33(2): 163–214.
Kuniholm, Bruce R. (1989). 'United States Policy in the Near East: The Triumph and Tribulations of the Truman Administration.' In: Michael J. Lacy, ed., *The Truman Presidency*. Cambridge, pp. 299–338.
Kyle, Keith (2003). *Suez*. London.
Lammpromm, Arnon, and Haggai Tsoref, eds. (2002). *Levy Eshkol: The Third Prime Minister – Selected Documents (1895–1969)*. Jerusalem (Hebrew).
Lammpromm, Arnonn (2009). Ed. *Chaim Herzog. The Sixth President of Israel: Selected Documents*. Jerusalem (Hebrew).
Laron, Guy (2009). '"Logic Dictates That They Attack Where They Feel They Can Win": The 1955 Czech–Egyptian Arms Deal, the Egyptian Army, and Israeli Intelligence.' *Middle East Journal* 63(1): 69–84.
Lawson, Fred H. (1996). *Why Syria Goes to War? Thirty Years of Confrontation*. Ithaca.
Leffler, Melvin, and David S. Painter, eds. (2005). *Origins of the Cold War: An International History* (2nd edition). London and New York.
Leffler, Melvin, and Odd Arne Westad, eds. (2010). *Cambridge History of the Cold War. Vol.1: Origins; Vol. 2: Crises and Détente*. Cambridge.
Levanon, Nechemia (1996). *The Code Was Nativ*. Tel Aviv (Hebrew).
Levey, Zach (1997). *Israel and the Western Powers, 1952–1960*. Chapel Hill and London.
Levey, Zach (2004). 'The United States Skyhawk Sale to Israel, 1966: Strategic Exigencies of an Arms Deal.' *Diplomatic History* 28(2): 255–76.
Little, Douglas (1988). 'The New Frontier on the Nile: JFK, Nasser, and Arab Nationalism.' *Journal of American History* 75 (1988): 501–27.
Little, Douglas (1989). 'From Even-Handed to Empty-Handed: Seeking Order in the Middle East.' In: Thomas G. Paterson, ed., *Kennedy's Quest for Victory: American Foreign Policy, 1961–1963*. New York and Oxford, pp. 156–77.
Little, Douglas (1993). 'The Making of Special Relationship: The United States and Israel, 1957–1968.' *International Journal of Middle East Studies* 25 (1993): 563–85.
Little, Douglas (1994). 'Choosing Sides: Lyndon Johnson and the Middle East.' In: Robert A. Divine, ed., *III: LBJ at Home and Abroad*. Lawrence, KS.
Little, Douglas (1999). '"Nasser Delenda Est": Lyndon Johnson, the Arabs, and the Six Day War.' In: Henry W. Brands, ed., *The Foreign Policies of Lyndon Johnson: Beyond Vietnam*. College Station, TX, pp. 145–67.
Little, Douglas (2001). 'His Finest Hour? Eisenhower, Lebanon, and the 1958 Middle East Crisis.' In: Peter L. Hahn and Mary A. Heiss, eds., *Empire and Revolution: The United States and the Third World Since 1945*. Columbus.
Little, Douglas (2002). *American Orientalism: The United States and the Middle East since 1945*. Chapel Hill and London.

Logvall, Frederik (2003). 'America Isolated: The Western Powers and the Escalation of the War.' In: Andreas W. Daum, Lloyd C. Gardner, and Wilfried Mausbach, eds., *America, the Vietnam War, and the World: Comparative and International Perspectives*. Cambridge.
Louis, William Roger (1984). *The British Empire in the Middle East, 1945–1951: Arab Nationalism, the United States, and Postwar Imperialism*. Oxford.
Louis, William Roger (1989). 'The Tragedy of the Anglo–Egyptian Settlement of 1954.' In: Wm. Roger Louis and Roger Owen, eds., *Suez 1956: The Crisis and its Consequences*. Oxford, pp. 43–71.
Louis, William Roger (2006). *Ends of British Imperialism: The Scramble for Empire, Suez and Decolonization*. London.
Louis, William Roger, and Roger Owen (2002). *A Revolutionary Year: The Middle East in 1958*. London and New York.
Louis, William Roger, and Avi Shlaim, eds. (2012). *The 1967 Arab–Israeli War: Origins and Consequences*. Cambridge.
Lucas, W. Scott (1990). 'Redefining the Suez "Collusion."' *Middle Eastern Studies* 26(1): 88–112.
Lucas, W. Scott (1996). *Divided We Stand: Britain, the US and the Suez Crisis*. London.
McDonald, James G. (1951). *My Mission to Israel, 1948–1951*. New York.
McGhee, George (1983). *Envoy to the Middle East: Adventures in Diplomacy*. New York.
Macmillan, Harold (1971). *Riding the Storm, 1956–1959*. New York.
McNamara, Robert (2000). 'Britain, Nasser and the Outbreak of the Six Day War.' *Journal of Contemporary History* 35(4): 619–39.
McNamara, Robert (2003). *Britain, Nasser and the Balance of Power in the Middle East, 1952–1967*. London.
Macomber, William (1975). *The Angels' Game: A Handbook of Modern Diplomacy*. New York.
McPherson, Harry (1999). 'The White House, American Jews, and the Six Day War.' In: Asher Sasser, ed., *Six Days, Thirty Years: New Perspectives on the Six Day War*. Tel Aviv (Hebrew), pp. 137–42.
Mak, Dayton, and Charles S. Kennedy (1992). *American Ambassadors in a Troubled World: Interviews with Senior Diplomats*. Westport.
Ma'oz, Moshe (1995). *Syria and Israel: From War to Peacemaking*. Oxford.
Morozov, Boris (1999). *Documents on Soviet Jewish Emigration*. London.
Morris, Benny (1993). *Israel's Border Wars, 1949–1956: Arab Infiltration, Israeli Retaliation, and the Countdown to the Suez War*. Oxford.
Namir, Mordechai (1971). *Mission to Moscow: 1948–1950*. Tel Aviv (Hebrew).
Naumkin, Vitali, ed. (2003). *Russia in the Twentieth Century: Documents from the Russian Federation Foreign Policy Archives*. Ed. Alexander Yakovlev. *The Middle Eastern Conflict. Volume 1: 1947–1956; Volume 2: 1957–1967*. Moscow (Russian).
Nitze, Paul H. (1983). *Tension Between Opposites: Reflections on the Practice and Theory of Politics*. New York.

Offner, Arnold A. (2002). *Another Such Victory: President Truman and the Cold War, 1945–1953*. Stanford.
Oren, Michael B. (2002). *Six Days of War: June 1967 and the Making of the Modern Middle East*. New York.
Ovendale, Ritchie (1996). *Britain, the United States, and the Transfer of Power, 1945–1962*. London.
Parker, Richard B. (1993). *The Politics of Miscalculation in the Middle East*. Bloomington.
Parker, Richard B. (1997). *Six Day War: A Retrospective*. Gainesville.
Pinkus, Benjamin (1984). *The Soviet Government and the Jews, 1948–1967: A Documentary Record*. Ed. Jonathan Frankel. Cambridge.
Pinkus, Benjamin (1989). *The Jews of the Soviet Union: The History of a National Minority*. Cambridge.
Pinkus, Benjamin (1996). 'The Soviet Rejection of Zalman Shazar as Israel's Minister to the USSR in Light of New Documentary Materia.' *Shvut* (New Series) 4: 183–212.
Podeh, Eli (1995). *The Quest for Hegemony in the Arab World: The Struggle over the Baghdad Pact*. Leiden.
Podeh, Eli (1999). *The Decline of Arab Unity: The Rise and Fall of the United Arab Republic*. Brighton.
Podeh, Eli (2004). 'Demonizing the Other: Israel's Perceptions of Nasser and Nasserism.' In: Eli Podeh and On Winkler, eds., *Rethinking Nasserism: Revolution and Historical Memory in Modern Egypt*. Gainesville, pp. 72–99.
Polk, William R. (1964). 'Social Modernization: The New Men.' In: Georgina G. Stevens, ed., *The United States and the Middle East*. Englewood, pp. 31–52.
Porter, Gareth (2005). *Perils of Dominance: Imbalance of Power and the Road to War in Vietnam*. Berkeley.
Primakov, Yevgeny (2004). *Russian Crossroads: Towards the New Millennium*. New Haven and London.
Quandt, William B. (1977). *Decade of Decisions: American Policy toward the Arab-Israeli Conflict, 1967–1976*. Berkeley.
Quandt, William B. (1992). 'Lyndon Johnson and the June 1967: What Color Was the Light?' *Middle East Journal* 46(2): 198–227.
Quandt, William B. (1993). *Peace Process: American Diplomacy and the Arab–Israeli Conflict Since 1967*. Berkeley and Los Angeles.
Rabin, Yitzhak (1979). *Memoirs*. Tel Aviv (Hebrew). (I used the Hebrew edition rather than the abridged English edition).
Rabinovich, Itamar (1972). *Syria under the Ba'ath, 1963–1966: The Army–Party Symbiosis*. Jerusalem.
Rafael, Gideon (1981). *Destination Peace: Three Decades of Israeli Foreign Policy*. London.
Raviv, Moshe (1998). *Israel at Fifty: Five Decades of Struggle for Peace*. London.
Redlich, Shimon (1995). *War, Holocaust and Stalinism: A Documentary Study of the Jewish Anti-Fascist Committee in the USSR*. Luxembourg.

Reynolds, David (1986). 'Anglo-American Relations Since 1945.' In: William Roger Louis and Hedly Bull, eds., *The 'Special Relationship': Anglo-American Relations Since 1945*. Oxford, pp. 17–41.
Ro'i, Yaacov (1974a). *From Encroachment to Involvement: A Documentary History of Soviet Policy in the Middle East, 1945–1973*. New York.
Ro'i, Yaacov (1974b). 'Soviet Policy in the Middle East: The Case of Palestine during World War II.' *Cahiers du Monde Russe et Sovietique* 15: 3–4 (July–December): 373–408.
Ro'i, Yaacov (1980). *Soviet Decision Making in Practice: The USSR and Israel, 1947–1953*. New Brunswick and London.
Ro'i, Yaacov (1991). *The Struggle for Soviet Jewish Immigration, 1948–1967*. Cambridge.
Ro'i, Yaacov (2003). 'The Deterioration of Relations: From Support to Severance.' *The Journal of Israeli History* 22(1): 21–36.
Ro'i, Yaacov, and Boris Morozov (2008). *The Soviet Union and the June 1967 Six Day War*. Washington D.C and Stanford.
Ro'i, Yaacov, et al., eds. (2000). *Documents on Israeli–Soviet Relations*. London.
Roosevelt, Kermit (1948). 'The Partition of Palestine: A Lesson in Pressure Politics.' *Middle East Journal* 2(1): 1–13.
Rosenthal, Yemima, ed. (2005). *Yitzhak Rabin, the Prime Minister of Israel, 1974–1977, 1992–1995: Selected Documents, Vol. 1: 1922–1967*. Jerusalem (Hebrew).
Rostow, Walt W. (1972). *The Diffusion of Power, 1957–1972: An Essay in Recent History*. New York.
Rubinstein, Alvin Z. (2008). *Moscow's Third World Strategy*. Princeton.
Rucker, Laurent (2001). 'The Soviet Union and the Suez Crisis.' In: David Tal, ed., *The 1956 War: Collusion and Rivalry in the Middle East*. London.
Rusk, Dean (1990). *As I Saw It*. Ed. Daniel S. Papp. New York. (As told to Richard Rusk.)
Rustow, Dankwart A., ed. (1970). *Philosophers and Kings: Studies in Leadership*. New York.
Schlesinger, Arthur M., Jr. (1992). 'Some Lessons of the Cold War.' In: Michael J. Hogan, ed., *The End of the Cold War: Its Meaning and Implications*. Cambridge, pp. 53–62.
Sebag Montefiore, Simon (2004). *Stalin: The Court of the Red Tsar*. London.
Segev, Tom (2007). *1967: Israel, the War, and the Year that Transformed the Middle East*. New York.
Sela, Avraham (1982). *Unity within Conflict in the Inter-Arab System: The Arab Summit Conferences, 1964–1982*. Jerusalem (Hebrew).
Sementenko, Nina, and Sergei Mirokhin (1995). 'Soviet Diplomacy and the Issue of Jewish Immigration to Israel, 1946–1953.' In: Yaacov Ro'i, ed., *Jews and Jewish Life in Russia and the Soviet Union*. London, pp. 316–26.
Service, Robert (2004). *Stalin: A Biography*. Cambridge, MA.

Shalom, Zaki (1997). 'Document: David Ben-Gurion and Chancellor Adenauer at the Waldorf Astoria on March 14, 1960.' *Israel Studies* 2(1): 56–67.

Shalom, Zaki (2004). *Between Dimona and Washington: The Development of Israel's Nuclear Option, 1960–1968*. Tel Aviv (Hebrew). Published in English in 2005 as: *Israel's Nuclear Option: Behind the Scenes Diplomacy between Dimona and Washington* (Portland).

Shaltiel, Eli, ed. (1996). *David Ben-Gurion, the First Prime Minister: Selected Documents (1947–1963)*. Jerusalem (Hebrew).

Shamir, Shimon (1989). 'The Collapse of Project Alpha.' In: William Roger Louis and Roger Owen, eds., *Suez 1956: The Crisis and its Consequences*. Oxford, pp. 73–100.

Sharett, Moshe (1966). 'Israel and the Arabs: War and Peace (Reflections on the Years 1947–1957).' In: *Ot* (September). Lecture given at Beit Berl October–November 1957. Tel Aviv (Hebrew).

Sharett, Moshe (1978). *Personal Diary*, Vols. 1–8. Tel Aviv (Hebrew).

Sheffer, Gabriel (1997). *Moshe Sharett: Biography of a Political Moderate*. Oxford.

Sheffy, Yigal (2008). *Early Warning on Trial: The Israeli Defense Perception and the Rotem Affair, 1957–1960*. Tel Aviv (Hebrew).

Shlaim, Avi (2000). *The Iron Wall: Israel and the Arab World*. London.

Shlaim, Avi (2007). *Lion of Jordan: The Life of King Hussein in Peace and War*. London.

Shuckburgh, Evelyn (1986). *Descent to Suez*. London.

Smith, Tony (2005). 'New Bottles for New Wine: A Pericentric Framework for the Study of the Cold War.' *Diplomatic History* 24(40): 567–91.

Spiegel, Steven L. (1985). *The Other Arab–Israeli Conflict: Making America's Middle East Policy from Truman to Reagan*. Chicago.

Spiegel, Steven L. (2001). 'Israel and Beyond: American Jews and United States Foreign Policy.' In: L. Sandy Meisel, ed., *Jews in American Politics*. Lanham, pp. 251–79.

Stola, Dariusz (2006). 'Anti–Zionism as a Multipurpose Policy Instrument: The Anti–Zionist Campaign in Poland, 1967–1968.' In: Jeffrey Herf, ed., *Anti-Semitism and Anti-Zionism in Historical Perspective: Convergence and Divergence*. London and New York.

Susser, Asher, ed. (1999). *Six Days–Thirty Years: New Perspectives on the Six Day War*. Tel Aviv (Hebrew).

Tal, David, ed. (2001). *The 1956 War: Collusion and Rivalry in the Middle East*. London.

Talbot, Strobe, ed. (1971). *Khrushchev Remembers*. London.

Talbot, Strobe, ed. (1974). *Khrushchev Remembers: The Last Testament*. Boston.

Taubman, William (2003). *Khrushchev: The Man and His Era*. New York.

Troen, Selwyn Ilan, and Moshe Shemesh, eds. (1990). *The Suez–Sinai Crisis, 1956: Retrospective and Reappraisal*. London.

Turner, Admiral Stansfield (2005). *Burn Before Reading*. New York.

Tsur, Jacob (1968). *An Ambassador's Diary in Paris, 1953–1956*. Tel Aviv (Hebrew).
United Nations (1947). *Official Records of the First Special Session of the General Assembly*. Vol. 1: *Plenary Meetings of the General Assembly*. Verbatim Record, 28 April–15 May 1947. Seventy-Seventh Plenary Meeting. 14 May 1947. Discussion of the First Committee on the Establishment of a Special Committee on Palestine, pp. 128–35.
Van Ree, Erik (2008). *The Political Thought of Joseph Stalin: A Study in Twentieth Century Revolutionary Patriotism*. London and New York.
Vassiliev, Alexei (1993). *Russian Policy in the Middle East: From Messianism to Pragmatism*. Reading.
Vaughan, James R. (2005). *The Failure of American and British Propaganda in the Arab Middle East, 1945–1957*. New York.
Vogt, Judith (1986). 'Nazism turned Zionism: Political Cartoons Analysis.' In: Shmuel Ettinger, ed., *Anti-Semitism in the Soviet Union*. Tel Aviv (Hebrew), pp. 206–22.
Weit, Erwin (1973). *At the Red Summit: Interpreter Behind the Iron Curtain*. New York.
Westad, Odd Arne (2005). *The Global Cold War: Third World Interventions and the Making of Our Time*. Cambridge.
Wilson, Harold (1971). *The Labour Government, 1964–1970: A Personal Record*. London.
Woods, Randall B. (2006). *LBJ: Architect of American Ambition*. New York.
Yakub, Salim (2004). *Containing Arab Nationalism: The Eisenhower Doctrine and the Middle East*. Chapel Hill.
Yazid, Sayegh, and Shlaim, Avi, eds. (1997). *The Cold War and the Middle East*. Oxford.
Yogev, Gedalia, ed. (1980) *Political and Diplomatic Documents of the State of Israel, November 1947–May 1948*. Jerusalem.
Yost, Charles W. (1968). 'The Arab–Israeli War: How It Began?' *Foreign Affairs* 46: 304–26.
Zak, Moshe (1988). *The Soviet Union and Israel: A Forty-Year Dialogue*. Tel Aviv (Hebrew).
Zubok, Vladislav, and Constantine Pleshakov (1996). *Inside the Kremlin Cold War: From Stalin to Khrushchev*. Cambridge, MA.
Zubok, Vladislav, and Constantine Pleshakov (2000). 'Soviet Policy Aims at the Geneva Conference, 1955.' In: Guenter Bischof and Saki Dockrill, eds., *The Cold War Respite*. Baton Rouge, pp. 55–74.
Zubok, Vladislav, and Constantine Pleshakov (2007). *(A Failed Empire): The Soviet Union in the Cold War from Stalin to Gorbachev*. Chapel Hill.

# Index

Abdullah, King of Jordan 68
Acheson, Dean 31
Adenauer, Konrad 103, 108, 211
aid programs 28–31, 50–2, 55–9, 66, 75, 79, 82, 86, 91, 107, 116, 122, 135–7, 141, 151, 168, 172, 177–82, 188, 191, 194–9, 254, 259, 268
al-Hammah bombing (1951) 27
Allen, George 106
Allon, Yigal 138, 215, 220, 243
American Jewry 47–50, 54, 56, 60, 72, 81–5, 111, 114, 116, 124–5, 130, 158, 166, 170, 173–4, 198–201, 205, 238, 264, 268
Amit, Meir 212, 232–3
Anderson, Robert 66, 234
Angleton, James 233
anti-Semitism 2–3, 6, 15, 19, 31, 52, 94, 97–9, 103, 129, 132, 140, 158–9, 162, 165–6, 204–6, 209, 213, 239, 263, 267
Aqaba, Gulf of 84, 91, 107–8, 116–17, 224, 228–31, 234, 237, 240, 243, 252, 255
Arab–Israeli conflict 26, 28, 32–5, 39, 50–5, 60–2, 64–5, 69, 86, 90–1, 106, 110, 112, 161–2, 167–8, 173, 175, 183–4, 189, 191, 197, 202, 215, 218, 250, 259–66
Arab states
  moderate 91, 108, 260
  'progressive' 2

Arab summits (Cairo and Alexandria, 1964) 169, 177–80, 204
Arab unity 8–9, 67, 109, 254
Arab world, the
  American policy towards 4, 47, 202
  Soviet policy towards 1, 18, 85, 93, 95, 98, 176, 123, 227
ARAMCO (company) 142
arms control 205
arms race 118, 121, 123, 128, 140, 150, 159, 161, 169, 173, 176–8, 185, 188, 190, 193, 199, 208, 210, 261
arms stockpiles 70–1
arms supplies 10, 12, 24, 26, 35, 44, 69, 72, 112, 116, 118, 140, 145, 152, 159–61, 164–5, 187, 190, 197, 199, 240, 262
assimilation 154, 161, 206, 210, 267
Avigur, Shaul 161, 164, 207

Ba'ath factions 212, 221
Badeau, John 136, 141–2, 168–70
Badran, Shams 227, 246–7
Baghdad Pact 61–6, 79–80, 99, 210
Ball, George 139, 229
Barbour, Walworth 141–2, 148, 194, 213, 230
Battle, Lucius D. 179, 226, 228
Ben Bella, Ahmed 163
Ben-Gurion, David
  on the Cold War 141
  influence on Israeli foreign policy 8–9, 16, 26–7, 39, 51, 62–90, 267

Index

on Israeli membership of
  NATO 114
political opinions expressed by
  1, 7, 10–17, 21–4, 28, 33, 35,
  56–7, 163
on relations with the Arab states
  117–18, 139, 144, 263–4
on relations with the Soviet
  Union 156–60
on relations with the United States
  92–104, 108–11, 137, 189
Ben-Nun, Yohai 178
Birobidzhan 96, 99–102, 155–6
Bodrov, Mikhail 164, 166
Bourguiba, Habib 193
Bowles, Chester 124
Brezhnev, Leonid 253–4, 266
Britain 6–8, 20–3, 34, 40, 44, 62, 70,
  73–4, 110–11, 184, 226–7, 231
Bulganin, Nikolai 45, 92
Bundy, McGeorge 134, 151, 169, 171
Bundy, William P. 121
Burns, E.L.M. 85
Byroade, Henry 29–30, 52–3, 57, 67

Cabinet minutes, Israeli 3
Califano, Joseph 238
Canada 70–1
Casablanca summit (1965) 187
Celler, Emanuel 232
Central Treaty Organization
  (CENTO) 210, 224
Chiang Kai-shek 24, 43
China 12, 24, 26, 55, 102, 104,
  151–2, 155, 157, 160–1, 164,
  214, 216, 249–50
Chuvakhin, Dmitri 204–7, 210–18,
  242–3, 249
Clifford, Clark 20, 229, 233
coexistence doctrine 99, 102–3, 117,
  156–62, 208–9
Cold War 1–4, 6, 9–10, 16, 19–23,
  28–9, 33–4, 40–4, 56–9, 63,
  66–7, 70, 72, 75, 91, 94–7, 100,
  107, 113–17, 121, 125, 130–3,
  139, 141, 145, 148–9, 154–60,
  164, 167, 169, 183–4, 188, 193,
  196–7, 202, 205–10, 214–18,
  221, 238, 240, 252, 259–68
colonialism and colonial rule
  160, 162
Comay, Michael 161
Communist ideology 93, 157
Crawford, William 137
Cuban Missile Crisis (1962) 119,
  124, 131–4, 159, 176, 231
Czech–Egyptian arms agreement
  (1955) 4, 38–42, 58–62, 67
Czechoslovakia 9, 15–16, 21

Davies, Rodger 188
Dayan, Moshe
  as a military commander 79, 85, 93
  as Minister for Agriculture 126
  as Minister of Defense 233, 235
  political views 146, 173
  as a war correspondent 193
Dean, Sir Patrick 235–6
Dedioulia, Ivan 204
defense pact between Israel and
  the US (proposed) 36–9, 43,
  55–61, 63, 65, 70, 110, 260, 262,
  265, 268
détente 49, 102–4, 115, 119, 154,
  160, 162, 166, 176, 186, 190,
  198, 206, 212, 215, 218, 244,
  253, 259, 265–8
  in the Middle East 193, 221
Dillon, Douglas 118
Dimona nuclear reactor 119–20,
  122, 132, 136–7, 140–1,
  145–6, 149–50, 170, 175–8,
  182, 185–93, 196–9, 203, 204,
  212, 261–4
disarmament 97, 142–3, 155, 158,
  160, 172, 185, 251
discrimination 163, 165
Dobrynin, Anatoly 222
Doctors' Plot 16, 33
Dominican Republic 244

Dulles, Alan 78, 111
Dulles, John Foster
　interventions in Middle East
　　crises 106–15
　role in relations with Israel
　　39, 47–91

Eban, Abba 3, 22, 29
　as Foreign Minister of Israel
　　188–96, 205–6, 210–16, 223–4,
　　227–32, 235, 242–3
　influence on Israeli foreign policy 3
　as an Israeli diplomat 22, 29, 54,
　　57–8, 67–8, 71–2, 78, 84, 87,
　　102, 108–16
　as a member of the Israeli Government
　　121, 126, 130, 134, 139,
　　146, 161, 171, 176, 179
Eddy, William 50
Eden, Sir Anthony 43, 59, 64
Egypt 30–1, 37–40, 44, 48, 50, 56–9,
　　64, 67, 69, 73–4, 78, 85, 90, 98,
　　117, 120, 124–7, 130, 133, 136,
　　147, 151, 164, 168, 179–80,
　　188, 203, 206, 217, 221–3,
　　227–34, 238, 242, 253–4; *see
　　also* Czech–Egyptian arms deal
Ehrenburg, Ilya 9–10
Eichmann trial (1960) 155
Eilat 66, 88, 229, 245
Eisenhower, Dwight D.
　as American President 53–7,
　　60–1, 64–5, 68–79, 82–91,
　　109–19, 263
　confidence in John Foster Dulles 113
　dealings with President Nasser 119
　Declaration of Common Purpose
　　with Macmillan (1958) 107
　seeking election 47–50
　summit with Khrushchev (1959)
　　101, 114–15
'Eisenhower Doctrine' 82, 85–7, 90–1,
　　95, 108, 113, 116–17, 260
emigration *see* migration
Eshkol, Levi 3, 87, 156, 161, 163, 166,
　　168, 172–83, 185, 188–91, 195–6,
　　199, 205, 209–14, 217, 220–3,
　　227, 230–5, 238, 242, 245–8
　influence on Israeli foreign policy 3
　as Israeli Minister of Finance 81
　as Israeli Prime Minister 146–9
Export–Import Bank of the United
　States 23, 91, 106

Faisal, King of Saudi Arabia 142, 217
Farkash, Yaakov 218–19, 256–7
fascism 7
Fatah 186, 214, 217
Feinberg, Abraham 200
Feldman, Myer 122, 128, 171–5
foreign bases 14
foreign policy in general
　American 179
　Israeli 3, 11, 13, 16, 193
　Soviet 6, 43, 209
Fortas, Abe 229
'fortress' mentality 174
France 2–3, 23, 39, 44–6, 57, 60–1,
　　63–6, 69, 73–6, 82, 84, 87–8,
　　91, 94, 100, 120, 125, 133, 141,
　　150–1, 184, 264
Franco, Francisco 61
Fulbright, William 226, 239

Gardosh, Kariel 239–40
De Gaulle, Charles 104, 118, 133,
　　200, 225, 239, 263
Gavish, David 213
Gaza Strip 84–5, 240
geopolitics 4
Germany 101, 103, 156–8, 190,
　　221, 255
Gilpatrick, Rosewell 126
Gilpatrick Committee 179–80
Ginsburg, David 198
Goldberg, Arthur 166, 201, 251
Goldmann, Nahum 35
Gomulka, Wladyslaw 254
Grechko, Marshal 246–7, 253, 255
Gromyko, Andrei 8–9, 44, 96, 157,
　　161, 188, 190, 205–10, 214, 225,
　　231, 241, 246, 248, 251, 253

Haifa 22, 56, 65, 83
Hammarskjöld, Dag 85
Harel, Aryeh 100, 154–8
Harel, Isser 155
Harman, Abraham 139–40,
    145–6, 168, 193, 195, 199,
    201, 234–5
Harriman, Averell 148, 181–2, 186
Hart, Parker 142
Hawk missiles 118–22, 126–31, 135,
    138, 143–5, 152, 159, 164, 170,
    199, 260, 264
Heikal, Mohamed Hassanein
    230, 241
Helms, Richard 225–6, 233
Herter, Christian 89
Herut movement 3
Herzog, Ya'akov 242
historical materialism, doctrine
    of 207
Hitler, Adolf 7, 109
Hoopes, Townsend 202
Hoover, Herbert Jr. 77
Humphrey, Hubert 197
Hungary 76–9, 161
Hussein, King of Jordan 74, 88,
    109–10, 138, 173, 178, 183,
    215, 231

ideology 4, 93, 157
immigration *see* migration
imperialism 243
India 35
International Atomic Energy
    Authority (IAEA) 174, 183, 185,
    187, 204
International Monetary Fund 234
Iraq 74, 113, 260
Israel, State of
    establishment 15
    relations with the Soviet Union
        1–3, 6–7, 10–14, 17–18, 22,
        33–46, 62, 157–8, 161–2, 199,
        205–18, 249, 254–5
    relations with the United States
        1–5, 10–18, 21–34, 51–5, 66, 82,
        103, 115–19, 135–7, 141, 150–2,
        168, 174–5, 179, 182–3, 185–6,
        189, 194, 198, 201–3, 242
Israel Defense Forces (IDF) 10–12,
    21, 29, 44, 47–8, 53, 79, 84–5,
    100–1, 109, 123, 137, 145,
    178–9, 186, 207–8, 220, 231,
    233, 238, 248–9
Israeli Air Force 199–200
Israel State Archives (ISA) 4
*Izvestia* 36, 43, 92, 159,
    221, 242

Javits, Jacob 80
Jerusalem 8, 12, 47
Johnson, Joseph 124, 131, 135, 173
Johnson, Lyndon 83, 260–1, 264–7
    as American President 166–80,
        183, 185–202, 221–40, 244,
        251–2, 255, 260–1, 264–7
    as Senate majority leader 83
    as Vice President 151, 153
'Johnson Doctrine' 188
Jones, George Lewis 118
Jordan, State of 74, 110, 138, 180–3,
    195, 264
Jordan River diversion project 51,
    69, 96, 103, 118, 122, 129, 133,
    135, 141, 150–1, 169–70, 173–7,
    181–6, 192, 210–11, 220

Kamel, Mustafa 196
Karami, Rashid 115
Katz, Katriel 208–9, 214, 242–8
Katzenbach, Nicholas 198–201
Kennedy, John F. 2, 104, 120–8,
    131–49, 152–3, 155, 167, 197,
    260, 264, 267–8
    assassination of (1963) 151
Khrushchev, Nikita 263, 267
    and Communism 122, 149
    dealings with President
        Eisenhower 114–15
    dealings with President Nasser 37,
        43, 121, 128
    and ethnic minorities 43

Khrushchev, Nikita (*cont*)
  ousting of (1964) 204
  and relations with Egypt 72, 151, 174–5, 267
  and relations with Israel 41–2, 45, 80, 92–105, 117, 154–67
  and relations with other Middle Eastern states 108, 134, 267
Kichko, Trofim 163
Kissinger, Henry 124, 176
Klutznik, Philip 116
Komer, Robert W. 127, 132, 135–6, 139–40, 144, 149–51, 168–76, 180–3, 196
Korean War 12–13, 24–6, 259
Kosygin, Alexei 186, 207, 211, 214, 224, 231, 244–8, 251–5
*Krasnaya Zvezda* 243
*Krokodil* 257–8

Lawson, Edward 68, 81
Lebanon 108–10
LeMay, Curtis 175
Lenin, V.I. 38, 41, 95
Levavi, Aryeh 156–7, 210–12, 217

McCloskey, Robert 238
McCloy, John 144
McElroy, Neil 106
Macmillan, Harold 58, 60, 63, 66, 96, 107
McNamara, Robert 137, 173, 188, 190, 198–200, 222, 226–36
Mak, Dayton 143
Malakhovka synagogue arson attack (1959) 102, 158
Malik, Yakov 156
Mao Zedong 104
Mapai party in Israel 3
Mapam party in Israel 10, 25, 87
Marshall, George 20
Marshall Plan 19
Meir (formerly Myerson), Golda 3, 10
  and the Cold War 206
  influence on Israeli foreign policy 72
  as Israeli Foreign Minister 43, 205
  and relations with Egypt 72, 125, 132, 181
  and relations with other Middle East countries 96, 110, 118, 121, 124–5, 162, 174, 187
  and relations with the Soviet Union 39, 85–6, 89, 97, 100–1, 133
  and relations with the United States 73, 81, 135–8, 177
Memorandum of Understanding between Israel and the United States 185–8, 261–2
Meyer, Armin 143–4, 173
Middle East Command (MEC) 14, 28, 30, 48–53
Middle East Defense Organization (MEDO) 30
Middle East policy
  of the Soviet Union 1–2, 4, 19, 23, 34, 38–40, 45, 100–1, 129, 135–7, 206, 212–16, 248
  of the United States 6–7, 21, 27–32, 53–5, 58, 62–3, 82, 113, 125, 128, 134, 136, 144, 175, 197–8, 202, 266
migration of Jews to Israel 16, 24–8, 49, 85–9, 102, 106–7, 128–31, 139, 184, 211, 259
  from America 1
  from the Soviet bloc 1–2, 4, 22–3, 8–18, 28, 33–7, 54, 57, 85–6, 93, 95, 100–1, 113–14, 118–19, 154–6, 159–67, 204–10, 252–3, 263, 267
Mikoyan, Anastas 43, 95, 103
missiles *see* Hawk missiles; surface-tosurface missiles
Mollet, Guy 69
Molotov, Vyacheslav 35–6, 41, 58, 61, 95
Morozov, Boris 4
Morris, Willy 184

Namir, Mordechai 10–11, 81
Nasser, Gamal Abdel 262–6
  and the Arab–Israeli conflict 56–77

armaments controlled by 148
and closure of the Tiran
   Straits 223–6
and the Cold War 120–40,
   185–8, 266
and the Gaza Strip 84–5
and relations with Israel 238,
   242–55, 262–5
and relations with other Middle
   East countries 107–19, 147, 150
and relations with the Soviet Union
   37–8, 43, 49, 92, 154–6, 159,
   162–5, 194–8, 204–8, 237
and relations with the United States
   145, 230
rivalry with King Faisal 217
standing as Egyptian leader 37,
   78–80, 90, 102, 146, 149, 151–2,
   231, 233–4, 236
and the US/Israeli alliance 168–83
nationalism 111, 114, 119, 139,
   255, 260
Near East policy, American 106
Nehru, Jawaharlal 43, 151
neutrality 22–3, 26–7, 30, 33, 43, 97,
   116, 119, 127, 154–5, 175, 190,
   195–6, 238, 259
Nitze, Paul 126
Nixon, Richard 54
Nolte, Richard 224–5
non-aligned countries 14, 22, 35,
   131, 259
North Atlantic Treaty Organization
   (NATO) 14, 22, 33, 68, 79, 91,
   97, 101, 118, 126, 139, 160, 166,
   186, 190, 207, 210, 217, 224
*Novoye Vremya* 7, 209, 248
Nuclear Non-Proliferation Treaty
   199, 201
nuclear power 14, 57, 104
Nuclear Test Ban Treaty 146,
   162, 185
nuclear weapons 35, 125, 139, 143,
   145, 154, 158, 166, 171–83,
   185–96, 201–2, 209, 211,
   233, 250
   testing of 99, 199

oil supplies 4–5, 9, 14, 39–40, 61–2,
   65, 68–71, 79, 109–14, 142, 197,
   229–30, 233–7, 264
Oppenheimer, Robert 100

Palestine 6–12, 19–21, 41, 67, 90, 99,
   136–9, 142, 150, 162–3, 176,
   184, 199, 203, 209, 211, 244
   partition of (proposed) 8–9,
   12, 19–20
patron–client relations with the
   United States and with the Soviet
   Union 265
peaceful coexistence *see* coexistence
Pearl Harbor 227
Pentagon, the *see* United States: Defense Department
Peres, Shimon
   as Deputy Defense Minister 126
   as a member and envoy of the
   Israeli Government 138, 147–8,
   151–2, 174–5, 178
Podgorny, Nikolai 252
Poland 208
Pozhidaev, Dmitri 244
*Pravda* 9–10, 13, 95, 155, 205, 208,
   213, 221, 242–3, 246
preemptive strikes 38, 40, 55, 59–61,
   65–6, 90, 108, 117, 130, 174,
   181–2, 185, 200
Project Alpha 55–60, 64–5, 74,
   86, 260
propaganda 94, 162–3, 205–6,
   209–14, 226, 242, 244, 263

Qibya 51

Rabin, Yitzhak
   as Israeli Deputy Chief of Staff
   133, 149
   promotion to Chief of Staff 172
   role as member and envoy of the
   Israeli Government 150, 178–91,
   190, 213, 217, 232, 242
racism 12, 52, 160
Ramat Gan bombing (1953) 16, 33
'realpolitik' 4, 87, 264, 268

recognition of Israel 9, 20, 32
refugees 2, 11, 22, 24, 29–31, 39, 41, 47–50, 56, 59, 63–4, 87, 89, 99, 101, 106–7, 110–12, 116–19, 121–5, 128–32, 135–7, 142, 150, 154–7, 169, 173, 184, 199, 234–7, 252, 260–1
Reid, Ogden 115, 120
religious discrimination 163
reparations 24–5, 29, 48, 101, 177
repatriation 118, 155
reprisals 51, 57, 64–5, 72, 74, 80, 82, 133, 198, 208, 211, 262
Richards, James P. 86
Robertson, Brian 13
Roosevelt, Franklin D. 6
Rostow, Eugene 222–4, 230
Rostow, Walt 126, 136, 191–2, 195–202, 220–2, 226, 234–7
Rountree, William M. 108, 114
Rusk, Dean
    as American Secretary of State 120
    interventions in the run-up to the Six Day War 220–38, 250
    as principal adviser to the American President 129–32, 145–7, 168–71, 176, 179–82, 187–8, 192–6
Russell, Bertrand 159, 162
Russell, Francis 55

Sadat, Anwar 241–2
Said, Nuri 74
sanctions 75, 77, 82–3, 112, 265
Sartre, Jean-Paul 162
Saudi Arabia 148, 197, 236
Saunders, Harold 192–3, 198, 221
Sayegh, Yezid 3
Schelling, Thomas 176
security guarantees for Israel (proposed) 2, 38, 56, 78, 80, 113, 127–8, 141–7, 152–3, 160, 169, 171, 177, 180, 185–8, 193, 200
Semyonov, Vladimir 97, 212, 217, 241–4

Sèvres agreements (1956) 44, 74
Sharett, Moshe 3, 7, 26, 36–9, 42, 48–9, 52–62, 64–8
Shchiborin, Alexander 209
Shelepin, Alexander 151, 179, 206
Shepilov, Dmitry 93
Shukeiry, Ahmad 212
Silver, Abba Hillel 50
Sinai Peninsula 54, 56, 78–84, 94, 96, 104, 117, 120, 146, 220–4, 232, 238, 240, 242–3, 268
Sisco, Joseph 199, 229
Six Day War (1967) 2, 4–5, 217–20, 240, 253, 263–4, 267–8
Skyhawk planes 188–93, 202
Sloan, Frank 173
Smua 194, 197–8
Smyth, Hugh 232
socialism 9
Soviet Jewry 117, 154, 157–67, 199, 204–9, 212–18, 266
Soviet Union
    Israeli relations with 1–3, 6–7, 10–14, 17–18, 22, 33–46, 62, 157–8, 161–2, 199, 205–18, 249, 254–5
    Middle East policy of 1–2, 4, 19, 23, 34, 38–40, 45, 100–1, 129, 135–7, 206, 212–16, 248
    objectives of policy 4, 6, 8–9
    policy towards the Arab world 1, 18, 85, 93, 95, 98, 176, 123, 227
*Sovietische Heimland* (newspaper) 156
'special relationship' 55, 135, 137, 141–2, 146, 152, 185–6, 262, 264, 268
spheres of influence 9, 59, 77, 158, 198
Sputnik launch (1957) 96
Stalin, Joseph 6–10, 14–17, 32, 41, 96
    hatred of Soviet Jews 17
Stalinism 160
Stassen, Harold 48
statesmanship 267

Index                                                                                          289

Stookey, Robert 143
Strauss, Lewis 106
Strong, Robert 127–8
Suez Campaign (1956) 2, 79, 95, 142, 172, 261, 263
Suez Canal 29, 43, 53, 56, 70–3, 78, 81, 101, 116, 233, 245, 255
  nationalization of 72, 170
surface-to-surface missiles 118, 146–51, 171, 174, 178, 201, 264
Suslov, Mikhail 103
Symington, Stuart 226
Syria 79–80, 87–8, 94–8, 133–4, 147, 151, 178–9, 192–200, 203, 211–18, 223, 225, 241–4, 247–9

Talbot, William Phillips 123–4, 127–8, 141–5
Tashkent summit (1966) 250
Tekoah, Yosef 159, 165, 208, 215
terrorism 195–6, 214, 217, 225, 243, 249
Thant, U 217, 223, 227, 229, 243–4
Thompson, Llewellyn 225, 243, 246
Tiran, Straits of 76, 84–5, 118–19, 222–40, 245–51
Tito, Marshal 43, 254
Tripartite Declaration (1950) 24, 64, 68, 75, 98, 222
*Trud* (newspaper) 157–8
Trudeau, Arthur G. 53
Truman, Harry S. 7, 20–3, 26–7, 30–2, 262, 264, 267
Tzur, Zvi 127, 138, 145

United Arab Republic (UAR) 98–103, 107–8, 115–19, 124, 138–9, 146, 149, 159, 201
United Nations (UN) 7–12, 15, 17, 20–2, 26–7, 49, 53, 68, 78–85, 91, 107, 110, 127–8, 137, 155–7, 165, 181–2, 190, 210, 223–31, 235–8, 247–51

Charter 84, 224, 248
General Assembly 82, 96, 131, 157, 208, 250
Security Council 34, 36, 42, 51, 161, 214, 224, 227, 238, 242, 247
United Press International (UPI) 245
United Sates
  Central Intelligence Agency (CIA) 19–20, 59–60, 83, 87–8, 137, 194, 200, 227–30, 243, 249
  Defense Department (the Pentagon) 19–24, 29, 32, 69, 91, 116–17, 128, 136, 178, 191, 197–202, 222, 228, 235
  Israeli relations with 1–5, 10–18, 21–34, 51–5, 66, 82, 103, 115–19, 135–7, 141, 150–2, 168, 174–5, 179, 182–3, 185–6, 189, 194, 198, 201–3, 242
  Joint Chiefs of Staff (JCS) 30, 57–8, 112, 123, 145, 174, 176, 191, 231
  Middle East policy of 6–7, 21, 27–32, 53–5, 58, 62–3, 82, 113, 125, 128, 134, 136, 144, 175, 197–8, 202, 266
  Mutual Security Agency 32, 226
  National Security Council (NSC) 20, 26, 28, 50, 53–4, 59–61, 65, 71, 78, 106, 110, 112, 119, 129, 195
  policy towards the Arab world 4, 47, 202
  State Department 19–27, 30–2, 47–56, 64, 69–74, 80, 84–91, 112–23, 126–32, 136–40, 144, 148–51, 160, 168–82, 185–6, 189–202, 205–6, 221–5, 229, 233, 238, 246–9, 262, 264, 268
  State Foreign Relations Committee 68

Vance, Cyrus 175
'victim' image of Israel 263–4

Vietnam War 5, 186, 188, 191–7, 201, 203, 207–10, 214, 216, 221, 231, 235, 245–6, 251

Warsaw Pact 101
Wattenberg, Ben 238
Webber, Robert 182, 187
Weizman, Ezer 178, 190
Wilson, Harold 216, 235, 239
worldviews 3

Yariv, Aharon 149, 178
Yemen 130–3, 135, 147–8, 210, 261
Yershov, Pavel 16–17

Yevtushenko, Yevgeny 157
Yom Kippur War 255, 265
Yost, Charles 234
Yugoslavia 9

zeitgeist 3
Zhivkov, Todor 254
Zhou Enlai 249
Zionism 4, 6–11, 17, 19–20, 32–3, 36–41, 48, 67, 100, 106, 143, 154–8, 165, 202, 205, 211, 215, 252, 259, 263, 266
Zorin, Valerian 246

EU authorised representative for GPSR:
Easy Access System Europe, Mustamäe tee 50,
10621 Tallinn, Estonia
gpsr.requests@easproject.com

www.ingramcontent.com/pod-product-compliance
Lightning Source LLC
Chambersburg PA
CBHW070235240426
43673CB00044B/1795